THE
CAMBRIDGE EDITION OF
THE LETTERS AND WORKS OF
D. H. LAWRENCE

THE WORKS OF D. H. LAWRENCE

EDITORIAL BOARD

SKETCHES OF ETRUSCAN PLACES

AND OTHER ITALIAN ESSAYS

D. H. LAWRENCE

EDITED BY
SIMONETTA DE FILIPPIS

CAMBRIDGE
UNIVERSITY PRESS

Published by the Press Syndicate of the University of Cambridge
The Pitt Building, Trumpington Street, Cambridge CB2 1RP
40 West 20th Street, New York, NY 10011-4211, USA
10 Stamford Road, Oakleigh, Victoria 3166, Australia

Printed in Great Britain at the University Press, Cambridge

A catalogue record for this book is available from the British Library

Library of Congress cataloguing in publication data
Lawrence, D. H. (David Herbert), 1885–1930.
Sketches of Etruscan places and other Italian essays.
p.   c.m. – (The Cambridge edition of the letters and
works of D. H. Lawrence)
Includes bibliographical references.
1. Etruscans.
2. Italy – Description and travel – 1901–1944.
3. Lawrence, D. H. (David Herbert), 1885–1930 –
Journeys – Italy.
I. De Filippis, Simonetta.   II. Title.
III. Series: Lawrence, D. H. (David Herbert), 1885–1930.
Works. 1979.
DG223.L374   1992   937'.5–dc20   91-34290

ISBN 0 521 25253 9 hard covers

CE

CONTENTS

GENERAL EDITORS' PREFACE

D. H. Lawrence is one of the great writers of the twentieth century – yet the texts of his writings, whether published during his lifetime or since, are, for the most part, textually corrupt. The extent of the corruption is remarkable; it can derive from every stage of composition and publication. We know from study of his MSS that Lawrence was a careful writer, though not rigidly consistent in matters of minor convention. We know also that he revised at every possible stage. Yet he rarely if ever compared one stage with the previous one, and overlooked the errors of typists or copyists. He was forced to accept, as most authors are, the often stringent house-styling of his printers, which overrode his punctuation and even his sentence-structure and paragraphing. He sometimes overlooked plausible printing errors. More important, as a professional author living by his pen, he had to accept, with more or less good will, stringent editing by a publisher's reader in his early days, and at all times the results of his publishers' timidity. So the fear of Grundyish disapproval, or actual legal action, led to bowdlerisation or censorship from the very beginning of his career. Threats of libel suits produced other changes. Sometimes a publisher made more changes than he admitted to Lawrence. On a number of occasions in dealing with American and British publishers Lawrence produced texts for both which were not identical. Then there were extraordinary lapses like the occasion when a typist turned over two pages of MS at once, and the result happened to make sense. This whole story can be reconstructed from the introductions to the volumes in this edition; cumulatively they will form a history of Lawrence's writing career.

The Cambridge edition aims to provide texts which are as close as can now be determined to those he would have wished to see printed. They have been established by a rigorous collation of extant manuscripts and typescripts, proofs and early printed versions; they restore the words, sentences, even whole pages omitted or falsified by editors or compositors; they are freed from printing-house conventions which were imposed on Lawrence's style; and interference on the part of frightened publishers has been eliminated. Far from doing violence to the texts Lawrence would have wished to see published, editorial intervention is essential to recover them. Though we have to accept that some cannot now be recovered in their entirety because early states have not survived, we must be glad that so much evidence remains. Paradoxical as it may seem, the outcome of this recension will be texts which differ, often radically and certainly frequently, from those seen by the author himself.

Editors have adopted the principle that the most authoritative form of the text is to be followed, even if this leads sometimes to a 'spoken' or a 'manuscript' rather than a 'printed' style. We have not wanted to strip off one house-styling in order to impose another. Editorial discretion has been allowed in order to regularise Lawrence's sometimes wayward spelling and punctuation in accordance with his most frequent practice in a particular text. A detailed record of these and other decisions on textual matters, together with the evidence on which they are based, will be found in the textual apparatus which records variant readings in manuscripts, typescripts and proofs; and printed variants in forms of the text published in Lawrence's lifetime. We do not record posthumous corruptions, except where first publication was posthumous. Significant MS readings may be found in the occasional explanatory note.

In each volume, the editor's introduction relates the contents to Lawrence's life and to his other writings; it gives the history of composition of the text in some detail, for its intrinsic interest, and because this history is essential to the statement of editorial principles followed. It provides an account of publication and reception which will be found to contain a good deal of hitherto unknown information. Where appropriate, appendixes make available extended draft manuscript readings of significance, or important material, sometimes unpublished, associated with a particular work.

Though Lawrence is a twentieth-century writer and in many respects remains our contemporary, the idiom of his day is not invariably intelligible now, especially to the many readers who are not native speakers of British English. His use of dialect is another difficulty, and further barriers to full understanding are created by now obscure literary, historical, political or other references and allusions. On these occasions explanatory notes are supplied by the editor; it is assumed that the reader has access to a good general dictionary and that the editor need not gloss words or expressions that may be found in it. Where Lawrence's letters are quoted in editorial matter, the reader should assume that his manuscript is alone the source of eccentricities of phrase or spelling. An edition of the letters is still in course of publication: for this reason only the date and recipient of a letter will be given if it has not so far been printed in the Cambridge edition.

ACKNOWLEDGEMENTS

I would like to thank Carl Baron for recommending me to edit this volume and for all his useful suggestions and friendly help.

I am deeply indebted to Lindeth Vasey for her valuable comments and meticulous help on editorial matters at every stage in the preparation of this volume. I am sincerely grateful to Michael Black, James Boulton and John Worthen for their expert advice and helpful suggestions.

Special thanks must go to Dorothy Armstrong, Helen Baron, Michael Burgoyne and Stephen Parkin for their constructive and friendly criticism and for the time they devoted to reading and discussing my work in progress.

For valuable help in particular matters I would like to express my personal thanks also to Andrew Brown, Giovanni Cerri, Vittorio Cicco, Rossella Ciocca, Bruno D'Agostino, Daniela de Filippis, Ornella De Zordo, Enrico Del Re, P. E. Easterling, Paul Eggert, Carla Esposito, Clemente Florio, Paola Giordano, E. W. Handley, Peter Honri, Christa Jansohn, David Johnson-Davis, Mara Kalnins, E. J. Kenney, Franco Lessi, Maurizio Martinelli, Dieter Mehl, Olimpia Mendia, Annegret Ogden, Gerald Pollinger, Gordon Poole, Maria Romano, Cornelia Rumpf-Worthen, Keith Sagar, R. W. Sharples, Nigel Spivey and Claudio Vicentini.

I am grateful to George Lazarus for allowing me access to his manuscript of 'Flowery Tuscany', and to the following libraries for making available the research materials in their collections: the photographs of *Sketches of Etruscan Places* and the typescripts of 'David', 'The Nightingale' and 'Flowery Tuscany', the Bancroft Library, University of California at Berkeley; the typescripts of 'Looking Down on the City' and 'The Nightingale', the University of California at Los Angeles; the typescript of 'Man is a Hunter', the University of New Mexico; the manuscripts of *Sketches of Etruscan Places*, 'Fireworks' and 'Man is a Hunter' and the typescripts of *Sketches of Etruscan Places*, 'David', 'Fireworks', 'Flowery Tuscany' IV, 'Germans and English', 'Man is a Hunter' and 'The Nightingale', the Harry Ransom Humanities Research Center, University of Texas at Austin; the typescripts and page proofs of *Sketches of Etruscan Places*, the McFarlin Library, University of Tulsa; the manuscript of 'The Nightingale', the Beinecke Library, Yale University.

My thanks go also, for their assistance, to the staff of the following libraries and institutions: American Consulate, Naples; Biblioteca Alessandrina, Rome; Biblioteca Nazionale, Naples; British Library; Cambridge University Library; Colindale Library; the Departments of English Studies and of Etruscology, Istituto Universitario Orientale, Naples; and Saint Louis Public Library.

I particularly wish to express my heartfelt gratitude to Fernando Ferrara for his teaching and encouragement throughout my career and for his contribution to this volume.

My final and special thanks go to my mother, Livia de Filippis, for her invaluable and constant support and for her extraordinary generosity.

My work was greatly helped by grants from the Ministry of Education of Italy and from the Centre for National Research (CNR).

June 1991   S.d.F.

CHRONOLOGY

11 September 1885	Born in Eastwood, Nottinghamshire
September 1898–July 1901	Pupil at Nottingham High School
1902–1908	Pupil teacher; student at University College, Nottingham
7 December 1907	First publication: 'A Prelude', in *Nottinghamshire Guardian*
October 1908	Appointed as teacher at Davidson Road School, Croydon
November 1909	Publishes five poems in *English Review*
3 December 1910	Engagement to Louie Burrows; broken off on 4 February 1912
9 December 1910	Death of his mother, Lydia Lawrence
19 January 1911	*The White Peacock* published in New York (20 January in London)
19 November 1911	Ill with pneumonia; resigns his teaching post on 28 February 1912
March 1912	Meets Frieda Weekley; they elope to Germany on 3 May
23 May 1912	*The Trespasser*
September 1912–March 1913	At Gargnano, Lago di Garda, Italy
February 1913	*Love Poems and Others*
29 May 1913	*Sons and Lovers*
June–August 1913	In England
August–September 1913	In Germany and Switzerland
30 September 1913–9 June 1914	At Lerici, Gulf of La Spezia, Italy
1 April 1914	*The Widowing of Mrs. Holroyd* (New York)
July 1914–December 1915	In London, Buckinghamshire and Sussex
13 July 1914	Marries Frieda Weekley in London
26 November 1914	*The Prussian Officer and Other Stories*
30 September 1915	*The Rainbow*; suppressed by court order on 13 November
June 1916	*Twilight in Italy*
July 1916	*Amores*
15 October 1917	After twenty-one months' residence in Cornwall, ordered to leave by military authorities
October 1917–November 1919	In London, Berkshire and Derbyshire

26 November 1917	*Look! We Have Come Through!*
October 1918	*New Poems*
14 November 1919	Travels to Italy
15–17 November 1919	At Val Selice, near Turin
19 November–10 December 1919	At the Pensione Balestra, Florence; probably writes 'David' and 'Looking Down on the City' (between November 1919 and May 1921)
20 November 1919	*Bay*
13–22 December 1919	At Picinisco
March 1920–February 1922	At Fontana Vecchia, Taormina, Sicily
May 1920	*Touch and Go*
September 1920	At Villa Canovaia, San Gervasio, Florence; the poem 'Cypresses' written at Fiesole
9 November 1920	Private publication of *Women in Love* (New York)
25 November 1920	*The Lost Girl*
5–13 January 1921	Visits Sardinia
April 1921	To Germany via Capri, Rome and Florence; on Capri meets Earl and Achsah Brewster; in Florence meets Rebecca West
May 1921	Writes the chapters 'Florence' and 'High Up over the Cathedral Square' of *Aaron's Rod*
10 May 1921	*Psychoanalysis and the Unconscious* (New York)
12 December 1921	*Sea and Sardinia* (New York)
26 February 1922	Leaves for Ceylon
March–August 1922	In Ceylon and Australia
14 April 1922	*Aaron's Rod* (New York)
September 1922–March 1923	In New Mexico
23 October 1922	*Fantasia of the Unconscious* (New York)
24 October 1922	*England, My England* (New York)
March 1923	*The Ladybird, The Fox, The Captain's Doll*
March–November 1923	In Mexico and USA
27 August 1923	*Studies in Classic American Literature* (New York)
September 1923	*Kangaroo*
9 October 1923	*Birds, Beasts and Flowers* (New York)
December 1923–March 1924	In England, France and Germany
March 1924–September 1925	In New Mexico and Mexico
28 August 1924	*The Boy in the Bush* (with Mollie Skinner)
10 September 1924	Death of his father, John Arthur Lawrence

14 May 1925	*St. Mawr together with the Princess*
September–November 1925	In England and Germany
15 November 1925–20 April 1926	At Spotorno (Liguria), and at Villa Bernarda from 23 November
Late November 1925	Writes 'Europe Versus America'
7 December 1925	*Reflections on the Death of a Porcupine* (Philadelphia)
21 January 1926	*The Plumed Serpent*
March–April 1926	Begins to plan to visit Etruria
Late March 1926	First visit to an Etruscan town, Perugia
25 March 1926	*David*
April 1926	'Europe Versus America' in *Laughing Horse*
May 1926	Reading Etruscan history in Mommsen, Weege, Ducati, Fell
6 May 1926–June 1928	At the Villa Mirenda, Scandicci (Florence)
25 June 1926	Probably writes 'Fireworks'
Late June 1926	Probably writes 'The Nightingale'
July–September 1926	In Germany and England
October 1926–19 March 1927	Back at the Villa Mirenda
October–November 1926	Writes 'Man is a Hunter' and *The First Lady Chatterley*
December 1926–February 1927	Writes *John Thomas and Lady Jane*
February 1927	New plan to visit the Etruscan places
February–April 1927	Writes 'Flowery Tuscany' I–III
22–8 March 1927	At Ravello (Salerno) with the Brewsters
5 April 1927	Etruscan tour with Earl Brewster starts in Rome: visit to the Villa Giulia Museum
6 April 1927	At Cerveteri
7–8 April 1927	At Tarquinia
9 April 1927	At Vulci
10 April 1927	At Volterra
11 April 1927–June 1928	At the Villa Mirenda
16 April 1927	'Fireworks' in *Nation & Athenæum*
13–28 April 1927	Writes Part I of *The Escaped Cock*, 'from that toy in Volterra'
27–9 April 1927	'Travel Sketches of Etruscan Places' begun; asks for copies of Dennis and Weege
30 April 1927	Suggests *Travel* might publish the Etruscan sketches; probably writes 'Flowery Tuscany' IV
Early May 1927	Probably writes 'Germans and English', later published by Insel-Verlag as 'Ein Brief von D. H. Lawrence an das Inselschiff' (Leipzig 1927); starts collecting photographs for the Etruscan book

May 1927	'Fireworks' in *Forum* (New York)
June 1927	*Mornings in Mexico*
6 June 1927	'About 80 pp. MSS.' written ('Cerveteri', 'Tarquinia', 'The Painted Tombs of Tarquinia' 1.)
14 June 1927	'Cerveteri' typed; 'The Painted Tombs of Tarquinia' 2. and 'Vulci' written. Sends 'Cerveteri' ('6000 words') and eight photographs to Curtis Brown
25 June 1927	'Volterra' written
26 June–22 July 1927	The other five Etruscan sketches are typed
July 1927	Plans a second Etruscan tour; 'The Florence Museum' possibly written July–October 1927
23 July 1927	Sends Curtis Brown the 'first' six Etruscan sketches and all the photographs
10 September 1927	'The Nightingale' in *Spectator* and also in the September *Forum* (a German translation, 'Die Nachtigall', published in the *Insel-Almanach auf das Jahr 1928*)
October–December 1927	'Flowery Tuscany' I–III in *New Criterion*
November 1927	'The City of the Dead at Cerveteri' ('Cerveteri') in *Travel*
December 1927	'The Ancient Metropolis of the Etruscans' ('Tarquinia') in *Travel*
December 1927–February 1928	Writes *Lady Chatterley's Lover*
January 1928	'The Painted Tombs of Tarquinia' (1) in *Travel*
February 1928	'The Wind-Swept Stronghold of Volterra' ('Volterra') in *Travel*
February–May 1928	The same four Etruscan essays in *World Today* with DHL's titles
24 May 1928	*The Woman Who Rode Away and Other Stories*
June 1928–March 1930	In Switzerland and, principally, in France
July 1928	*Lady Chatterley's Lover* privately published (Florence)
September 1928	*Collected Poems*
March 1929	Gives up the plan of writing more Etruscan sketches
April 1929	'The Year in Flowery Tuscany' ('Flowery Tuscany' I–III) in *Travel*
July 1929	Exhibition of paintings in London raided by police; *Pansies* (manuscript earlier seized in the mail)
September 1929	*The Escaped Cock* (Paris)

20 November 1929	Last mention of his interest in the Etruscans
2 March 1930	Dies at Vence, Alpes Maritimes, France
September 1932	*Etruscan Places* published by Martin Secker in England and Viking in America
November 1934	'Germans and English' published as 'Tedeschi e Inglesi' in *La Cultura* (Turin)
19 October 1936	*Phoenix: The Posthumous Papers of D. H. Lawrence*: contains 'Man is a Hunter', 'The Nightingale', 'Flowery Tuscany' I–III, 'David', 'Europe Versus America', 'Fireworks' (as 'Fireworks in Florence') and 'Flowery Tuscany' IV (as 'Germans and Latins')
15 January 1968	*Phoenix II: Uncollected, Unpublished and Other Prose Works by D. H. Lawrence*: contains 'Germans and English'

CUE-TITLES

A. Manuscript locations

GSArchiv	Goethe-und Schiller-Archiv, Weimar
Lazarus	Mr George Lazarus
NWU	Northwestern University
UCB	University of California at Berkeley
UCLA	University of California at Los Angeles
UNM	University of New Mexico
UT	University of Texas at Austin
UTul	University of Tulsa
YU	Yale University

B. Printed works

(The place of publication, here and throughout, is London unless otherwise stated.)

Aaron's Rod	D. H. Lawrence. *Aaron's Rod*. Ed. Mara Kalnins. Cambridge: Cambridge University Press, 1988.
Dennis	George Dennis. *The Cities and Cemeteries of Etruria*. 2nd edn. 2 volumes. J. Murray, 1878.
Ducati	Pericle Ducati. *Etruria Antica*. 2 volumes. Torino: G. B. Paravia, 1925.
Letters, iii.	James T. Boulton and Andrew Robertson, eds. *The Letters of D. H. Lawrence*. Volume III. Cambridge: Cambridge University Press, 1984.
Letters, v.	James T. Boulton and Lindeth Vasey, eds. *The Letters of D. H. Lawrence*. Volume V. Cambridge: Cambridge University Press, 1989.
Letters, vi.	James T. Boulton and Margaret H. Boulton with Gerald M. Lacy, eds. *The Letters of D. H. Lawrence*. Volume VI. Cambridge: Cambridge University Press, 1991.

OED	Sir James A. H. Murray and others, eds. *A New English Dictionary on Historical Principles*. 10 volumes. Oxford University Press, 1884–1928.
Phoenix	Edward D. McDonald, ed. *Phoenix: The Posthumous Papers of D. H. Lawrence*. New York: Viking Press, 1936.
Roberts	Warren Roberts. *A Bibliography of D. H. Lawrence*. 2nd edn. Cambridge: Cambridge University Press, 1982.

INTRODUCTION

INTRODUCTION

Sketches of Etruscan Places

The Genesis and Composition

In 1925 D. H. Lawrence and his wife Frieda left New Mexico to return to Europe: 'Myself, I hate the real U.S.A., Chicago and New York and all that. I feel very much drawn to the Mediterranean again: we may winter in Sicily.'[1] They sailed from New York on 21 September 1925, and after a few weeks in England and Germany, arrived at Spotorno on 15 November and rented the Villa Bernarda,[2] where they lived until April 1926.

Lawrence had already stayed in Italy on three previous occasions. The first was after his elopement with Frieda, from early September 1912 to the beginning of April 1913 when they lived at Gargnano (Lake Garda); the second period, from the end of September 1913 to the beginning of June 1914, was spent at Lerici (La Spezia), also in the north of Italy; Lawrence's impressions of these Italian experiences, particularly of his sojourn at Gargnano, were conveyed in a series of essays collected in the volume *Twilight in Italy*.[3] The third Italian period belongs to the years 1919–22, when the Lawrences chose the south and lived mostly near Taormina, Sicily.

Since 1912–14, Lawrence had been fascinated by Italy, by its landscape, climate, people, atmosphere: 'One must love Italy, if one has lived there. It is so non-moral. It leaves the soul so free. Over these countries, Germany and England, like the grey skies, lies the gloom of the dark moral judgment and condemnation and reservation of the people. Italy does not judge.'[4] Italy represented a completely different world to him, and he could see in it

---

[1] *Letters*, v. 277. (Subsequent references to *Letters*, iii., v. and vi. are given in the text with volume and page number.)

[2] Spotorno is a small town on the coast of Liguria, northern Italy. The Villa Bernarda was owned by Angelo Ravagli (1891–1976), who was to marry Frieda in 1950.

[3] Also called 'Italian Sketches', parts were first written in 1912–13; it was extended and revised for book publication in 1915 and published in 1916.

[4] James T. Boulton, ed., *The Letters of D. H. Lawrence* (Cambridge, 1979), i. 544.

the invitation for a more authentic way of life. 'Why is England so shabby. The Italians here sing ... And they go by the window proudly, and they don't hurry or fret. And the women walk straight and look calm. And the men adore children – they are glad of their children even if they're poor. I think they haven't many ideas, but they look well, and they have strong blood.'[5]

Although Lawrence's feelings about Italy were not always consistent, sometimes expressing great love and admiration, at other times being sharply critical, Italy provided a sympathetic context for his fast maturing beliefs. Italian rural life and culture gave him insights into an earlier more natural and spontaneous world, untouched by the corruption of modern industrialisation, power, money and intellectualism. Italy was thus a rich source of inspiration for a number of his writings.

The charm that Italy had exerted on Lawrence drew him back for a third sojourn in 1919. This time he stayed for two full years, mainly in Sicily, but he also spent some time in other Italian places.[6]

It was during this third period that Lawrence also visited Picinisco (13–22 December 1919) – a small village in the Abruzzi mountains where the last part of *The Lost Girl* is set – and Sardinia (5–13 January 1921), which provided him with the subject of his second Italian book *Sea and Sardinia*. Here, as in all his other writings inspired by his experiences in foreign countries, Lawrence offers the reader not only a description of the places he visited and of the people he met, but also clearly shows the impact they had on him and how they related to his own feelings and ideas.

His unending quest for unspoilt places where he could feel the natural impulses in their full and authentic power, however, drew him towards other continents, and he left Italy, with Frieda, on 26 February 1922. It was more than three years (spent principally in USA and Mexico) before they returned, drawn back by their rediscovered Europeanness and attracted by Italy once more. They arrived at Spotorno, on the Italian Riviera, on 15 November 1925; from the Villa Bernarda Lawrence wrote to Earl and Achsah Brewster ten days later: 'We've taken this house until end of March, but that doesn't mean we can't go away for a while. I should like to move south when the spring comes – to see Amalfi and Sicily in February'.[7]

---

[5] Ibid., p. 460.

[6] In March 1920 the Lawrences settled at Fontana Vecchia, in a villa 'out of Taormina on the green height over the sea, looking east' (*Letters*, iii. 494). For the specific places DHL visited and dates, see Chronology.

[7] *Letters*, v. 345. Earl Henry Brewster (1878–1957) and Achsah Barlow Brewster (1878–1945), American painters, and students of Eastern philosophy. DHL met them on Capri in

Indeed, Lawrence and Frieda left Spotorno for Florence at the end of April and, a short time later, they settled at Scandicci, near Florence, where they rented the Villa Mirenda in early May 1926 and where they lived for the rest of their fourth Italian sojourn, until June 1928. It was during March–April 1926 that Lawrence began to plan his visit to the various historical sites of Etruria in order to write a book about them. Ill health delayed his plans during the summer of 1926 and in the autumn he was involved in the writing of the first and second versions of *Lady Chatterley's Lover*. He was also growing impatient with his publishers and with the critics and reading public in general. Their persistent misunderstanding of his work, together with their readiness to condemn and censure, made him all the more committed to the writing of *Lady Chatterley's Lover*. These reasons, combined with his gradually worsening health, account for his fluctuating enthusiasm for the Etruscan project, and indeed, even after his tour of Etruria, prevented him from ever attempting a second trip to complete the book as originally planned.

Lawrence's fascination with the Etruscans predated the planning of the expedition by at least six years. He had long been interested in Etruscan culture and history, and in the Etruscans' ancient 'wisdom', that old, 'dark' conception of life which had disappeared with them when they were absorbed into Roman civilisation.

Lawrence's readings in his formative years may have awakened his curiosity in Etruscan culture. In 1908, for instance, as Jessie Chambers recalls, he 'was very impressed by Balzac's *La Peau de Chagrin*'. At the beginning of the novel, the hero observes 'an Etruscan vase of finest clay, the nut-brown maiden dancing before the god Priapus, to whom she joyously waved her hand'. In December 1915 Lawrence read *The Golden Bough*[8] and was very much taken by Frazer's account of tree-spirits in chapter IX, 'The Worship of Trees', where central Etruria and its 'rich fields' are mentioned.

An early mention of the Etruscans in Lawrence's own writing is contained in the poem 'Cypresses'. Written in September 1920 at Fiesole (Tuscany), it shows clearly how Lawrence had already traced the main elements which he later developed into the more complex and conscious vision offered in *Sketches of Etruscan Places*. In the poem, Lawrence's

April 1921 and visited them in Ceylon in March–April 1922. DHL toured the Etruscan area with Earl Brewster in April 1927; see the Brewsters' memoir, *D. H. Lawrence: Reminiscences and Correspondence* (1934).
[8] E. T. [Jessie Wood], *D. H. Lawrence: A Personal Record* (1935; reprinted Cambridge, 1980), p. 106; *La Peau de chagrin* was published in 1831. George J. Zytaruk and James T. Boulton, eds., *The Letters of D. H. Lawrence* (Cambridge, 1981), ii. 470 and n.

attitude to the Etruscans is still unresolved. The tone is exploratory, undecided, as the form of the first half of the poem shows, with its series of unanswered questions: 'Tuscan cypresses,/What is it? ... Is there a great secret?/Are our words no good? ... Is it the secret of the long-nosed Etruscans? ... Were they then vicious, the slender, tender-footed/Long-nosed men of Etruria? ...'[9] Rosalind Baynes recalled: 'Sometimes he came to Fiesole where I was now living, climbing by a steep track up through the olives and along under the remains of Fiesole's Etruscan walls ... It was here several ... poems were suggested – "Cypresses," for example.'[10] A year later, on 10 September 1921, Lawrence mentioned the Tuscan cypresses once more in a letter to his mother-in-law and, again, he drew a physical parallel with the Etruscans: 'This is Tuscany, and nowhere are the cypresses so beautiful and proud, like black-flames from primeval times, before the Romans had come, when the Etruscans were still here, slender and fine and still and with naked elegance, black haired, with narrow feet.'[11] Lawrence's keen interest in the Etruscans and his desire to penetrate their 'secret' were also shown in a letter to Catherine Carswell written about six weeks later: 'will you tell me *what* ʾ.en was the secret of the Etruscans, which you saw written so plainly in the place you went to? Please dont forget to tell me, as they really do rather puzzle me, the Etruscans.'[12]

During the same year, 1921, Lawrence wrote his second book on his theory of the unconscious, *Fantasia of the Unconscious*.[13] In its foreword, Lawrence attributes to ancient civilisations some kind of deep life-knowledge, which is completely lost and unknown to modern man:

I honestly think that the great pagan world of which Egypt and Greece were the last living terms, the great pagan world which preceded our own era once, had a vast and perhaps perfect science of its own, a science in terms of life. In our era this science crumbled into magic and charlatanry. But even wisdom crumbles ... Then

[9] Published in *Birds, Beasts and Flowers* (*The Complete Poems of D. H. Lawrence*, ed. Vivian de Sola Pinto and Warren Roberts, 1964, i. 296–7, ll. 1–2, 6–7, 14, 40–1).

[10] Edward Nehls, ed., *D. H. Lawrence: A Composite Biography* (Madison, 1957–9), ii. 49–50. Rosalind Baynes (1891–1973) met DHL in Berkshire in 1919. She arranged for him and Frieda to stay at Picinisco in December 1919. DHL stayed in her house at Fiesole in September 1920.

[11] Warren Roberts, James T. Boulton and Elizabeth Mansfield, eds., *The Letters of D. H. Lawrence* (Cambridge, 1987), iv. 84. Frieda's mother was the Baroness Anna von Richthofen (1851–1930). The same image of the Tuscan cypresses recurs in *Aaron's Rod* 265:31–4. The idea of lost wisdom, intuited through plants, goes back to *The White Peacock* (ed. Andrew Robertson, Cambridge, 1983, pp. 129–30).

[12] Roberts, Boulton and Mansfield, eds., *Letters of D. H. Lawrence*, iv. 105. Catherine Carswell (1879–1946), Scottish critic, novelist and biographer, met DHL in summer 1914, and often corresponded with him, particularly during the war years.

[13] *Psychoanalysis and the Unconscious* had been written in 1920.

came ... the world flood ... The refugees ... fled ... and some, like Druids or Etruscans or Chaldeans or Amerindians or Chinese, refused to forget, but taught the old wisdom, only in its half-forgotten, symbolic forms.

The old 'secret' was lost with the Etruscans and so for Lawrence man is no longer able to understand the real meaning of life: 'We are really far, far more life-stupid than the dead Greeks or the lost Etruscans.'[14] In *Sea and Sardinia*, written in the same year, Lawrence also refers to the Etruscans and their gods as an expression of man's 'conscious genius'.[15]

The fact that so little was known about the Etruscans and their civilisation helped to stimulate Lawrence's imagination and curiosity, and gave him the opportunity to interpret freely the Etruscan remains in terms of those symbols which best expressed his own ideas. So, for Lawrence, the Etruscans were the keepers of the old, great secret of life, and when finally he came to write the book, they were to symbolise naturalness, spontaneity and simplicity – aspects of the positive civilisation which was dramatically antithetical to the modern, mechanical and corrupted world.

Although Lawrence's interest in the Etruscans can be dated back at least to 1920, it was only in spring 1926 that he seriously started planning to visit the places where Etruscan culture had developed, and to write a book on them. At the end of March his interest in the Etruscans caused him to make a short trip to Perugia, accompanied by Millicent Beveridge and Mabel Harrison;[16] there he visited the National Archaeological Museum, famous for its Etruscan urns, and a few days later he wrote: 'I have an idea I might like to roam round in Umbria for a little while, and look at the Etruscan things, which interest me' (v. 416). The first contact with an Etruscan town and museum was – as one would expect – very stimulating and fired Lawrence's enthusiasm for writing 'a book about Umbria and the Etruscans: half travel-book, scientific too' (v. 412). As several letters written between 4 and 11 April indicate, he was considering spending a few weeks in Perugia in order to collect material; on the 4th, writing to his English publisher Martin Secker, he also mentioned his reading:

We might go to Perugia, and I might do a book on Umbria and the Etruscan remains ... It would be half a travel book – of the region round Perugia, Assisi, Spoleto, Cortona, and the Maremma – and half a book about the Etruscan things, which interest me very much. – If you happen to know any good book, modern, on

---

[14] *Fantasia of the Unconscious*, chap. VII.   [15] *Sea and Sardinia*, chap. VI.
[16] Anne Millicent Beveridge (1871–1955), Scottish painter, and her fellow-artist Mabel Harrison (*Letters*, v. 407, 412 and 403 n.1). The first shared his interest to the extent of sending him a book on the Etruscans (see p. xxviii below).

Etruscan things, I wish you'd order it for me. I've only read that old work, Dennis' –
Cities and Cemeteries of Etruria.[17]   (v. 413)

However, Lawrence had mixed feelings about the idea of writing a book;
as we see from a letter he wrote the next day to his English agent Curtis
Brown, shortly after having made his original plan, he was by no means
committed to the scheme: 'I fancied I might like to do a book, half travel
and half study, on Umbria and the Etruscans. The Etruscan things interest
me very much. We might stay at Perugia for a couple of months and get
material. But heaven knows if I'll really do it – the book, I mean. I'm "off"
writing – even letters – ' (v. 415).

In a letter to Richard Aldington of 18 April 1926, Lawrence explains
more clearly his interest in the Etruscans: 'the Etruscan things appeal *very
much* to my imagination. They are so curiously natural – somebody said
bourgeois, but that's a lie, considering all the phallic monuments'.[18] At this
point Lawrence had only visited the museums in Florence[19] and Perugia,
and yet he had already quite clearly defined his own idea and interpretation
of Etruscan culture as natural and anti-bourgeois, a judgement which was
later confirmed by his tour of Etruria.

The plan to go to Umbria seemed, by this time, less appealing to
Lawrence; on 25 April he wrote to Earl Brewster: 'I had thought of staying
perhaps a couple of months in and around Umbria, and doing a book on
the Etruscans. But I notice, if ever I say I'll do a thing, I never bring it off.
To tell the truth, I feel like going away – perhaps to Spain, or to Germany'
(v. 437). Nevertheless he was still interested in reading about the Etruscans, for he wrote to Secker on 29 April: 'I'm reading Italian books on the
Etruscans – very interesting indeed. I'll join Vieusseux's library here – they
will have more things.'[20] Even if he had deferred his visit to Umbria, the
idea of writing a book on the Etruscans was firmly fixed in his mind;
moreover,

[17] George Dennis's *The Cities and Cemeteries of Etruria* was published in two volumes of over
a thousand pages with close printing and many footnotes in 1848; a revised edn was
published thirty years later.
[18] *Letters*, v. 427. Richard Aldington (1892–1962), novelist, biographer, critic, poet; DHL
first met him in July 1914, and visited him in Berkshire in August 1926: 'As I knew he was
contemplating a book on the Etruscans, I had a dozen standard works on the subject sent
down from the London Library; and we spent a good deal of time turning them over and
discussing Etruria, which was very important at that time in Lawrence's private mythology'
(Nehls, *A Composite Biography*, iii. 84–5).
[19] Probably DHL had visited the Archaeological Museum in Florence when he first stayed
there in 1919, by which time he had also read Dennis. It contains mainly Etruscan and
Egyptian remains (see Explanatory note on 175:4).
[20] *Letters*, v. 444. Vieusseux is a well-known Florentine circulating library, founded in 1819;
see ibid. n. 3.

Secker has been urging me to write a travel book: and I don't want to do an ordinary travel book, just of places. So I thought I might stay here [at the Villa Mirenda] two months or so, and prepare a book on the Etruscan cities – the dead Etruscans. It would mean my travelling about a good deal ... That would be in June – at present I'm reading the Italian books on the Etruscans, getting the idea into shape. (v. 448–9)

The idea of travelling through Etruria became more feasible when the Lawrences left Spotorno and settled at the Villa Mirenda, in the Florentine countryside: 'we have taken a villa about 7 miles out of Florence here, in the country, and I can use that as a centre, when I have to go travelling round to ... quite a number of places in Tuscany and Umbria, where the best remains are. At present I am supposed to be reading up about my precious Etruschi!' (v. 447). In a number of letters written around mid-May, Lawrence, although professing to be undecided about writing his book on the Etruscans, confirmed that he was still reading about them, and he told Curtis Brown: 'I ... may this summer manage a book, half-travel and half description of Etruscan things, about those people. It would have quite a lot of photographs' (v. 460). The inclusion of photographs was, in Lawrence's opinion, essential for the book's success (v. 461).

Towards the end of May 1926 Lawrence sent a letter to his sister-in-law Else Jaffe which contains the roots of all the main ideas which were to be developed extensively a year later in the actual writing of the Etruscan sketches. After describing the kind of book he intended to write – 'nothing pretentious, but a sort of book for people who will actually be going to Florence ... and those places, to look at the Etruscan things' – he declared:

Etruscan things ... have a great attraction for me: there are lovely things in the Etruscan Museum here ... Mommsen hated everything Etruscan, said the germ of all degeneracy was in the race. But the bronzes and terra cottas are fascinating, so alive with physical life, with a powerful physicality which surely is as great, or sacred, ultimately, as the *ideal* of the Greeks and Germans. Anyhow, the real strength of Italy seems to me in this physicality, which is not at all Roman.[21]

---

[21] *Letters*, v. 464–5. DHL refers to the Archaeological Museum in Florence (see footnote 19 above). Theodor Mommsen (1817–1903), German historian and professor of law, author of *Römische Geschichte* (Berlin, 1861), trans. as *The History of Rome* by W. P. Dickson (rev. edn, 1894). Mommsen makes a number of critical remarks about the Etruscans and their life style which 'leave no doubt as to the deep degeneracy of the nation' (II. iv. 436). See also I. xii. 232; I. xv. 309; II. iv. 435; II. ix. 124–5, 128.

The reference to Mommsen is repeated, in a very similar style and tone, at the beginning of 'Cerveteri', the first of the six sketches.[22] Lawrence considers the Italian people not as the progeny of the Romans, but as the offspring of the Etruscans, whose 'physicality' is still alive in Italy. What Mommsen and others had interpreted as the 'germ of all degeneracy' is, in Lawrence's view, a virtue: the very source of authentic life and vivacity. The Italian people and their true ancestors, the Etruscans, come to symbolise naturalness, spontaneity and the inner and true freedom in contrast with all the misconceptions, artificialities and hypocrisy of Western industrialised society.

Two other books on the Etruscans are mentioned in this letter, though they are both damned with faint praise. Fritz Weege's *Etruskische Malerei* (Halle, 1920, 1921) seemed to interest Lawrence only for its reproductions, while Pericle Ducati's *Etruria Antica* (Turin, 1925) – like many books he had already read – he considered neither particularly original nor stimulating. Lawrence dismissed the so-called authoritative books on the subject as 'dreary, repetition and surmise', partly because their traditional, historical interpretation was based on a viewpoint so radically different from his own. A letter written in June 1926 to Millicent Beveridge particularly reveals this attitude:

Many thanks for Fell, his book came a few days ago. He's very thorough in washing out once more the few rags of information we have concerning the Etruscans: but not a thing has he to say. It's really disheartening: I shall just have to start in and go ahead, and be damned to all authorities! There really is next to nothing to be said, *scientifically*, about the Etruscans. Must take the imaginative line.[23]

In this letter and elsewhere, Lawrence still talks of visiting the Etruscan places in September, but two letters – the last written in 1926 in which the Etruscan plan is mentioned – have a rather different tone and the project seems to be set definitely aside for that year. Not only did he seem to have changed his mind about writing the book; he was also very hostile towards the idea of publishing in general as he always resented the pressure from publishers to meet the demands of what he regarded as a generally unqualified reading public. A letter written on 28 June 1926 has a challenging tone: 'I haven't done any of the Etruscan book yet: and shan't do it, unless the mood changes. Why write books for the swine, unless one absolutely must!' (v. 483). Three weeks later the tone is still negative, but a little more subdued: 'Of literary news, I have none. I wanted to write a

---

[22] See below 9:22–8.
[23] *Letters*, v. 473. DHL refers to Roland Arthur Lonsdale Fell, *Etruria and Rome* (Cambridge, 1924).

book on the Etruscans and Etruscan cities – sort of half travel book. But I
get such a distaste for committing myself into "solid print," I am holding
off. Let the public read what there is to read' (v. 496). He was also
conscious of the strain writing put upon his health; in a letter of 29 July
1926 he complained bitterly: 'I am not doing any work at all: feel
sufficiently disgusted with myself for having done so much and under-
mined my health, with so little return. Pity one has to write at all' (v. 504).

It was early 1927 before Lawrence resumed his planning for the
Etruscan tour, and by now he had found a companion, Earl Brewster.
Lawrence mentioned his new project to him in a letter of 27 February: 'If
you and Achsah ask me, I'll come to Ravello for a week or ten days, then
we'll go our walking trip ... Or should we meet in Rome and look at those
Etruscan tombs?'[24] A few days later he gave Earl more details of their
projected trip:

What *I* should most like to do, for the trip, would be to do the western half of the
Etruscans – the Rome museums – then Veii and Città Castellana and Cervet[e]ri
– which one does from Rome – then Corneto, just beyond Città Vecchia in
Maremma – then the Maremma coast-line – and Volterra ... If there were time, we
might get to Chiusi and Orvieto – we could see. I have a real feeling about the
Etruscans.[25]

Lawrence had an additional incentive for the trip because 'an American
magazine' wanted to publish the articles (v. 655, 653). However, of all the
places he mentioned in his letter, only Rome, Cerveteri, Corneto, the
Maremma coastline and Volterra were actually visited, probably for lack of
time. Orvieto and Chiusi were later mentioned, in several letters, as places
to be included in a second Etruscan tour and to be described in another six
sketches: 'I intended to do twelve sketches, on different places – but when
I was ill, I left off at Volterra ... if you felt at all keen about the Etruscan
book, I'd sweat round Arezzo and Chiusi and Orvieto and those places,
and do the other six sketches this autumn.'[26] Unfortunately that second
tour was never made; nor of course were those sketches written.

Another month was to pass before he actually set out. On 19 March
1927 Lawrence left the Villa Mirenda and joined the Brewsters in Ravello
on 22 March; after a week, on 28 March, he and Earl drove to Sorrento.

[24] *Letters*, v. 648. Ravello is a small village on a hill over the Amalfi coast, s. of Naples.
[25] *Letters*, v. 649–50. The places mentioned are all within the regions of Lazio, Umbria and
Tuscany (central Italy). Corneto is the ancient name of Tarquinia (see Explanatory note
on 25:2).
[26] *Letters*, vi. 182, to Alfred Knopf, DHL's current publisher in USA. DHL planned to do
an essay for each of the 'great' city-states – and possibly a second volume of the 'little
places' (vi. 89).

Brewster recalled: 'From Sorrento we started on our Etruscan pilgrimage, beginning with the museum of the Villa di Papa Giulia in Rome.'[27] From Rome, on 5 April 1927, Lawrence announced that he and Brewster were finally on their way to the Etruscan places: 'Brewster ... and I are going to stop off at various places on the east [i.e. west] coast, to look at Etruscan tombs and remains. Several people have asked me for travel articles, and I might do them on the Etruscan places' (vi. 25).

During and soon after their trip, Lawrence wrote several postcards and letters which make it possible to date and trace the itinerary he and Brewster followed through Etruria. On 6 April they left Rome for Cerveteri from where Lawrence wrote: 'Came here from Rome with Earl today – a fascinating place of Etruscan tombs' (vi. 27). On the 7th and the 8th they were in Tarquinia, as Lawrence wrote from there on 'Friday evening': 'We had two very delightful days here, looking at painted tombs ... And tomorrow we go to Vulci – expect to be in Volterra, the last place, by Monday' (vi. 27). It is likely that they were at Vulci on the 9th and at Volterra on 10 April; he almost certainly arrived at the Villa Mirenda on the evening of Monday, the 11th.[28]

In April Lawrence wrote a number of letters describing his Etruscan experience in enthusiastic terms. A letter to his mother-in-law, written in German on the 14th, contains what would be the core of his approach to the Etruscans: 'They were a lively, fresh, jolly people, lived their own life, without wanting to dominate the life of others. I am fond of my Etruscans. They had life in themselves, so they didn't have so much need to dominate. I should like to write a couple of sketches of Etruscan places – nothing scientific, but just as it is now, and the impression one has' (vi. 33–4).

In spite of his enthusiasm, Lawrence did not start writing on the Etruscans immediately. Instead, between 13 and 28 April, he wrote 'a story of the Resurrection ... It's called *The Escaped Cock*, from that toy in Volterra.'[29] After this, he briefly went back to his project on the Etruscan

---

[27] Brewster, *Reminiscences and Correspondence*, p. 122. The National Museum of Antiquities was built under Pope Giulio III and is commonly called 'Villa Giulia'.

[28] A letter to Nancy Pearn of the periodical department at Curtis Brown from the Villa Mirenda, dated 12 April, says: 'I got back here last night' (vi. 29). Two letters dated 13 April, suggest that the 12th was the date of DHL's return to the Villa Mirenda (vi. 30, 31); however, considering that in the Volterra sketch we are told that DHL and Brewster arrived there on a 'Sunday afternoon' and spent the Monday morning visiting the museum, DHL may well have returned to the Villa Mirenda on the evening of that same day.

[29] *Letters*, vi. 50. Brewster recalled that, when they were at Volterra on Easter morning, they 'passed a little shop, in the window of which was a toy white rooster escaping from an egg. I remarked that it suggested a title – "The Escaped Cock – a story of the Resurrection". Lawrence replied that he had been thinking about writing a story of the Resurrection: later

sketches: 'Now I really want to do a series of "Travel Sketches of Etruscan Places". I liked my trip to Cerveteri and Tarquinia and Vulci so much, I'd like to jot them down while they are fresh. Then later go to Cortona and Chiusi and Orvieto etc. . . . And so make a little book of Etruscan places' (vi. 42). Finally, only two days later, on 29 April, he informed Secker: 'I began my essays on the Etruscan things – I believe they'll be rather nice' (vi. 45) – but broke off almost immediately to write other essays[30] and to type *The Escaped Cock*.

However, during the month of May, Lawrence did not work much. He was ill with 'bronchial colds, mixed with malaria' (vi. 66) and was concerned about *Lady Chatterley's Lover*. He was deeply committed to the novel, and in it he tried to synthesise his most strongly held beliefs, many of which had come to their maturity during his long consideration of the Etruscans and their culture. In the description of the Tomb of the Painted Vases, included in the essay 'The Painted Tombs of Tarquinia' 1., he wrote:

the etruscan paintings: they really have the sense of touch; the people and the creatures are all really in touch. It is one of the rarest qualities, in life as well as in art . . . Here, in this faded etruscan painting, there is a quiet flow of touch that unites the man and the woman on the couch, the timid boy behind, the dog that lifts his nose, even the very garlands that hang from the wall.[31]

The concept of touch, in the sense of physical and pre-mental communication, is a major theme of *Lady Chatterley's Lover*, and Mellors, in the final part of the novel, preaches it as his gospel: 'Sex is really only touch, the closest of all touch. And it's touch we're afraid of. We're only half-conscious, and half alive. We've got to come alive and aware. Especially the English have got to get into touch with one another, a bit delicate and a bit tender. It's our crying need—'[32] There are many similar echoes between the Etruscan essays and the novel, one of which is particularly illuminating. It concerns the passage from 'Cerveteri' where Lawrence describes the Etruscan-like faces of the people he had seen there: 'warm faces still jovial with etruscan vitality, beautiful with the mystery of the unrifled ark, ripe with the phallic knowledge and the

---

in the book of that title which he gave to me, he has written: "To Earl this story, that began in Volterra, when we were there together"' (Brewster, *Reminiscences and Correspondence*, pp. 123–4). The story was revised and extended later.

[30] Probably 'Flowery Tuscany' IV and 'Germans and English'; see below.

[31] See below 54:3–14. DHL wrote 'etruscan' for the adjectival form in the manuscript, and sometimes in letters: his practice is followed in this edition; see below, p. xlviii and Note on the text.

[32] *Lady Chatterley's Lover* (ed. Michael Squires, Cambridge, 1992, 277:32–6).

etruscan carelessness!'[33] There is an obvious connection between this and his feelings about *Lady Chatterley's Lover*, expressed in a letter written about a year after the essay: 'It is a nice and tender phallic novel – not a sex novel in the ordinary sense of the word … I sincerely believe in restoring … the phallic consciousness, into our lives, because it is the source of all real beauty, and all real gentleness' (vi. 328).

In spite of all his ill health and his worries about the novel, Lawrence did not abandon his project on the Etruscan sketches; in fact, at times he demonstrated a serious and professional attitude towards the project, such as thinking about the book in its final form, as we can see from his letter to Secker on 29 April 1927: 'do send me Dennis' *Cities and Cemeteries of Etruria*. I should like to read it again, and my copy is in America. It's a good book … We can put thrilling illustrations in an Etruscan book!' (vi. 45). Taken by the idea of including photographs in his volume, on 1 June 1927 Lawrence wrote to his sister-in-law Else and asked her to buy him a copy of Weege's *Etruskische Malerei*, a book which only a year earlier had certainly not roused much interest in him.[34] He also started collecting photographs: 'I got photographs too from Alinari – and on the one from the Tomba dei Tori, the two little improper bits, "un poco pornografico," as brave as life. Amusing!'[35]

On 6 June 1927, Lawrence wrote to Secker:

I began doing the Etruscan book – have done about 80 pp. MSS. Of course it fascinates *me* – but the public is an ass I don't understand. I've got some lovely photographs, too, from Alinari. I might possibly, if the gods wish it, get these *Sketches of Etruscan Places* done by early autumn – and you might, if you liked, in that case get it out for Christmas. But God knows how it'll go. – It would have to be a book with many full illustrations – a hundred even – and as such it could be a standard popularish – not scientific – book on the Etruscan things and places, and might really sell, for the photographs at least are striking and beautiful. When I've finished 'Tarquinia', I'll let you see the essays on Cerveteri and Tarquinia, with some of the photographs, and you can let me know what you think, for the rest of the book. Perhaps in about two weeks I can send you so much.	(vi. 77)

Lawrence was already writing his third essay (the first '80 pp. MSS.' correspond to 'Cerveteri', 'Tarquinia' and 'The Painted Tombs of Tarquinia' 1., that is, the first part of the essay which was to be divided into

---

[33] See below 22:39–41.	[34] *Letters*, vi. 74. See above, p. xxviii.
[35] *Letters*, vi. 50. The *Tomba dei Tori* is described in 'The Painted Tombs of Tarquinia' 2. (see below, pp. 120–5).

Alinari, a publishing firm founded in Florence in 1852 by Leopoldo Alinari (1832–65), soon became famous for its excellent photographic reproductions and art books. DHL had considered using some of their photographic work in *Sea and Sardinia* (see *Letters*, iii. 696–7).

two parts).[36] However, despite his continuing enthusiasm, Lawrence had come to think that his was not a popular subject: 'I am working at my Etruscan book – a piece of hopeless unpopularity, as far as I can see. But the pictures may help it' (vi. 82). In fact, he was convinced that good photographs were essential if the book was to succeed at all, and he wrote to Earl Brewster: 'I am in rather a fix for some photographs for my Etruscan essays' (vi. 85), asking him to get information about some photographs, particularly of the *Tomba della Caccia e della Pesca* (Tarquinia) and of the *Ponte dell'Abbadia* (Vulci).[37]

Within another week Lawrence had written 'The Painted Tombs of Tarquinia' 2. and 'Vulci'; he then sent 'Cerveteri' to his agent Curtis Brown to forward to Secker, and wrote to the latter:

I am sending to Curtis Brown today the first of the *Sketches of Etruscan Places*: 'Cerveteri'. It is about 6000 words. I contemplate doing a dozen essays of that length – or perhaps 14. This one has eight photographs: and that might be the average. I have done four more essays, but am waiting to get them typed, and for photographs. I'll send them along in about a week. – Will you let me know at once what you think about a book of this sort. If you are doubtful of it, I won't press ahead with it. It would have to have about a hundred illustrations. (vi. 84)

On 25 June, Lawrence informed Earl Brewster that the last of the first batch of sketches had been written: 'I wrote my essay on Volterra – made me think of you' (vi. 89). On 2 July Lawrence pressed Secker again: 'I have done so far six essays of my Etruscans . . . *give me your candid opinion*. I want this book – which will be a bit expensive to you, owing to illustrations – to be as popular as I can make it. And I am open to any suggestions you can make me' (vi. 93). Obviously, as long as Secker was inclined to publish, in spite of the cost, Lawrence felt obliged to seek his opinion. Not long after, he received a reassuring letter from Nancy Pearn, saying: 'You will, I gather, already have heard from Secker, saying how pleased he is with the idea of a book on the "Etruscan Sketches".'[38]

Another attack of illness in July, however, forced Lawrence to bed again, and the project for his second tour with Brewster had to be postponed along with his writing of the second group of sketches: 'I want Frieda to post the rest of the Etruscan Sketches to Curtis Brown tomorrow – the first six. It is all I have done – but half the book: and all the photographs. But I

---

[36] See below, p. xxxix.
[37] DHL also asked Millicent Beveridge to look for photographs in the British Museum (vi. 93). See Appendix III on the photographs.
[38] Letter from Nancy Pearn to DHL, 30 June 1927, UT. All the correspondence between DHL and Nancy Pearn quoted hereafter is located at UT.

could not get any of Vulci ... I shant be able to do any more of my Etruscans this summer' (vi. 105).

This letter of 22 July to Secker indicates that, by this time, all the essays (except 'The Florence Museum') had been typed.[39] Lawrence never refers to typing arrangements for the Etruscan sketches in his letters. We do not know the identity of the typist – who appears to have been a professional – nor at what stage Lawrence made his revisions on the typescripts. 'Cerveteri' was typed by the 14th of June; the other five essays were typed by the 22nd of July;[40] it is probable that Lawrence expected to do a final revision of them all after he had written the other six sketches. 'The Florence Museum' was never mentioned in his correspondence; it may have been written in July, when he told Secker that he wanted to do Etruscan essays on 'Florence and Fiesole. – Cortona – Arezzo – Chiusi – Orvieto – Perugia' (vi. 93); or it may have been written in October – after his return to Florence from Austria and Germany – as an attempt on Lawrence's part to revive his commitment to the Etruscan book (vi. 195–6).

Lawrence wrote again to Secker on 17 August (vi. 130) and 17 September, asking once more for his opinion on the Etruscan essays, but apparently Curtis Brown had not forwarded the sketches to him: 'Stupid of Curtis Browns not to give you that Etruscan MS. and photographs, as I *insisted* they should at the time: I want your opinion' (vi. 151). On 30 September Lawrence was still writing to Secker: 'I hope you'll get those Etruscan essays soon' (vi. 168).

In autumn 1927, Lawrence was still talking about his plan for the second half of the book, but his energy, interest and will seemed to be fading away: 'I don't feel a bit like work . . . I *ought* to finish the Etruscan Essays, of which I've done just half. But I feel terribly indifferent to it all, whether it's done or not' (vi. 195–6).

Besides his ill health, Lawrence was by this time too concerned with *Lady Chatterley's Lover* to pay proper attention to anything else. The tone of a letter to Alfred Knopf, 1 January 1928, is very casual: Knopf had asked about the sketches, but it no longer seemed likely that Lawrence would make any serious attempt to finish the Etruscan book: 'As for the Etruscan Sketches – as you know, they are only one-half done – the other half would need a jaunt through middle Italy here – it's very cold – I cough – hotels are unwarmed in out-of-the-way places: so you see the chances. If I can get the

---

[39] For a discussion of 'The Florence Museum' see below, p. xxxviii.
[40] See above, pp. xxxii–xxxiii and *Letters*, vi. 77, 84.

MS in apple-pie order by the end of March, well and good. If I cant – there you are, and there am I' (vi. 253).

Several letters written in 1928 still refer to a possible little tour of Cortona, Arezzo, Chiusi and Orvieto, but the tone becomes increasingly doubtful. Moreover, in June 1928 the Lawrences left the Villa Mirenda and Italy to go to Switzerland where they stayed until October, when they went to France. In fact, Lawrence was thereafter based in France, mainly at Bandol, until his death.

However, until September 1928[41] he retained his idea of making that excursion in the second half of October with Aldous and Maria Huxley.[42] In November, in letters to friends and relations, he sounded however less and less willing to do it: 'The publishers are worrying me for a book, pestering me to finish the Etruscan book I have half done.'[43] At the same time, in a letter to Laurence Pollinger at Curtis Brown's office, he maintained an 'official' enthusiasm: 'I think by the end of the month I'll go back to Italy to finish those Etruscan essays. If I get that done, there's a nice book.'[44]

Despite the urgings of publishers, it was manifest that the Etruscan book would not be completed. As he told Koteliansky on 1 March 1929, he was 'out of temper for writing': 'Secker wants me to go back to Italy to finish my Etruscan Sketches, but I don't want to'.[45] Worsening health made Lawrence increasingly impatient, moody and understandably unable to face the fatigue of the trip necessary to finish the book. Moreover, the priority given in the last period of his life to what he regarded as more important writings made it inevitable that the work would never be finished.

---

[41] In September DHL was making an embroidery with an Etruscan motif. On the 13th he wrote in a letter to Earl Brewster: 'the Etruscan embroidery is done, save the background' (vi. 562).

[42] See *Letters*, vi. 538, 542, 546. Aldous Huxley (1894–1963) and his wife Maria (1898–1955) became close friends of DHL in the 1920s. Aldous Huxley portrayed DHL as Mark Rampion in *Point Counter Point* (1928), a character who sometimes refers to the Etruscans, probably in the way in which DHL must have talked to Huxley about them (cf. *Point Counter Point*, chaps IX–X).

[43] Letter to DHL's elder sister Emily King, 22 November 1928.

[44] 22 November 1928.

[45] Samuel Solomonovich ('Kot') Koteliansky (1880–1955), Russian born, was one of DHL's closest friends, from 1914, and his collaborator in several translations.

Publication

Lawrence never considered his Etruscan essays completed for book publication and, consequently, did not try to have a book published in his lifetime. However, in April 1927, he offered the individual sketches for publication in periodicals even before they were finished: 'I began doing *Sketches of Etruscan Places* ... They'd be travel sketches, but with stuff about the Etruscan tombs ... I don't know if you like a bit of mild and very easy archaeological interest in your *Travel*. – And there are lovely Etruscan photographs'.[46] On 14 June he wrote again to a member of the editorial staff of *Travel* saying that the sketches were meant for a book and were therefore too long for a magazine: 'But you can cut them as much as you like: just leave out what you like and take of the photographs what you please' (vi. 83). In a letter on the same day to Nancy Pearn, Lawrence confirmed his long-term aim of having the complete essays published in book-form, but again showed surprisingly little concern about their eventual shape in periodicals: 'He [the editor of *Travel*] can cut the essay up as much as he likes, for periodical use: the same in England – they can leave out of it whatever they like, for periodical purposes. But I want the MS. kept whole for the book later on.'[47] Lawrence gave the editor of *Travel* that freedom because, from years of experience, he knew that magazines cut what was too long for their purposes and that he had to give *Travel* 'carte blanche' if he wanted the publication of his essays, and some financial reward. But, aware of the unpopularity of his subject, he may well have been unsure whether Secker would publish the book and he did not want his effort to be wasted: 'I hear *Travel* is publishing four of the first six [essays], with pictures – beginning in November. So it's not work in vain' (vi. 168).

That Lawrence was also interested in the financial aspect of his work is confirmed in two letters from Nancy Pearn: she informed him that *Travel* would pay fifty dollars for each essay and that the editor of *World Today* was so fascinated by the Etruscan sketches that he was ready to pay 'the none-too-bad price of Ten Guineas each', though they were not the kind of things they usually published; to which Lawrence replied: 'I was glad that editor of *World* liked the Etruscan essays: shows somebody still has a

---

[46] *Letters*, vi. 48 to Coburn Gilman, the editor of the American magazine *Travel*. DHL actually addressed him as 'Mr Colman', an error arising presumably from the conflation of his names (ibid. n. 1).

[47] *Letters*, vi. 84. The 'essay' is 'Cerveteri' (see letter to Secker, ibid.). DHL had expressed the same acquiescence to cuts made in periodicals to stories, as long as the version published in book form was complete.

bit of sense.'[48] Although Nancy Pearn said in her November letter that the *World Today* 'had agreed to publish the same [essays] as have been taken by "Travel", namely, one, two, three and six', in a letter dated 9 January 1928 she was still saying that *World Today* 'have finally chosen one, two, three and six of the "ETRUSCAN SKETCHES"' and that they were also thinking of reproducing some photographs.

The publication of photographs was considered by Lawrence very important in the magazine publication of his essays too, as is evident in a letter to the Brewsters written on 21 October 1927: 'Four of the Etruscan Essays are to appear in *Travel* – beginning in November I think – with pictures. You see they have to go in a *picture* magazine' (vi. 196). In November 'The City of the Dead at Cerveteri' was published in *Travel*. Lawrence was more concerned about the photographs than about the editorial trimming of his essays, as his first comment shows: 'I'll send you a copy of *Travel* with the first of the Etruscan sketches. It has got pictures, but disappointing because they're too small' (vi. 209). *Travel* also printed 'Tarquinia' (as 'The Ancient Metropolis of the Etruscans'), 'The Painted Tombs of Tarquinia' 1. and 'Volterra' (as 'The Wind-Swept Stronghold of Volterra') between December 1927 and February 1928; all four had subtitles and introductory notes. The same essays appeared in England, in the *World Today*, between February and May 1928, under their original titles.[49]

On 10 October 1927 Lawrence had offered his essays for book publication to Knopf, at the same time expressing his bitterness at the lack of appreciation of his work shown by what he often contemptuously called 'the Philistine world', and his present indifference to writing and publishing (vi. 182). He made no effort to push Knopf into publishing the book: he professed no strong concern about it, saying that after all the book would stress him too much and bring too little reward.

A letter to Koteliansky of 1 March 1929 contains the first direct reference to Secker's intention to publish the Etruscan book.[50] There is no

---

[48] Letters from Rowena Killick, Nancy Pearn's secretary, and from Nancy Pearn to DHL, 22 September and 20 November 1927; *Letters*, vi. 232. For DHL's interest in the financial aspect of his publications, see letter to Pollinger, 3 September 1929, quoted below, p. lxvii fn. 41.

Nancy Pearn had also offered DHL's sketches to the editor of the *Argosy* and in her letter of 9 November 1927 she told DHL that 'he is considering [them] early next week'. However, *Argosy* is not mentioned further, and the essays were probably rejected as 'difficult stuff from the magazine point of view', as she had foreseen in her letter.

[49] The pagination for the first, second, third and sixth essays in *Travel* is 12–16, 50; 20–5, 55; 28–33, 40; 31–5, 44. The corresponding pagination in *World Today* is 280–8; 389–98; 552–66; 662–74.

[50] See above, p. xxxv.

further mention of the plan in Lawrence's later correspondence. Secker, however, published it posthumously about 16 September 1932, either he or someone at Curtis Brown choosing the title *Etruscan Places*. The American edition published by the Viking Press, under the same title, appeared simultaneously in USA.[51]

Of one essay, however, Lawrence never speaks in his correspondence, nor was it typed for inclusion in the Secker edition; 'The Florence Museum' has never been published. It is much shorter than the others, and probably incomplete. The Etruscan remains preserved in the Archaeological Museum of Florence are not even mentioned in the essay, and it is likely that Lawrence intended to comment on them in the light of his general approach. Indeed, the essay consists of a discussion of the historical development and the meaning of Etruscan civilisation, and proceeds along the lines Lawrence had followed in 'Volterra', as a result of his visit to the museum of that town: he describes the symbolic meaning of Etruscan art and what he defines as a 'culture-principle' and a 'cosmic consciousness' the Etruscan people felt and expressed. There is no evidence that 'The Florence Museum' was ever typed and, although incomplete in its surviving form, and, unlike the other essays, unrevised, it is published in this edition for the first time, being a thematic continuation of 'Volterra' and in some ways a conclusion to the book.

Texts

The autograph manuscript (Roberts E117a; hereafter MS) of *Sketches of Etruscan Places* is on loose sheets and gatherings pulled from two notebooks, totalling 192 pages, with individual pagination for each essay.[52]

[51] On 22 January 1932 Pollinger sent Secker a copy of the contract between the Lawrence Estate and Secker, covering several volumes, and including 'Etruscan Sketches'. On 17 February 1932 Pollinger received from Secker 'two sets of uncorrected proofs of "Etruscan Places", which, as at present arranged, will form our next Lawrence publication ... It will be a fully illustrated volume, containing certainly not less than 16 plates. It would be helpful if you could agree a date with the Vikings for its appearance in both countries' (UT). In July the contract with Viking for publication of *Etruscan Places* in USA was signed by Frieda. The book was expected to come out by late summer. On 8 September 1932, Pollinger wrote to Secker: 'Many thanks for passing to me the photographs and personal copy of this book. I think you have made a handsome looking volume of it' (UT).
For a discussion of the title see below, p. xlviii.

[52] In the MS at UT, 'Cerveteri' through p. 24 of 'Volterra' is on lined paper with rounded corners, measuring 8 1/16 × 5 13/16 inches; p. 25 of 'Volterra' through 'The Florence Museum' is on lined paper with square corners, 8¼ × 5 15/16 inches. The pagination is 'Cerveteri', 1–15, 17–27 (26pp.); 'Tarquinia', 1–5, 5a, 6, 6a, 7, 7–25 (28pp.); 'The Painted Tombs of Tarquinia', 1–60 (later divided: 1–26, 26–60) (6opp.); 'Vulci', 1–20, 22–33 (32pp.); 'Volterra' 1–34, 36–8 (37pp.); 'The Florence Museum', 1–9.

The title *Sketches of Etruscan Places* appears at the head of each essay and is followed by the number of the essay in Roman numerals[53] and by the individual title; full stops generally appear after the first two headings.[54] On the first page of MS the title was initially 'Studies of Etruscan Places'; 'Studies' was then replaced by 'Glimpses' which, in turn, was replaced by 'Glances at' (both deleted in pencil and then in ink); finally 'Sketches' was inserted (in pencil and then in ink). In the next two essays Lawrence wrote 'Glimpses of Etruscan Places', and then replaced the first word with 'Sketches'. 'Sketches of Etruscan Places' appears without correction in the last four essays.

The two essays on the painted tombs of Tarquinia were first written as one under the heading 'Sketches of Etruscan Places. / III. / The Painted Tombs of Tarquinia.' As the essay was much longer than the others, however, Lawrence drew a line on p. 26 of MS to divide it, and inserted 'Sketches of Etruscan Places. / The Painted Tombs of Tarquinia / II' in the narrow space left between lines 10 and 11. He went on to number the following essay ('Vulci') as 'V.', showing that he was thereafter thinking of the two parts of 'The Painted Tombs of Tarquinia' as separate essays (III. and IV.).

The MS is generally clear, though there are numerous corrections, sometimes of entire passages and pages. Differences in ink colour suggest that many of these alterations were made at a second reading. Although all the essays with the exception of the last were revised, sometimes extensively, MS in general serves as base-text for them all. The exceptions are the entirely rewritten and retyped portions of both parts of 'The Painted Tombs of Tarquinia' and 'Vulci'; see below.

Lawrence had three copies of a typescript prepared: of these, one complete and two partial sets survive, with only a few ribbon pages found in two of them.[55] These are designated:

---

[53] The Roman numeral 'I.' for 'Cerveteri' was added in MS (p. 1) after DHL wrote the volume title, his name and the individual title.

[54] Individual titles have stops only after 'The Painted Tombs of Tarquinia' 1., 'Volterra' and 'The Florence Museum' in MS.

[55] Ribbon-copy pages are 'Tarquinia' TSc, all pages; 'The Painted Tombs of Tarquinia' 1. TSa p. 14, TSc pp. 1–4, 7, 13, 15, 30; 'The Painted Tombs of Tarquinia' 2. TSa pp. 20–32, 35–40, 45–9, TSc pp. 33–4, 41–4; 'Vulci' TSa p. 1, TSc pp. 2–25. For pagination of the essays, see footnote 58.

TSa = 160pp. (Roberts E117b), complete and used as setting-copy for Secker's first edition (hereafter E1); 'Volterra' has a typed half-title page; now at UT[56]

TSb = 56pp. (Roberts E117c), composed of 'The Painted Tombs of Tarquinia' 2. and 'Vulci' (all carbon-copy) which have Curtis Brown of London stamps on Lawrence's autograph half-title pages; now at UT[57]

TSc = 56pp. (Roberts E117d), 'The Painted Tombs of Tarquinia' 2. and 'Vulci', from the Alfred A. Knopf collection; now at UT *and*
81pp. (Roberts E117e), 'Tarquinia', 'The Painted Tombs of Tarquinia' 1. and 'Volterra', of which the first two have Lawrence's autograph half-title pages and the last a typed half-title; all have Curtis Brown of New York stamps; now at UTul

In TSa each essay is numbered separately; typed numbers are placed top-centre.[58] Consecutive pagination in pencil in the top right-hand corner (25–160) begins with the second chapter (no such pagination occurs in the other typescripts) and does not appear to be in Lawrence's hand; it was probably provided by the editor of E1.

In 'The Painted Tombs of Tarquinia' 2. the typed numbers start with '20': this must be due to the fact that although Lawrence had divided the essay in MS, the consecutive page numbering led to the two essays being typed as though they were one. During revision of the second part of the essay, Lawrence inserted 'IV' between the volume and individual titles and changed 'II.' to '2.' to avoid having two Roman numerals in the heading, but failed to go back to add '1.' to the first part; for coherence and clarity, the present editor has inserted it. The original typescript of 'The Painted Tombs of Tarquinia' 1. must have been 19 pages, which is consistent with the length of MS, but most of it was retyped (all except pp. 1–5, 13–16)

---

[56] Throughout TSa there are neat pencil ticks just above some words; these represent either a Curtis Brown employee or someone associated with E1 counting the words in hundreds, sometimes with slight inaccuracies.

[57] There is also a title-page in an unknown hand ('Etruscan Places / D. H. Lawrence'), with a word count for the six essays and calculations.

[58] The pagination of the typescripts is: 'Cerveteri', 1–24; 'Tarquinia', 1–12, 12a, 13–19, 19a, 20–2 (24 pp.); 'The Painted Tombs of Tarquinia' 1., 1–8, 10–30 (29 pp.); 'The Painted Tombs of Tarquinia' 2., 20–49 (30 pp.); 'Vulci', 1–25 (TSb and TSc include an additional page – 12a – a typing of a long interlinear revision on pp. 12–13 of TSa); 'Volterra', 1–28.

after extensive authorial revisions (presumably on the original typescript, and perhaps on additional sheets: none of these survives) for a total of 29 pages. The retyping was done by a different typist from the original: see p. xliv below. Given the interest the original MS version of the essay has as Lawrence's first, most direct and spontaneous interpretation of the Etruscan paintings at Tarquinia, it is printed as Appendix I.

In the other essays, TSa contains some authorial revisions. Additions are usually interlinear, occasionally written vertically down the left-hand margin. Several pages in 'The Painted Tombs of Tarquinia' 2. must have been retyped because of extensive rewriting, since the number of lines per page is not the usual 24 or 25, but varies between 29 and 31; the typing style does not, however, change as in the previous essay, so these pages were perhaps done by the original typist. The omission of a word or line of MS is often clearly attributable to typist error; in 'Tarquinia' the typist missed a whole page, but as this did not make nonsense of the text, no-one – Lawrence included – realised the error.[59]

TSc is treated by this edition as a single document since three essays have the New York Curtis Brown stamp and the other two were passed on to Knopf, Lawrence's American publisher, indicating that all five went through the American branch office of the agent: TSc was probably the typescript copy sent to America. TSc and TSb were both divided up when periodicals decided to print only four of the essays, and returned the unwanted ones to the Curtis Brown agencies in New York and London respectively.

While TSa is the only copy to have survived whole – and 'The Painted Tombs of Tarquinia' 2. and 'Vulci' have 'keep' written in Lawrence's hand on blank sheets associated with them – it is not necessarily the last revised typescript. The texts of the essays in the periodicals *Travel* (American: hereafter Per1) and *World Today* (British: Per2) can help to determine the status of the authorial revisions in their missing typescript setting-copies. The surviving Per1 copies of three essays are heavily marked up, e.g. the spelling is Americanised, many cuts have been made for shortening and transitional words inserted – and a few cuts made for censorship;[60] words have been added to a short line to fill it out under a photograph or to make an extra line, a line reparagraphed to lengthen it or small cuts made to shorten a paragraph.[61] Per1 reproduced Lawrence's substantive revisions in the three typescripts and his accidentals fairly accurately. Per2 house-

---

[59] See text, Textual apparatus and Explanatory note at 34:14–34.
[60] Cf. apparatus for 19:25–21:1, 22:40. DHL expected his essays to be cut; see above, p. xxxvi.
[61] See apparatus for 27:22, 162:25, 163:9, 37:16, 158:23, 12:34–7.

styled accidentals heavily – though the extent varies from essay to essay and within essays – but otherwise followed setting-copy quite accurately, so the editor can trust its handling of substantives, except in the rare cases of censorship.[62] When substantive revisions printed in Per1 and Per2 match, they can generally be believed – within the above guidelines – to present Lawrence's own typescript revisions correctly; this enables an assessment to be made of the extent of the revision in the missing typescripts.

Lawrence did not think of individual typescripts as separate, whole entities. It has been shown in other volumes of this edition that, when reading and revising, he worked backwards and forwards between copies and between pages, and sometimes mixed pages from different copies.[63] He usually started working through to correct typing mistakes and infelicities, but he was a constantly revising author and seldom limited himself to simple correction; while, in transcribing a revision of more than a few words, he often made further changes, even if only to punctuation (e.g. 125:33, 128:18). It is known from his work on other texts that he did not always transcribe all his revisions from a first typescript copy to a second – much less to a third. Sometimes this was deliberate: on p. 45 in TSb he deleted 'Orcus' and then reinstated it (131:6); or he made a change in two copies and then thought better of it (see 'Vulci', p. xlvii below). At other times, differences in revision between the typescripts appear to have been due to his careless flipping through lightly revised pages or having his attention distracted by other, larger changes. Where all three copies of an essay can be examined, it is usually possible on heavily revised pages to say which copy was revised first, but it is often difficult to determine which was revised last. For example, 'The Painted Tombs of Tarquinia' 2. has fairly heavy revision on pp. 21–2, 31, 37 and 40, and for pp. 20–4, 28–9, 31 and 41, from the evidence of spacing and deletions and additions within revisions, TSb was the first corrected copy; for pp. 32, 36–7, 40, 45 and 47 the copy first corrected was TSa; for p. 35, TSc. TSc is likely to be the last corrected copy on pp. 31–2, 36, 40 and possibly 30 and 44; TSa on pp. 34 and 41.[64] The first corrected copy for pp. 20–31 was therefore TSb, but then Lawrence appears to have turned his attention to TSa (ribbon copy in some of these pages – see footnote 55);

---

[62] See apparatus for 60:24–7 and 61:5.

[63] See, e.g., *The Boy in the Bush*, ed. Paul Eggert (Cambridge, 1990), pp. xxxiv, lviii–lix and *Women in Love*, ed. David Farmer, Lindeth Vasey and John Worthen (Cambridge, 1987), p. lix.

[64] It is impossible to be certain when there were only slight (or no) corrections, as on pp. 25–7, 38–9, 42–3, 46, 48–9. On p. 33 it is likely that either TSa or TSb was the first corrected copy, but there are no variants.

where it can be determined, TSc was last corrected. In rare instances the editor can show that Lawrence went back to the first two corrected copies to inscribe a second, or possibly third, set of revisions (see 'Vulci' below).

Where two copies of a typescript survive, it is usually possible to say on the more heavily revised pages which is first corrected, and the periodical which used the missing copy can be of some help. 'Volterra' is the most lightly revised of all the essays (three added phrases with only a single-word variant and two added or substituted words), so the order in which revisions were inserted into its typescripts cannot be established for certain.

The editor has taken the latest revised copy of the typescript for each essay as the primary source of substantive revisions, and used the first (and where it survives, the second) revised copy only for altered punctuation and the occasional single-word variant where it seems likely that Lawrence missed them by mistake. It is not possible to follow Lawrence's zig-zag course through his revision of the typescripts with any certainty, so it has been deemed sensible to adopt one typescript of each essay for its set of the major revisions. MS has also been used to emend the punctuation of the texts of the first six essays, and to correct mistakes in the typescripts, such as missing words or lines, or the misreading of Lawrence's writing.

Cerveteri

TSa is the sole surviving typescript, and – on the evidence of matching missing substantive revisions in Per1 and Per2 (e.g. 11:15, 12:11, 13:26, 14:7) – it was also the latest revised.

Tarquinia

TSa is the later revised copy, TSc the earlier. A number of changes to accidentals (e.g. 'Etruscan' to 'etruscan') are made in both copies, but TSc has some underlining which does not appear in TSa. The alignment of the revision of p. 17 (see Explanatory note on 35:27) and the deletion in the revision on p. 20 (⌐seers, ⟨religious⟩ governors in religion; then⌐ 37:34) in TSc suggest that it was in general the first corrected copy, but TSa has one authorial deletion in a revision on p. 12 (little ⌐, lad in ⟨...⟩ long trousers⌐, 31:26).[65]

The substantive variants on pp. 3 and 19 in TSa (26:30–3, 37:2–10) appear to be later, and match Per2. But Per2 – set from the missing

[65] ⟨ ⟩ indicates a deletion; ⌐ ⌐ an addition (⟨...⟩ is a deletion that cannot be deciphered).

TSb – appears to have had an intermediate version of the revisions on p. 6 (28:11); it also has some additional variants from p. 19 of TSa (37:7–8) and misses out a revision from p. 20 (38:6). TSc seems to have the final state on p. 6. In view, however, of its more substantial changes on pp. 3 and 19 – and without the setting-copy of Per2, there remains some doubt about the authority of its variants – TSa's substantive revisions have been accepted throughout, with some of TSc's accidentals also incorporated.

The Painted Tombs of Tarquinia I.

TSa appears to be the first corrected copy on pp. 3, 4, 23 and 29, while TSc seems to have later revisions on pp. 3 and 4: its changes fit into the available space more neatly and an additional sentence is added to a revision (45:17–19); TSc's revisions also match the substantives in Per2 (set from the missing TSb copy). But TSc appears to be the first corrected copy on pp. 15, 19 and 20.

The retyped pages (5, 8, 10–30) replace MS as base-text because they constitute a total rewriting. These pages were typed on another typewriter and by another person, with different spacing and typing style.[66] Lawrence himself probably did the retyping: the work is amateurish, with obvious typographical mistakes (e.g. no space between words, strikeovers and transpositions of letters), most of which are corrected by hand; on almost every page (ribbon and carbon), two or three words (and their punctuation) at the end of lines have had to be finished by hand (e.g. p. 8 'colo⌐ur⌐' and 'alertne⌐ss⌐'); and two changes of wording in the typing – '⟨chaplet⟩ ⌐garland⌐' and '⟨oblivion⟩ a field of obliteration' (pp. 10, 18; 49:9, 55:7) are likely to have been made by Lawrence.[67] While it is difficult to be certain whether many of the letters added at the end of lines are by him – they are written with precision as is likely in such circumstances – he did make some further revisions by hand (e.g. see the Textual apparatus for 47:29, 48:38, 49:29 – correcting a typing mistake, 50:26); these, however, are so few that it is impossible to tell which copy he worked on first.

---

[66] In the original typing words divided at the end of lines are usually given hyphens at the end of the first line and the beginning of the next (e.g. interest-/ -ed, p. 2), but not compound words (e.g. south-/ west, p. 1); in the retyped pages all divided words are hyphenated only at the end of the first line.

[67] The original pp. 5–10 were removed, and the newly typed page has a typed '6' corrected by hand by DHL to '5'; the original pp. 11 and 12 became 6 and 7; the next retyped page has typed '9' which DHL altered to '8'. (There is no page 9.)

Per2 provides some evidence that its unlocated copy (TSb) had a few small variants in its revisions (see apparatus for 45:20–5, 46:33, 50:26, 59:17, 60:14), but the magazine copy-editor may have made some changes in sections where Lawrence did not revise the other two copies (e.g. 47:13, 29, 50:35–7, 51:4, 7, 8, 14–23, 58:26). There are two other possible explanations. First, since the missing TSb was ribbon copy, and Lawrence often, but not always, corrected the ribbon copy first, Per2's setting-copy may at these points have been an autograph revised text on the ribbon pages: compare pp. 12–13 of 'Vulci' below. Secondly, Lawrence may sometimes have failed to make two carbon copies, and Per2's copy could have been a further retyping. At least one page of the essay *was* typed twice: the final p. 30 in the surviving copies has the typed page number placed differently, and the lines end with different words. If an extra retyped page had ended up in Per2's copy, it would not be surprising if there were variants since Lawrence characteristically revised as he retyped.[68] But while it is possible that some of the variants in Per2 represent Lawrence's differing revisions, without the evidence of a surviving typescript none can be accepted.

Substantive variants in Per2 must always be viewed with caution, but where they match those in one typescript – see apparatus for 44:16, 45:15, 17, 18 (but see also 45:21–5) – they can help to determine the order of revision. Since in these instances they generally match TSc,[69] it has been chosen as the preferred text for all substantive revisions in this essay.

The Painted Tombs of Tarquinia 2.

The order of revision has been discussed above (see pp. xlii–xliii): the substantive revisions of TSc are accepted, with accidentals and minor changes taken from the first corrected and intermediate copies (e.g. 115:12, 117:25, 27, 40, 132:20).

Several pages were retyped (33–4 and 41–4; 123:13–124:28 'He wastes ... of fertility;' and 128:6–131:2 'moving, tomb ... '). The typewriter appears to be the same as that used for the retyping of 'The Painted Tombs of Tarquinia' 1., but the typing is better and the left margins much larger, with typed page numbers more nearly centred and followed by full stops; the repeated hyphen is used (see footnote 66). The added letters at the end of lines on pp. 33–4 and 41 are fewer and less like Lawrence's writing.

[68] Cf. *Women in Love*, ed. Farmer, Vasey and Worthen, p. lviii.
[69] But at 51:28 Per2 matches TSa in a single-word revision, and at 59:17 Per2 appears to be the intermediate revision.

There is one small autograph substantive revision on p. 44 (130:30) which
links an original passage to the preceding new paragraph, and the last two
lines on that page, completing the final paragraph, are also in autograph.
The typing ends with 'evid-' (130:40), suggesting either that the typist
typed the last two or three lines on a new page, or that – if the typist was
Lawrence – he stopped there; in either case he wrote out the last lines on
all three copies. Since the evidence about the typist is minimal and
inconclusive, the variants in accidentals from unrevised MS passages are
accepted in preference to those of one – and possibly two – unknown
typists. However, the variants at the end of p. 44 – although made under
the constraints of space – are accepted from TSc, because Lawrence could
have carried over the slightly longer MS version on to the next page if he
had chosen, as he did on pp. 21–2 of this essay and pp. 19–19a of
'Tarquinia'.

In one instance (p. 31) this means excluding a major revision of eight
autograph lines. In TSb Lawrence added a sentence in the second line (see
apparatus for 121:40), deleted a one-word parenthesis (122:10), added the
equivalent of four lines interlinearily to the end of a paragraph (122:16)
and revised a phrase a few lines later (122:25); he also crossed out five
lines (six lines from the top of the page) and substituted eight lines which
extend below the end of the typed paragraph and into the left margin (see
apparatus for 122:5). In TSa and TSc (probably the last corrected) he
made all the first mentioned changes (all, except the deletion, with
variants), but instead of adding the lines at 122:16 at the end of the
paragraph, he turned the page sideways and wrote them in the wide left
margin. He did not copy the eight-line change at 122:5 from TSb, and
could hardly have overlooked it; he must have intended to omit it.[70]

Vulci

TSa appears to be the copy first corrected on pp. 7–8, 12–13, 18, 21–3, 25
where punctuation is changed, and revisions containing deletions are
tightly spaced. The lengthy revision on pp. 12–13 was typed out – with
further changes – for TSb and TSc, while TSa has it squeezed by hand on
to the bottom of p. 12 and into the top and side margins of p. 13, with
some deletions and additions. The page may have been retyped by
Lawrence; the typographical mistakes and the typed change of 'acres‹, in
the months timeʸ. The Etruscans had … ᵇ (144:40) suggest this,

[70] Cf. 120:36, 127:29 and 127:33 where single-word changes would be easy to miss among
the other, longer revisions on pp. 29 and 40.

although the two letters added at the end of lines cannot confidently be attributed to him. On pp. 18, 22 and 25 TSb seems to be last revised (but first revised in the second revision on p. 23); the first revision on p. 23 seems to be latest in TSc (which has a first revision on p. 10). On p. 25 Lawrence revised all three copies a second time: 'probably' was altered to 'surely' in the first of the added sentences (153:3–4), while the opening word had been written as 'Anyway' and altered to 'Anyhow' in TSb, but only written 'Anyhow' in the other two copies; TSa retains 'famous' at 152:34 from MS, while TSb's alteration to 'so-called' is written at an angle which suggests that it was an afterthought. On p. 18 Lawrence deleted the first two words in 'hundreds, even thousands' and substituted 'many' in TSa and TSc, but, by the time he got to TSb, had decided that 'thousands of painted vases' (148:13) would do and deleted 'many' from the two other copies; in addition he substituted 'taken from' for 'found in' in TSb and TSc, but neglected to go back to TSa and alter it. The choice between TSb and TSc as the last corrected copy is not clear-cut, but on balance TSb has been selected as the source of substantive revisions.

Volterra

TSc has been chosen as the later corrected copy: it differs only in one single-word variant from TSa, and matches Per2 (167:7).

In summary, the last corrected typescripts adopted as the source of substantive revisions are TSa for 'Cerveteri' and 'Tarquinia', TSb for 'Vulci' and TSc for both of the 'Painted Tombs' essays and 'Volterra'.

The Florence Museum

This essay survives only in the MS version, which therefore is base-text.

The page proofs (hereafter PP)[71] of E1, consisting of 191 pages, were set from TSa and reproduce it more closely than E1: for instance in the use of the word 'etruscan' with a lower case 'e' when adjectival (see below), or of the Italian words which are usually not underlined in TSa. TSa punctuation was altered in a number of places in PP; furthermore, some of the changes introduced in PP were further altered in E1, as occurs in 'The Painted Tombs of Tarquinia' 1. where TSc reads 'or, in a feebler *de*

[71] At UTul.

crescendo', which became 'in a feebler *de crescendo*' in PP and 'in a feebler *decrescendo*' in E1 (58:7–8).

E1, published by Secker in September 1932, also differs from TSa in having a few words changed, inserted or omitted, as in 'Volterra', where the phrases '*Death to Lenin*' and '*Mussolini is always right!*' do not appear (158:39, 159:2). The first American edition (A1), published by Viking also in September 1932, was printed from the Secker sheets and therefore corresponds exactly to E1.

Title

Like MS, TSa has *Sketches of Etruscan Places* as a general title, followed by the number of the essay in Roman numerals and by the individual title. In 'Cerveteri', the first two words of the general title and 'Places' were deleted, with 'Sketches' written above the latter in an unknown hand ('Etruscan Sketches');[72] then the new word was crossed out and 'Places' was underlined with stet marks so that the resulting title was *Etruscan Places*, the form adopted either by the Curtis Brown office or by the editor of E1. The original, full title appears with no changes in the other essays of TSa and in TSb and TSc. Lawrence used the title *Sketches of Etruscan Places* frequently in his letters and on his photographs; given his intention to write another six essays or more, he probably never considered the book complete, and the successive changes he had made in his title in MS ('Glimpses' and 'Glances at') suggest that he knew he had not covered his topic fully. In a letter of 9 June 1927 to Earl Brewster he explicitly refers to the title: 'Perhaps Frieda and I will do a trip to Cortona, Arezzo, Chiusi, Orvieto, Perugia next week or the week after – before we go to Germany – so I could do enough essays – or Sketches – *Sketches of Etruscan Places* – for a book' (vi. 79–80). Lawrence's own title has been restored in this edition.

One peculiarity of both MS and the typescripts is the lack of capitalisation of the word 'etruscan'. Apart from the first eighteen pages of 'Cerveteri', where the usual initial capital is found, MS has 'etruscan' for the adjectival form and 'Etruscan(s)' for the noun. The typescripts follow the same rule (and this edition), with the exception of those first pages which read as MS. However, Lawrence's intention to use the lower case 'e' as the adjectival form is confirmed by his alterations when, in a few instances, he found the adjective typed with a capital by mistake.

---

[72] It is possible that this is in the same hand as the title-page mentioned in footnote 57.

Both the periodicals and E1 (but not its page proofs) capitalised all occurrences, but Lawrence's practice is followed in this edition.[73]

Reception

Etruscan Places[74] received on the whole favourable comments from its English and American reviewers who generally limited their criticism to the lack of scientific authority and to the predominance of Lawrence's beliefs, whereas the major focus for appreciation was the quality of its prose and style.

In October 1932, immediately following the publication of the Secker edition, three reviews appeared under similar headings: 'Lawrence Among the Etruscans', in the *New Statesman and Nation*; 'Lawrence's Etruria' in the *Observer*; 'Lawrence in Etruria', in the *Bookman*. The first two reviews were rather critical of the unscholarly nature of the book and denied it any historical and archaeological authority, although they both pointed out its artistic value and Lawrence's qualities as a writer. Indeed, the reviewer in the *New Statesman and Nation* was warmly enthusiastic about the style and Lawrence's attitude towards his subject:

It was Lawrence's habit when any subject profoundly interested him to throw his impression on to paper with an almost conversational ease and freshness. No scruples of style or scholarship stood in his way; it was enough that he should be interested in his theme. The literary side of his work could look after itself – which, since he was a born writer, it usually did ... He had but to touch a subject as he passed to brush it over with the vivid colours of imagination and give it a new, strange, penetrating charm ... He mixes knowledge, presumption and wild conjecture into a phantasmagoric but sharply distinctive whole.[75]

T. E. Welby in the *Observer* was much sharper and more critical of the extravagances and liberties that Lawrence allowed his genius to take:

the affair here is clearly less one of what Etruria was than of what a very modern and disordered man of genius took it to have been in his desperate search for a civilization untroubled by the intellect. Illustrations of extraordinary excellence provide the reader with some material whereby to check Lawrence if that prosaic meddlesomeness be thought worth while.[76]

[73] With words like 'Greek', 'Italian', 'Roman' and 'Latin' DHL usually observes the accepted rule of initial capital letter.
[74] This title is used in this section because the reviews refer to the first published title.
[75] 22 October 1932, pp. 490–2.
[76] 23 October 1932, p. 7.

Arthur Ball in the *Bookman* appreciated Lawrence's social commitment and his efforts to indicate to his fellow men a more lively and meaningful way of living; he also showed genuine enthusiasm for the writer: 'His descriptions of the painted tombs are marvellously precise ... And sometimes his prose passes into declamation that is splendid.'[77]

A totally different opinion on Lawrence's style was expressed by a reviewer in the *Saturday Review*: 'Lawrence was so shaken by his emotion that he became slipshod with his English. One has perhaps a vague idea of what he is driving at, but its translation into Etruscan would need more than the decyphering of the unknown script.' This critic, however, could not help admitting that 'Lawrence is a travelling companion, sensitive to all beauty and gifted with a power of instilling into what he appreciated his own view of life.'[78]

Aldous Huxley's review for the *Spectator* expressed thoroughly positive opinions of Lawrence and his book, defending him even from criticism on historical and scientific grounds. Huxley stated that an archaeologist could give data and information about remains but he could not explain their inner meaning, 'the psychological rather than the material plane'; he needed, then, the help of 'a diviner' and 'such a psychological diviner was D. H. Lawrence'. Huxley openly affirmed the importance of *Etruscan Places* from a historical point of view, saying that 'it is not only a beautiful and delicate work of literary art; it also makes a real contribution to historical knowledge ... any sensitive person ... is left with the inner certainty that Lawrence's interpretation is right'.[79]

A reply to Huxley's review was published in the *Spectator* a few weeks later. E. C. Oppenheim wrote a letter to the editor, saying he was an enthusiastic reader of Huxley's novels but disagreed with his review of *Etruscan Places*. He argued against Lawrence's interpretation of the Etruscans, doubting 'whether it wholly satisfied the Etruscans themselves', and gave an example of Lawrence's 'one-sided outlook on life':

I once had a heated argument with him. It was a superb spring morning, and we were coming down a Sicilian hillside covered with olives, asphodel and wild cyclamen. We had been talking of the Greeks, of course; and we went on to discuss the conquests of modern science. I expatiated on the wonder and mystery of existence – ... He was evidently irritated at what he considered my childish enthusiasm, and at last he turned on me almost fiercely. 'I don't believe a word of it,' he said. 'I am not sure I even believe that the Earth goes round the sun. I know it does, of course, with my reason; but to my innermost self all that does not really

[77] October 1932, p. 49.   [78] 'Never-Never Lands', 12 November 1932, p. 509.
[79] 'Lawrence in Etruria', 4 November 1932, p. 629.

exist.' 'What, then, really exists for you?' I asked. 'Men and women,' he replied, 'and human passions, from all eternity.'

It was a clear proof of how our beliefs depend on temperament, never on ratiocination.[80]

For Lorine Pruette, in the *New York Herald Tribune Books*, the starting point for an interpretation of *Etruscan Places* was Lawrence's endless travelling in search of 'a people in whom he could believe, who would seem to him to be truly alive'. She suggested that Lawrence succeeded in his quest at the end of his life, back in Italy, by turning to the old past and the Etruscan culture, visiting the remains of that old civilisation and giving us an account of great artistic value:

Lawrence restores to us those scenes from the life of the ancient people, making them surely more vivid than they would be for most of us were we to visit the tombs ourselves ... He makes us share with him the lightness and the joy, the casualness of the old Tuscan life ... The book is like a day in the country with Lawrence, happily enough, in a peculiarly benign mood.[81]

Percy Hutchison in the *New York Times Book Review* found that 'there is enough of the novelist in the book to give it the unmistakable twist of thought and style', and declared his preference for *Etruscan Places* 'above all previous books by D. H. Lawrence', giving as his reasons:

in it Lawrence seems articulate to a degree not before attained ... nowhere in the book does there appear to be that straining after something intangible and elusive which is so often present in Lawrence's writing. 'Etruscan Places' is not a book which will appeal to all; it is belles-lettres, however, in every sense of the word ... It is a book touched with a rare beauty.[82]

James W. Lane in the *Bookman* (New York) pointed out the supposed weaknesses in *Etruscan Places*, basing his criticism on moralistic and religious considerations: '[Lawrence's] non-moralism is always fizzing to the surface of the book, because he finds that he can talk of phallic stones and symbols. This he begins to do on page twenty-five, and makes a thorough job of it.' In the end, however, Lane could not deny the 'charm' and the 'vitality' of the book, and conceded: 'Lawrence is usually a very clear writer, adept at terse prose pictures. His love of animal life, his descriptions of the Mediterranean and of the Maremma are appealing ... But unfortunately he was a half-light, his beacon discovered things but did

[80] 'Lawrence and Etruria', 23 December 1932, p. 893.
[81] 'With the Etruscans Lawrence Found Peace', 13 November 1932, p. 5.
[82] 'D. H. Lawrence Delves In the Deep Past', 11 December 1932, p. 4.

not point the way to heaven, unless Paganism is still, with its ultimate despair, considered one.'[83]

Mixed feelings were also expressed by Hetty Goldman in the *Saturday Review of Literature* (New York):

There is no attempt to 'do' all the sites, but a great attempt to penetrate, to feel, and to understand. It is achieved in flashes of insight and sometimes with real profundity ... The book is full of Lawrence's philosophy ... and while it is frequently illuminating, there are moments when one wonders whether his vision was not at times as much obscured by his theory of phallic consciousness as that of any teutonic professor by his more ponderous ratiocinations.[84]

The Times Literary Supplement published a favourable review by A. J. B. Wace, a scholar in classical archaeology, with a particular mention of the two chapters on the painted tombs of Tarquinia:

Among these splendid vivid frescoes Lawrence could allow his thoughts free play as he felt the fascination of the scenes and the symbols depicted before him ... his impressions of the paintings ... are truly stimulating. These and the delicate, intimate sketches of the Etruscan countryside and country men and women revivify memories of the desolate, primitive grandeur of the earth where life and all it meant to a great race of men are found only in its tombs.[85]

The negative aspect of this review was in the by now standard criticism of the slight scholarly value of the book, which made (it claimed) no new contribution to our knowledge of Etruscan life and religion.

Max Plowman (poet and briefly one of Lawrence's correspondents), in the *Adelphi* defended the book against all previous criticism:

Etruscan Places has received less than its due: it has been described as 'slight, casual,' and cited as an example of the way Lawrence idealised people when he believed they shared his prejudices. But it is a superficial glance that gives such an impression. *Etruscan Places* is really a serious work of almost pure appreciation, and it has a rare quality which will only be hidden from those who believe that exquisiteness comes by labour rather than of natural grace.

Plowman felt so profoundly touched by Lawrence's writing in this book that at times he expressed himself more as a poet than a critic:

here, free from books and the contentions of society, free from the irk of modern civilisation, wandering under the open sky in places of natural or human interest, the poet in him buds and blossoms as spontaneously as a wild rose. The whole quality of the book is a wild rose quality; it has the same delicacy, the same open

[83] January 1933, p. 78.   [84] 28 January 1933, p. 400.
[85] 23 February 1933, p. 122.

inevitability, the same chance beauty and gentle insouciance, and the same prickliness on the stalk.[86]

[86] February 1933, pp. 383–4. Other reviews appeared in the *New Republic*, 'D. H. Lawrence: The Phoenix and the Grave', by Horace Gregory, 14 December 1932, pp. 131–3; *Nation*, 1 February 1933, p. 128; *Scrutiny*, 'More Lawrence', by F. R. Leavis, March 1933, pp. 404–5. *Etruscan Places* was listed in 'Books received' in the *Manchester Guardian*, 16 September 1932, p. 5. The book was also enthusiastically mentioned in Harold Jay Snyder's *A Catalogue of English and American First Editions of D. H. Lawrence* (New York, 1932).

Italian Essays, 1919–27

The sketches included in this section were all written during Lawrence's third and fourth Italian periods and were all inspired by Italy and by Tuscany in particular. They sometimes have a common or similar genesis but the problems connected with the individual texts and their publication are different and sometimes insoluble. Though some of the sketches were published in magazines during Lawrence's lifetime, they were all first collected in *Phoenix: The Posthumous Papers of D. H. Lawrence*, ed. Edward D. McDonald (New York), published in 1936 (hereafter A1), with the exceptions of 'Looking Down on the City', which is published in this edition for the first time, and of 'Germans and English' which appeared in the 1968 collection *Phoenix II: Uncollected, Unpublished and Other Prose Works by D. H. Lawrence*, ed. Warren Roberts and Harry T. Moore (E1).

David (November–December 1919 or April–May 1921)

Our information about Lawrence's essay on the sculpture by Michelangelo is inadequate and fragmentary, and the date of its composition remains uncertain. It appears to belong to Lawrence's third Italian period (1919–22) and could have been written during or soon after one of the several short trips to Florence which Lawrence made in those years.

Lawrence did not mention the essay in his letters. His only reference to Michelangelo's statue in his correspondence was on a picture postcard of it which he sent to his sister Emily on 4 December 1919: 'This statue of David, outside the Old Palace, is very famous.'[1] But the impact on Lawrence of Michelangelo's work went beyond that of simple aesthetic appreciation. Lawrence describes it in his sketch as 'the presiding genius of Florence' and sees in it a synthesis of the fundamental contradiction of the town, lying as it does on the borderline between north and south and, therefore, containing the elements of the two different civilisations: the cold, christian North and the warm, pagan South. In a letter written at Taormina on 1 June 1920, Lawrence asserted what he perceived as the difference between north and south in historical and philosophical terms: 'The south is so different from the north. I believe morality is a purely climatic thing ... Here the past is so much stronger than the present, that one seems remote like the immortals, looking back at the world from their otherworld. A great indifference comes over me – I feel the present isn't real' (iii. 538).

[1] *Letters*, iii. 427. DHL's interest in Michelangelo dates back to at least 1914 (see *Study of Thomas Hardy and Other Essays*, ed. Bruce Steele, Cambridge, 1985, pp. 73–4).

Several elements can be taken into account in the dating of 'David'. When Lawrence left England in November 1919, on his way south he stopped briefly near Turin (15–17 November), a city which is mentioned in the sketch.[2] Soon after, he stayed in Florence for three weeks and from the Pensione Balestra he wrote various letters, 20–6 November 1919, complaining about the heavy rain, the sound of which pervades 'David'. In one letter, particularly, there is a description which is echoed in the first part of the sketch in a strikingly similar way: 'The horses and mules, as they cross the bridge, have nice grey bonnets on their heads, and the carters are hidden under big green umbrellas. On they trot in the rain, busy as ever' (iii. 422). In 'David' Lawrence writes: 'Over the bridge, carriages trotting under great ragged umbrellas. Two white bullocks urged from beneath a bright green umbrella, shambling into a trot as the whip-thong flickers between their soft shanks' (185:8–11).

On 3 December, Lawrence wrote to Benjamin Huebsch: 'I am going to do various small things – on Italy and on Psycoanalysis – for the periodicals' and a few days later he informed Koteliansky that he had sent 'Murry an essay from here'. The essay might well have been 'David'.[3] These considerations suggest, therefore, that November–December 1919 could be taken as the first possible date for the composition of this sketch.

A later dating is suggested by a comparison of the essay with the chapter 'Florence' in *Aaron's Rod*, probably written in May 1921, where Michelangelo's statue is described as 'the genius of Florence ... The physical, self-conscious adolescent, Michelangelo's David, shrinking and exposing himself, with his white, slack limbs!'[4] The description and interpretation of the statue of David are virtually the same in both the sketch and the novel; so is the development of Lawrence's narrative, which gradually moves from the window overlooking the Arno, to the Piazza della Signoria and then to *David*. The following chapter of *Aaron's Rod*, 'High Up over the Cathedral Square' – also written in May 1921 – echoes 'David' in the mention of Florence as 'the flowery town'.[5] 'David' could therefore have been written just before those two chapters, in April 1921, or at the same time, in May.

[2] See below 186:8–12.

[3] *Letters*, iii. 426–7, 428 and n. 1. DHL was working on *Psychoanalysis and the Unconscious* in January 1920. Benjamin W. Huebsch (1876–1964), a New York publisher, had published an expurgated edition of *The Rainbow* on 30 November 1915.

[4] *Aaron's Rod* 211:36 and 212:23–5; cf. below 186:31–5. Cf. also *Aaron's Rod* 210:28–212:32, and note the description of rain and carriages with 'pale-green huge umbrellas' at 211:3–13. For the date of composition of the chapters 'Florence' and 'High Up over the Cathedral Square', see Introduction to *Aaron's Rod* xxii–xxiv.

[5] Ibid. 232:22–6.

The April dating is supported by an anecdote of Rebecca West's. She met Lawrence in Florence in April 1921, on his way from Sicily to Germany, and remembers him writing something about Florence while he was staying in a 'hotel that overlooked the Arno ... he sat tapping away at a typewriter ... we went in and asked if he were already writing an article about the present state of Florence; and Lawrence answered seriously that he was'.[6]

Even though the most likely date would seem to be April 1921, we cannot be certain when 'David' was first written, or whether it was subsequently revised; we can only date it between November 1919 and May 1921.

Two carbon typescripts of 'David' have survived, although no manuscript appears to be extant and nothing is known about the typing of it (but see next essay). One typescript (hereafter TCCI; Roberts E88a) consists of seven pages and has a few corrections and revisions in Lawrence's hand, the latter usually of single words which are written directly above the rejected reading; these authorial revisions have led to its choice as the base-text for this edition. The second typescript (TCCII; Roberts E88b)[7] was typed later: it incorporates the autograph corrections of TCCI and has no revisions. TCCII – or perhaps its ribbon copy (there are no editing marks on TCCII) – was used as the setting-copy for A1 as the correspondence of some mistypings confirms.[8]

Looking Down on the City (November–December 1919 or April–May 1921)

This sketch echoes 'David' in a number of references: Botticelli's *Venus*, *David*'s self-conscious adolescence and self-realisation, Turin and the Alps beyond, Leonardo's *Madonna of the Rocks*, the image of Florence – 'the flowery town' – having 'something tender and exposed about it', *David* 'frowning' (194:30–1, 195:21–2). Although there is no information about this sketch nor mention of it in the correspondence, we can be sure that it was written in the same period as 'David', between November 1919 and May 1921.

If Lawrence's reference to his writing small articles about Italy in the letter of 3 December 1919 to Huebsch could be to 'David' as well as to

---

[6] *D. H. Lawrence*, 1930, p. 21. Rebecca West was the pseudonym of Cicily Isabel Andrews, née Fairfield (1892–1983), novelist, journalist and critic. She met DHL in 1921.

[7] TCCI located at UCB; TCCII at UT.

[8] See Textual apparatus, particularly at 185:12 and 187:13. DHL's corrections of the many obvious typing mistakes in TCCI are not recorded.

'Looking Down on the City', the article about Florence that Lawrence was typing when Rebecca West visited him in April 1921 could also be 'Looking Down on the City'. The two essays, in fact, appear to have been typed by the same person, a non-professional typist who, most likely, was Lawrence himself: spacing is very similar in the typescripts, and so are the strikeovers, the hyphenation at the end of lines and the kinds of errors. Moreover, the typeface characters match exactly, indicating that 'David' and 'Looking Down on the City' were prepared on the same typewriter. Another common feature, which supports the argument that both essays were written at the same time, between April and May 1921, is the many echoes which link them with the second half of *Aaron's Rod*; indeed, the similarities and parallels between 'Looking Down on the City' and the novel are even more numerous and more revealing than those in 'David': the description of the men with torches carrying a body and the brief mention of a bomb thrown in a café, become narrative matter in the novel; the references in the sketch to morning concerts at a friend's house and to 'a Florentine girl playing a violin concerto—her father's music' (196:14–15) recur in the novel in much the same way: 'We have music on Saturday mornings. Next Saturday a string quartette, and violin solos by a young Florentine woman—a friend—very good indeed, daughter of our Professor Tortoli, who composes—' Another parallel can be found in the misquotation of the first line of Dante Gabriel Rossetti's poem, 'The Blessed Damozel'.[9]

The essay appears to have been written in April–May 1921, but there is no final evidence to prove it; we can only date it for certain between November–December 1919 and April–May 1921.

The only surviving text (Roberts E206) is the carbon typescript (hereafter TCC) of five pages, rather badly typed,[10] with a few corrections and additions of single words in Lawrence's hand; it is the base-text for this edition. 'Looking Down on the City' is published for the first time in this volume.

Europe Versus America (November 1925)

In the autumn of 1925 Lawrence left the United States and went back to Italy. He often mentioned his American experience in letters at that time, frequently in comparison with Europe and Italy. From the Villa Bernarda

---

[9] Cf. *Aaron's Rod* 275–6; chap. XX; 221:10–13; 235:11–12, and 'Looking Down on the City' at 195:31–40; 196:5–6; 196:10–16, 194:25–6. See Explanatory note at 194:26.

[10] Located at UCLA. TCC and 'David's TCCI both end with a row of percentage signs ('David' has them after the title), have a blank space between a word and closing punctuation, use a spaced hyphen for a dash and have many corrections of typographical mistakes.

at Spotorno where he and Frieda had settled, Lawrence wrote to Earl and Achsah Brewster on 25 November 1925: 'Italy feels very familiar: almost too familiar, like the ghost of one's own self. But I am very glad to be by the Mediterranean again for a while. It seems so versatile and so young, after America, which is everywhere tense' (v. 345). Very similar feelings are described in the sketch 'Europe Versus America', where he confronts his recent experience of the New World with Europe and, in particular, with the atmosphere of Italy:

> coming back to Europe, I realise how much more *tense* the European civilisation is, in the Americans, than in the Europeans ... the Americans are tense, somewhere inside themselves, as if they felt that once they slackened, the world would really collapse ... Now, back in Europe, I feel a real relief ... it's a relief to be by the Mediterranean ...   (199:19–21, 23–5, 200:25, 36)

The composition of 'Europe Versus America' can therefore be most likely dated to November 1925; and this dating is confirmed in a letter to Dorothy Brett, written on 25 November, where Lawrence mentioned the forthcoming publication of a special Lawrence issue of the magazine *Laughing Horse* in which the sketch was first printed in April 1926.[11] Although he expected it to be 'awful' (v. 343), Lawrence was sufficiently pleased with the magazine publication to send it to his sister Emily: 'I'm sending a copy of the *laughing Horse* – a little magazine published by a young American friend away in Santa Fe.[12] You'll be amused by it' (v. 475). 'Europe Versus America' appeared in *Laughing Horse* with two illustrations: a pen and ink drawing of Lawrence in profile by Witter Bynner – an American poet Lawrence had met in New Mexico in 1922 – and a linocut, 'Rancho de Taos', by Loren Mozley.

There is no surviving manuscript or typescript of 'Europe Versus America'. The *Laughing Horse* (Per) was the essay's only publication in Lawrence's lifetime, and is the base-text for this edition; the Textual apparatus records the few variant readings of A1.

---

[11] No. 13, pp. 6–9. The special DHL issue of *Laughing Horse* (Roberts C139) also contained an essay – 'A Little Moonshine with Lemon' – which was published in *Mornings in Mexico*; two poems – 'Mediterranean in January' and 'Beyond the Rockies'; a letter – 'Paris Letter' – later collected in *Phoenix*; and a drawing – 'Pueblo Indian Dance' (pp. 1–15).

[12] Willard Johnson (1897–1968), an American journalist, was co-founder and editor of *Laughing Horse*, 1922–39.

Fireworks (June 1926)

During the summer of 1926, Lawrence had not been completely inactive despite his illness and his unwillingness to commit himself too much to writing.[13] In June he wrote the story 'The Man Who Loved Islands' and two of his Italian sketches: 'Fireworks' and 'The Nightingale'.

'Fireworks' was written – or at least started – on 25 June 1926, since it begins 'Yesterday being the twenty-fourth of June, and St. John's Day' (203:2). In two letters Lawrence mentions the celebrations for St John's Day in Florence: to Dorothy Brett he wrote on the 23rd: 'it's San Giovanni tomorrow, Florence's saint, and big festa-day' (v. 478); and to his niece Margaret King, he announced: 'Today is San Giovanni, the Saint of Florence, and a great festa. So we shall go in to town this evening for dinner, and stay for the fireworks. They will illuminate the town, and everybody will be in full holiday rig' (v. 479). One can detect here a note of anticipation: the sketch, however, expresses his disappointment at the show. In fact, he does not put much effort into describing the festivities, but prefers to discuss the 'crowd', which clearly annoyed him. The reaction of a dog, frightened by the noise of the rockets, is described in more detail than the display itself, and only in the last part of the article does he admit that the fireworks were attractive.[14]

There is no reason to doubt that 'Fireworks' was written, if not on 25 June itself, then immediately afterwards. This date for its composition (and that of 'The Nightingale'; see below) seems to be confirmed by a letter Lawrence wrote to Nancy Pearn on 27 June 1926: '*Vogue* told Richard Aldington to ask me to do them little articles: paying £10. for … 1,500 words. I'm not doing anything else, so have written three little things – though they come about 2,000 – and I'll send them along in a day or two, soon as they're typed. And will you offer them to *Vogue* – unless you think any of them quite unsuitable' (v. 482). It is reasonable to conjecture that two of the 'three little things' Lawrence refers to are 'Fireworks' and 'The Nightingale', both just over 2,000 words. They were never published in *Vogue*; whether Nancy Pearn or the magazine judged them 'unsuitable', we do not know.

'Fireworks' was published in two magazines during Lawrence's lifetime: the *Nation & Athenæum* (16 April 1927) and the American *Forum* (May 1927). A letter from Nancy Pearn on 6 October 1926 informed Lawrence that they had 'sold that little piece called FIREWORKS to The Forum for $75,00'; on 12 January 1927 Nancy Pearn wrote again to announce that

[13] See above, pp. xxviii–xxix.   [14] See below 205–206, 207:12–15.

she had 'just heard from the New York Office that the *Forum* are planning
to use "Fireworks" in their May number'.[15]

The extant texts of 'Fireworks' are: an autograph manuscript of 8 pages
(hereafter MS; Roberts E134); a carbon typescript of 10 pages (TCC),[16]
which reproduces MS and was probably prepared posthumously, and a
copy of which served as setting-copy for A1; the two periodical publications, the *Nation & Athenæum* (Per1) and the *Forum* (Per2).[17] The
periodical versions differ from the other texts to such an extent that one
must assume that they derived from another source, probably a heavily
corrected typescript, now missing. They are thus the result of a later stage
of Lawrence's writing and contain passages typical of Lawrence's biting
criticism of mechanical life which do not appear in MS.[18]

The two periodical versions differ from each other mainly in punctuation and new paragraphing, together with the American orthography of a
few words in Per2. Moreover, Per2 contains some clear errors: for
example Per2 has 'Siva dancing his dance' whereas Per1 more correctly
reads 'Shiva dancing her dance', matching, in this case, MS.[19] On these
grounds, Per1 has been chosen as base-text for this edition and the
variants in Per2 are recorded in the apparatus. Base-text has occasionally
been emended from MS when there is an exact correspondence with it.[20]
MS is printed in Appendix V and the variants in TCC and A1 are
recorded.

The title was chosen by Lawrence for MS and used in his correspondence with Nancy Pearn; three years later, when he asked Pino Orioli for a
copy of the sketch, he called it 'Fireworks'.[21] Both periodicals printed his
title. A1, however, has 'Fireworks in Florence', and 'in Florence' has been
added on the title-page (only) of TCC in an unidentified hand – whether

---

[15] All of Nancy Pearn's letters cited below are at UT.   [16] Both located at UT.

[17] No. 3, pp. 47–9; vol. lxxvii, pp. 648–54. *Forum* is illustrated with drawings by Thomas
Handforth. The first, above the title, shows the Piazza della Signoria with (right to left)
Michelangelo's *David*, a car with two people and 'two women with a police-dog on a chain'
(205:34); and in the background buildings and fireworks. On pp. [650–1] a drawing of
the Palazzo Vecchio, with its tower on fire and a crowd below, is printed at the outer
margins of the pages, in mirror-images. At the bottom of p. 654 is the Lungarno, with a
bridge in the background (most probably the Ponte Vecchio) and fireworks, and the faces
of two lovers and a man in the foreground.

[18] See below 206:22–7 and cf. the MS version at 290:10–15, and 204:7–13.

[19] See apparatus at 204:2.

[20] See apparatus at 203:16; 203:22; 205:37; 206:1; 206:34 (1) and (2), etc.

[21] Letter of 18 December 1929: 'They want to publish a volume of my newspaper articles in
spring, and some are missing ... There is one "The Nightingale" and another
"Fireworks" – I want those two especially'. Pino Orioli, Florentine publisher, published
the first edition of *Lady Chatterley's Lover* (1928).

before or after the publication of A1 is not known – but the original title is on p. 1. Someone must have modified the title for A1, perhaps to differentiate the essay from the periodical version. Lawrence's title has been restored in this edition, and the familiar title of A1 appears as a subtitle to Appendix V because of its association with that version.

The Nightingale (June 1926)

In the letter of 24 June 1926 to his niece Margaret King where Lawrence speaks of St John's Day, he also describes the beauty of the Tuscan countryside and the singing of the nightingales: 'Then the evening comes cooler, and the nightingale starts singing again. There are many nightingales, in every little wood you can hear half a dozen singing away all day long, except in the hot hours, very lively' (v. 479). The first two lines of 'The Nightingale' echo the words of this letter, suggesting that it may well have been written at the same time: 'Tuscany is full of nightingales, and in spring and summer they sing all the time, save in the middle of the night and the middle of the day' (211:2–3). Characteristically, Lawrence does not confine himself to a mere description of the singing of a nightingale, but proposes a symbolic meaning: 'it's a male sound, a most intensely and undilutedly male sound. A pure assertion . . . he's got that tender, hopping mystery about him, of a thing that is rich alive inside' (212:2–3, 28–30).

Late June 1926 is also suggested as the probable date of composition of 'The Nightingale' by the letter to Nancy Pearn where Lawrence recommends that some of his 'little things' should be offered to *Vogue* for publication.[22] He wrote to her again on 31 August: 'Show Harraps any little essays of mine that you have – if you wish. There is "The Nightingale" and those others I sent for *Vogue*' (v. 520–1). But *Vogue* never published the essay.

Two other periodicals, however, were interested. Nancy Pearn wrote to Lawrence on 19 November 1926 to inquire whether he would accept the essay's publication in the *Spectator* with a significant cut, of about five hundred words, on the understanding that they would submit proofs to him. On 4 January 1927 she wrote again to inform him that the *Spectator* was pressing to publish the sketch but that they had to wait for simultaneous appearance with the American *Forum*, and concluded on an ironical note: 'why the "Spectator" should be wanting necessarily to talk about nightingales in January when they might just as well wait a month or two, I don't know'. A second letter from her on 12 January informed Lawrence that *Forum* were not after all planning to publish 'The

22 See above, p. lix.

Nightingale' until September: 'I am afraid the "Spectator" will kick, particularly as they seem to want their "Nightingales" early in the year. Does America have hers always in the Fall? Or perhaps they don't have them at all over there.' However, Lawrence had received an excellent offer from *Forum*, and he replied on 17 January: 'The *Forum* paid $75– for the nightingale, so I'm afraid they've put salt on the poor bird's tail, and will serve him out of season, to be luxurious. As for the *Spectator*, they wanted to cut him up, didn't they? So they can wait. Damn them all' (v. 625–6). An agreement was reached in the end, as Nancy Pearn reported to Lawrence on 27 January: 'At last we have comfortably settled "The Nightingale" – *The Spectator* having agreed to wait until September and be caviare along with the "Forum".'[23] Later, Lawrence commented on the appearance of the sketch in the *Forum*: 'They ... seem to have got off with it very well' (vi. 196).

'The Nightingale' was also sought for publication in Germany: in May 1927 Lawrence asked Nancy Pearn if she could 'possibly get a copy of "The Nightingale" – that little article which you sold to somebody – and could you send it to Frau Dr. Anton Kippenberg, Insel Verlag, Kurze-strasse, *Leipsig, Germany*. They want to print it in translation in the *Insel-Almanach*.'[24] Nancy Pearn agreed to send the article to Germany; a set of *Spectator* galley proofs with two single-letter corrections, possibly in Lawrence's hand, survives. The essay appeared as 'Die Nachtigall' in the *Insel-Almanach auf das Jahr 1928* (Leipzig, 1927), translated by Karl Lerbs.

The pertinent surviving texts of 'The Nightingale' are: an autograph manuscript (hereafter MS; Roberts E272a) of 8 pages;[25] the slightly-corrected set of galley proofs for *Spectator* (G) of 2 pages;[26] and the periodical publications in *Forum* (Per1) and *Spectator* (Per2).[27]

---

[23] *Forum*, lxxviii (September 1927), 382–7 and *Spectator* (10 September 1927), 377–8. *Forum* was illustrated by C. LeRoy Baldridge: above the title, a poet, from his romanticised style of dress and his quill pen, gazes upwards as if searching for inspiration whilst shedding tears, and next to him is an open cage with a singing bird on top. At the end are two startled lovers sitting slightly apart and turning to look at a bush from which musical notes appear (cf. 214:33–215:5).

[24] *Letters*, vi. 52. Kippenberg was the Director of the Insel-Verlag, DHL's publisher in Germany, and his wife an editor.

[25] Located at YU.

[26] Located at GSArchiv; for the corrections see apparatus at 215:25, 34, which are possibly in DHL's hand.

[27] An incomplete copy of MS has a note at the top of p. 1 in Frieda's hand: 'We copied it for you, Pino – I believe it was printed in a little magazine'; pp. 1–5 are in an unidentified hand and end with the bottom of p. 4 of MS, while pp. 6–8 were copied by Frieda (p. 9 with the

The three almost identical published versions – Per1, Per2 and A1 – show remarkable differences from MS. The nature of these variants, which include additions and substantial rewriting of some paragraphs, makes it legitimate to assume that Lawrence made extensive alterations on a now lost typescript. The *Spectator* galley proofs of 'The Nightingale' were sent to Lawrence by Nancy Pearn on 26 July 1927 with an accompanying letter specifying that they were 'only sent in case you feel you would like to look through them, otherwise shoot them back uncorrected, and we will see that they are looked through at this end'. Lawrence's reply on the 31st – 'The "Nightingale" seems all right, without any more corrections' (vi. 110) – shows that he had already made the major revisions at a previous stage.

The text published in Per2 was extensively altered, most cuts being made before G but some copy-editing changes and a few further cuts were made before publication;[28] Per1, however, printed the complete essay. The base-text chosen for this edition is MS emended from Per1. The Textual apparatus records the variants in the two periodicals and in A1.

MS (without the revisions found in Per1) was published in Frieda's memoir "*Not I, But the Wind ...* " (A2) in 1934, a ribbon-copy typescript (TS; Roberts E272c) of 7 pages served as setting-copy as some copy-editing marks show.[29] TS and A2 are recorded in the apparatus, as the first publication of MS.

Man is a Hunter (October–November 1926)
This sketch about the hunting of birds in Italy was probably written in the autumn of 1926. Lawrence mentioned the killing of birds in Italy as early as January 1926, when he was still at the Villa Bernarda: 'We actually had two days of snow here, and the cacciatori are banging away at the tiny birds, it's like a festa with all the crackers going off. The robins and finches fly about in perfect bewilderment – and occasionally in bits – La caccia!'[30] But

last three paragraphs is missing), in the Lazarus collection (Roberts E272e). It may have been made for one of the posthumous volumes proposed by Orioli.

　Three different typescripts, all of the MS version and apparently posthumous, survive: a ribbon copy of 7 pp. (see end of this section above), a ribbon copy and its carbon of 8 pp. (Roberts E272d, UT) and a single-spaced carbon of 5 pp. (Roberts E272b, UCB). The 8-page ribbon copy has markings indicating it was considered for inclusion in A1.

　None of these texts (except the 7-page typescript) has any authority; their variants are not recorded.

[28] E.g. apparatus for 211:19, 21, 22, 29; for cuts see 212:4 and 212:30–213:2.

[29] "*Not I, But the Wind ...* " (pp. 115–21) was first published in Santa Fe; TS is located at UT.

[30] *Letters*, v. 379. 'Cacciatori' and 'caccia' are 'hunters' and 'hunting' (Italian).

there are three letters written on 17 and 18 October 1926 where Lawrence describes the same events in Tuscany – the setting of the essay. In the first letter he refers to 'an enormous fusillade going on in the boschi – shooting little birds as they go south'.[31] The second reads: 'This is a pretty, hilly part of Tuscany. The little pink cyclamens are out in the woods, the pines smell sweet, the "cacciatori" are banging away all day at the little birds' (v. 559–60). In the last letter the subject of hunting in Italy is more widely discussed and similarities with the essay are more extensive:

In the woods the little wild cyclamens, pink ones, are dotted under the leaves. I am very fond of them. And all the time, the famous Italian 'hunters' are banging away at the little birds, sparrows, larks, finches, any little bird that flutters. They are awful fools, in some respects, these people. To see a middle-aged man stalking a sparrow with as much intensity as if it were male rhinocerous, and letting bang at it with a great gun, is too much for my patience. They will offer you a string of little birds for a shilling, robins, finches, larks, even nightingales. Makes one tired!

(v. 560)

Since Lawrence's letters often reflect his current work, a mid-October date seems likely for the composition of this essay, but late November 1926 is also possible. In a letter to Nancy Pearn of 23 November, Lawrence expressed his intention to write some 'little sketches' (v. 584), and about a week later he sent her one for magazine publication which might well be 'Man is a Hunter': 'Here's a little article – Surely short enough – – let's see if that's the sort they want, and if it is, I'll do more' (v. 590). Miss Pearn replied on 6 December 1926: 'Very many thanks for the two copies of "MAN IS A HUNTER". I do hope this will just fit the "Spectator" opening.' About a month later, on 4 January 1927 she wrote: 'The *Spectator* returned "Man is a Hunter" intimating they felt that it contained too many political implications and might have given offence in Italy.' It is not unreasonable to assume that this was the principal obstacle to the publication of this sketch during Lawrence's lifetime; 'Man is a Hunter' made its first appearance posthumously in A1.

Three texts survive: an autograph manuscript with a few corrections (hereafter MS; Roberts E226a); a carbon-copy typescript of 3 pages, with a few revisions in Lawrence's hand (TCCI; Roberts E226b); and a carbon-copy typescript of 5 pages (TCCII; Roberts E226c).[32] TCCI has many substantive differences from MS: it was typed by Lawrence who

---

[31] Ibid. 558. 'Boschi' is 'woods' (Italian).
[32] MS and TCCII are located at UT; TCCI at UNM.

revised as he typed.[33] TCCII was typed from TCCI, and A1 was probably set from a copy of TCCII.

The base-text chosen for this edition is MS, emended from TCCI for substantive and accidental variants. The variants of TCCII and A1 are recorded in the apparatus.

Flowery Tuscany (February–April 1927)

Between the planning of the Etruscan tour with Earl Brewster and its actual realisation,[34] Lawrence stayed at the Villa Mirenda, enjoying the early spring. Between 16 February and 11 March 1927 he wrote several letters in which he describes the beauty of the Tuscan countryside: 'It is already beginning to be spring. Under the olive trees the winter aconites, such pretty pale yellow bubbles, are all out, and many daisies: and I found the first purple anemone ... The wild tulips are peeping through, though they won't flower till Easter, and the grape hyacinths also are coming. We've had a week of lovely sunshine'.[35]

The beauty of the spring in the Tuscan landscape inspired him to write four sketches entitled 'Flowery Tuscany'. They were probably composed at about the same time as these letters. However, some passages contained in the sketches themselves suggest that they were written over a more extended period, between February and April 1927: 'In a fortnight, before February is over, the yellow bubbles of the aconite are crumpling to nothingness' (I, 228:6–7); 'And now that it is March, there is a rush of flowers' (II, 231:1); 'But as yet it is neither May nor June, but end of April' (III, 237:3); 'To-morrow, however, is the first of May' (IV, 238:39). Of course Lawrence might only be notating the passing of time, as marked by the blooming of different flowers, and the sketches might have been written all at the same time. However, similarities with some of his letters seem to confirm the longer span of February to April as the date of composition. A letter to his sister Ada, dated 16 February, reads: 'under the olives all the pale-gold bubbles of winter aconites, and many daisies' (v. 643); in the first essay Lawrence writes: 'early in February, you will notice on a bit of fallow land, under the olive trees, tight, pale-gold little balls ... It is the winter aconite suddenly come' (227:19–23). In a letter to Secker written on 15 March, Lawrence says: 'It's lovely spring

---

[33] TCCI appears to have been typed on the same typewriter as the first typescript (Roberts E116b) for Part I of *The Escaped Cock* – they share a distinctive exclamation mark, made up of an apostrophe and full stop, with the upper part printing to the right of the dot – which DHL is known to have typed and which was extensively revised from manuscript as he typed.

[34] See above, pp. xxviii–xxix.   [35] *Letters*, v. 644. See also pp. 643–5, 650, 653–4.

here – the wheat full of big blue anemones, and primroses and many violets and grape hyacinths by the stream – and purple anemones and scarlet, and the wild tulips all in bud. Tuscany is very flowery' (v. 655); the penultimate words recur in Part II – 'The wild tulips are in bud' (233:9) – and the last ones provided Lawrence with his title. The third and fourth sketches show how Lawrence, having toured Etruria at the beginning of April and having started to write his Etruscan sketches, was by then in an 'Etruscan' frame of mind. In the third, after describing the April flowers, he talks of the symbolic contrast between sunshine and darkness and of the different attitudes to death in northern and southern Europe, and he combines those two themes in the conclusion to the essay: 'For my part, if the sun always shines, and always will shine, in spite of millions of clouds of words, then death, somehow, does not have many terrors. In the sunshine, even death is sunny. And there is no end to the sunshine' (238:17–21). It is almost the same attitude as that he attributed to the Etruscans when he described the banquet scene in the Tomb of Hunting and Fishing: 'the underworld of the Etruscans was a gay place. While the living feasted out of doors, at the tomb of the dead, the dead himself feasted in like manner, with a lady to offer him garlands and slaves to bring him wine, away in the underworld. For the life on earth was so good, the life below could but be a continuance of it.'[36] This latter argument is developed further in Part IV of 'Flowery Tuscany' by means of comparisons between the Germans and the Italians, and then, in a wider perspective, between the nations of thought and the nations of the sun.[37]

In July 1927 'Flowery Tuscany' I–III were offered for publication to the *New Criterion*; on 27 July Nancy Pearn informed Lawrence that '"The Criterion" … wants to run my treasured "FLOWERY TUSCANY" sketches',[38] and on 24 August she announced: '"The Criterion" is rushing into print with "FLOWERY TUSCANY", beginning in the October number.' Parts II and III appeared in the November and December issues.[39]

'Flowery Tuscany' I–III were also published in *Travel* in the USA two years later, under the title 'The Year in Flowery Tuscany'.[40] Nancy Pearn

[36] See 46:5–10.   [37] Cf. 242:32–243:4.

[38] Letter from Nancy Pearn to DHL, 5 July 1927: 'at present we have "FLOWERY TUSCANY" on offer'.

[39] Vol. vi., pp. 305–10, 403–8, 516–22.

[40] Vol. xlix (April 1929), pp. 25–9, 56, 58, 60. The subtitle reads: 'How Italy Built Her Gardens and Vineyards – Garlands of the Seasons on the Tuscan Hillsides – The Magic of the Mediterranean Sun'. There are seven photographs of peasant life and Tuscan landscapes, with titles and detailed captions.

wrote to Lawrence on 5 July 1928: 'We have heard that the *Travel* magazine is publishing parts of "Flowery Tuscany"', thus implying that the sketches were to be cut. Only a few paragraphs were omitted, however, when *Travel* published the three sections as one unusually long article.

'Flowery Tuscany' IV, separated from the first three, was never published during Lawrence's lifetime and appeared for the first time in *Phoenix* as 'Germans and Latins'. A comment in Nancy Pearn's letter of 2 May 1927 – 'The MS of "FLOWERY TUSCANY" has arrived safely and gone to be typed' – is extended and clarified in a letter to her which Lawrence wrote three days later: 'I suppose you got the three little sketches: "Flowery Tuscany"' (vi. 52). In late April, Lawrence could have sent only the first three sketches, since the fourth was almost certainly written on or after 30 April and could not have reached Curtis Brown's office by 2 May. It must have been sent later: Lawrence's first reference to it is in a letter of 3 September 1929 to Pollinger, in which he discusses pieces for limited editions: 'Another small thing – rather "sweet" – which would do for limited publication is the "Flowery Tuscany" articles, which Nancy Pearn liked so much. The *New Criterion* published three of the sketches – I thought there were four. But the magazine dept has them.'[41] This is the first indication of confusion over the number of 'Flowery Tuscany' essays.

In the surviving Curtis Brown archives there is an undated list which includes a handwritten manuscript, identified as: 'Untitled, "It is already summer in Tuscany ... ".'[42] Lawrence Clark Powell listed in his 1937 catalogue a 10-page manuscript in ink on ruled paper which was apparently entitled 'Summer in Tuscany, or, Germans and Latins';[43] it is likely that the manuscript originally had no title, being the fourth part of a series of articles; it had probably never been united with the first three parts at Curtis Brown's and someone must have provided a title, taking it from the first line ('Summer in Tuscany') and from the general content ('Germans and Latins'); the latter provided the title for A1.

A few further references to 'four' 'Flowery Tuscany' sketches can be found in the Curtis Brown files. In particular, there is an undated list of

---

[41] The letter continues: 'The thing to do is to make the most of this boom of limited editions – it's the only way to make money, and without so much fuss. I shall get much more from my 500 *Pansies* than from Secker's 3000 – and no taxes and all that.' For the complications of another version of Part IV, see next section 'Germans and English'.

[42] Located at UT; probably made after DHL's death, as there are several inventories of items in London and New York.

[43] *The Manuscripts of D. H. Lawrence: A Descriptive Catalogue* (Los Angeles), item 81. This manuscript is unlocated.

Lawrence's manuscripts including '"Flowery Tuscany" / I–II–III *Criterion* / IV unpublished'.[44]

The first three parts of 'Flowery Tuscany' survive in a manuscript (hereafter MS; Roberts E135a) of 31 pages;[45] Part I was first entitled 'Flowery Spring', and the last word was replaced by 'Tuscany' at a later stage in paler ink. A 25-page carbon typescript (TCC; Roberts E135b) appears to have been prepared from *New Criterion*.[46] A copy of TCC was used in setting A1, as is shown by a number of variants in common, especially a missing line.[47] Another typescript, prepared for Curtis Brown and now unlocated, must have served as the original setting-copy for *New Criterion* (Per1); *Travel* (Per2) may have been set from a copy of this typescript or from Per1.

For Part IV, three carbon-copy typescripts survive. TCCI, 8 pp., has the typed title '*FLOWERY TUSCANY.*' and on a label in an unidentified hand, someone has inked over a pencil note: 'Part IV' (Roberts E135c). TCCII, also 8 pp., is untitled.[48] Although a title sheet with '*FLOWERY TUSCANY. / By / D. H. LAWRENCE.*' and 'Part IV' in an unidentified hand is now associated with TCCII, the similarity of the typeface and the typing style makes it certain that the title sheet actually belongs to TCCI. On p. 1 of TCCI and the title sheet occur the notation 'no corrections/ C[?]R':[49] these initials are found on other typescripts, and probably indicate that someone at Curtis Brown was verifying the status of the typescripts for the posthumous lists (see above). A third typescript (Roberts E143.7, hereafter referred to as the 'Texas copy'), another carbon copy from the typing of TCCII, is titled only by a handwritten note: 'Germans & Latins / (Unpublished)'.[50] This typescript was probably used for A1, and thus it is likely that it (like TCCII) was posthum-

[44] A letter of 8 May 1934 from the Curtis Brown office to Secker contains a proposal for a miscellaneous volume 'tentatively entitled "A World of Men and Women. Last Essays by D. H. Lawrence"' and gives details such as: 'PART III – "Flowery Tuscany" (to include these 4 essays, or to be called "Travel Essays" and to include other essays on places chosen from PART I).' (Part I was supposed to include the Italian sketches published in this CUP volume, except for 'Looking Down on the City', 'Europe Versus America' and 'Germans and English').

[45] In George Lazarus's collection; on lined paper torn from a notebook (8⅛ × *c.* 6 inches), the three parts are numbered separately: 1–10; 1–10; 1–11.

[46] Located at UCB; the three parts are numbered consecutively. See apparatus at 229:28 and 229:35.

[47] See apparatus at 229:21; cf. also entries at 228:29 and 229:9.

[48] Both are located at UCB.

[49] The title sheet also has a note 'Pub[?] in Criterion in England'.   [50] Located at UT.

ous.[51] The unlocated manuscript (see above) almost certainly had no title, so TCCI was probably the first typing while Nancy Pearn or her secretary, knowing that it was part of the 'Flowery Tuscany' set, saw to it that TCCI was so labelled. TCCII (and the Texas copy) was typed later probably from the same untitled manuscript. Someone subsequently, having both TCCI and TCCII, transferred the title sheet to TCCII as a means of identifying it (hence the duplicate note about 'no corrections'). The Texas copy remained untitled and, when used for printing A1, someone must have added the title 'Germans and Latins', perhaps inspired by parts of the sketch itself. That title was adopted by the editor of A1, E. D. McDonald, who explained in his Introduction that it was not Lawrence's title, but that it 'was chosen as reasonably descriptive'.[52]

The essay, previously published as 'Germans and Latins', is included in this edition as Part IV of 'Flowery Tuscany'. The contents of all four parts also provide further support for the argument that they form a quartet. The first three parts describe flowers and nature in the Tuscan country-side with references, for comparison, to the English countryside, implicitly contrasting the two different cultures. The last few paragraphs of Part III become more openly ideological, dealing with the contrast between north and south, dark and light, as revealing elements of a wider conflict between a tragic life-death vision in the Northerners and a vital one in the Southerners. Part IV, despite its different textual history, is manifestly a development of Part III. It opens with a bridging paragraph in which spring and nightingales are celebrated,[53] before Lawrence turns to concentrate on the description of two German boys walking fast, instinctively, towards the south and the sun; by this means the author works his way towards contrasting the Germans with the Latin peoples – French and Italian – who live according to the influence of the sun, which is 'anti-thought' and 'non-mental consciousness'. Part IV thus develops the same theme presented in the first three sections, and elaborates it in theoretical terms.

The base-texts used for this edition are MS emended from Per1 for Parts I–III and TCCI (slightly more accurate than TCCII)[54] emended from A1 for Part IV.

---

[51] See pp. lxii–lxiii footnote 27 where the 8-page ribbon-copy typescript has markings in the same hand.

[52] *Phoenix* xv.

[53] The mention of the birds is reminiscent of the earlier sketch, 'The Nightingale'; cf. 238:35–6 with 211:23–4.

[54] See apparatus for 241:26 and 241:39.

Germans and English (May 1927)

The first part of 'Flowery Tuscany' IV is echoed – sometimes literally – in passages of another article posthumously entitled 'Germans and English', which must have been written at about the same time, probably early in May 1927, and which was first published in *Phoenix II*.

At the end of April Lawrence broke off from the writing of his Etruscan sketches for about a month[55] and wrote a number of short pieces which partly reflect his Etruscan experience and his thinking on Etruscan civilisation. Neither 'Flowery Tuscany' IV nor 'Germans and English' contains any specific reference to the Etruscans, but the Etruscan spirit and attitude to life are always implicitly present, if only by contrast.

Despite the similarity in the initial description of the two German boys, 'Germans and English' is rather different in style from the other sketch and its ideological development proceeds along the lines of a comparison between German and English people. Even though the parallel phrasing of the two articles might lead the reader to see one as a rewriting of the other, their differences in form and substance justify their publication in this edition under two different titles.

The publication history of 'Germans and English' has rightly been defined as 'a bibliographical puzzle'.[56] A German translation appeared in the quarterly *Das Inselschiff. Eine Zeitschrift für die Freunde des Insel-Verlages* (Leipzig, 1927)[57] with the generic title 'Ein Brief von D. H. Lawrence an das Inselschiff'. Unfortunately, the Insel-Verlag archives were partly destroyed during the bombing of Leipzig, and nothing is known about the text which was submitted: whether it was a manuscript or a typescript, whether it was in English or in German, and if the latter, by whom it had been translated. The German printed version was published in an Italian translation in 1934, in the monthly review *La Cultura*, with the title 'Tedeschi e Inglesi'.[58] This title, translated into English, appeared within square brackets in *Phoenix II* (hereafter E1).

[55] See above, pp. xxx–xxxi.
[56] Cf. Horst E. Meyer, 'An Addendum to the D. H. Lawrence Canon', in *Papers of the Bibliographical Society of America*, No. 67 (1973), 458–9.
[57] No. 8, pp. 285–93.
[58] Turin: Einaudi, xii (November 1934), 125–7. The text, trans. Emma Sola, was accompanied by an editor's note which reads, in translation, as follows:
    As we read in *The Letters of D. H. Lawrence* edited by Aldous Huxley (London, Heinemann 1932) this essay was written in Florence in the early days of 1927 in response to a request from Insel Verlag, Leipzig, who wanted from Lawrence 'a more or less personal article to put in their Almanach, in German' (p. 678). Thanks to the kind

'Germans and English' exists in a 10-page typescript (hereafter TS) and its two carbon copies (Roberts E143.7c).[59] It is untitled and is headed '*E S S A Y – (No title).*' and has a number of remarkable and unusual mistypings – e.g. 'pur' (249:29); 'ethis' (250:27); 'Europian' (252:20) – all corrected in E1.[60]

Since the typescripts are uncorrected and the many mistypings had already been emended in E1, E1 has been chosen as base-text for this edition. The title used in E1 has been retained because it is the title by which the essay has been known, and, also, because it is reasonably descriptive of the essential matter of the sketch. The generic title given in the German version was obviously adopted for the readers of that particular publication and Lawrence was probably not consulted about the matter.

Reception

Phoenix included all but two of the sketches published in this edition; it was reviewed by various critics who all praised McDonald's 'skilful, unobtrusive editing' of a book which 'provides samples of Lawrence's development as a writer, as an artist and as a thinker, at all stages of his life'; in a word, 'a well-edited book' and 'an invaluable compilation' that 'comble plusieurs lacunes', the Introduction to which is 'extremely useful, strictly dealing with the circumstances of the pieces and dating where possible'.[61]

Most of the critics were struck by the contents, which exhibited, more

---

permission previously given by Lawrence, Emma Sola has been able to translate for us, from the German, this article hitherto unknown to us. For its psychological observations on Germans and English (the title is ours) it seemed to us particularly topical, especially the two sentences showing the lack of understanding of 'Romanness' [the Roman character] by the Germans. As authoritatively recorded in the Italian newspapers, these sentences were to find exact correspondence in later events, which Lawrence seems to have almost foreseen.

The information about the date is wrong, since we know that the essay was actually written in early May 1927; the Italian editor had obviously been misled by the words quoted, which are in fact contained in DHL's letter to Nancy Pearn of 9 January 1927 and which refer to an autobiographical sketch published in the *Insel-Almanach* in 1930 as 'D. H. Lawrence über Sich Selbst' (see Roberts C217).

[59] Located at UT (the carbon copies are identical to TS).

[60] One mistake led to further misinterpretation: see Explanatory note to 251:23.

[61] H. T. Moore, 'A Lawrence Budget', *Nation* (24 October 1936), 492; David Garnett, *New Statesman and Nation* (21 November 1936), 812; Mina Curtiss, *Living Age* (New York, December 1936), 370; Kerker Quinn, 'Lawrence as Critic and Artist', *Yale Review* (June 1937), 847; Emile Delavenay, *Études Anglaises* (March 1937), 157; Peter Monro Jack, 'Papers D. H. Lawrence Wrote', *New York Times Book Review* (29 November 1936), 29. The French quotation means 'fills many gaps'.

than any other volume, 'Lawrence's multiplicity – a fairer word, perhaps, than inconsistency' and his 'omnivorous interest in all things, from the tiniest object to a vast concept, and his talent for electric, mettlesome description of them'.[62] Lawrence's style also drew the attention of critics who mostly agreed on its special character, even when they pointed out its faults.

Lawrence had died only six years before the publication of *Phoenix* and his name, although respected as that of an 'artist', was still considered devilish, or, at least, still caused resentment and visceral reactions. This explains how it was that so many critics appreciated the artist Lawrence proved to be in the pieces collected in *Phoenix*, but could not come to terms with his ideas.

Those reviewers who gave details of the various sections in which the book was divided never omitted an enthusiastic mention of 'Nature and Poetical Pieces',[63] and specific references to the individual articles published in this edition are also contained in a number of reviews. Geoffrey West, in *The Times Literary Supplement*, mentioned 'Flowery Tuscany' among those 'few lovely essays' where 'the artist also appears', whereas 'the expositor takes to himself the bulk of the volume'.[64] Edward Garnett also commented on 'Flowery Tuscany' 'which conveys all the charm of Lawrence's passionate love of flowers'. He then mentioned 'the gay sharp mockery of "Man is a Hunter"' as 'another characteristic facet of his passion for wild nature',[65] thus presenting it in a much more lively way than McDonald had proposed in his Introduction: 'Lawrence, who could kill no living thing, and least of all a bird, found it impossible to understand the appeal of hunting, especially as practised in Italy. In "Man is a Hunter" he satirises mildly, merely half-contemptuously, the idiotic doings of the Nimrods of Italy.'[66] In the same review, Garnett devoted a few lines to Section II – 'Peoples, Countries, Races' – which contains 'many good examples of Lawrence's rare sensibility to the atmosphere of place and to racial distinctions between peoples'.[67]

---

[62] Granville Hicks, 'D. H. Lawrence as Messiah', *New Republic* (28 October 1936), 358; Quinn, *Yale Review*, p. 847.

[63] This section includes 'Man is a Hunter', 'The Nightingale', 'Flowery Tuscany' I–III and 'David'.

[64] 'The Flame of Another Phoenix: D. H. Lawrence as Expositor and Artist' (21 November 1936), 956.

[65] 'D. H. Lawrence: His Posthumous Papers', *London Mercury* (December 1936), 156.

[66] *Phoenix* xii.

[67] *London Mercury*, p. 156. The sketches included in this section are: 'Europe Versus America', 'Fireworks in Florence' and 'Germans and Latins', that is 'Flowery Tuscany' IV.

These two sections were also singled out for special mention by Peter Monro Jack: 'The nature pieces ... reprint the lovely essays on the flowers of Tuscany that appeared originally in the London *Criterion. Peoples, Countries, Races* ranges from Nottingham coal mines to Germany, Paris, Florence and Taos.'[68] C. Henry Warren, after appreciating the volume as a whole, asked: 'Who, for instance, could describe nature as sensitively and vividly as Lawrence? Certainly there is an exasperating essay on Keats and the nightingale ... But "Flowery Tuscany" is unforgettable'.[69]

Emile Delavenay appreciated the art of Lawrence particularly as it appeared in the first two sections: 'Mais surtout le voyageur, le conteur, l'observateur puissant et délicat des bêtes et des plantes, se retrouvent dans mainte page de ce fort volume qui, s'il contient quelques spécimens du pire style lawrencien, les rachète par les plus beaux morceaux de lyrisme.'[70] Among these *morceaux*, 'l'étude sur les fleurs de Toscane' receives a special mention. A. Desmond Hawkins reminded the readers of the *Criterion* that 'Flowery Tuscany' had been originally published in that periodical, but he attributed more importance to 'the travel sketches, which range from pre-war adventures in Germany and Italy to more sombre studies of Mexico and post-war Europe'.[71]

If the critics' opinions of *Phoenix* as a whole varied from enthusiasm to contempt and reproof, they all shared a thorough appreciation of most of those 'Italian essays', included in the present volume, in which Lawrence describes nature and gives his impressions of people and places, showing once again his capacity to express his sensitivity, passion and ideology perfectly combined in his art.

[68] *New York Times Book Review*, p. 29.
[69] 'Ark Under Rainbow: Last Papers from D. H. Lawrence', *Observer Christmas Supplement* (13 December 1936), 19.
[70] *Études Anglaises*, p. 158. ('But above all the traveller, the story-teller, the powerful and delicate observer of beasts and plants can be found again in many pages of this great volume which, if it contains some specimens of the worst Lawrencian style, redeems them thanks to the most beautiful passages of lyricism.')
[71] July 1937, p. 749.

SKETCHES OF
ETRUSCAN PLACES

Note on the text

The base-text for *Sketches of Etruscan Places* is the manuscript (MS), located at UT, with the typescripts adopted as the primary sources for substantive emendation as follows: 'Cerveteri', TSa (UT); 'Tarquinia', TSa (UT); 'The Painted Tombs of Tarquinia' 1., TSc (UTul); 'The Painted Tombs of Tarquinia' 2., TSc (UT); 'Vulci', TSb (UT); and 'Volterra', TSc (UTul).

The Textual apparatus records all the variants from the base-text in subsequent texts. The apparatus for 'The Florence Museum' records all the deletions and corrections in MS since that is the only surviving text. Secker's first edition (E1) follows the page proofs (PP) unless otherwise indicated.

DHL's use of an initial capital letter in 'Dazio' and 'Museum'; the capitalisation of his 'c', which is often difficult to distinguish in his handwriting (though he generally writes 'christian' when the word is used as an adjective); and the Italian names of the tombs generally italicised and capitalised by DHL have all been regularised according to DHL's most usual practice, and the variants have been recorded in the apparatus.

DHL is often inconsistent when using the ancient and modern names of the Etruscan cities. His inconsistencies have been preserved in this edition except in 'Vulci' where, particularly in the first two pages, DHL is actually mistaken. 'Volci' and 'Vulci' – the first being the old name of the city and the second the modern one – have been standardised throughout the essay, with the variants recorded in the apparatus.

The apparatus records all textual variants, except for the following silent emendations which have only been recorded when they form part of another variant:

1 Clearly inadvertent spelling and typesetting errors have been corrected. When a variant occurs only in an unpublished text (i.e. the typescripts or PP) it has not been recorded.

2 Omitted or misplaced apostrophes in possessive cases and contractions, incomplete quotation marks and full stops omitted at the end of sentence where no other punctuation exists, have all been supplied or corrected.

3 DHL did not usually italicise punctuation, and variants have only been recorded when they are part of an entry.

4 Per2 and PP consistently printed 'to-day', whereas DHL wrote it as one unhyphenated word; Per2 and PP printed 'for ever' as two words, whereas DHL generally wrote it as one word; DHL's spelling has been preserved in this

edition. The American spelling of words such as 'center' and 'color' in Per1 and TScC (i.e. non-Lawrentian corrections to TSc) has not been recorded. DHL consistently wrote 'fulness', which was typed as 'fullness', and so printed in Per2 and PP; and he regularly wrote 'maremma' which was generally capitalised in E1; DHL's spelling has been preserved.

5 Per1, TScC and PP house-styled '-is-' to '-iz-', e.g. DHL's 'realise' became 'realize'; DHL's practice has been retained in this edition. The diphthongs 'ae' and 'oe' were printed as 'æ' and 'œ' in Per2, and PP and Per1 often printed 'e' instead of 'ae' in words such as 'mediaeval' and 'archaeologist'; this edition follows DHL's practice.

6 DHL often followed a full stop, question mark or exclamation mark with a dash before beginning the next sentence with a capital letter, e.g. 'spinach.—The' (11:32). His typist occasionally and the typesetter consistently omitted the dash, which has been restored in this edition.

7 Inconsistencies in the placing of quotation marks for a single word or short sentence before, over or after the punctuation, e.g. 'norm".' (39:14) '"Volterra,"' (160:24) 'uplift."' (39:16), have been regularised to have the quotation marks following the punctuation, as it occurs most often. DHL's preferred practice was also used in PP. When quotation marks have an emphatic function, they have been regularised from single to double, e.g. '"classical"' (130:36), respecting DHL's usual practice.

8 In MS, at the beginning of each essay, the chapter title is preceded by the general title of the volume; both titles are in upper and lower case letters. In the extant typescripts the general title is given in capitals. PP dropped the general title and printed the chapter titles in capitals. In this edition the general title has also been dropped, whereas the chapter title follows the MS reading.

9 In MS and in the typescripts a full stop always follows the roman numerals which number the essays; the stops were dropped in PP and have been restored in this edition. A full stop also follows the individual titles of each essay in three cases in MS and always in the revised typescripts; they were dropped in PP and do not appear in this edition.

10 With very few exceptions, 'Etruscan' in its adjectival form always appears uncapitalised in MS, the typescripts and PP, whereas in Per1, Per2 and E1 it is always capitalised (see Introduction). DHL's preferred practice has been restored in this edition.

11 In 'Vulci' the dialogues are always introduced by dashes in MS and in the typescripts whereas PP substituted quotation marks; DHL's practice has been retained in this edition. E1 always italicised the Italian 'carretto'; italics have been dropped in this edition following DHL's practice.

12 For the captions and order of the Illustrations see Appendix III, pp. 275–8.

Contents

I.
CERVETERI

I.

Cerveteri*

The Etruscans, as everyone knows, were the people who occupied
the middle of Italy in early Roman days, and whom the Romans, in
their usual neighbourly fashion, wiped out entirely in order to make 5
room for Rome with a very big R.* They couldn't have wiped them all
out, there were too many of them. But they did wipe out the
etruscan* existence as a nation and a people. However, this seems to
be the inevitable result of expansion with a big E, which is the sole
raison d'être of people like the Romans.* 10

Now, we know nothing about the Etruscans except what we find in
their tombs. There are references to them in Latin writers.* But of
first-hand knowledge we have nothing except what the tombs offer.

So to the tombs we must go: or to the museums containing the
things that have been rifled from the tombs. 15

Myself, the first time I consciously saw etruscan things, in the
museum at Perugia,* I was instinctively attracted to them. And it
seems to be that way. Either there is instant sympathy, or instant
contempt and indifference. Most people despise everything B.C.
that isn't Greek, for the good reason that it ought to be Greek if it 20
isn't. So etruscan things are put down as a feeble Graeco-Roman
imitation. And a great scientific historian like Mommsen* hardly
allows that the Etruscans existed at all. Their existence was antipa-
thetic to him. The Prussian in him was enthralled by the Prussian in
the all-conquering Romans. So being a great scientific historian, he 25
almost denies the very existence of the etruscan people. He didn't
like the idea of them. That was enough for a great scientific
historian.

Besides, the Etruscans were vicious. We know it, because their
enemies and exterminators said so.* Just as we knew the unspeakable 30
depths of *our* enemies in the late war. Who isn't vicious, to his
enemy? To my detractors, I am a very effigy of vice. A la bonne
heure!*

However, those pure, clean-living, sweet-souled Romans, who
smashed nation after nation and crushed the free soul in people after 35

9

people, and were ruled by Messalina and Heliogabalus* and such-
like snowdrops, they said the Etruscans were vicious. So *basta!*
Quand le maître parle, tout le monde se tait.* The Etruscans were
vicious! The only vicious people on the face of the earth, pre-
5 sumably. You and I, dear reader, we are two unsullied snow-flakes,
aren't we? We have every right to judge.

Myself, however, if the Etruscans were vicious, I'm glad they
were. To the Puritan all things are impure, as somebody says.* And
those naughty neighbours of the Romans at least escaped being
10 Puritans.

But to the tombs, to the tombs! On a sunny April morning we set
out for the tombs. From Rome, the eternal city, now in a black
bonnet. It was not far to go—about twenty miles over the campagna
towards the sea, on the line to Pisa.*

15 The campagna, with its great green spread of growing wheat, is
almost human again. But still there are damp empty tracts, where
now the little narcissus stands in clumps, or covers whole fields. And
there are places queer and foam-white, all with camomile, on a
sunny morning in early April.

20 We are going to Cerveteri, which was the ancient Caere, or Cere,
and which had a Greek name too, Agylla. It was a gay and gaudy
etruscan city when Rome put up her first few hovels: probably.
Anyhow, there are tombs there now.

The inestimable big Italian railway-guide says the station is Palo,
25 and that Cerveteri is eight-and-a-half kilometres away: about five
miles. But there is a post omnibus.*

We arrive at Palo, a station in nowhere, and ask if there is a bus to
Cerveteri. No! An ancient sort of wagon with an ancient white horse
stands outside. Where does that go? To Ladispoli.* We know we
30 don't want to go to Ladispoli, so we stare at the landscape.—Could
we get a carriage of any sort?—It would be difficult. That is what they
always say: difficult! meaning impossible. At least they won't lift a
finger to help.—Is there an hotel at Cerveteri? They don't know.
They have none of them ever been, though it is only five miles away,
35 and there are tombs.—Well, we will leave our two bags at the
station.—But they cannot acccept them. Because they are not
locked. But when did a hold-all ever lock? Difficult! Well then, let us
leave them, and steal if you want to. Impossible! Such a moral
responsibility! Impossible to leave an unlocked small holdall at the
40 station. So much for the officials!

However, we try the man at the small buffet. He is very laconic, but seems all right. We abandon our things in a corner of the dark little eating-place, and set off on foot. Luckily it is only something after ten in the morning.

A flat, white road with a rather noble avenue of umbrella pines for the first few hundred yards. A road not far from the sea, a bare, flattish, hot white road with nothing but a tilted oxen-wagon in the distance like a huge snail with four horns. Beside the road the tall asphodel is letting off its spasmodic pink sparks, rather at random, and smelling of cats. Away to the left is the sea, beyond the flat green wheat, the Mediterranean glistening flat and deadish, as it does on the low shores. Ahead are hills, and a ragged bit of a grey village with an ugly big grey building:* that is Cerveteri. We trudge on along the dull road. After all, it is only five miles and a bit.

We creep nearer, and climb the ascent. Caere, like most etruscan cities, lay on the crown of a hill with cliff-like escarpments. Not that this Cerveteri is an etruscan city. Caere, the etruscan city, was swallowed by the Romans, and after the fall of the Roman empire* it fell out of existence altogether. But it feebly revived, and today we come to an old Italian village, walled in with grey walls, and having a few new, pink, box-shaped houses and villas outside the walls.

We pass through the gateway, where men are lounging talking and mules are tied up, and in the bits of crooked grey streets look for a place where we can eat. We see the notice, *Vini e Cucina,** Wines and Kitchen*; but it is only a deep cavern where mule drivers are drinking blackish wine.

However, we ask the man who is cleaning the post-omnibus in the street, if there is any other place. He says no, so in we go, into the cavern, down a few steps.

Everybody is perfectly friendly. But the food is as usual, meat broth, very weak, with thin macaroni in it: the boiled meat that made the broth: and tripe: also spinach.—The broth tastes of nothing, the meat tastes almost of less, the spinach, alas, has been cooked over in the fat skimmed from the boiled beef. It is a meal—with a piece of so-called sheep's cheese, that is pure salt and rancidity, and probably comes from Sardinia; and wine that tastes like, and probably is, the black wine of Calabria* wetted with a good proportion of water. But it is a meal. We will go to the tombs.

Into the cave swaggers a spurred shepherd wearing goatskin trousers with the long, rusty-brown goat's hair hanging shaggy from

his legs. He grins and drinks wine, and immediately one sees again the shaggy-legged faun.* His face is a faun-face, not deadened by morals. He grins quietly, and talks very subduedly, shyly, to the fellow who draws the wine from the barrels. It is obvious fauns are
5 shy, very shy, especially of moderns like ourselves. He glances at us from a corner of his eye, ducks, wipes his mouth on the back of his hand, and is gone, clambering with his hairy legs on to his lean pony, swirling, and rattling away with a neat little clatter of hoofs, under the ramparts and away to the open. He is the faun escaping again out of
10 the city precincts, far more shy and evanescent than any christian virgin. You cannot hard-boil him.

It occurs to me, how rarely one sees the faun-face now, in Italy, that one used to see so often before the war: the brown, rather still, straight-nosed face* with a little black moustache and often a little
15 tuft of black beard; yellow eyes, rather shy under long lashes, but able to glare with a queer glare, on occasion; and mobile lips that had a queer way of showing the teeth when talking, bright white teeth. It was an old, old type, and rather common in the south. But now you will hardly see one of these men left, with the unconscious,
20 ungrimacing faun-face. They were all, apparently, killed in the war: they would be sure not to survive such a war. Anyway the last one I know, a handsome fellow of my own age—forty and a bit—is going queer and morose, crushed between war-memories that have revived, and remorseless go-ahead women-folk. Probably, when I go
25 south again, he will have disappeared. They can't survive, the faun-faced men, with their pure outlines and their strange non-moral calm. Only the deflowered faces survive.

So much for a maremma* shepherd! We went out into the sunny April street of this Cerveteri, Cerevetus, the old Cere.* It is a
30 worn-out little knot of streets shut in inside a wall. Rising on the left is the citadel, the acropolis,* the high place, that which is the arx in etruscan cities. But now the high place is forlorn, with a big, weary building like a governor's palace, or a bishop's palace, spreading on the crest behind the castle gate, and a desolate sort of yard tilting
35 below it, surrounded by ragged, ruinous enclosure. It is forlorn beyond words, dead, and still too big for the grey knot of inhabited streets below.

The girl of the cavern, a nice girl but a bad cook, has found us a guide, obviously her brother, to take us to the necropolis. He is a lad
40 of about fourteen, and like everybody in this abandoned place, shy

and suspicious, holding off. He bids us wait while he runs away somewhere. So we drink coffee in the tiny café outside which the motor-omnibus reposes all day long, till the return of our guide and another little boy, who will come with him and see him through. The two boys cotton together,* make a little world secure from us, and 5 move on ahead of us, ignoring us as far as possible. The stranger is always a menace. B. and I are two very quiet-mannered harmless men. But that first boy could not have borne to go alone with us. Not alone! He would have been afraid, as if he were in the dark.

They led us out of the only gate of the old town. Mules and ponies 10 were tied up in the sloping, forlorn place outside, and pack-mules arrived, as in Mexico.* We turned away to the left, under the rock cliff from whose summit the so-called palace goes up flush, the windows looking out on to the world. It seems as if the Etruscans may once have cut this low rock-face, and as if the whole crown on which the 15 wall-girt village of Cerveteri now stands may once have been the arx, the ark, the inner citadel and holy place of the city of Caere, or Agylla, the splendid etruscan city, with its Greek quarters. There was a whole suburb of Greek colonists, from Ionia, or perhaps from Athens, in busy Caere, when Rome was still a rather crude place. 20 About the year 390 B.C. the Gauls came swooping down on Rome. Then the Romans hurried the Vestal Virgins* and other women and children away to Caere, and the Etruscans took care of them, in their rich city. Perhaps the refugee Vestals were housed on this rock.

And perhaps not. The site of Caere may not have been exactly 25 here. Certainly it stretched away on this same hill-top, east and south, occupying the whole of the small plateau, some four or five miles round, and spreading a great city thirty times as big as the present Cerveteri. But the Etruscans built everything of wood, houses, temples, all save walls for fortification, great gates, bridges, 30 and drainage works. So that the etruscan cities vanished as completely as flowers. Only the tombs, like bulbs, were underground.

But the Etruscans built their cities, whenever possible, on a long narrow plateau or headland above the surrounding country, and they liked to have a rocky cliff for their base, as in Cerveteri. Round the 35 summit of this cliff, this headland, went the enclosure wall, sometimes miles of the great cincture. And within the walls they liked to have one inner high place, the arx, the citadel. Then outside, they liked to have a sharp dip or ravine, with a parallel hill opposite. And on the parallel hill opposite, they liked to have their city of the dead, 40

their necropolis. So they could stand on their ramparts and look over
the hollow where the stream flowed among its bushes, across from
the city of life, gay with its painted houses and temples, to the
near-at-hand city of their dear dead, pleasant with its smooth walks
5   and stone symbols, and painted fronts.

So it is at Cerveteri. From the sea-plain—and the sea was
probably a mile or two miles nearer in, in etruscan days—the land
heaves in an easy slope to the low, crowned cliffs of the city. But
behind, turning out of the gate away from the sea, you pass under the
10 low but sheer cliff of the town, down the stony road to the little
ravine, full of bushes.

Down here in the gully, the town—village, rather—has built its
wash-house, and the women are quietly washing the linen. They are
good-looking women, of the old world, with that very attractive look
15 of noiselessness and inwardness, which women must have had in the
past. As if, within the woman, there were again something to seek,
that the eye can never search out. Something that can be lost, but can
never be found out.

Up the other side the ravine is a steep, rocky little climb along a
20 sharp path, the two lads scrambling subduedly ahead. We pass a
door cut in the rock face. I peep in to the damp, dark cell of what was
apparently once a tomb. But this must have been for unimportant
people, a little room in a cliff-face, now all deserted. The great tombs
in the Banditaccia* are covered with mounds, tumuli. No-one looks
25 at these damp little rooms in the low cliff-face, among the
bushes.—So I scramble on hastily, after the others.

To emerge on to the open, rough, uncultivated plain. It was like
Mexico, on a small scale: the open, abandoned plain; in the distance
little, pyramid-shaped mountains set down straight upon the level, in
30 the not-far distance; and between, a mounted shepherd galloping
round a flock of mixed sheep and goats, looking very small. It was
just like Mexico, only much smaller and more human.

The boys went ahead across the fallow land, where there were
many flowers, tiny purple verbena, tiny forget-me-nots, and much
35 wild mignonette, that had a sweet little scent. I asked the boys what
they called it. They gave the usual dumb-bell answer: It is a flower!
On the heaping banks towards the edge of the ravine the asphodel
grew wild and thick, with tall flowers up to my shoulder, pink and
rather spasmodic. These asphodels are very noticeable, a great
40 feature* in all this coast landscape, I thought the boys surely would

have a name for it. But no! Sheepishly they make the same answer: "*È un fiore! Puzza!*"—It is a flower. It stinks!—Both facts being self-evident, there was no contradicting it. Though the smell of the asphodel is not objectionable, to me: and I find the flower, now I know it well, very beautiful, with its way of opening some pale, big, starry pink flowerets, and leaving many of its buds shut, with their dark, reddish stripes.

Many people, however, are very disappointed with the Greeks, for having made so much of this flower. It is true, the word "asphodel" makes one expect some tall and mysterious lily, not this sparky, assertive flower with just a touch of the onion about it. But for me, I don't care for mysterious lilies, not even for that weird shyness the mariposa lily has. And having stood on the rocks in Sicily,* with the pink asphodel proudly sticking up like clouds at sea, taller than myself, letting off pink different flowerets with such sharp and vivid éclat, and saving up such a store of buds in ear, stripey, I confess I admire the flower. It has a certain reckless glory, such as the Greeks loved.

One man said he thought we were mistaken in calling this the Greek asphodel, as somewhere in Greek the asphodel is called yellow. Therefore, said this scholastic Englishman, the asphodel of the Greeks was probably the single daffodil.

But not it! There is a very nice and silky yellow asphodel on Etna,* pure gold. And heaven knows how common the wild daffodil is in Greece? It does not seem a very Mediterranean flower. The narcissus, the polyanthus narcissus, is pure Mediterranean, and Greek. But the daffodil, the lent lily!

However, trust an Englishman and a modern for wanting to turn the tall, proud, sparky, dare-devil asphodel into the modest daffodil! I believe we don't like the asphodel because we don't like anything proud and sparky. The myrtle opens her blossoms in just the same way as the asphodel, explosively, throwing out the sparks of her stamens. And I believe it was just this that the Greeks *saw*. They were that way themselves.

However, this is all on the way to the tombs: which lie ahead, mushroom-shaped mounds of grass, great mushroom-shaped mounds, along the edge of the ravine.—When I say ravine, don't expect a sort of Grand Canyon. Just a modest, Italian sort of ravine-gully, that you could almost jump down.

When we come near, we see the mounds have bases of stone

masonry, great girdles of carved and bevelled stone, running round
touching the earth in flexible, uneven lines, like the girdles on big,
uneasy buoys half sunk in the sea. And they are sunk a bit in the
ground. And there is an avenue of mounds, with a sunken path
5 between, parallel to the ravine. This was evidently the grand avenue
of the necropolis, like the million-dollar cemetery in New Orleans.
Absit omen!*

Between us and the mounds is a barbed-wire fence. There is a
wire gate on which it says you mustn't pick the flowers, whatever that
10 may mean, for there are no flowers. And another notice says, you
mustn't tip the guide, as he is gratuitous.

The boys run to the new little concrete house just by, and bring
the guide: a youth with red eyes and a bandaged hand. He lost a
finger on the railway a month ago. He is shy, and muttering, and
15 neither prepossessing nor cheerful, but he turns out quite decent.
He brings keys and an acetylene lamp, and we go through the wire
gate into the place of tombs.

There is a queer stillness, and a curious peaceful repose about the
etruscan places I have been to, quite different from the weirdness of
20 Celtic places, the slightly repellant feeling of Rome and the old
campagna, and the rather horrible feeling of the great pyramid places
in Mexico, Teotihuacán and Cholula, and Mitla in the south;* or the
amiably idolatrous Buddha places in Ceylon. There is a stillness and
a softness in these great grassy mounds with their ancient stone
25 girdles, and down the central walk there lingers still a kind of
homeliness and happiness. True, it was a still and sunny afternoon in
April, and larks rose from the soft grass of the tombs. But there was a
stillness and a soothingness in all the air, in that sunken place, and a
feeling that it was good for one's soul to be there.

30 The same when we went down the few steps, and into the
chambers of rock, within the tumulus. There is nothing left. It is like
a house that has been swept bare: the inmates have left: now it waits
for the next comer. But whoever it is that has departed, they have left
a pleasant feeling behind them, warm to the heart, and kindly to the
35 bowels.

They are surprisingly big and handsome, these homes of the dead.
Cut out of the living rock, they are just like houses. The roof has a
beam cut to imitate the roof-beam of the house. It is a home.

As you enter, there are two small chambers, one to the right, one
40 to the left, ante-chambers. They say that here the ashes of the slaves

were deposited, in urns, upon the great benches of rock. For the slaves were always burned, presumably. Whereas at Cerveteri the masters were laid full-length, sometimes in the great stone sarco-phagi, sometimes in big coffins of terra cotta, in all their regalia. But most often they were just laid there on the broad rock-bed that goes 5
round the tomb, and is empty now, laid there calmly upon an open bier, not shut in sarcophagi, but sleeping as if in life.

The central chamber is large, perhaps there is a great square column of rock left in the centre, apparently supporting the solid roof as a roof-tree supports the roof of a house. And all round the 10
chamber goes the broad bed of rock, sometimes a double tier, on which the dead were laid, in their coffins, or lying open upon carved litters of stone or wood, a man glittering in golden armour, or a woman in white and crimson robes, with great necklaces round their necks, and rings on their fingers. Here lay the family, the great chiefs 15
and their wives, the Lucumones,* and their sons and daughters, many in one tomb.

Beyond again is a rock doorway, rather narrow, and narrowing upwards, like Egypt. The whole thing suggests Egypt; but on the whole, here all is plain, simple, usually with no decoration, and with 20
those easy, natural proportions whose beauty one hardly notices, they come so naturally, physically. It is the natural beauty of proportion of the phallic consciousness, contrasted with the more studied or ecstatic proportion of the mental and spiritual conscious-ness we are accustomed to. 25

Through the inner doorway is the last chamber, small and dark and culminative. Facing the door goes the stone bed on which was laid, presumably, the Lucumo and the sacred treasures of the dead, the little bronze ship of death that should bear him over to the other world,* the vases of jewels for his arraying, the vases of small dishes, 30
the little bronze statuettes and tools, the weapons, the armour: all the amazing impedimenta of the important dead. Or sometimes, in this inner room, lay the woman, the great lady, in all her robes, with the mirror in her hand, and her treasures, her jewels and combs and silver boxes of cosmetics, in urns or vases ranged alongside. 35
Splendid was the array they went with, into death.*

One of the most important tombs is the Tomb of the Tarquins, the family that gave etruscan kings to early Rome.* You go down a flight of steps, and into the underworld home of the Tarchne, as the Etruscans wrote it. In the middle of the great chamber there are two 40

pillars, left from the rock. The walls of the big living-room of the dead Tarquins, if one may put it so, are stuccoed, but there are no paintings. Only there are the writings on the wall, and in the burial niches in the wall above the long, double-tier stone bed, little
5 sentences freely written in red paint or black, or scratched in the stucco with the finger, slanting with the real etruscan carelessness and fulness of life, often running downwards, written from right to left. We can read these debonair inscriptions, that look as if someone had just chalked them up yesterday without a thought, in the archaic
10 etruscan letters, quite easily. But when we have read them, we don't know what they mean. Avle—Tarchnas—Larthal—Clan. That is plain enough. But what does it mean? Nobody knows precisely. Names, family names, family connections, titles of the dead—we may assume so much. "Aule, son of Larte Tarchna," say the
15 scientists, having got so far. But we cannot read one single sentence. The etruscan language is a mystery. Yet in Caesar's day it was the everyday language of the bulk of the people in central Italy—at least, east-central. And many Romans spoke Etruscan as we speak French. Yet now the language is entirely lost.* Destiny is a queer
20 thing.

The tomb called the *Grotta Bella** is interesting because of the low relief carvings and stucco reliefs on the pillars and the walls round the burial niches and above the big stone death-bed that goes round the tomb. The things represented are mostly warriors' arms and
25 insignia: shields, helmets, corselets, greaves for the legs, swords, spears, shoes, belts, the necklace of the noble: and then the sacred drinking bowl, the sceptre, the dog who is man's guardian even on the death journey, the two lions that stand by the gateway of life or death, the triton, or merman, and the goose, the bird that swims on
30 the waters and thrusts its head deep into the flood of the Beginning and the End.* All these are represented on the walls. And all these, no doubt, were laid, the actual objects, or figures to represent them, in this tomb. But now nothing is left. But when we remember the great store of treasure that every notable tomb must have contained:
35 and that every large tumulus covered several tombs: and that in the necropolis of Cerveteri we can still discover hundreds of tombs: and that other tombs exist in great numbers on the other side of the old city, towards the sea; we can have an idea of the vast mass of wealth this city could afford to bury with its dead, in days when Rome had
40 very little gold, and even bronze was precious.

The tombs seem so easy and friendly, cut out of rock under-ground. One does not feel oppressed, descending into them. It must be partly owing to the peculiar charm of natural proportion which is in all etruscan things of the unspoilt, unRomanised centuries. There is a simplicity, combined with a most peculiar, free-breasted natural-   5
ness and spontaneity in the shapes and movements of the under-world walls and spaces, that at once reassures the spirit. The Greeks sought to make an impression, and Gothic still more seeks to impress the mind. The Etruscans, no. The things they did, in their easy centuries, are as natural and as easy as breathing. They leave the   10
breast breathing freely and pleasantly, with a certain fulness of life. Even the tombs. And that is the true etruscan quality: ease, naturalness, and an abundance of life, no need to force the mind or the soul in any direction.

And death, to the Etruscan, was a pleasant continuance of life,   15
with jewels and wine and flutes playing for the dance. It was neither an ecstasy of bliss, a heaven, nor a purgatory of torment. It was just a natural continuance of the fulness of life. Everything was in terms of life, of living.

Yet everything etruscan, save the tombs, has been wiped out. It   20
seems strange. One goes out again into the April sunshine, into the sunken road between the soft, grassy-mounded tombs, and as one passes one glances down the steps at the doorless doorways of tombs. It is so still and pleasant and cheerful. The place is so soothing.

B., who has just come back from India, is so surprised to see the   25
phallic stones by the doors of many tombs.—Why, it's like the Shiva lingam at Benares!* It's exactly like the lingam stones in the Shiva caves and the Shiva temples!—

And that is another curious thing. One can live one's life, and read all the books about India or Etruria, and never read a single word   30
about the thing that impresses one in the very first five minutes, in Benares or in an etruscan necropolis: that is, the phallic symbol. Here it is, in stone, unmistakeable, and everywhere, around these tombs. Here it is, big and little, standing by the doors, or inserted, quite small, into the rock: the phallic stone! Perhaps some tumuli   35
had a great phallic column on the summit: some perhaps by the door. There are still small phallic stones, only seven or eight inches long, inserted in the rock outside the doors: they always seem to have been outside. And these small lingams look as if they were part of the rock. But no, B, lifts one out. It is cut, and is fitted into a socket, previously   40

cemented in. B. puts the phallic stone back into its socket, where it
was placed, probably, five or six hundred years before Christ was
born.—The big phallic stones that, it is said, probably stood on top
of the tumuli are sometimes carved very beautifully, sometimes with
5   inscriptions. The scientists call them cippus—cippi.* But surely the
cippus is a truncated column used usually as a grave-stone: a column
quite squat, often square, having been cut across, truncated, to
represent maybe a life cut short. Some of the little round phallic
stones are like this—truncated. But others are tall, huge and
10   decorative and with the double cone that is surely phallic, and little
inserted phallus stones are not cut short.

By the doorway of some tombs there is a carved stone house, or a
stone imitation chest with sloping lids like the two sides of the roof of
an oblong house. The guide-boy, who works on the railway and is no
15   profound scholar, mutters that every woman's tomb had one of these
stone houses or chests over it—over the doorway, he says—and
every man's tomb had one of the phallic stones, or lingams. But since
the great tombs were family tombs, perhaps they had both.

The stone house, as the boy calls it, suggests the Noah's Ark
20   without the boat-part: the Noah's Ark box we had as children, full of
animals. And that is what it is, the Ark, the arx, the womb. The womb
of all the world, that brought forth all the creatures. The womb, the
arx, where life retreats in the last refuge. The womb, the ark of the
covenant, in which lies the mystery of eternal life, the manna and the
25   mysteries.* There it is, standing displaced outside the doorway of
etruscan tombs at Cerveteri.

And perhaps in the insistence on these two symbols, in the
etruscan world, we can see the reason for the utter destruction and
annihilation of the etruscan consciousness. The new world wanted
30   to rid itself of these fatal, dominant symbols of the old world, the old
physical world. The etruscan conscious was rooted, quite blithely, in
these symbols, the phallus and the arx. So the whole consciousness,
the whole etruscan pulse and rhythm, must be wiped out.

Now we see again, under the blue heavens where the larks are
35   singing in the hot April sky, why the Romans called the Etruscans
vicious. Even in their palmy days, the Romans were not exactly
saints. But they thought they ought to be. They hated the phallus and
the ark, because they wanted empire and dominion and above all,
riches: social gain. You cannot dance gaily to the double flute,* and at
40   the same time conquer nations or rake in large sums of money.

Delenda est Cartago.* To the greedy man, everybody that is in the way of his greed is vice incarnate.

There are many tombs, though not many of the great mounds are left. Most must have been levelled. There are many tombs: some were standing half full of water: some were in process of being 5 excavated, in a kind of quarry-place, though the work for the time was silent and abandoned. Many tombs, many, many, and you must descend to them all, for they are all cut out below the surface of the earth; and where there was a tumulus, it was piled above them afterwards, loose earth, within the girdle of stone. Some tumuli have 10 been levelled, yet the whole landscape is lumpy with them. But the tombs remain, here all more or less alike, though some are big and some are small, and some are noble and some are rather mean. But most of them seem to have several chambers, beyond the ante-chambers. And all these tombs along the dead high-way would seem 15 to have been topped, once, by the beautiful roundness of tumuli, the great mounds of fruition, for the dead, with the tall phallic cone rising from the summit.

The necropolis, as far as we are concerned, ends on a waste place of deserted excavations and flood-water. We turn back, to leave the 20 home of dead Etruscans. All the tombs are empty. All have been rifled. The Romans may have respected the dead, for a certain time, while their religion was sufficiently etruscan to exert a power over them. But later, when the Romans started collecting etruscan antiques—as we collect antiques today—there must have been a 25 great sacking of the tombs. Even when all the gold and silver and jewels had been pilfered from the urns—which no doubt happened very soon after the Roman dominion—still the vases and the bronze must have remained in their places. Then the rich Romans began to collect vases, "Greek" vases with the painted scenes. So these were 30 stolen from the tombs. Then the little bronze figures, statuettes, animals, bronze ships, of which the Etruscans put thousands in the tombs, became the rage with the Roman collectors. Some smart Roman gentry would have a thousand or two choice little etruscan bronzes to boast of. Then Rome fell, and the barbarians pillaged 35 whatever was left. So it went on.

And still some tombs remained virgin, for the earth had washed in and filled the entrance way, covered the stone bases of the mounds, trees, bushes grew over the graves, you had only hilly, humpy, bushy waste country. 40

Under this the tombs lay silent, either ravaged, or, in a few wonderful cases, still virgin. And still absolutely virgin lay one of the tombs of Cerveteri, alone and apart from the necropolis, buried on the other side of the town, until 1836, when it was discovered: and,
5 of course, denuded. General Galassi and the arch-priest Regolini unearthed it: so it is called the Regolini-Galassi tomb.*

It is still interesting, a primitive narrow tomb like a passage, with a partition half-way, and covered with an arched roof, what they call the false arch, which is made by letting the flat horizontal stones of
10 the roof jut out step by step, as they pile upwards, till they almost meet. Then big flat stones are laid as cover, and make the flat top of the almost gothic arch: an arch built, probably, in the eighth century before Christ.

In the first chamber lay the remains of a warrior, with his bronze
15 armour, beautiful and sensitive as if it has grown in life for the living body, sunk on his dust. In the inner chamber beautiful frail, pale-gold jewellery lay on the stone bed, ear-rings where the ears were dust, bracelets in the dust that once was arms, surely, of a noble lady, nearly three thousand years ago.*

20 They took away everything. The treasure, so delicate and sensitive and wistful, is mostly in the Gregorian Museum in the Vatican. On two of the little silver vases from the Regolini-Galassi tomb, is the scratched inscription—Mi Larthia—Almost the first written etruscan words we know. And what do they mean, anyhow? "This is
25 Larthia"—Larthia being a lady—??*

Caere, even seven hundred years before Christ, must have been rich and full of luxury, fond of soft gold and of banquets, dancing, and great Greek vases. But you will find none of it now. The tombs are bare: what treasure they yielded up, and even to us Cerveteri has
30 yielded a great deal, is in the museums. If you go, you will see, as I saw, a grey, forlorn little township in tight walls—perhaps having a thousand inhabitants—and some empty burying places.

But when you sit in the post-automobile, to be rattled down to the station, about four o'clock in the sunny afternoon, you will probably
35 see the bus surrounded by a dozen buxom, handsome women, saying goodbye to one of their citizenesses. And in the full, dark, handsome, jovial faces surely you see the lustre still of the life-loving Etruscans! There are some level Greek eyebrows. But surely there are other vivid, warm faces still jovial with etruscan vitality, beautiful with the
40 mystery of the unrifled ark, ripe with the phallic knowledge and the etruscan carelessness!

II.

TARQUINIA

II.

Tarquinia*

In Cerveteri, there is nowhere to sleep, so the only thing to do is to go
back to Rome, or forwards to Cività Vecchia.* The bus landed us at
the station of Palo at about 5.0 o'clock: in the midst of nowhere: to   5
meet the Rome train. But we were going on to Tarquinia, not back to
Rome, so we must wait two hours, till seven.

In the distance we could see the concrete villas and new houses of
what was evidently Ladispoli, a sea-side place, some two miles away.
So we set off to walk to Ladispoli, on the flat sea-road. On the left, in   10
the wood that forms part of the great park, the nightingales had
already begun to whistle, and looking over the wall, one could see
many little rose-coloured cyclamens glowing on the earth in the
evening light.

We walked on, and the Rome train came surging round the bend.   15
It misses Ladispoli, whose two miles of branch line only runs in the
hot bathing months. As we neared the first ugly villas on the road, the
ancient wagonette drawn by the ancient white horse, both looking
sun-bitten almost to ghostliness, clattered past. It just beat us.

Ladispoli is one of those ugly little places on the Roman coast,   20
consisting of new concrete villas, new concrete hotels, kiosks and
bathing establishments, bareness and non-existence for ten months
in the year, seething solid with fleshy bathers, in July and August.
Now it was deserted, quite deserted, save for two or three officials
and four wild children.   25

B. and I lay on the grey-black lava sand, by the flat, low sea, over
which the sky, grey and shapeless, emitted a flat, wan evening light.
Little waves curled green out of the sea's dark greyness, from the
curious low flatness of the water. It is a peculiarly forlorn coast, the
sea peculiarly flat and sunken, lifeless-looking, the land as if it had   30
given its last gasp, and was now forever inert.

Yet this is the Tyrrhenian sea of the Etruscans, where their
shipping spread sharp sails, and beat the sea with slave-oars, roving
in from Greece and Sicily, Sicily of the Greek tyrants;* from Cumae,
the city of the old Greek colony of Campania, where the province of   35

25

Naples now is; and from Elba, where the Etruscans mined their
iron-ore. The Etruscans sailed the seas. They are even said to have
come by sea, from Lydia in Asia Minor, at some date far back in the
dim mists before the eighth century B.C. But that a whole people,
5 even a whole host sailed in the tiny ships of those days, all at once, to
people a sparsely-peopled central Italy, seems hard to imagine.
Probably ships did come—even before Ulysses. Probably men
landed on the strange flat coast, and made camps, and then treated
with the natives. Whether the newcomers were Lydians, or Hittites*
10 with hair curled in a roll behind, or men from Mycenae or Crete, who
knows. Perhaps men of all these sorts came, in batches. For in
Homeric days a restlessness seems to have possessed the Mediterranean basin, and ancient races began shaking ships like seeds over
the sea. More people than Greeks, or Hellenes, or Indo-Germanic
15 groups, were on the move.

But whatever little ships were run ashore on the soft, deep,
grey-black volcanic sand of this coast, three thousand years ago, and
earlier, their mariners certainly did not find those hills inland empty
of people. If the Lydians or Hittites pulled up their long little
20 two-eyed ships on to the beach, and made a camp behind a bank, in
shelter from the wet strong wind, what natives came down curiously
to look at them? For natives there were, of that we may be certain.
Even before the fall of Troy, before even Athens was dreamed of,
there were natives here. And they had huts on the hills, thatched huts
25 in clumsy groups most probably; with patches of grain, and flocks of
goats and probably cattle. Probably it was like coming on an old Irish
village, or a village in the Scottish Hebrides in Prince Charlie's day,*
to come upon a village of these Italian aborigines, by the Tyrrhenian
sea, three thousand years ago. But by the time etruscan history starts
30 in Caere, some eight centuries B.C., there was certainly more than a
village on the hill. There was a native city, of that we may be sure;
and a busy spinning of linen and beating of gold, long before the
Regolini-Galassi tomb was built.

However that may be, somebody came, and somebody was already
35 here:* of that we may be certain: and, in the first place, none of
them were Greeks or Hellenes. It was the days before Rome rose
up: probably, when the first comers arrived, it was the days even
before Homer. The newcomers, whether they were few or many,
seem to have come from the east, Asia Minor or Crete or Cyprus.
40 They were, we must feel, of an old, primitive Mediterranean and

Asiatic or Aegean stock. The twilight of the beginning of our history was the nightfall of some previous history, which will never be written. Pelasgian is but a shadow-word. But Hittite and Minoan, Lydian, Carian,* Etruscan, these words emerge from shadow, and perhaps from one and the same great shadow come the peoples to whom the names belong. 5

The etruscan civilisation seems a shoot, perhaps the last, from the pre-historic Mediterranean world, and the Etruscans, newcomers and aborigines alike, probably belonged to that ancient world, though they were of different nations and levels of culture. Later, of course, the Greeks exerted a great influence. But that is another matter. 10

Whatever happened, the newcomers in ancient central Italy found many natives flourishing in possession of the land. These aboriginals, now ridiculously called Villanovans,* were neither wiped out nor suppressed. Probably they welcomed the strangers, whose pulse was not hostile to their own. Probably the more highly-developed religion of the newcomers was not hostile to the primitive religion of the aborigines: no doubt the two religions had the same root. Probably the aborigines formed willingly a sort of religious aristocracy from the newcomers: the Italians might almost do the same today. And so the etruscan world arose. But it took centuries to arise. Etruria was not a colony, it was a slowly developed country. 15, 20

There was never an etruscan nation: only, in historical times, a great league* of tribes or nations using the etruscan language and the etruscan script—at least officially—and uniting in their religious feeling and observances. The etruscan alphabet seems to have been borrowed from the old Greeks, apparently from the Chalcidians of Cumae*—the Greek colony just north of where Naples now is. But the etruscan language is not akin to any of the Greek dialects, nor, apparently, to the Italic. But we don't know. It is probably to a great extent the language of the old aboriginals of southern Etruria, just as the religion is in all probability basically aboriginal, belonging to some vast old religion of the prehistoric world. From the shadow of the prehistoric world emerge dying religions that have not yet invented gods or goddesses, but live by the mystery of the elemental powers in the universe, the complex vitalities of what we feebly call Nature. And the etruscan religion was certainly one of these. The gods and goddesses don't seem to have emerged in any sharp definiteness. 25, 30, 35, 40

But it is not for me to make assertions. Only, that which half emerges from the dim background of time is strangely stirring; and after having read all the learned suggestions, most of them contradicting one another; and then having looked sensitively at the tombs
5 and the etruscan things that are left, one must accept one's own resultant feeling.

Ships came along this low, inconspicuous sea, coming up from the Near East, we should imagine, even in the days of Solomon, even, maybe, in the days of Abraham.* And they kept on coming. As the
10 light of history dawns and brightens, we see them winging along with their white or scarlet sails. Then, as the Greeks came crowding into colonies in Italy, and the Phoenicians began to exploit the western Mediterranean, we begin to hear of the silent Etruscans, and to see them.

15 Just north of here Caere founded a port called Pyrgi, and we know that the Greek vessels flocked in, with vases and stuffs and colonists coming from Hellas or from Magna Graecia, and that Phoenician ships came rowing sharply, over from Sardinia, up from Carthage, round from Tyre and Sidon; while the Etruscans had their own
20 fleets, built of timber from the mountains, caulked with pitch from northern Volterra, fitted with sails from Tarquinia, filled with wheat from the bountiful plains, or with the famous etruscan articles of bronze and iron, which they carried away to Corinth or to Athens or to the ports of Asia Minor. We know of the great and finally
25 disastrous sea-battles with the Phoenicians and the tyrant of Syracuse.* And we know that the Etruscans, all except those of Caere, became ruthless pirates, almost like the Moors and the Barbary corsairs later on. This was part of their viciousness, a great annoyance to their loving and harmless neighbours, the law-abiding
30 Romans—who believed in the supreme law of conquest.

However, all this is long ago. The very coast has changed since then. The smitten sea has sunk and fallen back, the weary land has emerged when, apparently, it didn't want to, and the flowers of the new coast-line are miserable bathing places such as Ladispoli and
35 sea-side Ostia,* desecration put upon desolation, to the triumphant trump of the mosquito.

The wind blew flat and almost chill from the darkening sea, the dead waves lifted small bits of pure green out of the leaden greyness, under the leaden sky. We got up from the dark-grey, but soft sand,
40 and went back along the road to the station, peered-at by the few

people and officials who were holding the place together till the next bathers came.

At the station there was general desertedness. But our things still lay untouched in a dark corner of the buffet, and the man gave us a decent little meal of cold meats and wine and oranges. It was already night. The train came rushing in, punctually.

It is an hour or more to Città Vecchia, which is a port of not much importance, except that from here the regular steamer sails to Sardinia. We gave our things to a friendly old porter, and told him to take us to the nearest hotel. It was night, very dark as we emerged from the station.

And a fellow came furtively shouldering up to me.

"You are foreigners, aren't you?"

"Yes."

"What nationality?"

"English."

"You have your permission to reside in Italy—or your passport?"

"My passport I have—what do you want?"

"I want to look at your passport."

"It's in the valise! And why? Why is this?"

"This is a port, and we must examine the papers of foreigners."

"And why?—Genoa is a port, and no one dreams of asking for papers—"

I was furious. He made no answer. I told the porter to go on to the hotel, and the fellow furtively followed at our side, half a pace to the rear, in the mongrel way these spy-louts have.

In the hotel I asked for a room and registered, and then the fellow asked again for my passport. I wanted to know why he demanded it, what he meant by accosting me outside the station as if I was a criminal, what he meant by insulting us with his requests, when in any other town in Italy one went unquestioned—and so forth, in considerable rage.

He did not reply, but obstinately looked as though he would be venomous if he could. He peered at the passport—though I doubt if he could make head or tail of it—asked where we were going, peered at B.'s passport, half excused himself in a whining, disgusting sort of fashion, and disappeared into the night. A real lout.

I was furious. Supposing I had not been carrying my passport—and usually I don't dream of carrying it—what amount of trouble would that lout have made me! Probably I should have spent the night in prison, and been bullied by half a dozen low bullies.

Those poor rats at Ladispoli had seen me and B. go to the sea and sit on the sand for half an hour, then go back to the train. And this
5 was enough to arouse their suspicions, I imagine, so they tele-graphed to Città Vecchia. Why are officials *always* fools?—Even when there is no war on? What *could* they imagine we were doing!

The hotel-manager, propitious, said there was a very interesting museum in Città Vecchia,* and wouldn't we stay the next day and
10 see it—Ah! I replied. But all it contains is Roman stuff, and we don't want to look at that.—It was malice on my part, because the present régime* considers itself purely ancient Roman. The man looked at me scared, and I grinned at him.—But what do they mean, I said, behaving like this to a simple traveller, in a country where foreigners
15 are invited to travel!—Ah! said the porter softly and soothingly. It is the Roman province. You will have no more of it when you leave the Provincia di Roma.—And when the Italians give the soft answer to turn away wrath,* the wrath somehow turns away.

We walked for an hour in the dull street of Città Vecchia. There
20 seemed so much suspicion, one would have thought there were several wars on. The hotel manager asked if we were staying. We said we were leaving by the eight o'clock train in the morning, for Tarquinia.

And sure enough, we left by the eight o'clock train. Tarquinia is
25 only one station from Città Vecchia—about twenty minutes over the flat maremma country, with the sea on the left, and the green wheat growing luxuriantly, the asphodel sticking up its spikes.

We soon saw Tarquinia, its towers pricking up like antennae on the side of a low bluff of a hill, some few miles inland from the sea.
30 And this was once the metropolis of Etruria, chief city of the great etruscan league. But it died like all the other etruscan cities, and had a more or less mediaeval re-birth, with a new name. Dante knew it, as it was known for centuries, as Corneto—Corgnetum or Cornetium—and forgotten was its etruscan past. Then there was a
35 feeble sort of wakening to remembrance, a hundred years ago, and the town got Tarquinia tacked on to its Corneto: Corneto-Tarquinia! The Fascist régime, however, glorying in the Italian origins of Italy, has now struck out the Corneto, so the town is once more, simply, Tarquinia. As you come up in the motor-bus from the
40 station, you see the great black letters on a white ground, painted on

the wall by the city gateway: Tarquinia! So the wheel of revolution turns. There stands the etruscan word—Latinised etruscan—beside the mediaeval gate, put up by the Fascist power to name and unname.

But the Fascists, who consider themselves in all things Roman, Roman of the Caesars, heirs of empire and world power, are beside the mark restoring the rags of dignity to etruscan places. For of all the Italian people that ever lived, the Etruscans were surely the least Roman. Just as, of all the people that ever rose up in Italy, the Romans of ancient Rome were surely the most un-Italian, judging from the natives of today.

Tarquinia is only about three miles from the sea. The omnibus soon runs one up, charges through the widened gateway, swirls round in the empty space inside the gateway, and is finished. We descend in the bare place, which seems to expect nothing. On the left is a beautiful stone palazzo*—on the right is a café, upon the low ramparts above the gate. The man of the Dazio,* the town customs, looks to see if anybody has brought food-stuffs into the town—but it is a mere glance. I ask him for the hotel. He says, Do you mean to sleep?—I say I do. Then he tells a small boy to carry my bag and take us to Gentile's.

Nowhere is far off, in these small wall-girdled cities. In the warm April morning the stony little town seems half-asleep. As a matter of fact, most of the inhabitants are out in the fields, and won't come in through the gates again till evening. The slight sense of desertedness is everywhere—even in the inn, when we have climbed up the stairs to it, for the ground floor does not belong. A little lad in long trousers, who would seem to be only twelve years old but who has the air of a mature man, confronts us with his chest out. We ask for rooms. He eyes us, darts away for the key, and leads us off upstairs another flight, shouting to a young girl, who acts as chambermaid, to follow on. He shows us two small rooms, opening off a big, desert sort of general assembly room common in this kind of inn. "And you won't be lonely," he says briskly, "because you can talk to one another through the wall. *Teh! Lina!*" He lifts his finger and listens. —"Eh!" comes through the wall, like an echo, with startling nearness and clearness. "Fai presto!" says Albertino.— "È pronto!" comes the voice of Lina.— "Ecco!"* says Albertino to us. "You hear!"—We certainly did. The partition wall must have been butter-muslin. And Albertino was delighted, having reassured us we should not feel lonely nor frightened in the night.

He was, in fact, the most manly and fatherly little hotel manager I
have ever known, and he ran the whole place. He was in reality
fourteen years old, but stunted. From five in the morning till ten at
night he was on the go, never ceasing, and with a queer, abrupt,
5   sideways-darting alacrity that must have wasted a great deal of
energy. The father and mother were in the background—quite
young and pleasant. But they didn't seem to exert themselves.
Albertino did it all.—How Dickens would have loved him! But
Dickens would not have seen the queer wistfulness, and trustfulness,
10 and courage in the boy.—He was absolutely unsuspicious of us
strangers. People must be rather human and decent in Tarquinia,
even the commercial travellers: who, presumably, are chiefly buyers
of agricultural produce, and sellers of agricultural implements and
so forth.
15   We sallied out, back to the space by the gate, and drank coffee at
one of the tin tables outside. Beyond the wall there were a few new
villas—the land dropped green and quick, to the strip of coast plain
and the indistinct, faintly gleaming sea, which seemed somehow not
like a sea at all.
20   I was thinking, if this were still an etruscan city, there would still
be this cleared space just inside the gate. But instead of a rather
forlorn vacant lot, it would be a sacred clearing, with a little temple to
keep it alert.
        Myself, I like to think of the little wooden temples of the early
25 Greeks and of the Etruscans: small, dainty, fragile, and evanescent
as flowers. We have reached the stage where we are weary of huge
stone erections, and we begin to realise that it is better to keep life
fluid and changing, than to try to hold it fast down in heavy
monuments. Burdens on the face of the earth, are man's ponderous
30 erections.
        The Etruscans made small temples, like little houses with pointed
roofs, entirely of wood. But then, outside, they had friezes and
cornices and crests of terra-cotta, so that the upper part of the
temple would seem almost made of earthenware, terra-cotta plaques
35 fitted neatly, and alive with freely-modelled, painted figures in relief,
gay dancing creatures, rows of ducks, round faces like the sun, and
faces grinning and putting out a big tongue, all vivid and fresh and
unimposing. The whole thing small and dainty in proportion, and
fresh, somehow charming instead of impressive. There seems to
40 have been in the etruscan instinct a real desire to preserve the natural

humour of life. And that is a task surely more worthy, and even much more difficult in the long run, than conquering the world or sacrificing the self or saving the immortal soul.

Why has mankind had such a craving to be imposed upon! Why this lust after imposing creeds, imposing deeds, imposing buildings, imposing language, imposing works of art? The thing becomes an imposition and a weariness at last. Give us things that are alive and flexible, which won't last too long and become an obstruction and a weariness. Even Michelangelo becomes at last a lump and a burden and a bore. It is so hard to see past him.

Across the space from the café is the Palazzo Vitelleschi, a charming building, now a national museum—so the marble slab says. But the heavy doors are shut. The place opens at ten, a man says. It is nine-thirty. We wander up the steep but not very long street, to the top.

And the top is a fragment of public garden, and a look-out. Two old men are sitting in the sun, under a tree. We walk to the parapet, and suddenly are looking into one of the most delightful landscapes I have ever seen: as it were, into the very virginity of hilly green country. It is all wheat-green and soft and swooping, swooping down and up, and glowing with green newness, and no houses. Down goes the declivity below us, then swerving the curve and up again, to the neighbouring hill that faces in all its greenness and long-running immaculateness. Beyond, the hills ripple away to the mountains, and far in the distance stands a round peak, that seems to have an enchanted city on its summit.

Such a pure, uprising, unsullied country, in the greenness of wheat on an April morning!—and the queer complication of hills! There seems nothing of the modern world here—no houses, no contrivances, only a sort of fair wonder and stillness, an openness which has not been violated.

The hill opposite is like a distinct companion. The near end is quite steep and wild, with ever-green oaks and scrub, and specks of black-and-white cattle on the slopes of common. But the long crest is green again with wheat, running and drooping to the south. And immediately one feels: that hill has a soul, it has a meaning.

Lying thus opposite to Tarquinia's long hill, a companion across a suave little swing of valley, one feels at once that, if this is the hill where the living Tarquinians had their gay wooden houses, then that is the hill where the dead lie buried and quick, as seeds, in their

painted houses underground. The two hills are as inseparable as life
and death, even now, on the sunny, green-filled April morning with
the breeze blowing in from the sea. And the land beyond seems as
mysterious and fresh as if it were still the morning of Time.

5   But B. wants to go back to the Palazzo Vitelleschi: it will be open
now. Down the street we go, and sure enough, the big doors are
open, several officials are in the shadowy courtyard entrance. They
salute us in the Fascist manner: alla Romana. Why don't they
discover the etruscan salute, and salute us all'etrusca!* But they are
10   perfectly courteous and friendly. We go on into the courtyard of the
palace.

The museum is exceedingly interesting and delightful, to anyone
who is even a bit aware of the Etruscans. It contains a great number
of things found at Tarquinia, and only things found at Tarquinia: at
15   least, so the guide said.

Which is exactly as should be. It is a great mistake to rape
everything away from its setting, and huddle it together in the "great
centres." It is all very well to say, the public can then see the things.
The public is a hundred-headed ass, and can see nothing. A few
20   intelligent individuals do wander through the splendid etruscan
museum in Florence, struggling with the abstraction of many
fascinating things from all parts of Etruria confusing the sensitive
soul. But the public, if it straggles in, straggles out again in utter
boredom. When shall we learn that it is no use approaching the
25   still-vital creations of dead men as if they were so many machine-
parts which, fitted together, would make a "civilisation"! Oh, the
weary, asinine stupidity of man's desire to "see the thing as a whole."
There *is* no whole—the wholeness no more exists than the equator
exists. It is the dreariest of abstractions.

30   What one wants is to be aware. If one looks at an etruscan helmet,
then it is better to be fully aware of that helmet, in its own setting, in
its own complex of associations, than it is to "look over" a thousand
museums of stuff. Any one impression that goes really down into the
soul, is worth a million hasty impressions of a million* important
35   things.

If only we would realise it, and not tear things from their settings.
Museums anyhow are wrong. But if one must have museums, let
them be small, and above all, let them be local. Splendid as the
etruscan museum is in Florence, how much happier one is in the
40   museum at Tarquinia, where all the things are Tarquinian, and at

least have some association with one another, and form some sort of *organic* whole.

In an entrance-room from the cortile* lie a few of the long sarcophagi in which the nobles were buried. It seems as if the primitive inhabitants of this part of Italy always burned their dead, 5 and then put the ashes in a jar, sometimes covering the jar with the dead man's helmet, sometimes with a shallow dish for a lid, and then laid the urn with its ashes in a little round grave like a little well. This is called the Villanovan way of burial, in the well-tomb.

The newcomers to the country, however, apparently buried their 10 dead whole. Here, at Tarquinia, you may still see the hills where the well-tombs of the aboriginal inhabitants are discovered, with the urns containing the ashes inside. Then come the graves where the dead were buried unburned, graves very much like those of today. But tombs of the same period with cinerary urns are found near to, 15 or in connection. So that the new people, and the old apparently lived side by side in harmony, from very early days, and the two modes of burial continued side by side, for centuries, long before the painted tombs were made.

At Tarquinia, however, the main practice seems to have been, at 20 least from the seventh century on, that the nobles were buried in the great sarcophagi, or laid out on biers, and placed in chamber tombs: while the slaves apparently were cremated, their ashes laid in urns, and the urns often placed in the family tomb, where the stone coffins of the masters rested. The common people, on the other hand, were 25 apparently sometimes cremated, sometimes buried in graves very much like our graves of today, though the sides were lined* with stone.

The mass of the common people was mixed in race, and the bulk of them were probably serf-peasants, with many half-free artizans. 30 These must have followed their own desire in the matter of burial: some had graves, many must have been cremated, their ashes saved in an urn or jar which takes up little room in a poor man's burial place. Probably even the less important members of the noble families were cremated, their remains placed in the vases which 35 became more beautiful, as the connection with Greece grew more extensive.

It is a relief to think that even the slaves—and the luxurious Etruscans had many, in historical times—had their remains decently stored in jars and laid in a sacred place. Apparently the "vicious 40

Etruscans" had nothing comparable to the vast dead-pits which lay outside Rome beside the great highway, in which the bodies of slaves were promiscuously flung.

It is all a question of sensitiveness. Brute force and overbearing may make a terrific effect. But in the end, that which lives lives by delicate sensitiveness. If it were a question of brute force, not a single human baby would survive for a fortnight. It is the grass of the field, most frail of all things, that supports all life all the time. But for the green grass, no empire would rise, no man would eat bread: for grain is grass; and Hercules or Napoleon or Henry Ford would alike be denied existence.

Brute force crushes many plants. Yet the plants rise again. The pyramids will not last a moment, compared with the daisy. And before Buddha or Jesus spoke the nightingale sang, and long after the words of Jesus and Buddha are gone into oblivion, the nightingale still will sing. Because it is neither preaching nor teaching nor commanding nor urging. It is just singing. And in the beginning was not a Word, but a chirrup.*

Because a fool kills a nightingale with a stone, is he therefore greater than the nightingale? Because the Roman took the life out of the Etruscan, was he therefore greater than the Etruscan? Not he! Rome fell, and the Roman phenomenon with it. Italy today is far more etruscan in its pulse, than Roman: and will always be so. The etruscan element is like the grass of the field and the sprouting of corn, in Italy: it will always be so. Why try to revert to the Latin-Roman mechanism and suppression?

In the open room upon the courtyard of the Palazzo Vitelleschi lie a few sarcophagi of stone, with the effigies carved on top, something as the dead crusaders in English churches. And here, in Tarquinia the effigies are more like crusaders than usual, for some lie flat on their backs, and have a dog at their feet; whereas usually, the carved figure of the dead rears up as if alive, from the lid of the tomb, resting upon one elbow, and gazing out proudly, sternly. If it is a man, his body is exposed to just below the navel, and he holds in his hand the sacred patera, or mundum,* the round saucer with the raised knob in the centre, which represents the round germ of heaven and earth. It stands for the plasm, also, of the living cell, with its nucleus, which is the indivisible God of the beginning, and which remains alive and unbroken to the end, the eternal quick of all things, which yet divides and subdivides, so that it becomes the sun of the firmament and the

lotus of the waters under the earth, and the rose of all existence upon
the earth: and the sun maintains its own quick, unbroken for ever;
and there is a living quick of the sea, and of all the waters; and every
living created thing has its own unfailing quick. So within each man
is the quick of him, when he is a baby, and when he is old, the same   5
quick; some spark, some unborn and undying vivid life-electron.
And this is what is symbolised in the patera, which may be made to
flower like a rose or like the sun, but which remains the same, the
germ central within the living plasm.

And this patera, this symbol, is almost invariably found in the hand   10
of a dead man. But if the dead is a woman, her dress falls in soft
gathers from her throat, she wears splendid jewellery, and she holds
in her hand not the mundum, but the mirror, the box of essence, the
pomegranate, some symbols of her reflected nature, or of her
woman's quality. But she, too, is given a proud, haughty look, as is   15
the man: for she belongs to the sacred families that rule and that read
the signs.

These sarcophagi and effigies here all belong to the centuries of
the etruscan decline, after there had been long intercourse with the
Greeks, and perhaps most of them were made after the conquest of   20
Etruria by the Romans. So that we do not look for fresh, spontaneous
works of art, any more than we do in modern memorial stones. The
funerary arts are always more or less commercial. The rich man
orders his sarcophagus while he is still alive, and the monument-
carver makes the work more or less elaborate, according to the price.   25
The figure is supposed to be a portrait of the man who orders it, so
we see well enough what the later Etruscans look like. In the third
and second centuries B.C., at the fag end of their existence as a
people, they look very like the Romans of the same day, whose busts
we know so well. And often they are given the tiresomely haughty air   30
of people who are no longer rulers indeed, only by virtue of wealth.

Yet, even when the etruscan art is Romanised and spoilt, there still
flickers in it a certain naturalness and feeling. The etruscan Lucumones, or prince-magistrates, were in the first place religious seers,
governors in religion, then magistrates; then princes. They were not   35
aristocrats in the germanic sense, nor even patricians in the Roman.
They were first and foremost leaders in the sacred mysteries, then
magistrates, then men of family and wealth. So there is always a
touch of vital life, of life-significance.

And you may look through modern funerary sculpture in vain for   40

anything so good even as the Sarcophagus of the Magistrate, with his
written scroll* spread before him, his strong, alert old face gazing
sternly out, the necklace of office round his neck, the ring of rank on
his finger. So he lies, in the museum at Tarquinia. His robe leaves
5   him naked to the hip, and his body lies soft and slack, with the soft
effect of relaxed flesh the etruscan artists render so well, and which
is so difficult. On the sculptured side of the sarcophagus, the two
death-dealers wield the hammer of death, the winged figures wait for
the soul, and will not be persuaded away. Beautiful it is, with the easy
10 simplicity of life. But it is late in date. Probably this old etruscan
magistrate is already an official under Roman authority: for he does
not hold the sacred mundum, the dish, he has only the written scroll,
probably of laws. As if he were no longer the religious lord or
Lucumo.—Though possibly, in this case, the dead man was not one
15 of the Lucumones anyhow.

Upstairs in the museum are many vases, from the ancient crude
pottery of the Villanovans to the early black ware decorated in
scratches, or undecorated, called bucchero,* and on to the painted
bowls and dishes and amphoras which came from Corinth or
20 Athens, or to those painted pots made by the Etruscans themselves
more or less after the Greek patterns. These may or may not be
interesting: the Etruscans are not at their best, painting dishes. Yet
they must have loved them. In the early days, these great jars and
bowls, and smaller mixing bowls, and drinking cups and pitchers,
25 and flat wine cups, formed a valuable part of the household treasure.
In very early times, the Etruscans must have sailed their ships to
Corinth and to Athens, taking perhaps wheat and honey, wax and
bronze-ware, iron and gold, and coming back with these precious
jars, and stuffs, essences, and perfumes and spice. And jars brought
30 from overseas for the sake of their painted beauty must have been
household treasures.

But then the Etruscans made pottery of their own, and by the
thousand they imitated the Greek vases. So that there must have
been millions of beautiful jars in Etruria. Already in the first century
35 B.C. there was a passion among the Romans for collecting Greek
and etruscan painted jars from the Etruscans, particularly from the
etruscan tombs:* jars and the little bronze votive figures and
statuettes, the *sigilla Tyrrhena** of the Roman luxury. And when the
tombs were first robbed, for gold and silver treasure, hundreds of
40 fine jars must just have been thrown over and smashed. Because

even now, when a part-rifled tomb is discovered and opened, the fragments of smashed vases lie around.

As it is, however, the museums are full of vases. If one looks for the Greek form of elegance and convention, those elegant "still-unravished brides of quietness,"* one is disappointed. But get over 5 the strange desire we have for elegant convention, and the vases and dishes of the Etruscans, especially many of the black bucchero ware, begin to open out like strange flowers, black flowers with all the softness and the rebellion of life against convention, or red-and-black flowers painted with amusing free, bold designs. It is there 10 nearly always in etruscan things, the naturalness verging on the commonplace, but usually missing it, and often achieving an originality so free and bold and so fresh, that we, who love convention and things "reduced to a norm," call it a bastard art, and commonplace. 15

It is useless to look in etruscan things for "uplift." If you want uplift, go to the Greek and the gothic. If you want mass, go to the Roman. But if you love the odd spontaneous forms that are never to be standardised, go to the Etruscans. In the fascinating little Palazzo Vitelleschi one could spend many an hour, but for the fact that the 20 very fulness of museums makes one rush through them.

III.

THE PAINTED TOMBS OF
TARQUINIA 1.

III.

The Painted Tombs of Tarquinia
I.

We arranged for the guide to take us to the painted tombs,* which are
the real fame of Tarquinia. After lunch we set out, climbing to the   5
top of the town, and passing out through the south-west gate, on the
level hill-crest. Looking back, the wall of the town, mediaeval, with a
bit of more ancient black wall lower down, stands blank. Just outside
the gate are one or two forlorn new houses, then ahead, the long,
running tableland of the hill, with the white highway dipping and   10
going on to Viterbo,* inland.

"All this hill in front," said the guide, "is tombs! All tombs! The
city of the dead."

So! Then this hill is the necropolis hill! The Etruscans never
buried their dead within the city walls. And the modern cemetery   15
and the first etruscan tombs lie almost close up to the present city
gate. Therefore, if the ancient city of Tarquinia lay on this hill, it can
have occupied no more space, hardly, than the present little town of a
few thousand people. Which seems impossible. Far more probably,
the city itself lay on that opposite hill there, which lies splendid and   20
unsullied, running parallel to us.

We walk across the wild bit of hill-top, where the stones crop out,
and the first rock-rose flutters, and the asphodels stick up. This is
the necropolis. Once it had many a tumulus, and streets of tombs.
Now there is no sign of any tombs: no tumulus, nothing but the   25
rough bare hill-crest, with stones and short grass and flowers, the sea
gleaming away to the right, under the sun, and the soft land inland
glowing very green and pure.

But we see a little bit of wall, built perhaps to cover a water-trough.
Our guide goes straight towards it. He is a fat, good-natured young   30
man, who doesn't look as if he would be interested in tombs. We are
mistaken, however. He knows a good deal, and has a quick, sensitive
interest, absolutely unobtrusive, and turns out to be as pleasant a
companion for such a visit as one could wish to have.

The bit of wall we see is a little hood of masonry with an iron gate,   35
covering a little flight of steps leading down into the ground. One

43

comes upon it all at once, in the rough nothingness of the hillside. The guide kneels down to light his acetylene lamp, and his old terrier lies down resignedly in the sun, in the breeze which rushes persistently from the south-west, over these long, exposed hilltops.

5   The lamp begins to shine and smell, then to shine without smelling: the guide opens the iron gate, and we descend the steep steps down into the tomb. It seems a dark little hole underground: a dark little hole, after the sun of the upper world! But the guide's lamp begins to flare up, and we find ourselves in a little chamber in
10   the rock, just a small, bare little cell of a room that some anchorite might have lived in. It is so small and bare and familiar, quite unlike the rather splendid spacious tombs at Cerveteri.

But the lamp flares bright, we get used to the change of light, and see the paintings on the little walls. It is the Tomb of Hunting and
15   Fishing,* so-called from the pictures on the walls, and it is supposed to date from the sixth century B.C. But it is very badly damaged. Pieces of the wall-face are shattered away, damp has eaten into the tempera colours, nothing seems to be left but disappointment. Yet in the dimness, as we get used to the light, we see flights of birds flying
20   through the haze, rising from the sea with the draught of life still in their wings. And we take heart and look closer. The little room was frescoed all round with sea and sky of light, birds flying and fishes leaping, and fragmentary little men hunting, fishing, rowing in boats. The lower part of the wall is all a blue-green of sea with a silhouette
25   surface that ripples all round the room. From the sea rises a tall rock, off which a naked man, shadowy but still distinct, is beautifully and cleanly diving into the sea, while a companion climbs up the rock after him, and on the water a boat waits with rested oars, in it three men watching the diver, the middle man standing up naked, holding
30   out his arms. Meanwhile a great dolphin leaps behind the boat, a flight of birds soars upwards to pass the rock, in the clear air. Above all, from the bands of colour that border the wall at the top hang the regular loops of garlands, garlands of flowers and leaves and buds and berries, garlands which belong to maidens and to women, and
35   which represent the flowery circle of the female life and sex. The top border of the wall is formed of horizontal stripes or ribbands of colour that go all round the room, red and black and dull-gold and blue and primrose, and these are the colours that occur invariably. Men are nearly always painted a darkish red, which is the colour of
40   many Italians when they go naked in the sun, as the Etruscans went.

Women are coloured paler, because women did not go naked in the sun.

At the end of the room, where there is a recess in the wall, is painted another rock rising from the sea, and on it a man with a sling is taking aim at the birds which rise scattering this way and that. A boat with a big paddle oar is holding off from the rock, a naked man amidships is giving a queer salute to the slinger, a man kneels over the bows with his back to the others, and is letting down a net. The prow of the boat has a beautifully painted eye, so the vessel shall see where it is going. In Syracuse you will see many a two-eyed boat today come swimming in to quay. One dolphin is diving down into the sea, one is leaping out. The birds fly, and the garlands hang from the border.

It is all small and gay and quick with life, spontaneous as only young life can be. If only it were not so much damaged, one would be happy, because of the young liveliness of it. There is nothing impressive or grand. But through the paleness of time and the damage of men one still sees the quick ripple of life here, the eternity of the naïve moment, which the Etruscans knew.

The little tomb is empty, save for its shadowy paintings. It has no bed of rock around it: only a deep niche for holding vases, perhaps vases of precious things. The sarcophagus stood on the floor, perhaps under the slinger on the end wall. And it stood alone, for this is an individual tomb, for one person only, as is usual in the older tombs of this necropolis.

In the gable triangle of the end wall, above the slinger and the boat, the space is filled in with one of the frequent etruscan banqueting scenes of the dead. The dead man, sadly obliterated, reclines upon his banqueting couch with his flat wine-dish in his hand, resting on his elbow, and beside him, also half risen, reclines a handsome and jewelled lady in fine robes, apparently resting her left hand upon the naked breast of the man, and in her right holding up to him the garland, the garland of the female festive offering. Behind the man stands a naked slave-boy, perhaps with music, while another naked slave is just filling a wine-jug from a handsome amphora or wine-jar at the side. On the woman's side stands a maiden, apparently playing the flute; for a woman was supposed to play the flute at classical funerals; and beyond sit two maidens with garlands, one turning round to watch the banqueting pair, the other with her back to it all. Beyond the maidens in the corner are more garlands, and two birds, perhaps doves. On the wall behind the head of the banqueting lady is a problematic object, perhaps a bird-cage.

The scene is natural as life, and yet it has a heavy archaic fulness of meaning. It is the death-banquet; and at the same time it is the dead
5 man banqueting in the underworld; for the underworld of the Etruscans was a gay place. While the living feasted out of doors, at the tomb of the dead, the dead himself feasted in like manner, with a lady to offer him garlands and slaves to bring him wine, away in the underworld. For the life on earth was so good, the life below could
10 but be a continuance of it.

This profound belief in life, acceptance of life, seems character-istic of the Etruscans. It is still vivid in the painted tombs. There is a certain dance and glamour in all the movements, even in those of the naked slave-men. They are by no means downtrodden menials, let
15 later Romans say what they will.* The slaves in the tombs are surging with full life.

We come up the steps into the upper world, the sea-breeze and the sun. The old dog shambles to his feet, the guide blows out his lamp and locks the gate, we set off again, the dog trundling apathetic
20 at his master's heels, the master speaking to him with that soft Italian familiarity which seems so very different from the spirit of Rome, the strong-willed Latin.

The guide steers across the hill-top, in the clear afternoon sun, towards another little hood of masonry. And one notices there is
25 quite a number of these little gateways, built by the government to cover the steps that lead down to the separate small tombs. It is utterly unlike Cerveteri, though the two places are not forty miles apart. Here there is no stately tumulus city, with its highroad between the tombs, and inside, rather noble, many-roomed houses
30 of the dead. Here the little one-room tombs seem scattered at random on the hill-top, here and there: though probably, if exca-vations were fully carried out, here also we should find a regular city of the dead, with its streets and crossways. And probably each tomb had its little tumulus of piled earth, so that even above-ground there
35 were streets of mounds with tomb entrances. But even so, it would be different from Cerveteri, from Caere: the mounds would be so small, the streets surely irregular. Anyhow, today there are scattered little one-room tombs, and we dive down into them just like rabbits popping down a hole. The place is a warren.
40 It is interesting to find it so different from Cerveteri. The

Etruscans carried out perfectly what seems to be the Italian instinct: to have single, independent cities, with a certain surrounding territory, each district speaking its own dialect and feeling at home in its own little capital, yet the whole confederacy of city states loosely linked together by a common religion and a more-or-less common interest. Even today, Lucca is very different from Ferrara,* and the language is hardly the same. In ancient Etruria, this isolation of cities developing according to their own idiosyncrasy, within the loose union of a so-called nation, must have been complete. The contact between the plebs, the mass of the people, of Caere and Tarquinii must have been almost null. They were, no doubt, foreigners to one another. Only the Lucumones, the ruling sacred magistrates of noble family, the priests and the other nobles, and the merchants, must have kept up an intercommunion, speaking "correct" Etruscan, while the people, no doubt, spoke dialects varying so widely as to be different languages. To get any idea of the pre-Roman past, we must break up the conception of oneness and uniformity, and see an endless confusion of differences.

We are diving down into another tomb, called, says the guide, the Tomb of the Leopards.* Every tomb has been given a name, to distinguish it from its neighbours. The Tomb of the Leopards has two spotted leopards in the triangle of the end wall, between the roof-slopes. Hence its name.

The Tomb of the Leopards is a charming, cosy little room, and the paintings on the walls have not been so very much damaged. All the tombs are ruined to some degree by weather and vulgar vandalism, having been left and neglected like common holes, when they had been broken open again and rifled to the last gasp.

But still the paintings are fresh and alive, the ochre reds and blacks and blues and blue-greens are curiously alive and harmonious on the creamy yellow walls. Most of the tomb walls have had a thin coat of stucco, but it is of the same paste as the living rock, which is fine and yellow, and weathers to a lovely creamy gold, a beautiful colour for a background.

The walls of this little tomb are a dance of real delight. The room seems inhabited still by Etruscans of the sixth century before Christ; a vivid, life-accepting people, who must have lived with real fulness. On come the dancers and the music-players, moving in a broad frieze towards the front wall of the tomb, the wall facing us as we enter from the dark stairs, and where the banquet is going on in all its glory. Above the banquet, in the gable angle, are the two spotted leopards, heraldically facing each other across a little tree. And the ceiling of rock has chequered slopes of red and black and yellow and blue squares, with a roof-beam painted with coloured circles, dark-red and blue and yellow. So that all is colour, and we do not seem to be underground at all, but in some gay chamber of the past.

The dancers on the right wall move with a strange, powerful alertness onwards. They are men dressed only in a loose coloured scarf, or in the gay handsome *chlamys* draped as a mantle. The subulo* plays the double flute the Etruscans loved so much, touching the stops with big, exaggerated hands, the man behind him touches the seven-stringed lyre, the man in front turns round and signals with his left hand, holding a big wine-bowl in his right. And so they move on, on their long sandalled feet, past the little berried olive trees, swiftly going with their limbs full of life, full of life to the tips.

This sense of vigorous, strong-bodied liveliness is characteristic of the Etruscans, and is somehow beyond art. You cannot think of art, but only of life itself, as if this were the very life of the Etruscans, dancing in their coloured wraps with massive yet exuberant naked limbs, ruddy from the air and the sea-light, dancing and fluting along through the little olive trees, out in the fresh day.

The end wall has a splendid banqueting scene. The feasters recline upon a checked or tartan couch-cover, on the banqueting couch, and in the open air, for they have little trees behind them. The six feasters are bold and full of life like the dancers, but they are strong, they keep their life so beautifully and richly inside themselves, they are not loose, they don't lose themselves even in their wild moments. They lie in pairs, man and woman, reclining equally on the couch, curiously friendly. The two end women are called hetaerae,* courtesans; chiefly because they have yellow hair, which seems to have been a favourite feature in a woman of pleasure. The men are dark and ruddy, and naked to the waist. The women, sketched in on the creamy rock, are fair, and wear thin gowns, with rich mantles round their hips. They have a certain free bold look, and perhaps really are courtesans.

The man at the end is holding up, between thumb and forefinger, an egg, showing it to the yellow-haired woman who reclines next to him, she who is putting out her left hand as if to touch his breast. He, in his right hand, holds a large wine-dish, for the revel.

The next couple, man and fair-haired woman, are looking round and making the salute with the right hand curved over, in the usual etruscan gesture. It seems as if they too are saluting the mysterious egg held up by the man at the end; who is, no doubt, the man who has died and whose feast is being celebrated. But in front of the second couple, a naked slave with a chaplet on his head is brandishing an 5 empty wine-jug, as if to say, he is fetching more wine. Another slave further down is holding out a curious thing like a little axe, or fan. The last two feasters are rather damaged. One of them is holding up a garland to the other, but not putting it over his head, as they still put a garland over your head, in India, to honour you. 10

Above the banqueters, in the gable angle, the two great spotted male leopards hang out their tongues and face each other heraldically, lifting a paw, on either side of a little tree. They are the leopards or panthers of the underworld Bacchus,* guarding the exits and the entrances of the passion of life. 15

There is a mystery and a portentousness in the simple scenes which goes deeper than common-place life. It seems all so gay and light. Yet there is a certain weight, or depth of significance that goes beyond aesthetic beauty.

If one once starts looking, there is much to see. But if one glances 20 merely, there is nothing but a pathetic little room with unimposing, half-obliterated, scratchy little paintings in tempera.

There are many tombs. When we have seen one, up we go, a little bewildered, into the afternoon sun, across a tract of rough, tormented hill, and down again to the underground, like rabbits in a warren. 25 The hill-top is really a warren of tombs. And gradually, the underworld of the Etruscans becomes more real than the above day of the afternoon. One begins to live with the painted dancers and feasters and mourners, and to look eagerly for them.

A very lovely dance tomb is the *Tomba del Triclinio,** or *del Convito*, 30 both of which mean: Tomb of the Feast. In size and shape this is much the same as the other tombs we have seen. It is a little chamber, about 15 feet by 11 feet, six feet high at the walls, about eight feet at the centre. It is again a tomb for one person, like nearly all the old painted tombs here. So there is no inner furnishing. Only the further 35 half of the rock floor, the pale yellow-white rock, is raised two or three inches, and on one side of this raised part are the four holes where the feet of the sarcophagus stood. For the rest, the tomb has only its painted walls and ceiling.

And how lovely these have been, and still are! The band of 40

dancing figures that go round the room still is bright in colour,
fresh, the women in thin spotted dresses of linen muslin and
coloured mantles with fine borders, the men merely in a scarf.
Wildly the bacchic woman* throws back her head and curves out
5 her long strong fingers, wild and yet contained within herself, while
the broad-bodied young man turns round to her, lifting his dancing
hand to hers till the thumbs all but touch. They are dancing in the
open, past little trees, and birds are running, and a little fox-tailed
dog is watching something with the naïve intensity of the young.
10 Wildly and delightedly dances the next woman, every bit of her, in
her soft boots and her bordered mantle, with jewels on her arms; till
one remembers the old dictum, that every part of the body and of
the anima shall know religion, and be in touch with the gods.*
Towards her comes the young man piping on the double flute, and
15 dancing as he comes. He is clothed only in a fine linen scarf with a
border, that hangs over his arms, and his strong legs dance of themselves, so full of life. Yet too, there is a certain solemn intensity in
his face, as he turns to the woman beyond him, who swoops in a
bow to him as she vibrates her castanets.
20   She is drawn fair-skinned, as all the women are, and he is of a
dark red colour. That is the convention, in the tombs. But it is more
than convention. In the early days, men smeared themselves with
scarlet when they took on their sacred natures. The Red Indians
still do it. When they wish to figure in their sacred and portentous
25 selves, they smear their bodies all over with red. That must be why
they are called Red Indians. In the past, for all serious or solemn
occasions, they rubbed red pigment into their skins. And the same
today. And today, when they wish to put strength into their vision,
and to see true, they smear round their eyes with vermilion, rubbing
30 it in the skin. You may meet them so, in the streets of the American
towns.*

It is a very old custom. The American Indian will tell you: The
red paint, it is medicine, make you see!—But he means medicine in
a different sense from ours. It is deeper even than magic. Vermilion
35 is the colour of his sacred or potent or god body. Apparently it was
so in all the ancient world. Man all scarlet was his bodily godly self.
We know the kings of ancient Rome, who were probably Etruscans,
appeared in public with their faces painted vermilion with *minium*.*
And Ezekiel says (ch. xxiii. 14, 15): She saw men portrayed upon
40 the wall, the images of the Chaldeans portrayed with vermilion—all

of them princes to look to, after the manner of the Babylonians of
Chaldea, the land of their nativity.—*

It is then partly a convention, and partly a symbol, with the
Etruscans, to represent their men red in colour, a strong red. Here in
the tombs everything is in its sacred or inner-significant aspect. But   5
also the red colour is not so very unnatural. When the Italian today
goes almost naked on the beach, he becomes of a lovely dark ruddy
colour, dark as any Indian. And the Etruscans went a good deal
naked. The sun painted them with the sacred minium.

The dancers dance on, the birds run, at the foot of a little tree a   10
rabbit crouches in a bunch, bunched with life. And on the tree hangs
a narrow fringed scarf, like a priest's stole; another symbol.

The end wall has a banqueting scene, rather damaged, but still
interesting. We see two separate couches, and a man and a woman
on each. The woman this time is dark-haired, so she need not be a   15
courtesan. The Etruscans shared the banqueting bench with their
wives; which is more than the Greeks or Romans did, at this period.
The classic world thought it indecent for an honest woman to recline
as the men did, even at the family table. If the woman appeared at all,
she must sit up straight, in a chair.*   20

Here, the women recline calmly with the men, and one shows a
bare foot at the end of the dark couch. In front of the lecti, the
couches, is in each case a little low square table bearing delicate
dishes of food for the feasters. But they are not eating. One woman is
lifting her hand to her head in a strange salute to the robed piper at   25
the end, the other woman seems with the lifted hand to be saying No!
to the charming maid, perhaps a servant, who stands at her side
apparently offering the *alabastron*,* or ointment jar, while the man at
the end apparently is holding up an egg. Wreaths hang from the
ivy-border above, a boy is bringing a wine-jug, the music goes on,   30
and under the beds a cat is on the prowl, while an alert cock watches
him. The silly partridge, however, turns his back, stepping inno-
cently along.

This lovely tomb has a pattern of ivy and ivy berries, the ivy of the
underworld Bacchus,* along the roof-beam and in a border round   35
the top of the walls. The roof-slopes are chequered in red and black,
white, blue, brown and yellow squares. In the gable angle, instead of
the heraldic beasts, two naked men are sitting reaching back to the
centre of an ivy-covered altar, arm outstretched across the ivy. But
one man is almost obliterated. At the foot of the other man, in the   40

tight angle of the roof, is a pigeon, the bird of the soul that coos out of the unseen.

This tomb has been open since 1830, and is still fresh. It is interesting to see, in Fritz Weege's book *Etruskische Malerei*,* a
5   reproduction of an old water-colour drawing of the dancers on the right wall. It is a good drawing, yet as one looks closer, it is quite often out, both in line and position. These etruscan paintings, not being in our convention, are very difficult to copy. The picture shows my rabbit all spotted, as if it were some queer cat. And it shows a
10 squirrel in the little tree in front of the piper, and flowers, and many details that have now disappeared.

But it is a good drawing, unlike some that Weege reproduces, which are so Flaxmanised* and Greekified and made according to what our great-grandfathers thought they *ought* to be, as to be really
15 funny, and a warning forever against thinking how things *ought* to be, when already they are quite perfectly what they are.

We climb up to the world, and pass for a few minutes through the open day. Then down we go again. In the Tomb of the Bacchanti* the colours have almost gone. But still we see, on the end wall, a
20 strange, wondering dancer out of the mists of time carrying his zither, and beyond him, beyond the little tree, a man of the dim ancient world, a man with a short beard, strong and mysteriously male, is reaching for a wild archaic maiden who throws up her hands . and turns back to him her excited, subtle face. It is wonderful, the
25 strength and mystery of old life that comes out of these faded figures. The Etruscans are still there, upon the wall.

Above the figures, in the gable angle, two spotted deer are prancing heraldically towards one another, on either side the altar, and behind them, two dark lions with pale manes and with tongues
30 hanging out, are putting up a paw to seize them on the haunch. So the old story repeats itself.

From the striped border rude garlands are hanging, and on the roof are little painted stars, or four-petalled flowers. So much has vanished! Yet even in the last breath of colour and form, how much
35 life there is!

In the *Tomba del Morto*,* the Tomb of the Dead Man, the banqueting scene is replaced by a scene, apparently, of a dead man on his bed, with a woman leaning gently over to cover his face. It is almost like a banquet scene. But it is so badly damaged!—In the
40 gable above, two dark heraldic lions are lifting the paw against two

leaping, frightened, backward-looking birds. This is a new variation.—On the broken wall are the dancing legs of a man, and there is more life in these etruscan legs, fragment as they are, than in the whole bodies of men today. Then there is one really impressive dark figure of a naked man who throws up his arms so that his great wine-bowl stands vertical, and with spread hand and closed face gives a strange gesture of finality. He has a chaplet on his head, and a small pointed beard, and lives there shadowy and significant.

Lovely again is the *Tomba delle Leonesse,** the Tomb of the Lionesses. In its gable, two spotted lionesses swing their bell-like udders heraldically facing one another across the altar. Beneath is a great vase, and a flute player playing to it on one side, a zither player on the other, making music to its sacred contents. Then on either side of these goes a narrow frieze of dancers, very strong and lively in their prancing. Under the frieze of dancers is a lotus dado, and below that again, all round the room the dolphins are leaping, leaping all downwards into the rippling sea, while birds fly between the fishes.

On the right wall reclines a very impressive dark red man wearing a curious cap, or head-dress that has long tails like long plaits. In his right hand he holds up an egg, and in his left is the shallow wine-bowl of the feast. The scarf or stole of his human office hangs from a tree before him, and the garland of his human delight hangs at his side. He holds up the egg of resurrection, within which the germ sleeps as the soul sleeps in the tomb, before it breaks the shell and emerges again.— There is another reclining man, much obliterated, and beside him hangs a garland or chain like the chains of dandelion-stems we used to make as children. And this man has a naked flute-boy, lovely in naked outline, coming towards him.

The *Tomba della Pulcella,** or Tomb of the Maiden, has faded but vigorous figures at the banquet, and very ornate couch-covers in squares and the key pattern,* and very handsome mantles.

The *Tomba dei Vasi Dipinti,** Tomb of the Painted Vases, has great amphoras painted on the side wall, and springing towards them is a weird dancer, the ends of his waist-cloth flying. The amphoras, two of them, have scenes painted on them, which can still be made out.—On the end wall is a gentle little banquet scene, the bearded man softly touching the woman with him under the chin, a slave boy standing childishly behind, and an alert dog under the couch. The *cylix* or wine-bowl that the man holds, is surely the biggest on record; exaggerated, no doubt, to show the very special importance of the

feast. Rather gentle and lovely is the way he touches the woman under the chin, with a delicate caress. That again is one of the charms of the etruscan paintings: they really have the sense of touch; the people and the creatures are all really in touch. It is one of the
5 rarest qualities, in life as well as in art. There is plenty of pawing and laying hold, but no real touch. In pictures especially, the people may be in contact, embracing or laying hands on one another. But there is no soft flow of touch. The touch does not come from the middle of the human being. It is merely a contact of surfaces, and a juxta-
10 position of objects. This is what makes so many of the great masters boring, in spite of all their clever composition. Here, in this faded etruscan painting, there is a quiet flow of touch that unites the man and the woman on the couch, the timid boy behind, the dog that lifts his nose, even the very garlands that hang from the wall.

15   Above the banquet, in the triangle, instead of lions or leopards we have the hippocampus, a favourite animal of the etruscan imagin-ation. It is a horse that ends in a long, flowing fish-tail. Here these two hippocampi face one another prancing their front legs, while their fish-tails flow away into the narrow angle of the roof. They are a
20 favourite symbol of the sea-board Etruscans.

In the *Tomba del Vecchio*,* the Tomb of the Old Man, a beautiful woman with her hair dressed backwards into the long cone of the east,* so that her head is like a sloping acorn, offers her elegant twisted garland to the white-bearded old man, who is now beyond
25 garlands. He lifts his left hand up at her, with the rich gesture of these people, that must mean something each time.

Above them, the prancing spotted deer are being seized in the haunch by two lions. And the waves of obliteration, wastage of time and damage of men, are silently passing over all.

30   So we go on, seeing tomb after tomb, dimness after dimness, divided between the pleasure of finding so much, and the dis-appointment that so little remains. One tomb after another, and nearly everything faded or eaten away, or corroded with alkali, or broken wilfully! Fragments of people at banquets, limbs that dance
35 without dancers, birds that fly in nowhere, lions whose devouring heads are devoured away!—Once it was all bright and dancing; the delight of the underworld; honouring the dead with wine and flutes playing for a dance, and limbs whirling and pressing. And it was deep and sincere honour rendered to the dead and to the mysteries. It is
40 contrary to our ideas; but the ancients had their own philosophy for

it. As the pagan old writer says: For no part of us nor of our bodies shall be, which doth not feel religion: and let there be no lack of singing for the soul, no lack of leaping and of dancing for the knees and heart; for all these know the gods.—

Which is very evident in the etruscan dancers. They know the gods in their very finger-tips. The wonderful fragments of limbs and bodies that dance on in a field of obliteration still know the gods, and make it evident to us.

But we can hardly see any more tombs. The upper air seems pallid and bodiless, as we emerge once more, white with the light of the sea and the coming evening. And spent and slow the old dog rises once more to follow after.

We decide that the *Tomba delle Iscrizioni,** the Tomb of the Inscriptions, shall be our last for today. It is dim but fascinating, as the lamp flares up, and we see in front of us the end wall, painted with a false door studded with pale studs, as if it led to another chamber beyond; and riding from the left, a trail of shadowy tall horsemen; and running in from the right, a train of wild shadowy dancers, wild as demons.

The horsemen are naked on the four naked horses, and they make gestures as they come towards the painted door. The horses are alternately red and black, the red having blue manes and hoofs, the black, red ones, or white. They are tall archaic horses on slim legs, with necks arched like a curved knife. And they come pinking daintily and superbly along, with their long tails, towards the dark red death-door.

From the left, the stream of dancers leaps wildly, playing music, carrying garlands or wine-jugs, lifting their arms like revellers, lifting their live knees, and signalling with their long hands. Some have little inscriptions written near them: their names.

And above the false door in the angle of the gable is a fine design: two black, wide-mouthed, pale-maned lions seated back to back, their tails rising like curved stems, between them, as they each one lift a black paw against the cringing head of a cowering spotted deer, that winces to the death-blow. Behind each deer is a smaller dark lion, in the acute angle of the roof, coming up to bite the shrinking deer in the haunch, and so give the second death-wound. For the wounds of death are in the neck and in the flank.

At the other end of the tomb are wrestlers and gamesters; but so shadowy now! We cannot see any more, nor look any further in the

shadows for the unconquerable life of the Etruscans, whom the
Romans called vicious, but whose life, in these tombs, is certainly
fresh and cleanly vivid.

   The upper air is wide and pale, and somehow void. We cannot see
5 either world any more, the etruscan underworld nor the common
day. Silently, tired, we walk back in the wind to the town, the old dog
padding stoically behind. And the guide promises to take us to the
other tombs tomorrow.

---

10 There is a haunting quality in the etruscan representations. Those
leopards with their long tongues hanging out: those flowing hippocampi: those cringing spotted deer, struck in flank and neck; they get
into the imagination, and will not go out. And we see the wavy edge
of the sea, the dolphins curving over, the diver going down clean, the
15 little man climbing up the rock after him so eagerly. Then the men
with beards who recline on the banqueting beds: how they hold up
the mysterious egg! And the women with the conical head-dress,
how strangely they lean forward, with caresses we no longer know!
The naked slaves joyfully stoop to the wine-jars. Their nakedness is
20 its own clothing, more easy than drapery. The curves of their limbs
show pure pleasure in life, a pleasure that goes deeper still in the
limbs of the dancers, in the big, long hands thrown out and dancing
to the very ends of the fingers, a dance that surges from within, like a
current in the sea. It is as if the current of some strong different life
25 swept through them, different from our shallow current today: as if
they drew their vitality from different depths, that we are denied.

   Yet in a few centuries they lost their vitality. The Romans took the
life out of them.* It seems as if the power of resistance to life,
self-assertion and overbearing, such as the Romans knew; a power
30 which must needs be moral, or carry morality with it, as a cloak for its
inner ugliness; would always succeed in destroying the natural
flowering of life.—And yet there still are a few wild flowers and
creatures.

   The natural flowering of life! It is not so easy for human beings as
35 it sounds. Behind all the etruscan liveliness was a religion of life,
which the chief men were seriously responsible for. Behind all the
dancing was a vision, and even a science of life, a conception of the
universe and man's place in the universe which made men live to the
depth of their capacity.

40   To the Etruscan, all was alive: the whole universe lived: and the

business of man was himself to live amid it all. He had to draw life
into himself, out of the wandering huge vitalities of the world. The
cosmos was alive, like a vast creature. The whole thing breathed and
stirred. Evaporation went up like breath from the nostrils of a whale,
steaming up. The sky received it in its blue bosom, breathed it in and   5
pondered on it and transmuted it, before breathing it out again.
Inside the earth were fires like the heat in the hot red liver of a beast.
Out of the fissures of the earth came breaths of other breathing,
vapours direct from the living physical underearth, exhalations
carrying inspiration. The whole thing was alive, and had a great soul,   10
or anima: and in spite of one great soul, there were myriad roving,
lesser souls; every man, every creature and tree and lake and
mountain and stream was animate, had its own peculiar consciousness. And has it today.

The cosmos was one, and its anima was one; but it was made up of   15
creatures. And the greatest creature was earth, with its soul of inner
fire. The sun was only a reflection, or off-throw, or brilliant handful
of the great inner fire.—But in juxtaposition to earth lay the sea, the
waters that moved and pondered and held a deep soul of their own.
Earth and waters lay side by side, together, and utterly different.   20

So it was. The universe, which was a single aliveness with a single
soul, instantly changed, the moment you thought of it, and became a
dual creature with two souls, fiery and watery, forever mingling and
rushing apart, and held by the great aliveness of the universe in an
ultimate equilibrium. But they rushed together and they rushed   25
apart, and immediately they became myriad: volcanoes and seas,
then streams and mountains, trees, creatures, men. And everything
was dual, or contained its own duality, forever mingling and rushing
apart.*

The old idea of the vitality of the universe was evolved long before   30
history begins, and elaborated into a vast religion before we get a
glimpse of it. When history does begin, in China or India, Egypt,
Babylonia,* even in the Pacific and in aboriginal America, we see
evidence of one underlying religious idea: the conception of the
vitality of the cosmos, the myriad vitalities in wild confusion, which   35
still is held in some sort of array: and man, amid all the glowing
welter, adventuring, struggling, striving for one thing, life, vitality,
more vitality: to get into himself more and more of the gleaming
vitality of the cosmos. That is the treasure. The active religious idea
was that man, by vivid attention and subtlety and exerting all his   40

strength, could draw more life into himself, more life, more and
more glistening vitality, till he became shining like the morning,
blazing like a god. When he was all himself he painted himself
vermilion like the throat of dawn, and was god's body, visibly, red
5 and utterly vivid. So he was a prince, a king, a god, an etruscan
Lucumo; Pharaoh or Belshazzar or Ashurbanipal, or Tarquin; or,
in* a feebler *de crescendo*, Alexander, or Caesar, or Napoleon.

This was the idea at the back of all the great old civilisations. It was
even, half-transmuted, at the back of David's mind, and voiced in the
10 Psalms. But with David the living cosmos became merely a personal
god.* With the Egyptians and Babylonians and Etruscans, strictly
there were no personal gods. There were only idols or symbols. It
was the living cosmos itself, dazzlingly and gaspingly complex, which
was divine, and which could be contemplated only by the strongest
15 soul, and only at moments. And only the peerless soul could draw
into itself some last flame from the quick. Then you had a king-god
indeed.

There you have the ancient idea of kings, kings who are gods by
vividness, because they have gathered into themselves core after core
20 of vital potency from the universe, till they are clothed in scarlet, they
are bodily a piece of the deepest fire. Pharaohs and kings of
Nineveh,* kings of the east, and etruscan Lucumones, they are the
living clue to the pure fire, to the cosmic vitality. They are the vivid
key to life, the vermilion clue to the mystery and the delight of death
25 and life. They, in their own body, unlock the vast treasure house of
the cosmos for their people, and bring out life, and show the way into
the dark of death, which is the blue burning of the one fire. They, in
their own bodies, are the life-bringers and the death-guides, leading
ahead in the dark, and coming out in the day with more than sunlight
30 in their bodies. Can one wonder that such dead are wrapped in gold;
or were?

The life-bringers, and the death-guides. But they set guards at the
gates both of life and death. They keep the secrets, and safe-guard
the way. Only a few are initiated into the mystery of the bath of life,
35 and the bath of death: the pool within pool within pool, wherein,
when a man is dipped, he becomes darker than blood, with death,
and brighter than fire, with life; till at last he is scarlet royal as a piece
of living life, pure vermilion.

The people are not initiated into the cosmic ideas, nor into the
40 awakened throb of more vivid consciousness. Try as you may, you

can never make the mass of men throb with full awakenedness. They *cannot* be more than a little aware. So you must give them symbols, ritual and gesture, which will fill their bodies with life up to their own full measure. Any more is fatal. And so the actual knowledge must be guarded from them, lest knowing the formulae, without undergoing at all the experience that corresponds, they may become insolent and impious, thinking they have the all, when they have only an empty monkey-chatter. The esoteric knowledge will always be esoteric, since knowledge is an experience, not a formula. But it is foolish to hand out the formulae. A little knowledge is indeed a dangerous thing.* No age proves it more than ours. Monkey-chatter is at last the most disastrous of all things.

The clue to the etruscan life was the Lucumo, the religious prince. Beyond him were the priests and warriors. Then came the people and the slaves. People and warriors and slaves did not think about religion. There would soon have been no religion left. They felt the symbols and danced the sacred dances. For they were always kept *in touch*, physically, with the mysteries. The "touch" went from the Lucumo down to the merest slave. The blood-stream was unbroken. But "knowing" belonged to the high-born and the pure-bred.

So, in the tombs we find only the simple, uninitiated vision of the people. There is none of the priest-work of Egypt.* The symbols are to the artist just wonder-forms, pregnant with emotion and good for decoration. It is so all the way through etruscan art. The artists evidently were of the people, artizans. Presumably they were of the old Italic stock, and understood nothing of the religion in its intricate form, as it had come in from the east: though doubtless the crude principles of the official religion were the same as those of the primitive religion of the aborigines. The same crude principles ran through the religions of all the barbaric world of that time, Druid or Teutonic or Celtic. But the newcomers in Etruria held secret the science and philosophy of their religion, and gave the people the symbols and the ritual, leaving the artists free to use the symbols as they would; which shows that there was no priest-rule.

Later, when scepticism came over all the civilised world, as it did after Socrates, the etruscan religion began to die, Greeks and Greek rationalism flooded in, and Greek stories more or less took the place of the old etruscan symbolic thought. Then again the etruscan artists, uneducated, used the Greek stories as they had used the etruscan symbols, quite freely, making them over again just to please themselves.

But one radical thing the etruscan people never forgot, because it was in their blood as well as in the blood of their masters: and that was the mystery of the journey out of life, and into death; the death-journey, and the sojourn in the after-life. The wonder of their soul continued to play round the mystery of this journey and this sojourn.

In the tombs we see it; throes of wonder and vivid feeling throbbing over death. Man moves naked and glowing through the universe. Then comes death: he dives into the sea, he departs into the underworld.

The sea is that vast primordial creature that has a soul also, whose inwardness is womb of all things, out of which all things emerged, and into which they are devoured back. Balancing the sea is the earth of inner fire, of after-life and before-life. Beyond the waters and the ultimate fire lay only that oneness of which the people knew nothing: it was a secret the Lucumones kept for themselves, as they kept the symbol of it in their hand.

But the sea the people knew. The dolphin leaps in and out of it suddenly, as a creature that suddenly exists, out of nowhere. He was not: and lo! there he is! the dolphin which gives up the sea's rainbows only when he dies. Out he leaps; then, with a head-dive, back again he plunges into the sea. He is so much alive, he is like the phallus carrying the fiery spark of procreation down into the wet darkness of the womb. The diver does the same, carrying like a phallus his small hot spark into the deeps of death. And the sea will give up her dead like dolphins that leap out and have the rainbow within them.

But the duck that swims on the water, and lifts his wings, is another matter: the blue duck, or goose, so often represented by the Etruscans. He is the same goose that saved Rome, in the night.*

The duck does not live down within the waters as the fish does. The fish is the anima, the animate life, the very clue to the vast sea, the watery element of the first submission. For this reason Jesus was represented in the first christian centuries as a fish, in Italy especially, where the people still thought in the etruscan symbols. Jesus was the anima of the vast, moist ever-yielding element which was the opposite and the counterpart of the red flame the pharaohs and the kings of the east had sought to invest themselves with.

But the duck has no such subaqueous nature as the fish. It swims upon the waters, and is hot-blooded, belonging to the red flame of the animal body of life. But it dives underwater, and preens itself upon the flood. So it became, to man, the symbol of that part of himself which delights in the waters, and dives in, and rises up and shakes its wings. It is the symbol of a man's own phallus and phallic 5 life. So you see a man holding on his hand the hot, soft, alert duck, offering it to the maiden. So today the Red Indian makes a secret gift to the maiden, of a hollow, earthenware duck in which is a little fire and incense. It is that part of his body and his fiery life that a man can offer to a maid. And it is that awareness or alertness in him, that 10 other consciousness that wakes in the night and rouses the city.

But the maid offers the man a garland, the rim of flowers from the edge of the "pool," which can be placed over the man's head and laid on his shoulders, in symbol that he is invested with the power of the maiden's mystery and different strength, the female power. For 15 whatever is laid over the shoulders is a sign of power added.

Birds fly portentously on the walls of the tombs. The artist must often have seen those priests, the augurs, with their crooked, bird-headed staffs in their hand, out on a high place watching the flight of larks or pigeons across the quarters of the sky. They were 20 reading the signs and the portents, looking for an indication, how they should direct the course of some serious affair. To us it may seem foolish. To them, hot-blooded birds flew through the living universe as feelings and premonitions fly through the breast of a man, or as thoughts fly through the mind. In their flight, the 25 suddenly-roused birds, or the steady, far-coming birds moved wrapped in a deeper consciousness, in the complex destiny of all things. And since all things corresponded, in the ancient world, and man's bosom mirrored itself in the bosom of the sky, or vice versa, the birds were flying to a portentous goal, in the man's breast who 30 watched, as well as flying their own way in the bosom of the sky. If the augur could see the birds flying *in his heart*, then he would know which way destiny too was flying for him.

The science of augury certainly was no exact science. But it was as exact as our sciences of psychology or political economy. And the 35 augurs were as clever as our politicians, who also must practise divination, if ever they are to do anything worth the name. There is no other way, when you are dealing with life. And if you live by the cosmos, you look in the cosmos for your clue. If you live by a personal god, you pray to him. If you are rational, you think things over. But it 40

all amounts to the same thing, in the end. Prayer, or thought, or
studying the stars, or watching the flight of birds, or studying the
entrails of the sacrifice, it is all the same process, ultimately: of
divination. All it depends on, is the amount of *true*, sincere, religious
5 concentration you can bring to bear on your object. An act of pure
attention, if you are capable of it, will bring its own answer. And you
choose that object to concentrate upon, which will best focus your
consciousness. Every real discovery made, every serious and significant decision ever reached, was reached and made by divination.
10 Columbus discovered America by a sort of divination. The soul stirs,
and makes an act of pure attention, and that is a discovery.

The science of the augur and the haruspex was not so foolish as
our modern science of political economy. If the hot liver of the victim
cleared the soul of the haruspex,* and made him capable of that
15 ultimate inward attention which alone tells us the last thing we need
to know, then why quarrel with the haruspex? To him, the universe
was alive, and in quivering *rapport*. To him, the blood was conscious;
he thought with his heart. To him, the blood was the red and shining
stream of consciousness* itself. Hence, to him, the liver, that great
20 organ where the blood struggles and "overcomes death," was an
object of profound mystery and significance. It stirred his soul and
purified his consciousness; for it was also his victim. So he gazed into
the hot liver, that was mapped out in fields and regions like the sky of
stars, but these fields and regions were those of the red, shining
25 consciousness that runs through the whole animal creation. And
therefore it must contain the answer to his own blood's question.

It is the same with the study of stars, or the sky of stars. Whatever
object will bring the consciousness into a state of pure attention, in a
time of perplexity, will also give back an answer to the perplexity. But
30 it is truly a question of *divination*. As soon as there is any pretence of
infallibility and pure scientific calculation, the whole thing becomes
a fraud and a jugglery. But the same is true not only of augury and
astrology, but also of prayer and of pure reason, and even of the
discoveries of the great laws and principles of science. Men juggle
35 with prayer today as once they juggled with augury; and in the same
way they are juggling with science. Every great discovery or decision
comes by an act of divination. Facts are fitted round afterwards. But
all attempt at divination, even prayer and reason and research itself,
lapses into jugglery when the heart loses its purity. In the impurity of
40 his heart, Socrates often juggled logic unpleasantly. And no doubt,

when scepticism came over the ancient world, the haruspex and the augur became jugglers and pretenders. But for centuries they held real sway. It is amazing to see, in Livy, what a big share they must have had in the building up of the great Rome of the Republic.*

Turning from birds to animals, we find in the tombs the continual repetition of lion against deer. As soon as the world was created, according to the ancient idea, it took on duality. All things became dual, not only in the duality of sex, but in the polarity of action. This is the "impious pagan duality." It did not, however, contain the later pious duality of good and evil.

The leopard and the deer, the lion and the bull, the cat and the dove, or the partridge, these are part of the great duality, or polarity of the animal kingdom. But they do not represent good action and evil action. On the contrary, they represent the polarised activity of the divine cosmos, in its animal creation.

The treasure of treasures is the soul, which, in every creature, in every tree or pool, means that mysterious conscious point of balance or equilibrium between the two halves of the duality, the fiery and the watery. This mysterious point clothes itself in vividness after vividness, from the right hand, and vividness after vividness from the left. And in death it does not disappear, but is stored in the egg, or in the jar, or even in the tree which brings forth again.

But the soul itself, the conscious spark of every creature, is not dual; and being the immortal, it is also the altar on which our mortality and our duality is at last sacrificed.

So as the key-picture in the tombs, we have over and over again the heraldic beasts facing one another across the altar, or the tree, or the vase; and the lion is smiting the deer in the hip and the throat. The deer is spotted, for day and night, the lion is dark and light the same.

The deer, or lamb, or goat or cow is the gentle creature with udder of overflowing milk and fertility; or it is the stag or ram or bull, the great father of the herd, with horns of power set obvious on the brow, and indicating the dangerous aspect of the beasts of fertility. These are the creatures of prolific, boundless procreation, the beasts of peace and increase. So even Jesus is the lamb.* And the endless endless gendering of these creatures will fill all the earth with cattle,* till herds rub flanks over all the world, and hardly a tree can rise between.

But this must not be so, since they are only half, even of the animal creation. Balance must be kept. And this is the altar we are all sacrificed upon: it is even death; just as it is our soul and purest treasure.

So, on the other hand from the deer we have lionesses and leopards. These too are male and female. These too have udders of milk and nourish young; as the wolf nourished the first Romans;* prophetically, as the destroyers of many deer, including the etruscan. So these fierce ones guard the treasure and the gateway, which the prolific ones would squander or close up with too much gendering. They bite the deer in neck and haunch, where the great blood-streams run.

So the symbolism goes all through the etruscan tombs. It is very much the symbolism of all the ancient world. But here it is not exact and scientific, as in Egypt. It is simple and rudimentary, and the artist plays with it as a child with fairy stories. Nevertheless, it is the symbolic element which rouses the deeper emotion, and gives the peculiarly satisfying quality to the dancing figures and the creatures. A painter like Sargent,* for example, is so clever. But in the end he is utterly uninteresting, a bore. He never has an inkling of his own triviality and silliness. One etruscan leopard, even one little quail is worth all the miles of him.

ILLUSTRATIONS

17. Sketches of Etruscan Places./III.   The Painted Tombs of Tarquinia/ Tomb of the Leopards. 1.
18. Sketches of Etruscan Places./III.   The Painted Tombs of Tarquinia./ Tomb of the Leopards. 2.
19. Sketches of Etruscan Places./III.   The Painted Tombs of Tarquinia./ Tomb of the Feast. 1.
20. Sketches of Etruscan Places/III.   The Painted Tombs of Tarquinia/ Tomb of the Feast. 2.
    (DHL also noted 'Tomba del Triclinio (o Convito)', deleted 'dei Leopardi' on the front and substituted 'Convito')
21. [Sketches of Etruscan Places/III.   The Painted Tombs of Tarquinia/ Tomb of the Feast. 3.]
22. Sketches of Etruscan Places./III.   The Painted Tombs of Tarquinia/ Tomb of the Lionesses. 1.
23. Sketches of Etruscan Places/III.   The Painted Tombs of Tarquinia/ Tomb of the Lionesses. 2.
24. Sketches of Etruscan Places./IV.   The Painted Tombs of Tarquinia (2)/The Tomb of the Bulls: showing inner chamber & stone beds for sarcophagi
25. Sketches of Etruscan Places/IV.   The Painted Tombs of Tarquinia (2)/Tomb of the Augurs: the Augur-priest lifting his curved sceptre—wrestlers—boy bringing a stool.
26. Sketches of Etruscan Places/IV.   The Painted Tombs of Tarquinia (2)/*Tomb of the Augurs*: the fight of the blindfold man with the dog.
27. Sketches of Etruscan Places/IV.   The Painted Tombs of Tarquinia (2)/Tomb of the Augurs:
28. Sketches of Etruscan Places/IV./The Painted Tombs of Tarquinia. (2)/————/Tomb of the Baron.
29. Sketches of Etruscan Places/IV. —The Painted Tombs of Tarquinia (2)/*Tomb of the Baron*.
30. Sketches of Etruscan Places/IV./The Painted Tombs of Tarquinia. 2./ ————/Interior of the Tomb of Typhon
31. Sketches of Etruscan Places./III.   The Painted Tombs of Tarquinia/ Tomb of Orcus.
32. [Sketches of Etruscan Places V. Vulci *Ponte della Badia, Vulci* by S. J. Ainsley]
33. Sketches of Etruscan Places/————/VI./Volterra: view of the city, with the mediaeval castle, now a prison, on the right
34. Sketches of Etruscan Places/VI/Volterra: The Porta dell'Arco: etruscan gate.
35. Sketches of Etruscan Places/VI./Volterra: Alabaster workers.
36. Sketches of Etruscan Places/VI./Volterra: Ash-chest showing the boar-hunt.
37. Sketches of Etruscan Places. VI./Volterra.   Farewell scene & departure by boat for the underworld.
38. Sketches of Etruscan Places/VI./Volterra: Ash-chest showing journey of a woman to the underworld—followed by husband & child.

39. Sketches of Etruscan Places/VI./Volterra—Ash-chest showing an attack upon a woman.
40. VI./Volterra. Ash-chest showing Paris recognised as Priam's son.
41. Sketches of Etruscan Places/VI./Volterra—ash-chest showing Acteon and the dogs
42. Sketches of Etruscan Places./VI/Volterra.—Ash-chest showing attack on a city
43. Sketches of Etruscan Places/VI/Volterra. ash-chest showing fight between barbarians and Italic people.
44. Sketches of Etruscan Places/VI./Volterra. : The Inghirami Tomb with ash-chests as found in Volterra—now moved to the Florence Museum.
45. Sketches of Etruscan Places./II./*Tarquinia* : The earliest Italic tombs, or ash-jars, found in many parts of Italy. The jar often has a double volute, and i⟨t⟩⌐s⌐ covered by a smaller dish. Sometimes the jar containing the ashes is placed inside a bigger urn, like a kernel.

(Ed.ⁿⁱ Alinari) N.° 35846. CERVETERI – *Lazio*. Panorama della Necropoli Etrusca.

Figure 1

(Ed.^a Alinari) N.° 35850. CERVETERI. – *Lazio*. Necropoli Etrusca, ingressi di Tombe a Camera con Iscrizioni Etrusche.

Figure 2

(Edⁿ Alinari) N.° 35860. CERVETERI — *Laxio*. Necropoli Etrusca. Tomba degli Stucchi, o Grotta Bella, interno.

Figure 3

Figure 4

(Ed.ne Alinari) N. 35859. CERVETERI – *Lazio*. Necropoli Etrusca. Tomba dei Sarcofagi, interno.

Figure 5

(Ed." Alinari) N.° 35855. CERVETERI – *Lazio*. Necropoli Etrusca. Tomba dell' Alcova. Interno.

Figure 6

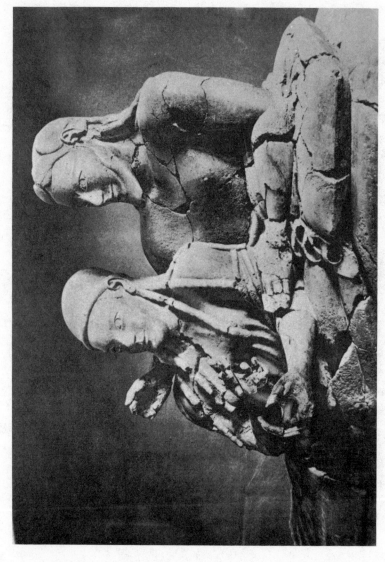

Figure 7

Ed.ᵐ Alinari-Riproduzione interdetta) N.° 35616. ROMA — Vaticano. Museo Etrusco Gregoriano. Umbone di Scudo con animali. (Bronzo - Arte Etrusca - Cervetari)

Figure 8

(Ed.^{ne} Alinari) N.° 26094. CORNETO TARQUINIA — Panorama.

Figure 9

(Ed.ni Alinari) N.º 26018. CORNETO TARQUINIA — Chiesa di S. Maria in Castello. (XIIº secolo).

Figure 10

(Ed.** Alinari) N.º 26058. CORNETO TARQUINIA — Museo Municipale. Sarcofago di un Magistrato. (Etrusco–Romano).

Figure 11

Figure 12

(Ed.ne Brogi) 18466. CORNETO TARQUINIA. Museo Etrusco. Bronzi e terrecotte dell'epoca arcaica.

Figure 13

Figure 14

Figure 15

Figure 16

(Ed.ⁿⁱ Alinari) N.º 26089. CORNETO TARQUINIA — Dintorni. Tombe Etrusche. Affresco nella Tomba dei Leopardi.

Figure 17

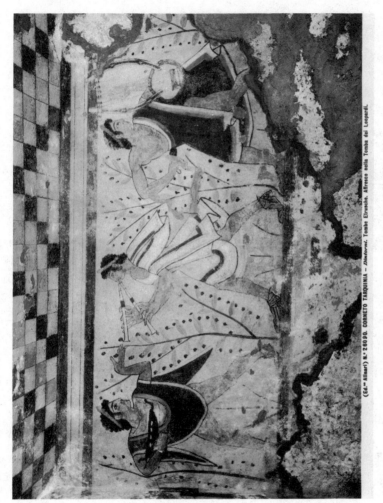

(Ed.ⁿ Alinari) N.° 26090. CORNETO TARQUINIA – *Diadorni*. Tombe Etrusche. Affresco nella Tomba del Leopardi.

Figure 18

(Ed.ⁿⁱ Alinari) N.º 26093. CORNETO TARQUINIA — *Dintorni*. Tombe Etrusche. Affresco nella Tomba del Convito.

Figure 19

Figure 20

(Ed.ne Alinari) N.º 23093. CORNETO TARQUINIA – *Dintorni*. Tomba Etrusca. Tomba Etrusca. Affresco nella Tomba del Convito.

Figure 21

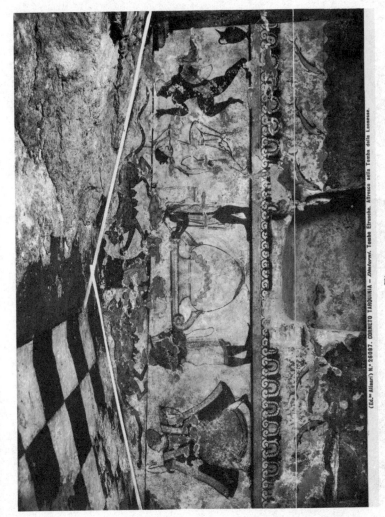

(Ed.re Alinari) N.º 26097. CORNETO TARQUINIA – *Dintorni.* Tomba Etrusche. Affresco nella Tomba delle Leonesse.

Figure 22

(Ed.ne Alinari) N.° 26088. CORNETO TARQUINIA – *Dintorni*. Tombe Etrusche. Affresco nella Tomba delle Leonesse.

Figure 23

(Ed.^{ne} Alinari) N.° 26104 CORNETO TARQUINIA. — *Antichità*. Tombe Etrusche. Affresco nella Tomba dei Tori.

Figure 24

(Ed.ᵐ Alinari) N.° 26107. CORNETO TARQUINIA – *Dintorni.* Tombe Etrusche. Affresco nella Tomba degli Auguri.

Figure 25

(Ed.^{ne} Alinari) N.° 26108. CORNETO TARQUINIA – *Dintorni*. Tombe Etrusche. Affresco nella Tomba degli Auguri.

Figure 26

(Ed.ne Alinari) N.° 26109. CORNETO TARQUINIA – *Dintorni.* Tombe Etrusche. Affresco nella Tomba degli Auguri.

Figure 27

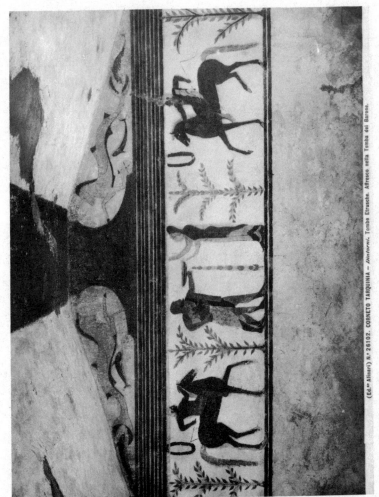

(Ed.nr Alinari) N.º 26102. CORNETO TARQUINA — *Dintorni*. Tombe Etrusche. Affresco nella Tomba del Barone.

Figure 28

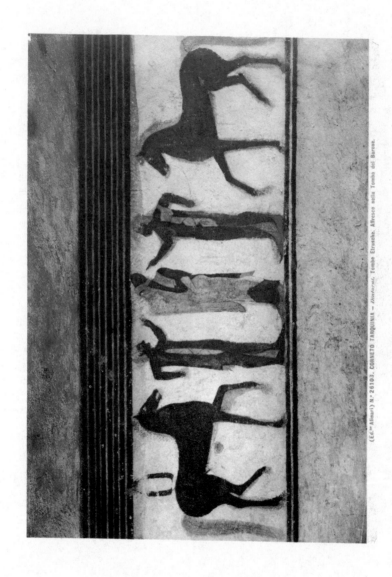

(Ed.ne Alinari) N.° 26103, CORNETO TARQUINIA – *Dintorni*. Tombe Etrusche. Affresco nella Tomba dei Barone.

Figure 29

(Ed.^{re} Alinari) N.° 26097. CORNETO TARQUINIA – *Dintorni*. Tombe Etrusche. Interno della Tomba del Tifone

Figure 30

Figure 31

Figure 32

Figure 33

(Ed.™ Alinari) N.º 24685. VOLTERRA. — Porta dell'Arco. (Epoca Etrusca.)

Figure 34

(Ed.ⁿⁱ Alinari) N.° 34688. VOLTERRA – Laboratorio di Alabastri.

Figure 35

Figure 36

Figure 37

(Ed.ni Brogi) 13664. VOLTERRA. Museo Guarnacci. Urna cineraria col Viaggio agl'Inferi.

Figure 38

Figure 39

Figure 40

Figure 41

(Ed.ne Alinari) N.° 8734. VOLTERRA — Museo Guarnacci. Urna Cineraria Romano-Etrusca, con l'Assedio di Tebe.

Figure 42

Figure 43

Figure 44

Figure 45

IV.

THE PAINTED TOMBS OF TARQUINIA 2.

IV.

The Painted Tombs of Tarquinia
2.

We sit at the tin tables of the café above the gate, watching the peasants coming in this evening from the fields, with their implements and their asses. As they drift in through the gate, the man of the Dazio, the town customs, watches them, asks them questions if they carry bundles, prods the pack on the ass, and when a load of brush-wood rolls up, keeps it halted while he pierces the load with a long steel rod, carefully thrusting to see if he can feel hidden barrels of wine or demijohns of oil, bales of oranges or any other food-stuffs. Because all food-stuffs that come into an Italian town—other things too, besides comestibles—must pay a duty, in some instances a heavy one.

Probably in etruscan days the peasants came in very much the same, at evening, to the town. The Etruscans were instinctively citizens. Even the peasants dwelt within walls. And in those days, no doubt the peasants were serfs very much as they are today in Italy, working the land for no wages, but for a portion of the produce: and working the land intensely, with that careful, almost passionate attention the Italian still gives to the soil: and living in the city, or village, but having straw huts out in the fields, for summer.

But in those days, on a fine evening like this, the men would come in naked, darkly ruddy-coloured from the sun and wind, with strong, insouciant bodies: and the women would drift in, wearing the loose, becoming smock of white or blue linen: and somebody, surely, would be playing on the pipes, and somebody, surely, would be singing, because the Etruscans had a passion for music, and an inner carelessness the modern Italians have lost. The peasants would enter the clear, clean, sacred space inside the gates, and salute the gay-coloured little temple as they passed along the street that rose uphill towards the arx, between rows of low houses with gay-coloured fronts, painted, or hung with bright terra cottas. One can almost hear them still, calling, shouting, piping, singing, driving in the mixed flocks of sheep and goats, that go so silently, and leading the slow, white, ghost-like oxen with the yokes still on their necks.

And surely, in those days, young nobles would come splashing in on horseback, riding with naked limbs on an almost naked horse, carrying probably a spear, and cantering ostentatiously through the throng of red-brown, full-limbed, smooth-skinned peasants. A
5 Lucumo, even, sitting very noble in his chariot driven by an erect charioteer, might be driving in at sundown, halting before the temple, to perform the brief ritual of entry into the city. And the crowding populace would wait; for the Lucumo of the old days, glowing ruddy in flesh, his beard stiffly trimmed, in the oriental
10 style,* the torque of gold round his neck, and the rich mantle bordered with scarlet falling in full folds, leaving the breast bare, he was divine, sitting on the chair of his chariot in the stillness of power. And the people drew strength even from looking at him.

The chariot drew forward a little from the temple; the Lucumo,
15 sitting on his chair in his chariot, would drop his mantle from his shoulders and wait, seated with bare breast and shoulders. Then the peasants would shrink back in fear. And perhaps some citizen in a white tunic would lift up his arms in the salute, and come forward to state some difficulty or ask for justice. And the Lucumo, seated silent
20 within another world of power, disciplined to his own responsibility of knowledge and inner wisdom, listened till all was said. Then a few words—and the chariot of gilt bronze swirls off up the hill to the house of the chief, the citizens drift on to their houses, the music sounds in the dark streets, torches flicker, the whole place is eating,
25 feasting, and as far as possible, having a gay time.

It is different now. The drab peasants, muffled in ugly clothing, straggle in across the waste bit of space, and trail home songless and meaningless. We have lost the art of living, and in the most important science of all, the science of daily life, the science of behaviour, we
30 are complete ignoramuses. We have psychology instead. Today, in Italy, in the hot Italian summer, if a navvy working in the street takes off his shirt to work with free, naked torso, a policeman rushes to him and commands him insultingly into his shirt again. One would think the human being was such a foul indecency altogether, that life was
35 only feasible when the indecent thing was as far as possible blotted out. The very exposure of female arms and legs in the street is only done as an insult to the whole human body. "Look at that! it doesn't matter!"

Neither does it!—But then, why did the torso of the workman
40 matter?

At the hotel, in the dark emptiness of the place, there are three
Japanese staying: little yellow men. They have come to inspect the
salt works down on the coast below Tarquinia, so we are told, and
they have a government permit. The salt works, the extracting of salt
from the pools shut off from the low sea, are sort of prisons, worked 5
by convict labour. One wonders why Japanese men should want to
inspect such places, officially. But we are told that these salt works
are "very important."

Albertino is having a very good time with the three Japanese, and
seems to be very deep in their confidence, bending over their table, 10
his young brown head among the three black ones, absorbed and on
the *qui vive*. He rushes off for their food—then rushes to us to see
what we want to eat.

"What is there?"

"Er—c'è—"* he always begins with wonderful deliberation, as if 15
there was a menu fit for the Tzar. Then he breaks off, suddenly,
says: "I'll ask the mamma!"—darts away—returns, and says exactly
what we knew he'd say—in a bright voice, as if announcing the New
Jerusalem.—"There are eggs—er—and beefsteak—er—and there
are some little potatoes—" We know the eggs and beefsteak well! 20
However, I decide to have beefsteak once more, with the little
potatoes—left over by good fortune from lunch—fried. Off darts
Albertino—only to dart back and announce that the potatoes and
beefsteak are finished (by the Chinese, he whispers)—but there are
frogs. There are what? *Le rane*, the frogs!—What sort of frogs?—I'll 25
show you!—Off he darts again, returns with a plate containing eight
or nine pairs of frogs' naked hind-legs. B. looks the other way, and I
accept frogs—they look quite good. In the joy of getting the frogs
safely to port, Albertino skips, and darts off: to return in a moment
with a bottle of beer, and whisper to us all the information about the 30
Chinese, as he calls them.—They can't speak a word of Italian.
When they want a word, they take the little book, French and Italian.
Bread?—eh? They want bread. Er!—Albertino gives little grunts, like
commas and semi-colons, which I write as *er*!—Bread they want,
eh?—er!—they take the little book,—here he takes an imaginary 35
little book, lays it on the table-cloth, wets his finger and turns over
the imaginary leaves—*bread*!—er!—p—you look under 'p'—er!—
ecco! pane!—pane!—si capisce!—bread! they want bread. Then
wine! er! take the little book—(he turns over imaginary little leaves
with fervour)—er! here you are, *vino*!*—*pane, e vino*! So they do! 40

Every word! They looked out *name*! Er! Name! You! Er! I tell him, *Albertino*!—And so the boy continues, till I ask what about le rane? Ah! *Er*! *Le rane*!—Off he darts, and swirls back with a plate of fried frogs' legs, in pairs.

5   He is an amusing and vivacious boy, yet underneath, a bit sad and wistful, with all his responsibility. The following day he darted to show us a book of views of Venice, left behind by the Chinese, as he persists in calling them, and asks if I want it. I don't. Then he shows us two Japanese postage-stamps, and the address of one of the 10 Japanese gentlemen, written on a bit of paper. The Japanese gentleman and Albertino are to exchange picture postcards. I insist that the Japanese are not Chinese.—Er! says Albertino. But the Japanese are also Chinese!—I insist they are not, that they live in a different country. He darts off, and returns with a school atlas.—Er! 15 China is in Asia! Asia! Asia!—he turns the leaves. He is really an intelligent boy, and ought to be going to school instead of running an hotel at the tender age of fourteen.

The guide to the tombs, having had to keep watch at the museum all night, wants to get a sleep after dawn, so we are not to start till ten. 20 The town is already empty, the people gone out to the fields. A few men stand about with nothing doing. The city gates are wide open. At night they are closed, so that the Dazio man can sleep: and you can neither get in nor out of the town. We drink still another coffee—Albertino's morning dose was a very poor show.

25   Then we see the guide, talking to a pale young fellow in old corduroy velveteen knee-breeches and an old hat and thick boots: most obviously German. We go over, make proper salutes, nod to the German boy, who looks as if he'd had vinegar for breakfast—and set off. This morning we are going out a couple of miles, to the furthest 30 end of the necropolis. We have still a dozen tombs to look at. In all, there are either twenty-five or twenty-seven painted tombs one can visit.

This morning there is a stiff breeze from the south-west. But it is blowing fresh and clear, not behaving in the ugly way the libeccio can 35 behave. We march briskly along the high-way, the old dog trundling behind. He loves spending a morning among the tombs. The sea gives off a certain clearness, that makes the atmosphere doubly brilliant and exhilarating, as if we were on a mountain top. The omnibus rolls by, from Viterbo. In the fields the peasants are 40 working, and the guide occasionally greets the women, who give him a sally back again. The young German tramps firmly on: but his spirit is not as firm as his tread. One doesn't know what to say to him, he vouchsafes nothing, seems as if he didn't want to be spoken to, and yet is probably offended that we don't talk to him. The guide chatters to him in unfailing cheerfulness, in Italian: but after a while, 5 drops back with evident relief to the milder company of B., leaving me to the young German, who has certainly swallowed vinegar some time or other.

But I feel with him as with most of the young people of today: he has been sinned against more than he sins. The vinegar was given 10 him to drink.* Breaking reluctantly into German, since Italian seems foolish, and he won't come out in English, I find, within the first half mile, that he is twenty-three (he looks nineteen), has finished his university course, is going to be an archaeologist, is travelling doing archaeology, has been in Sicily and Tunis, whence he has just 15 returned; didn't think much of either place—*mehr Schrei wie Wert*—he jerks out, speaking as if he were throwing his words away like a cigarette-end he was sick of—; doesn't think much of any place; doesn't think much of the Etruscans—*nicht viel Wert*;* doesn't, apparently, think much of me; knows a professor or two whom I have 20 met; knows the tombs of Tarquinia very well, having been here, and stayed here, twice before; doesn't think much of them; is going to Greece; doesn't expect to think much of it; is staying in the other hotel, not Gentile's, because it is still cheaper: is probably staying a fortnight, going to photograph all the tombs, with a big photographic 25 apparatus— has the government authority, like the Japs—apparently has very little money indeed, marvellously doing everything on nothing—expects to be a famous professor in a science he doesn't think much of—and I wonder if he always has enough to eat.

He certainly is a fretful and peevish, even if in some ways silent 30 and stoical young man. *Nicht viel Wert!—not much worth—doesn't amount to anything*—*seems to be his favourite phrase, as it is the favourite phrase of almost all young people today. Nothing amounts to anything, for the young.

Well, I feel it's not my fault, and try to bear up. But though it is bad 35 enough to have been of the war generation, it must be worse to have grown up just after the war. One can't blame the young, that they don't find that anything amounts to anything. The war cancelled most meanings for them.

And my young man is not really so bad: he would even rather like 40 to be *made* to believe in something. There is a yearning pathos in him somewhere.

We have passed the modern cemetery, with its white marble head-stones, and the arches of the mediaeval aqueduct mysteriously
5 spanning a dip, and left the highroad, following a path along the long hill-crest, through the green wheat that flutters and ripples in the sea-wind like fine feathers, in the wonderful brilliance of morning. Here and there are tassels of mauve anemones, bits of verbena, many daisies, tufts of camomiles. On a rocky mound which was once a
10 tumulus, the asphodels have the advantage, and send up their spikes on the bright, fresh air, like soldiers clustered on the mount. And we go on along this vivid green headland of wheat, which still is rough and uneven, because it was once all tumuli, with our faces to the breeze, the sea-brightness filling the air with exhilaration, and all the
15 country still and silent, and we talk German in the wary way of two dogs sniffing at one another.

Till suddenly we turn off to an almost hidden tomb—the German boy knows the way perfectly. The guide hurries up and lights the acetylene lamp, the dog slowly finds himself a place out of the wind,
20 and flings himself down: and we sink slowly again into the etruscan world, out of the present world, as we descend underground.

One of the most famous tombs at this far-off end of the necropolis is the Tomb of the Bulls. It contains what the guide calls: *un po' di pornografico!*—but a very little. The German boy shrugs his
25 shoulders as usual: but he informs me that this is one of the oldest tombs of all, and I believe him, for it looks so to me.

It is a little wider than some tombs, the roof has not much pitch, there is a stone bed for sarcophagi along the side walls, and in the end wall are two doorways, cut out of the rock of the end and opening
30 into a second chamber, which seems darker and more dismal. The German boy says this second chamber was cut out later, from the first one. It has no paintings of any importance.

We return to the first chamber, the old one. It is called the Tomb of the Bulls from the two bulls above the doorways of the end wall,
35 one a man-faced bull charging at the "po' di pornografico," the other bull lying down serenely and looking with mysterious eyes into the room, his back turned calmly to the second bit of a picture which the guide says is not "pornografico,"—"because it is a woman." The young German smiles with his sour-water expression.
40 Everything in this tomb suggests the old east: Cyprus,* or the

Hittites, or the culture of Minos of Crete. Between the doorways of the end wall is a charming painting of a naked horseman with a spear, on a naked horse, moving towards a charming little palm-tree and a well-head or fountain head, on which repose two sculptured, black-faced beasts, lions with queer black faces. From the mouth of the one near the palm-tree water pours down into a sort of altar-bowl, while on the far side a warrior advances, wearing a bronze helmet and shin-greaves, and apparently menacing the horseman with a sword which he brandishes in his left hand, as he steps up on to the base of the well-head. Both warrior and horseman wear the long, pointed boots of the east:* and the palm-tree is not very Italian.

This picture has a curious charm, and is evidently symbolical. I said to the German: What do you think it means?—Ach, nothing! The man on the horse has come to the drinking trough to water his horse: no more!—And the man with the sword?—Oh, he is perhaps his enemy.—And the black-faced lions?—Ach, nothing! Decorations of the fountain.— Below the picture are trees on which hang a garland and a neck-band. The border pattern, instead of the egg and dart, has the sign of Venus, so-called, between the darts: a ball surmounted by a little cross.—And that, is that a symbol?—I asked the German.—Here no! he replied abruptly.— Merely a decoration!—Which perhaps is true. But that the etruscan artist had no more idea of its being a symbol, than an English house-decorator today would have, we cannot believe.

I gave up for the moment. Above the picture is a sentence lightly written, almost scribbled, in etruscan.—Can you read it? I said to the German boy. He read it off quickly—myself, I should have had to go letter by letter.—Do you know what it means? I asked him. He shrugged his shoulders. Nobody knows.

In the shallow angle of the roof the heraldic beasts are curious. The squat centre-piece, the so-called altar, has four rams' heads at the corners. On the right a pale-bodied man with a dark face is galloping up with loose rein, on a black horse, followed by a galloping bull. On the left is a bigger figure, a queer galloping lion with his tongue out. But from the lion's shoulders, instead of wings, rises the second neck of a dark-faced, bearded goat: so that the complex animal has a second, backward-leaning neck and head, of a goat, as well as the first maned neck and menacing head, of a lion. The tail of the lion ends in a serpent's head. So that this is the proper

Chimaera.*—And galloping after the end of the lion's tail comes a winged female sphinx.

What is the meaning of this lion with the second head and neck?—I asked the German. He shrugged his shoulders, and said:

5 Nothing!—It meant nothing to him, because nothing, except the A. B. C. of facts, means anything to him. He is a scientist, and when he doesn't want a thing to have a meaning, it is ipso facto meaningless.

But the lion with the goat's head springing backwards from its shoulders must mean something, because there it is, very vivid, in

10 the famous bronze Chimaera of Arezzo, which is in the Florence museum, and which Benvenuto Cellini restored, and which is one of the most fascinating bronzes in the world. There, the bearded goat's head springs twisting backwards from the lion's shoulders, while the right horn of the goat is seized in the mouth of the serpent which is

15 the tail of the lion, whipped forward over his back.

Though this is the correct Chimaera, with the wounds of Bellerophon in hip and neck, still it is not merely a big toy. It has, and was intended to have, an exact esoteric meaning. In fact, the Greek myths are only gross representations of certain very clear and very ancient

20 esoteric conceptions, that are much older than the myths: or the Greeks. Myths, and personal gods are only the decadence of a previous cosmic religion.

The strange potency and beauty of these etruscan things arises, it seems to me, from the profundity of the symbolic meaning the artist

25 was more or less aware of. The etruscan religion, surely, was never anthropomorphic: that is, whatever gods it contained were not *beings*, but symbols of elemental powers, just symbols: as was the case earlier in Egypt. The undivided Godhead, if we can call it such, was symbolised by the mundum, the plasm-cell with its nucleus: that

30 which is the very beginning; instead of, as with us, a *personal* god, a person being the very end of all creation or evolution. So it is all the way through: the etruscan religion is concerned with all those physical and creative powers and forces which go to the building up and the destroying of the soul: the soul, the personality, being that

35 which gradually is produced out of chaos, like a flower, only to disappear again into chaos, or the underworld.—We, on the contrary, say: In the beginning was the Word!—and deny the physical universe true existence. We exist only in the Word, which is beaten out thin to cover, gild, and hide all things.

40 The human being, to the Etruscan, was a bull or ram, a lion or a

deer, according to his different aspects and potencies. The human being had in his veins the blood of the wings of birds and the venom of serpents. All things emerged from the blood-stream, and the blood-relation, however complex and contradictory it became, was never interrupted or forgotten. There were different currents in the blood stream, and some always clashed: bird and serpent, lion and deer, leopard and lamb. Yet the very clash was a form of unison, as we see in the lion which also has a goat's head.

But the young German will have nothing of this. He is a modern, and the obvious alone can have true existence for him. A lion with a goat's head as well as its own head is unthinkable. That which is unthinkable is non-existent, is nothing. So, all the etruscan symbols are to him non-existent and mere crude incapacity to think. He wastes not a thought on them. They are spawn of mental impotence, hence negligible.

But perhaps also he doesn't want to give himself away, or divulge any secret that is going to make him a famous archaeologist later on. Though I don't think that was it. He was very nice, showing me details, with his flashlight, that I should have overlooked. The white horse, for example, has had its drawing most plainly altered. You can see the old outline of the horse's back legs and breast, and of the foot of the rider, and you can see how considerably the artist changed the drawing, sometimes more than once. He seems to have drawn the whole thing complete, each time, then changed the position, changed the direction, to please his feeling. And as there was no india-rubber to rub out the first attempts, there they are, from at least six hundred years before Christ: the delicate mistakes of an Etruscan who had the instinct of a pure artist in him, as well as the blithe insouciance which makes him leave his alterations for anyone to spy out, if they want to.

The etruscan artists either drew with the brush or scratched, perhaps, with a nail, the whole outline of their figures on the soft stucco, and then applied their colour *al fresco*. So they had to work quickly. Some of the paintings seemed to me tempera, and in one tomb, I think the Francesco Giustiniani,* the painting seemed to be done on the naked, creamy rock. In that case, the blue colour of the man's scarf is marvellously vivid.

The subtlety of etruscan painting, as of Chinese and Hindu, lies in the wonderfully suggestive *edge* of the figures. It is not outlined. It is not what we call "drawing." It is the flowing contour where the body

suddenly leaves off, upon the atmosphere. The etruscan artist seems to have seen living things surging from their own centre to their own surface. And the curving and contour of the silhouette-edge suggests the whole movement of the modelling within. There is actually no
5   modelling. The figures are painted in the flat. Yet they seem of a full, almost turgid muscularity. It is only when we come to the late Tomb of Typhon* that we have the figure *modelled*, Pompeian style, with light and shade.

It must have been a wonderful world, that old world where
10   everything appeared alive and shining in the dusk of contact with all things, not merely as an isolated individual thing played upon by daylight; where each thing had a clear outline, visually, but in its very clarity was related emotionally or vitally to strange other things, one thing springing from another, things mentally contradictory fusing
15   together emotionally, so that a lion could be at the same moment also a goat, and not a goat. In those days, a man riding on a red horse was not just Jack Smith on his brown nag; it was a suave-skinned creature, with death or life in its face, surging along on a surge of animal power that burned with travel, with the passionate movement
20   of the blood, and which was swirling along on a mysterious course, to some unknown goal, swirling with a weight of its own. Then also, a bull was not merely a stud animal worth so much, due to go to the butcher in a little while. It was a vast wonder-beast, a well-head of the great, furnace-like passion that makes the worlds roll and the sun
25   surge up, and makes a man surge with procreative force: the bull, the herd-lord, the father of calves and heifers, of cows: the father of milk: he who has the horns of power on his forehead, symbolising the warlike aspect of the horn of fertility;* the bellowing master of force, jealous, horned, charging against opposition. The goat was in the
30   same line, father of milk, but instead of huge force he had cunning, the cunning *consciousness* and self-consciousness, of the jealous, hard-headed father of procreation. Whereas the lion was most terrible, yellow and roaring with a blood-drinking energy, again like the sun, but the sun asserting himself in drinking up the life of the
35   earth. For the sun can warm the worlds, like a yellow hen sitting on her eggs. Or the sun can lick up the life of the world with a hot tongue. The goat says: let me breed forever, till the world is one reeking goat. But then the lion roars from the other blood-stream, which is also in man, and he lifts his paw to strike, in the passion of
40   the other wisdom.

So all creatures are potential in their own way, a myriad manifold consciousness storming with contradictions and oppositions that are eternal, beyond all mental reconciliation. We can only know the living world symbolically. Yet every consciousness, the rage of the lion and the venom of the snake, *is*, and therefore is divine. All emerges out of the unbroken circle with its nucleus, the germ, the One, the God, if you like to call it so. And man, with his soul and his personality, emerges in eternal connection with all the rest. The blood-stream is one, and unbroken, yet storming with oppositions and contradictions.

The ancients saw, consciously, as children now see unconsciously: the everlasting *wonder* in things. In the ancient world, the three compelling emotions must have been emotions of wonder, fear, and admiration: admiration in the Latin sense* of the word, as well as our sense; and fear in its largest meaning, including repulsion, dread, and hate: then arose the last, individual emotion of pride. Love is only a subsidiary factor in wonder and admiration.

But it was by seeing all things alert in the throb of inter-related passional significance that the ancients kept the wonder and the delight in life, as well as the dread and the repugnance. They were like children: but they had the force, the power, and the sensual *knowledge* of true adults. They had a world of valuable knowledge, which is utterly lost to us. Where they were truly adult, we are children; and vice versa.

Even the two bits of "pornografico" in the Tomb of the Bulls are not two little dirty drawings. Far from it. The German boy felt this, as we did. The drawings have the same naïve wonder in them, as the rest, the same archaic adult innocence of complete acceptance, the same seeing things through the eyes of the bull and the eyes of the panther, and the conclusion according to the bull and the panther. The two little pictures have a symbolic meaning, quite distinct from a *moral* meaning—or an immoral. They are set in heraldic opposition, in relation to the man-faced bull; not, this time, to the panther. There is the peace of the bull, or the charge of the man-faced bull with lowered horns. It is not judgement. It is the sway of passional action and reaction: the action and reaction of the father of milk and procreation.

There are beautiful tombs, in this far off wheat-covered hill. The Tomb of the Augurs* is very impressive. On the end wall is painted a doorway-to-a-tomb, and on either side of it is a man making what is

probably the mourning gesture, strange and momentous, one hand
to the brow. The two men are mourning at the door of the tomb.

No! says the German. The painted door does not represent the
door to the tomb, with mourners on either side. It is merely the
5 painted door which later they intended to cut out, to make a second
chamber to the tomb. And the men are not mourning—

Then what are they doing?

Shrug!

In the triangle above the painted door two lions, a white-faced one
10 and a dark-faced, have seized a goat or an antelope: the dark-faced
lion turns over and bites the side of the goat's neck, the white-faced
bites the haunch. Here we have again the two heraldic beasts: but
instead of their roaring at the altar or the tree, they are biting the
goat, the father of milk-giving life, in throat and hip.

15 On the side walls are very fine frescoes of nude wrestlers, and then
of a scene which has started a lot of talk about etruscan cruelty. A
man with his head in a sack, wearing only a skin girdle, is being bitten
in the thigh by a fierce dog which is held, by another man, on a string
attached to what is apparently a wooden leash, this wooden handle
20 being fastened to the dog's collar. The man who holds the string
wears a peculiar high conical hat, and he stands, big limbed and
excited, striding behind the man with his head in the sack. This
victim is by now getting entangled in the string, the long, long cord
which holds the dog; but with his left hand he seems to be getting
25 hold of the cord to drag the dog off from his thigh, while in his right
hand he holds a huge club, with which to strike the dog when he can
get it into striking range.

This picture is supposed to reveal the barbarously cruel sports of
the Etruscans. But since the tomb contains an augur with his curved
30 sceptre, tensely lifting his hand to the dark bird that flies by: and the
wrestlers are wrestling over a curious pile of three great bowls; and
on the other side of the tomb, the man in the conical pointed hat, he
who holds the string in the first picture, is now dancing with a
peculiar delight, as if rejoicing in victory or liberation: we must
35 surely consider this picture as symbolic, along with all the rest: the
fight of the blind-folded man with some raging attacking element. If
it were sport, there would be onlookers, as there are at the sports in
the Tomb of the Chariots;* and here there are none.

However, the scenes portrayed in the tomb are all so *real*, that it
40 seems they must have taken place in actual life. Perhaps there was

some form of test or trial which gave a man a great club, tied his head
in a sack, and left him to fight a fierce dog which attacked him, but
which was held on a string, and which even had a wooden grip-
handle attached to its collar, by which the man might seize it and
hold it firm, while he knocked it on the head. The man in the sack   5
has very good chances against the dog. And even granted the thing
was done for sport, and not as some sort of trial or test, the cruelty is
not excessive, for the man has a very good chance of knocking the
dog on the head quite early. Compared with Roman gladiatorial
shows, this is almost "fair play."—But it must be more than sport.   10
The dancing of the man who held the string is too splendid. And the
tomb is, somehow, too intense, too meaningful. And the dog—or
wolf or lion—that bites the thigh of the man is too old a symbol. We
have it very plainly on the top of the Sarcophagus of the painted
Amazons,* in the Florence museum. This sarcophagus comes from   15
Tarquinia—and the end of the lid has a carved naked man, with legs
apart, a dog on each side biting him in the thigh. They are the dogs of
disease and death, biting at the great arteries of the thigh, where the
elementary life surges in a man.—The motive is common in ancient
symbolism. And the esoteric idea of malevolent influences attacking   20
the great arteries of the thighs was turned by the Greeks into the
myth of Actaeon and his dogs.*

Another very fine tomb is the Tomb of the Baron,* with its frieze of
single figures, dark on a light background, going around the walls.
There are horses and men, all in dark silhouette, and very fasci-   25
nating in drawing. These archaic horses are so perfectly satisfying *as*
horses: so far more horse-like, to the soul, than those of Rosa
Bonheur or Rubens or even Velasquez,* though he comes nearer to
these; so that one asks oneself, what, after all, is the horsiness of a
horse? What is it that man sees, when he looks at a horse? what is it,   30
that will never be put into words? For a man who sees sees not as a
camera does when it takes a snapshot, not even as a cinema-camera,
taking its succession of instantaneous snaps; but in a curious rolling
flood of vision, in which the image itself seethes and rolls; and only
the mind *picks out* certain factors which shall *represent* the image seen.   35
We have made up our minds to see things *as they are*: which is camera
vision. But the camera can neither feel the heat of the horse, his
strange body; nor smell his horsiness; nor hear him neigh. Whereas
the eye, seeing him, wakes all our other sensual experience of him:
not to speak of our terror of his frenzy, and admiration of his   40

strength. The eye really "sees" all this. It is the complete vision of a
child, full and potent. But this potent vision in us is maimed and
pruned as we grow up, till as adults we see only one dreary bit of the
horse, his static external form.*

5   We go from tomb to tomb, down into the dark, up again into the
wind and brilliance; and the day rolls by. But we are moving, tomb by
tomb, gradually nearer the city. The new cemetery draws near. We
have passed the aqueduct, which crosses the dip, then takes an
underground channel towards the town. Near the cemetery we
10   descend into a big tomb,* the biggest we have yet seen—a great
under-ground cavern with great wide beds for sarcophagi and biers,
and in the centre a massive square pillar or shaft on which is painted
a Typhon—the sea-man with coiled snake legs, and wings behind
his arms, his hands holding up the roof; two Typhons, another on the
15   opposite face of the pillar, almost identical with the first.

In this place, almost at once, the etruscan charm seems to vanish.
The tomb is big, crude, somehow ugly, like a cavern. The Typhon,
with his reddish flesh and light-and-shade modelling, is clever, and
might be modern, done for effect. He is rather Pompeian*—and a
20   little like Blake. But he is done from quite a new consciousness,
external; the old inwardness has gone. Dennis who saw him eighty
years ago thinks him far more marvellous than the archaic dancers.*
But we do not.

There are some curly-wig dolphins sporting over a curly border
25   which, but for experience, we should not know was the sea. And
there is a border of "roses," really the sacred symbol of the "one"
with its central germ, here for the first time vulgarly used. There is
also a fragment of a procession to Hades, which must have been
rather fine in the Graeco-Roman style. But the true archaic charm is
30   utterly gone. The dancing etruscan spirit is dead.

This is one of the very latest tombs: said to be of the second
century B.C. when the Romans had long been masters of Tarquinia.
Veii,* the first great etruscan city to be captured by Rome, was taken
about 388 B.C. and completely destroyed. From then on, Etruria
35   gradually weakened and sank, till the peace of 280 B.C., when we
may say the military conquest of Etruria was complete.

So that the tombs suddenly change. Those supposed to be of the V
century, like the Tomb of the Baron, with the frieze of horses and
men, or the Tomb of the Leopards, are still perfectly etruscan, no
40   matter what touch of the Orient they may have, and perfectly

charming. Then suddenly we come to the Tomb of Orcus, or Hell,* which is given the fourth century as a date, and here the whole thing utterly changes. You get a great, gloomy, clumsy, rambling sort of underworld, damp and horrid, with large but much damaged pictures on the walls.

These paintings, though they are interesting in their way, and have scribbled etruscan inscriptions, have suddenly lost all etruscan charm. They still have a bit of etruscan freedom, but on the whole they are Graeco-Roman, half suggesting Pompei, half suggesting Roman things. They are more free* than the paintings of the little old tombs; at the same time, all the motion is gone; the figures are stuck there without any vital flow between them. There is no touch.

Instead of the wonderful old silhouette forms, we have modern "drawing," often quite good. But to me it is an intense disappointment.

When the Roman took the power from the hands of the etruscan Lucumones—in the fourth century B.C.—and made them merely Roman magistrates, at the best, the mystery of Etruria died almost at once. In the ancient world of king-gods, governing according to a religious conception, the deposition of the chiefs and the leading priests leaves the country at once voiceless and mindless. So it was in Egypt and Babylonia, in Assyria, in the Aztec and Maya* lordships of America. The people are governed by the flower of the race. Pluck the flower, and the race is helpless.

The Etruscans were not destroyed. But they lost their being. They had lived, ultimately, by the *subjective* control of the great natural powers. Their subjective power fell before the objective power of the Romans. And almost at once, the true race-consciousness finished. The etruscan knowledge became mere superstition. The etruscan princes became fat and inert Romans. The etruscan people became expressionless and meaningless. It happened amazingly quickly, in the third and second centuries B.C.

Yet the etruscan *blood* continued to beat. And Giotto and the early sculptors* seem to have been a flowering again of the etruscan blood, which is always putting forth a flower, and always being trodden down again by some superior "force." It is a struggle between the endless patience of life, and the endless triumph of force.

There is one other huge late tomb—the Tomb of the Shields*— said to be of the third century. It contains many fragmentary paintings. There is a banqueting scene, with a man on the banquet-

ing bench taking the egg from the woman, and she is touching his
shoulder. But they might as well be two chairs from a "suite." There
is nothing between them. And they have those "important" sorts of
faces—all on the outside, nothing inside—that are so boring. Yet
5 they are interesting. They might almost be done today, by an
ultra-modern artist bent on being absolutely child-like and naïve and
archaic. But after the real archaic paintings, these are empty. The air
is empty. The egg is still held up. But it means no more to those men
and women than the chocolate Easter egg does to us. It has gone
10 cold.

In the Tomb of Orcus begins that representation of the grisly
underworld, hell and its horrors, which surely was reflected on to the
Etruscans from the grisly Romans. The lovely little tombs of just one
small chamber, or perhaps two chambers, of the earlier centuries
15 give way to these great sinister caverns underground, and hell is fitly
introduced.

The old religion of the profound attempt of man to harmonise
himself with nature, and hold his own and come to flower in the great
seething of life, changed with the Greeks and Romans into a desire
20 to resist nature, to produce a mental cunning and a mechanical force
that would outwit Nature and chain her down completely, completely, till at last there should be nothing free in nature at all, all
should be controlled, domesticated, put to man's meaner uses.
Curiously enough, with the idea of the triumph over nature arose the
25 idea of a gloomy Hades, a hell and purgatory. To the peoples of
the great natural religions, the afterlife was a continuing of the
wonder-journey of life. To the peoples of the Idea, the afterlife is
hell, or purgatory, or nothingness, and paradise is an inadequate
fiction.

30 But naturally enough, historians seized on these essentially non-
etruscan evidences in the etruscan late tombs, to build up a picture of
a gloomy, hellish, serpent-writhing, vicious etruscan people who
were quite rightly stamped out by the noble Romans. This myth is
still not dead. Men *never* want to believe the evidence of their senses.
35 They would far rather go on elaborating some mean little lie they
have read in some "classical" author. The whole science of history
seems to be the picking of old fables and old lies into fine threads,
and weaving them up again. Theopompus collected some scanda-
lous tales, and that is quite enough for historians. It is written down,
40 so that's enough. The evidence of fifty million gay little tombs

wouldn't weigh a straw. In the beginning was the Word, indeed! Even the word of a Theopompus is enough.*

Perhaps the favourite painting for representing the beauties of the etruscan tombs is the well-known head of a woman, seen in profile with wheat-ears for a head-wreath—or fillet. This head comes from the Tomb of Orcus, and is chosen because it is far more Greek-Roman than it is etruscan. As a matter of fact, it is rather stupid and self-conscious—and modern. But it belongs to the classic convention, and men can only see according to a convention. We haven't exactly plucked our eyes out, but we've plucked out three-fourths of their vision.

After the Tomb of the Typhon, one has had enough. There is nothing really etruscan left. It is better to abandon the necropolis altogether: and to remember that almost everything we know of the Etruscans from classic authors is comparable to the paintings in the late tombs. It refers to the fallen, Romanised Etruscans of the decadence.

———

It is very pleasant to go down from the hill on which the present Tarquinia stands, down into the valley and up to the opposite hill, on which the etruscan Tarquinii surely stood. There are many flowers, the blue grape-hyacinth and the white, the mauve tassel anemone, and in a corner of a field of wheat, the big purple anemone, then a patch of the big, pale-pink anemone with the red, sore centre—the big-petalled sort. It is curious how the anemone varies. Only in this one place in Tarquinia have I found the whitey-pink kind, with the dark, sore-red centre. But probably that is just chance.

The town ends really with the wall. At the foot of the wall is wild hillside, and down the slope there is only one little farm, with another little house made of straw. The country is clean of houses. The peasants live in the city.

Probably in etruscan days it was much the same, but there must have been far more people on the land, and probably there were many little straw huts, little temporary houses, among the green corn: and fine roads, such as the Etruscans taught the Romans to build, went between the hills: and the high black walls, with towers, wound along the hill-crest.

The Etruscans, though they grew rich as traders and metal-workers, seem to have lived chiefly by the land. The intense culture of the land by the Italian peasant of today seems like the remains of the etruscan system. On the other hand, it was Roman, and not etruscan, to have large villas in the country, with the great compound or "factory" for the slaves, who were shut in at night, and in gangs taken out to labour during the day. The huge farms of Sicily and Lombardy and other parts of Italy must be a remains of this Roman system: the big "fattorie."* But one imagines the Etruscans had a different system: that the peasants were serfs rather than slaves: that they had their own small portions of land, which they worked to full pitch, from father to son, giving a portion of the produce to the masters, keeping a portion for themselves. So they were half-free, at least, and had a true life of their own, stimulated by the religious life of their masters.

The Romans changed it all. They did not like the country. In palmy days they built great villas, with barracks for slaves, out in the country. But even so, it was easier to get rich by commerce or conquest. So the Romans gradually abandoned the land, which fell into neglect and prepared the way for the Dark Ages.

The wind blows stiffer and stiffer from the south-west. There are no trees: but even the bushes bend away from it. And when we get to the crown of the long, lonely hill on which stood the etruscan Tarquinii, we are almost blown from our feet, and have to sit down behind a thicket of bushes, for a moment's shelter: to watch the great black-and-white cattle stepping slowly down to the drinking place, the young bulls curving and playing. All along the hill-top, the green wheat ruffles like soft hair. Away inland, the green land looks empty, save for a far off town perched on a hill-top, like a vision. On the next hill towards the sea, Tarquinia holds up her square towers, in vain.

And we are sitting on the high place, where was once the arx of Tarquinii. Somewhere here the augurs held up their curved staffs, and watched the birds moving across the quarters of the sky. We can do as much today. But of the city of Tarquinii I cannot find two stones left together. Only openness and loneliness.

One can go back up a different road, and in through another gate of the present town across there. We drop quickly down, in the fierce wind, down to calm. The road winds up slowly from the little valley, but we are in shelter from the wind. So, we pass the first wall, through the first mediaeval gateway. The road winds inside the wall, past the Dazio, but there are no houses. A bunch of men are excitedly playing *morra*,* and the shouts of the numbers come like

explosions, with wild excitement. The men glance at us appre-
hensively, but laugh as we laugh.

So we pass on through a second frowning gateway, inside the
second circle of walls. And still we are not in the town. There is still a
third wall, and a third massive gate. And then we are in the old part of 5
the town, where the graceful little palazzos of the Middle Ages are
turned into stables and barns, and into houses for poor peasants. In
front of the lower storey of one little old palace, now a blacksmith's
shop, the smith is shoeing a refractory mule, which kicks and
plunges, and brings loud shouts from the inevitable little group of 10
onlookers.

Queer and lonely and slummy the waste corners and narrow
streets stem, forlorn, as if belonging to another age. On a beautiful
stone balcony a bit of poor washing is drying. The houses seem dark
and furtive, people lurking like rats. And then again rises another 15
tall, sharp-edged tower, blank and blind. They have a queer effect on
a town, these sharp, rigid, blind, meaningless towers, soaring away
with their sharp edges into the sky, for no reason, beyond the
house-roofs; and from the far distance, when one sees the little city
from far-off, suggesting the factory chimneys of a modern town. 20

They are the towers which in the first place were built for retreat
and defense, when this coast was ravaged by sea-rovers, Norman
adventurers, or Barbary pirates* that were such a scourge to the
Mediterranean. Later, however, the mediaeval nobles built towers
just for pure swank, to see who should have the tallest, till a town like 25
Bologna must have bristled like a porcupine in a rage, or like
Pittsburgh with chimney-stacks*—but square ones. Then the law
forbade towers—and towers, after having scraped the heavens,
began to come down. There are some still, however, in Tarquinia,
where age overlaps age. 30

V.
VULCI

V.

Vulci[*]

Ancient Etruria consisted of a league, or loose religious confederacy of twelve cities, each city embracing some miles of country all around, so that we may say there were twelve states, twelve city states, the famous *dodecapolis* of the ancient world, the Latin *duodecim populi Etruriae*. Of these twelve city states, Tarquinii was supposed to be the oldest, and the chief. Caere is another city: and not far off, to the north, Volci.

Volci is now called Vulci—though there is no city, only a hunting-ground for treasure in etruscan tombs. The etruscan city fell into decay in the decline of the Roman empire, and either lapsed owing to the malaria which came to fill this region with death, or else was finally wiped out, as Ducati says, by the Saracens.[*] Anyhow there is no life there now.

I asked the German boy about the etruscan places along the coast: Vulci, Vetulonia, Populonia.[*] His answer was always the same: Nothing! Nothing! There is nothing there!—

However, we determined to look at Vulci. It lies only about a dozen miles north of Tarquinia. We took the train, one station only, to Montalto di Castro, and were rattled up to the little town on the hill, not far inland. The morning was still fairly early—and Saturday.[*] But the town, or village on the hill was very quiet and dead-alive. We got down from the bus in a sort of nowhere-seeming little piazza: the town had no centre of life. But there was a café, so in we went, asked for coffee, and where could we get a carriage to take us to Vulci.

The man in the little café was yellow and slow, with the slow smile of the peasants. He seemed to have no energy at all: and eyed us lethargically. Probably he had malaria—though the fevers were not troubling him at the time. But it had eaten into his life.

He said, did we want to go to the Bridge—the Ponte? I said yes, the Ponte della Badia:[*] because I knew that Volci was near to this famous old Bridge of the Monastery. I asked him if we could get a light cart to drive us out. He said it would be difficult. I said, then we

could walk: it was only five miles, eight kilometres.—Eight kilometres! he said, in the slow, laconic malarial fashion, looking at me
with a glint of ridicule in his black eyes.—It is at least twelve.

The book says eight! I insisted stoutly.—They always want to
5 make distances twice as long, if you are to hire a carriage. But he
watched me slowly, and shook his head. Twelve! he said.—Then we
must have a carriage, said I.—You wouldn't find your way anyhow,
said the man.—Is there a carriage?—He didn't know. There was
one, but it had gone off somewhere this morning, and wouldn't be
10 back till two or three in the afternoon. The usual story.

I insisted, was there no little cart, no barroccino, no carretto?* He
slowly shook his head. But I continued to insist, gazing at him
fixedly, as if a carriage *must* be produced. So at last he went out, to
look. He came back, after a time, shaking his head. Then he had a
15 colloquy with his wife. Then he went out again, and was gone ten
minutes.

A dusty little baker, a small man very full of energy, as little Italians
often are, came in and asked for a drink. He sat down a minute and
drank his drink, eyeing us from his floury face. Then he got up and
20 left the shop again. In a moment the café man returned, and said that
perhaps there was a carretto. I asked where it was. He said the man
was coming.

The drive to the Ponte was apparently two hours—the road being
dry. If we stayed two hours, then the trip would be six hours. We
25 should have to take a little food with us—there was nothing there.

A small-faced, weedy sort of youth appeared in the doorway: also
malaria! We could have the carretto.—For how much?—Seventy
Liras!—Too much! said I. Far too much! Fifty, or nothing. Take it
or leave it, fifty!—The youth in the doorway looked blank. The café
30 man, always with his faint little sardonic smile, told the youth to go
and ask. The youth went. We waited. Then the youth came back, to
say all right! So!—How long?—*Subito!*—*Subito!* means immediately,
but it is as well to be definite.—Ten minutes? said I.—Perhaps
twenty! said the youth.—Better say twenty! said the café man: who
35 was an honest man, really, and rather pleasant in his silent way.

We went out to buy a little food! and the café man went with us.
The shops in the place were just holes. We went to the baker. Outside
stood a cart being loaded with bread, by the youth and the small,
quicksilver baker. Inside the shop, we bought a long loaf, and a few
40 bits of sliced sausage, and asked for cheese. There was no cheese—

but they would get us some. We waited an infinite while. I said to the café man, who waited alongside, full of interest: Won't the carretto be ready?—He turned round and pointed to the tall, randy mare between the shafts of the bread-cart outside.—That's the horse that will take you. When the bread is delivered, they will hitch her into the carretto, and the youth will drive you.—There was nothing for it but patience, for the baker's mare and the baker's youth were our only hope. The cheese came at last. We wandered out to look for oranges. There was a woman selling them on a low bench beside the road, but B., who was getting impatient, didn't like the look of them. So we went across to a little hole of a shop—where another woman had oranges. They were tiny ones, and B. was rejecting them with impatient scorn. But the woman insisted they were sweet, sweet as apples, and full of juice.—We bought four: and I bought a finocchio* for a salad.—But she was right. The oranges were exquisite, when we came to eat them, and we wished we had ten.

On the whole, I think the people in Montalto are honest and rather attractive: but most of them slow and silent. It must be the malaria every time.

The café man asked if we would stay the night. We said, was there an inn? He said: oh yes, several! I asked where—and he pointed up the street. But, said I, what do you want with several hotels here?—For the agents who come to buy agricultural produce, he said. Montalto is the centre of a great agricultural industry, and many agents come, many!—However, I decided that if we could, we would leave in the evening. There was nothing in Montalto to keep us.

At last the carretto was ready: a roomy, two-wheeled gig hung rather low. We got in, behind the dark, mulberry mare, and the baker's youth, who certainly hadn't washed his face for some days, started us on the trip. He was in an agony of shyness, stupefied.

The town is left behind at once. The green land, with squares of leaden-dark olives planted in rows, slopes down to the railway line, which runs along the coast parallel with the ancient Via Aurelia.* Beyond the railway is the flatness of the coastal strip, and the whitish emptiness of the sea's edge. It gives a great sense of nothingness, the sea down there.

The mulberry mare, lean and sparse,* reaches out and makes a good pace. But very soon we leave the road and are on a wide, wide trail of pinkish clayey earth, made up entirely of ruts. In part, the

mud is still deep, water stands in the fathomless mud holes. But fortunately, for a week it hasn't rained, so the road is passable, most of the ruts are dry, and the wide trail, wide as a desert road which has no confines, is not difficult, only jolty. We run the risk of having our
5   necks jerked out of their sockets by the impatient long-striding mare.

The boy is getting over his shyness, now he is warmed up to driving, and proves outspoken and straightforward. I said to him: What a good thing the road is dry!—If it had been fifteen days ago, he said, you couldn't have passed.—But in the late afternoon, when
10 we were returning on the same road, and I said: In bad wet weather we should have to come through here on horseback!—he replied: Even with the carretto you can get through.—Always! said I. —Always! said he.

And that was how he was. Possibility or impossibility was just a
15 frame of mind with him.

We were on the maremma, that flat, wide plain of the coast that has been water-logged for centuries, and one of the most abandoned, wildest parts of Italy. Under the Etruscans, apparently, it was an intensely fertile plain. But the Etruscans seem to have been very
20 clever drainage-engineers, they drained the land so that it was a waving bed of wheat, with their methods of intensive peasant culture. Under the Romans, however, the elaborate system of canals and levels of water fell into decay, and gradually the streams threw their mud along the coast and choked themselves, then soaked into the
25 land and made marshes and vast stagnant shallow pools where the mosquitoes bred like fiends, millions hatching on a warm May day; and with the mosquitoes came the malaria, called the marsh fever in the old days. Already in late Roman times this evil had fallen on the etruscan plains and on the campagna of Rome. Then, apparently,
30 the land rose in level, the sea-strip was wider but even more hollow than before, the marshes became deadly, and human life departed or was destroyed, or lingered on here and there.

In etruscan days, no doubt, large tracts of this coast were covered with pine-forest, as are the slopes of the mountains that rise a few
35 miles inland, and stretches of the coast still, further north. The pleasant *pineta*, or open, sparse forest of umbrella pines once spread on and on, with tall arbutus and heather covering the earth from which the reddish trunks rose singly, as from an endless moor, and tufts of arbutus and broom making thickets. The pine-woods further
40 north are still delightful, so silent and bosky, with the umbrella roofs.

But the pine will not bear being soaked. So as the great pools and marshes spread, the trees of etruscan days fell for ever, and great treeless tracts appeared, covered with an almost impenetrable low jungle of bush and scrub and reeds, spreading for miles, and quite manless. The arbutus, that is always glossy green, and the myrtle, the mastic tree, heaths, broom, and other spiney, gummy, coarse moorland plants rose up in dense luxuriance, to have their tops bent and whipped off by the ever-whipping winds from the sea, so that there was a low, dark jungle of scrub, less than man-high, stretching in places from the mountains almost to the sea. And here the wild-boar roamed in herds, foxes and wolves hunted the rabbits, the hares, the roe-buck, the innumerable wild fowl, and flamingoes walked the sickly, stricken shores of the great pools, and the sea.

So the maremma country lay for centuries, with cleared tracts between, and districts a little elevated, and therefore rich in produce, but for the most part a wilderness, where the herdsmen pastured sheep, if possible, and the buffaloes roamed unherded. In 1828, however, the Grand-duke Leopold of Tuscany* signed the decree for the reclaiming of the maremma, and lately the Italian government has achieved splendid results, great tracts of farm-land added on to the country's resources, and new farms stuck up.

But still, there are large tracts of moorland. We bowled along the grassy ruts, towards the distant mountains, and first all was wheat; then it was moorland, with great, grey-headed carrion crows floating around in the bareness; then a little thicket of ilex-oak; then another patch of wheat; and then a desolate sort of farm-house, that somehow reminded one of America, a rather dismal farm on the naked prairie, all alone.

The youth told me he had been for two years *guardiano*, or herdsman, at this place. The large cattle were lingering around the naked house, within the wire enclosure. But there was a notice, that the place was shut off, because of foot-and-mouth disease. The driver saluted a dismal woman and two children, as he drove past.

We made a good pace. The driver, Luigi,* told me his father had been also a guardiano, a herdsman, in this district—his five sons following him. The youth would look round, into the distance, with that keen, far-off look of men who have always lived* wild and apart, and who are in their own country. He knew every sign. And he was so glad to get out again, out of Montalto.

The father, however, had died, a brother had married and lived in

the family house, and Luigi had gone to help the baker in Montalto.
But he was not happy: caged. He revived and became alert, once
more out in the maremma spaces. He had lived more or less alone all
his life—he was only eighteen—and loneliness, space, was precious
5 to him, as it is to a moorland bird.

The great hooded crows floated round, and many big meadow-
larks rose up from the moor. Save for this, everything to us was
silent. Luigi said that now the hunting season was closed: but still, if
he had a gun, he could take a shot at those hooded crows. It was
10 obvious he was accustomed to have a gun in his hand, when he was
out in the long, hot malarial days, mounted on a pony, watching the
herds of cattle roving on the maremma. Cattle do not take malaria.

I asked him about game. He said there was much, in the foot-hills
there. And he pointed away ahead, to where the mountains began to
15 rise, six or eight miles away. Now so much of the maremma itself is
drained and cleared, the game is in the hills. His father used to
accompany the hunters in winter: they still arrive in winter time, the
hunters in their hunting outfit, with dogs and a great deal of fuss and
paraphernalia, from Rome or from Florence. And still they catch the
20 wild boar, the fox, the capriolo: which I suppose means the roe-deer,
rather than the wild goat. But the boar is the *pièce de résistance*. You
may see his bristling carcase in the market-place in Florence, now
and again, in winter. But, like every other wild thing on earth, he is
becoming scarcer and scarcer. Soon, the only animals left will be
25 tame ones: man the tamest and most swarming. Adieu even to
maremma!

There! said the boy. There is the bridge of the monastery!—We
looked into the shallow hollow of green land, and could just see a
little, black sort of tower by some bushes, in the empty landscape.
30 There was a long, straight ditch or canal, and digging evidently going
on. It was the government irrigation works.

We left the road and went bowling over rough grass, by tracts of
poor-looking oats. Luigi said they would cut these oats for fodder.
There was a scrap of a herdsman's house, and new wire fences along
35 the embankment of the big irrigation canal. This was new to Luigi.
He turned the mare uphill again, towards the house, and asked an
urchin where he was to get through the wire fence. The urchin
explained—Luigi had it in a moment. He was intelligent as a wild
thing, out here in his own spaces.
40 Five years ago, he said, there was none of this!—and he pointed

around.—No canal, no fences, no oats, no wheat. It was all maremma, moorland, with no life save the hooded crows, the cattle, and the herdsmen. Now the cattle are all going—the herds are only remnants. And the ranch-houses are being abandoned.—He pointed away to a large house some miles off, on the nearest hill-foot.—There, there are no more cattle, no more herdsmen. The steam plough comes and ploughs the earth, the machinery sows and reaps the wheat and oats, the people of the maremma, instead of being more, are fewer. The wheat grows by machinery.—

We were on a sort of trail again, bowling down a slight incline towards a bushy hollow and a black old ruin with a tower. Soon we saw that in the hollow was a tree-filled ravine, quite deep. And over the ravine went a queer bridge, curving up like a rainbow, and narrow and steep and fortified-seeming. It soared over the ravine in one high curve, the stony path nipped in like a gutter between its broken walls, and charging straight at the black lava front of the ruin opposite, which once was a castle* of the frontier. The little river in the gully, the Fiora, formed the boundary between the Papal States and Tuscany, so the castle guarded the bridge.

We wanted to get down, but Luigi made us wait, while he ran ahead to negotiate. He came back, climbed in, and drove up between the walls of the bridge. It was just wide enough for the cart: just. The walls of the bridge seemed to touch us. It was like climbing up a sort of gutter. Far below, way down in a thicket of bushes, the river rushed—the Fiora, a mere torrent or rain-stream.

We drove over the bridge, and at the far end the lava wall of the monastery seemed to shut us back, the mare's nose almost touched it. The road, however, turned to the left under an arched gateway. Luigi edged the mare round cleverly. There was just room to get her round with the carretto, out of the mouth of the bridge and under the archway, scraping the wall of the castle.

So! We were through. We drove a few yards past the ruin, and got down on a grassy place over the ravine. It was a wonderfully romantic spot. The ancient bridge, built in the first place by the Etruscans of Volci, of blocks of black tufo, goes up in the air like a black bubble, so round and strange. The little river is in the bushy cleft, a hundred feet below. The bridge is in the sky, like a black bubble, most strange and lonely, with the poignancy of perfect things long forgotten. It has, of course, been restored in Roman and mediaeval days. But essentially it is etruscan, a beautiful etruscan movement.

Pressing on to it, on this side, is the black building of the castle, mostly in ruin, with grass growing from the tops of the walls and from the black tower. Like the bridge, it is built of blocks of reddish-black, spongy lava-stone, but its blocks are much squarer.

5   And all around is a peculiar emptiness. The castle is not entirely ruined. It is a sort of peasant farmstead. Luigi knows the people who live there. And across the stream, there are patches of oats, and two or three cattle feeding, and two children. But all on this side, towards the mountains, is heathy, waste moorland, over which the trail goes
10   towards the hills, and towards a great house among trees, which we had seen from the distance.

That is the Badia, or monastery, which gave the name to the bridge. It is no longer a monastery, but a great villa. It belonged, along with the land on this side of the stream, to Lucien Bonaparte,*
15   brother of Napoleon; here, he was Prince of Canino. After the death of Napoleon, the Prince of Canino still flourished in the great ugly villa, and was lord of this bit of the maremma.

In 1828, some oxen ploughing the land near the castle suddenly went through, and found themselves in an etruscan tomb containing
20   broken vases. This at once brought on excavations. It was the hey-day of the "Grecian urn." Lucien Bonaparte had no interest in vases, save in the price they fetched. He hired a boor of an overseer to superintend his excavations, giving orders that every painted fragment must be saved, but that coarse ware must be smashed, to
25   prevent cheapening the market. The work went rudely on. Vases and basketfuls of broken pieces were harvested, things that were "of no value" were destroyed. Dennis saw the work still going on, in 1845 or 1846, in the days of Lucien's widow. The overseer sat with his gun across his knees, the workmen dug rudely in. And when they brought
30   out pieces of old rough black etruscan pottery, they dashed them to smithereens on the ground. In vain Dennis asked for a piece of this old ware. He was rudely denied. Orders were, such stuff must be smashed.

But the bits of painted pottery were skilfully fitted together, by the
35   Princess' expert workmen, and she would sell for a thousand crowns some patera or cylix that had been a handful of potsherds. Tombs that had been rifled were filled in again. The work went ahead, all the neighbouring landowners were excavating. In two months, at his first start, Lucien Bonaparte had got some two thousand etruscan objects
40   out of tombs covering a few acres. The Etruscans had left fortunes to

the Bonapartes. And by 1847, it was estimated that some six thousand tombs had been opened. The great find was thousands of "Greek" vases, the "brides of quietness" only too much ravished.*

We ate our food, the mare cropping the grass. And I wondered, seeing youths on bicycles, four or five, come swooping down the trail across-stream, out of emptiness, dismount and climb the high curve of the bridge, then disappear into the castle. From the mountains a man came riding on an ass: a pleasant young man in corduroy-velveteens. He was riding without a saddle. He had a word or two with Luigi, in the low, secretive tones of the country, and went on towards the bridge. Then across, two men on mules came trotting down to the bridge: and a peasant drove in two bullocks, whose horns pricked the sky from the tall poise of the bridge.

The place seemed very populous, for so lonely a spot. And still, all the air was heavy with isolation, suspicion, guardedness. It was like being in the Middle Ages. I asked Luigi to go to the house for some wine. He said he didn't know if he could get it: but he went off, with the semi-barbaric reluctance and fear of approaching a strange place.

After a while, he came back to say the *dispensa** was shut, and he couldn't get any.—Then, said I, let us go to the tombs! Do you know where they are?—He pointed vaguely into the distance of the moorland, and said they were there, but that we should want candles. The tombs were dark, and no-one was there.—Then let us get candles from the peasants, I said.—He answered again, the *dispensa* was shut, and we couldn't get candles. He seemed uneasy and depressed, as the people always are when there is a little difficulty. They are so afraid and mistrustful of one another.

We walked back to the black ruin, through a dark gateway that had been portcullised, into a half-ruined black courtyard, curiously gloomy. And here seven or eight men were squatting or standing about, their shiny bicycles leaning against the ruined walls. They were queer-looking, youngish fellows, smallish, unshaven, dirty; not peasants, but workmen of some sort, who looked as if they had been swept together among the rubbish. Luigi was evidently nervous of them: not that they were villains, merely he didn't know them. But he had one friend among them: a queer young fellow of about twenty, in a close-fitting blue jersey, a black, black beard on his rather delicate but *gamin* face, and an odd sort of smile. This young fellow came roving round us, with a queer uneasy, half-smiling curiosity. The men all seemed like that, uneasy and as it were outcast, but with another unknown quality too. They were, in reality, the queer, poorest sort of natives of this part of the maremma.

The courtyard of the castle was black and sinister, yet very
5   interesting in its ruined condition. There were a few forlorn, rat-like signs of peasant farming. And an outside stair-case, once rather grand, went up to what was now apparently the inhabited quarter, two or three rooms facing the bridge.

The feeling of suspicion and almost of opposition, negative rather
10 than active, was still so strong, we went out again and on to the bridge. Luigi, in a dilemma, talked mutteringly to his black-bearded young friend with the bright eyes: all the men seemed to have queer, quick, bright black eyes, with a glint on them such as a mouse's eyes have.

15 At last I asked him, flatly: Who are all those men?—He muttered that they were the workmen and navvies. I was puzzled to know *what* workmen and navvies, in this loneliness? Then he explained they were working on the irrigation works, and had come in to the *dispensa* for their wages and to buy things—it was Saturday afternoon—but
20 that the overseer, who kept the dispensa, and who sold wine and necessaries to the workmen, hadn't come yet to open the place, so we couldn't get anything.

At least, Luigi didn't explain all this. But when he said these were the workmen from the irrigation diggings, I understood it all.

25 By this time, we and our desire for candles had become a feature in the landscape. I said to Luigi, why didn't he ask the *peasants*. He said they hadn't any. Fortunately at that moment an unwashed woman appeared at an upper window in the black wall. I asked her if she couldn't sell us a candle. She retired to think about it—then
30 came back to say, surlily, it would be sixty centimes. I threw her a Lira, and she dropped a candle. So!

Then the black-bearded young fellow glintingly said we should want more than one candle. So I asked the woman for another, and threw her fifty centimes—as she was contemplating giving me the
35 change for the Lira. She dropped another candle.

B. and I moved away towards the carretto, with Luigi. But I could see he was still unhappy.—Do you know where the tombs are? I asked him.—Again he waved vaguely—Over there!—But he was unhappy.—Would it be better to take one of those men for a guide? I
40 said to him.—And I got that inevitable answer: It is as you think.—If

you don't know the tombs well, I said to him, then find a man to come
with us.—He still hesitated, with that dumb uncertainty of these
people.—Find a man anyhow! I said, and off he went, feebly.

He came back in relief with the peasant, a short but strong
maremmano* of about forty, unshaven but not unclean. His name   5
was Marco—and he had put on his best jacket, to accompany us. He
was quiet and determined seeming—a brownish blond, not one of
the queer black natives with the queer round soft contours. His boy
of about thirteen came with him, and they two climbed on to the back
of the carretto.   10

Marco gave directions, and we bowled down the trail, then away
over a slight track, on to the heathy, stony moorland. After us came a
little black-eyed fellow on a bicycle. We passed on the left a small
encampment of temporary huts made of planks, with women coming
out to look. By the trail were huge sacks of charcoal, and the black   15
charcoal-burners, just down from the mountains, for the week-end,
stood aside to look at us. The asses and mules stood drooping.

This was the winter camp of the charcoal-burners. In a week or so,
Marco told me, they would abandon this camp and go up into the
mountains, out of reach of the fevers which begin in May. Certainly   20
they looked a vigorous bunch, if a little wild. I asked Marco if there
was much fever—meaning malaria. He said, not much. I asked him if
he had had any attacks. He said, No, never!—It is true he looked
broad and healthy, with a queer, subdued, explosive sort of energy.
Yet there was a certain motionless, rather worn look in his face, a   25
certain endurance and sallowness, which seemed like malaria to me.
I asked Luigi, our driver, if he had had any fever. At first he too said
no. Then he admitted, he had had a touch now and then. Which was
evident, for his face was small and yellowish, evidently the thing had
eaten into him. Yet he too, like Marco, had a strong, *manly* energy,   30
more than the ordinary Italians.—It is evidently the thing, in these
parts, to deny that the malaria has ever touched you.

To the left, out of the heath, rose great flattish mounds, great
tumuli, bigger than those of Cerveteri. I asked Marco, were those the
tombs? He said, those were the tumuli, Coccumella and Coc-   35
cumelletta*—but that we would go first to the river tombs.*

We were descending a rocky slope towards the brink of the ravine,
which was full of trees as ever. Far away, apparently, behind us to the
right, stood the lonely black tower of the castle, across the moorland
whence we had come. Across the ravine was a long, low hill, grassy   40

and moorland: and farther down the stream were the irrigation
works. The country was all empty and abandoned-seeming, yet with
that peculiar, almost ominous poignancy of places where life has
once been intense.—Where do they say the city of Volci was?—I
5 asked Marco. He pointed across-stream, to the long, low elevation
along the opposite side of the ravine. I guessed it had been
there—since the tombs were on this side. But it looked very low and
undefended, for an etruscan site: so open to the world! I supposed it
had depended on its walls, to seawards, and the ravine inland.—I
10 asked Marco if anything was there. He said, nothing!—some sign of
where the walls had gone round. It had evidently not been a very
large city, like Caere and Tarquinia. But it was one of the cities of the
League, and very rich indeed, judging from the thousands of painted
vases which have been taken from the tombs here.

15   The rocky descent was too uneven. We got out of the cart, and
went on foot. Luigi left the mare, and Marco led us on, down to a
barb-wire fence. We should never, never have found the place
ourselves. Marco expertly held the wire apart, and we scrambled
through, on to the bushy, rocky side of the ravine. The trees rose
20 from the river-side, some leaves bright green. And we descended a
rough path, past the entrance-passage to a tomb most carefully
locked with an iron gate, and defended with barbed wire, like a
hermit's cave with the rank vegetation growing up to choke it again.

Winding among rank vegetation and fallen rocks of the face of the
25 ravine, we came to the openings of the tombs, which were cut into
the face of the rock, and must have been a fine row once, like a row of
rock houses with a pleasant road outside, along the ravine. But now
they are gloomy holes down which one must clamber through the
excavated earth. Once inside, with the three candles—for the
30 black-faced youth on the bicycle had brought a stump too—we were
in gloomy wolves' dens of places, with large chambers opening off
one another as at Cerveteri, damp beds of rock for the coffins, and
huge grisly stone coffins, seven feet long, lying in disorder, among
fallen rocks and rubble: in some of them the bones and man-dust
35 still lying dismally. There was nothing to see but these black damp
chambers, sometimes cleared, sometimes with coarse great sarcophagi and broken rubbish and excavation-rubble left behind, in the
damp, grisly darkness.

Sometimes we had to wriggle into the tombs on our bellies, over
40 the mounds of rubble, going down into holes like rats, while the bats

flew blindly in our faces. Once inside, we clambered in the faint darkness over huge pieces of rock and broken stone, from dark chamber to chamber, four or five or even more chambers to a tomb, all cut out of the rock and made to look like houses, with the sloping roof tilts and the central roof-beam. From these roofs hung clusters 5 of pale-brown, furry bats, in bunches like bunches of huge, furry hops. One could hardly believe they were alive: till I saw the squat little fellow of the bicycle holding his candle up to one of the bunches, singeing the bats' hair, burning the torpid creatures, so the skinny wings began to flutter, and half-stupefied, half-dead bats fell 10 from the clusters of the roof, then groped on the wing, and began to fly low, staggering towards the outlet. The dark little fellow took a pleasure in burning them. But I stopped him at it, and he was afraid, and left them alone.

He was a queer fellow, quite short, with the fat, soft round curves, 15 and black hair and sallow face and black bats' eyes of a certain type of this district. He was perhaps twenty years old—and like a queer burrowing dumb animal. He would creep into holes in the queerest way, with his queer, soft, round hindquarters jutting behind: just like some uncanny animal. And I noticed the backs of his ears were all 20 scaly and raw with sores, whether from dirt or some queer disease, who can say! He seemed healthy and alive enough, otherwise. And he seemed quite unconscious of his sore ears, with an animal unconsciousness.

Marco, who was a much higher type, knew his way about and led 25 us groping and wriggling and clambering from tomb to tomb, among the darkness and brokenness and bats and damp—then out among the fennel and bushes of the ravine top—then in again into some hole. He showed us a tomb whence only last year they had taken a big stone statue—he showed me where it had stood, there, in the 30 innermost chamber, with its back to the wall. And he told me of all the vases, mostly broken pieces, that he too had lifted from the dirt, on the stone beds.

But now there is nothing, and I was tired of climbing into these gruesome holes, one after another, full of damp and great fallen 35 rocks. Nothing living or beautiful is left behind—nothing. I was glad when we came to the end of the excavated tombs, and saw beyond only the ravine bank grown over with bushes and fennel and great weeds. Probably many a vase and many a stone coffin still lies hidden there—but let them lie. 40

We went back along the path the way we had come, to climb back

to the upper level. As we came to the gangway leading to the locked tomb, Marco told me that in here were paintings and some things left behind. Probably it was the famous François Tomb* with the paintings that are copied in the Vatican Museum. It was opened by
5 the excavator A. François in 1857, and is one of the very few painted tombs found at Vulci.

We tried in vain to get in. Short of smashing the lock, it was impossible. Of course, in these expeditions, one should arm oneself with official permits. But it means having officials hanging round.
10 So we climbed up to the open world, and Luigi made us get into the carretto. The mare pulled us jolting across towards the great tumuli, which we wanted to see. They are huge grassy-bushy mounds, like round, low hills. The band of stone-work round the base, if it be there, is buried.
15 Marco led us into the dense passage of brambles and bushes which leads to the opening into the tumulus. Already this passage is almost blocked up, overgrown. One has to crawl under the scratching brambles, like a rabbit.

And at last one is in the plain doorway of the tumulus itself.
20 Here, even in 1829, two weird stone sphinxes guarded the entrance. Now there is nothing.—And inside the passage or at the angles were lions and gryphons on guard. What now shall we find, as we follow the candle-light in the narrow winding passage? It is like being in a mine, narrow passages winding on and on, from
25 nowhere to nowhere. We had not any great length of candle left: four stumps. Marco left one stump burning at the junction of the passages, as a sign-post, and on and on we went, from nowhere to nowhere, stooping a little, our hats brushing the clusters of bats that hung from the ceiling, as we went on, one after the other,
30 pinned all the time in the narrow stone corridors that never led anywhere or did anything. Sometimes there was a niche in the wall—that was all.

There must, surely, be a central burial chamber, to which the passages finally lead. But we didn't find it, and Marco said there
35 was no such thing—the tumulus was all passages and nothing but passages—But Dennis says that when the tumulus was opened in 1829 there were two small chambers in the heart of the mound, and rising from these, two shafts of masonry which passed up to the apex of the mound, and there no doubt supported great phallic
40 monuments, or cippi, seen for miles around. On the floor of the

chamber were fragments of bronze and frail gold. But now there is nothing. The centre of the tumulus has no doubt collapsed.*

It was like burrowing* inside some ancient pyramid. This was quite unlike any other etruscan tomb we had seen: and if this tumulus was a tomb, then it must have been a very important person whose coffin formed the nut inside all this shell: a person important as a Pharaoh, surely. The Etruscans were queer people, and this tumulus, with no peripheral tombs, only endless winding passages, must be either a reminiscence of prehistoric days, or of Egyptian pyramids.

When we had had enough of running along passages in nowhere, we got out, scrambled through the bramble-tangle, and were thankful to see clear heaven again. We all piled into the carretto, and the mare nobly hauled us up to the trail. The little dark fellow sailed ahead silently, on his bicycle, to open the gate for us. We looked round once more at the vast mound of the Coccumella, which strange dead hands piled in soft earth over two tiny death-chambers, so long ago: and even now it is weirdly conspicuous on the flat maremma. A strange nut indeed, with a kernel of perpetual mystery! And once it rose suave as a great breast, tipped with the budded monuments of the cippi. It is too problematic. We turn our backs on it, as the carretto jolts over the tomb-rifled earth. There is something gloomy, if rather wonderful, about Vulci.

The charcoal-burners were preparing to wash their faces for Sunday, in the little camp. The women stood smiling as we drove by on the moor. "Oh, how fat thou hast got!" Luigi shouted to one plump and smiling woman. "*You* haven't though!" she shouted back at him. "*Tu pure, no?*"*

At the bridge, we said goodbye! to Marco and his boy, then we pulled over the arch once more. But on the other side, Luigi wanted to drink. So he and I scrambled down to the spring, the old, thin-trickling spring, and drank cool water. The river rushed below: the bridge arched its black, soaring rainbow above: and we heard the shouts of mule-drivers driving the mules over the arch.

Once this old bridge carried an aqueduct, and it is curious to see the great stalactitic mass that hangs like a beard down the side facing the mountain. But the aqueduct is gone, the muddy stalactitic mass is itself crumbling.* Everything passes!

So we climbed up and into the carretto, and away went the mare, at a spanking pace. We passed the young man in velveteens, on the

donkey: a peasant from the hills, Luigi said he was. And we met horsemen riding towards us, towards the hills, away from Montalto. It was Saturday afternoon, with a bright sea-wind blowing strong over the maremma, and men travelling away from work, on
5 horseback, on mules, or an asses. And some drove laden donkeys out to the hills.

   It would be a good life, I said to Luigi, to live here, and have a house on the hills, and a horse to ride, and space: except for the malaria. All except for the malaria!
10   Then, having previously confessed to me that the malaria was still pretty bad, though children often escaped it, but grown people rarely: the fever inevitably came to shake them sometimes; and that Montalto was more stricken than the open country; and that in the time of rains the roads were impassable, one was cut off: now Luigi
15 changed his tune, said there was almost no fever any more, the roads were always passable, in Montalto people came at bathing season to bathe in the sea, having little cane huts on the coast: the roads were always easily passable, easily: and that you never got fever at all, at all, if you were properly fed, and had a bit of meat now and then, and a
20 decent glass of wine.—He wanted me so much to come and have some abandoned house in the foot-hills; and he would look after my horses; and we would go hunting together—even out of season, for there was no-one to catch you.

   B. dozed lightly while we drove joltingly on. It was a dream too. I
25 would like it well enough—if I were convinced about that malaria. And I would certainly have Luigi to look after the horses. He hasn't a grand appearance, but he is solitary and courageous and surely honest, solitary and far more manly than the townsmen or the grubbing peasants—
30   So, we have seen all we could see of Vulci. If we want to see what the Etruscans buried there, we must go to the Vatican, or to the Florence museum, or to the British Museum in London, and see vases and statues, bronzes, sarcophagi and jewels. In the British Museum lie the contents, for the most part, of the so-called Tomb of
35 Isis,* where lay buried a lady whom Dennis thought was surely Egyptian, judging from her statue, that is stiff and straight, and from the statuette of "Isis," the six ostrich eggs and other imported things that went to the grave with her: for in death she must be what she was in life, as exactly as possible. This was the etruscan creed.—How the
40 Egyptian lady came to Volci, and how she came to be buried there

along with a lady of ancient Etruria, down in that bit of the Volci necropolis now called Polledrara, who knows? But all that is left of her is now in the British Museum. Vulci has nothing. Anyhow she was surely not Egyptian at all. Anything of the archaic east-Mediterranean seemed to Dennis Egyptian.   5

So it is. The site of Volci was* lost from Roman times till 1828. Once found, however, the tombs were rapidly gutted by the owners, everything precious was taken away, then the tombs were either closed again, or abandoned. All the thousands of vases that the Etruscans gathered so lovingly and laid by their dead, where are   10 they? Many are still in existence. But they are everywhere except at Vulci.

VI.
VOLTERRA

VI.

Volterra*

Volterra is the most northerly of the great etruscan cities of the west. It lies back some thirty miles from the sea, on a towering great bluff of rock that gets all the winds and sees all the world, looking out down the valley of the Cecina to the sea, south over vale and high land to the tips of Elba, north to the imminent mountains of Carrara,* inward over the wide hills of the Pre-Apennines, to the heart of Tuscany.

You leave the Rome-Pisa train at Cecina, and slowly wind up the valley of the stream of that name, a green, romantic, forgotten sort of valley, in spite of all the come-and-go of ancient Etruscans and Romans, mediaeval Volterrans and Pisans, and modern traffic. But the traffic is not heavy. Volterra is a sort of inland island, still curiously isolated, and grim.

The small, forlorn little train comes to a stop at the *Saline di Volterra*, the famous old salt-works* now belonging to the State, where brine is pumped out of deep wells. What passengers remain in the train are transferred to one old little coach across the platform, and at length this coach starts to creep like a beetle up the slope, up a cog-and-ratchet line, shoved by a small engine behind. Up the steep but round slope among the vineyards and olives you pass almost at walking pace, and there is not a flower to be seen, only the beans make a whiff of perfume now and then, on the chill air, as you rise and rise, above the valley below, coming level with the high hills to south, and the bluff of rock with its two or three towers, ahead.

After a certain amount of backing and changing, the fragment of a train eases up at a bit of a cold wayside station, and is finished. The world lies below. You get out, transfer yourself to a small ancient motor-omnibus, and are rattled up to the final level of the city, into a cold and gloomy little square, where the hotel is.

The hotel is simple and somewhat rough, but quite friendly, pleasant in its hap-hazard way. And what is more, it has central

heating, and the heat is on, this cold, almost icy April afternoon.
Volterra lies only 1800 feet above the sea, but it is right in the wind,
and cold as any alp.

5   The day was Sunday, and there was a sense of excitement and
fussing, and a bustling in and out of temporarily important persons,
and altogether a smell of politics in the air. The waiter brought us tea
of a sort, and I asked him what was doing. He replied that a great
banquet was to be given this evening to the new *podestà** who had
come from Florence to govern the city, under the new régime. And
10 evidently he felt that this was such a hugely important "party"
occasion, we poor outsiders were of no account.

It was a cold grey afternoon, with winds round the hard dark
corners of the hard, narrow mediaeval town, and crowds of black-
dressed, rather squat little men and pseudo-elegant young women
15 pushing and loitering in the streets, and altogether that sense of
furtive grinning and jeering and threatening which always accom-
panies a public occasion—a political one especially—in Italy, in the
more out-of-the-way centres. It is as if the people, alabaster-workers
and a few peasants, were not sure which side they wanted to be on,
20 and therefore were all the more ready to exterminate anyone who
was on the other side. This fundamental uneasiness, indecision, is
most curious in the Italian soul. It is as if the people could never be
whole-heartedly anything: because they can't trust anything. And
this inability to trust is at the root of the political extravagance and
25 frenzy. They don't trust themselves, so how can they trust their
"leaders" or their "party"?

Volterra, standing sombre and chilly alone on her rock, has
always, from etruscan days on, been grimly jealous of her own
independence. Especially she has struggled against the Florentine
30 yoke.* So what her actual feelings are, about this new-old sort of
village tyrant, the podestà, whom she is banqueting this evening, it
would be hard, probably, even for the Volterrans themselves to say.
Anyhow the cheeky girls salute one with the "Roman" salute, out of
sheer effrontery: a salute which has nothing to do with me, so I don't
35 return it. Politics of all sorts are anathema. But in an etruscan city
which held out so long against Rome, I consider the Roman salute
unbecoming, and the Roman *imperium* unmentionable.

It is amusing to see on the walls, too, chalked fiercely up: *Morte a
Lenin*: *Death to Lenin*: though that poor gentleman has been long
40 enough dead,* surely, even for a Volterran to have heard of it. And

more amusing still is the legend permanently painted: *Mussolini ha sempre ragione*! *Mussolini is always right*! Some are born infallible, some achieve it, and some have infallibility thrust upon them.*

But it is not for me to put even my little finger in any political pie. I am sure every post-war country has hard enough work to get itself governed, without outsiders interfering or commenting. Let those rule who can rule.

We wander on, a little dismally, looking at the stony stoniness of the mediaeval town. Perhaps on a warm sunny day it might be pleasant, when shadow was attractive and a breeze welcome. But on a cold, grey, windy afternoon of April, Sunday, always especially dismal, with all the people in the streets, bored and uneasy, and the stone buildings peculiarly sombre and hard and resistant, it is no fun. I don't care about the bleak but truly mediaeval piazza: I don't care if the Palazzo Pubblico has all sorts of amusing coats of arms on it: I don't care about the cold cathedral,* though it is rather nice really, with a glow of dusky candles and a smell of Sunday incense: I am disappointed in the wooden sculpture of the taking down of Jesus, and the bas reliefs don't interest me. In short, I am hard to please.

The modern town is not very large. We went down a long stony street, and out of the Porta all'Arco,* the famous old etruscan gate. It is a deep old gateway, almost a tunnel, with the outer arch facing the desolate country on the skew, built at an angle to the old road, to catch the approaching enemy on his right side, where the shield did not cover him. Up handsome and round goes the arch, at a good height, and with that peculiar weighty richness of ancient things; and three dark heads, now worn featureless, reach out curiously and inquiringly one from the keystone of the arch, one from each of the arch-bases, to gaze from the city out into the steep hollow of the world beyond.

Strange, dark old etruscan heads of the city gate, even now they are featureless they still have a peculiar, out-reaching life of their own. Ducati says they represented the heads of slain enemies hung at the city gate. But they don't hang. They stretch with curious eagerness forward. Nonsense about dead heads. They were city deities of some sort.

And the archaeologists say that only the door-posts of the outer arch, and the inner walls, are etruscan work. The Romans restored the arch, and set the heads back in their old positions. Unlike the

Romans to set anything back in its old position!—While the wall
above the arch is merely mediaeval.*

But we'll call it etruscan still. The roots of the gate, and the dark
heads, these they cannot take away from the Etruscans. And the
5   heads are still on the watch.

The land falls away steeply, across the road in front of the arch.
The road itself turns east, under the walls of the modern city, above
the world: and the sides of the road, as usual outside the gates, are
dump heaps, dump-heaps of plaster and rubble, dump-heaps of
10   the white powder from the alabaster works, the waste edge of the
town.

The path turns away from under the city wall,* and dips down
along the brow of the hill. To the right we can see the tower of the
church of Santa Chiara, standing on a little platform of the
15   irregularly-dropping hill. And we are going there. So we dip downwards above a Dantesque, desolate world, down to Santa Chiara,
and beyond. Here the path follows the top of what remains of the
old etruscan wall. On the right are little olive gardens and bits of
wheat. Away beyond is the dismal sort of crest of modern Volterra.
20   We walk along, past the few flowers and the thick ivy, and the
bushes of broom and marjoram, on what was once the etruscan
wall, far out from the present city wall. On the left the land drops
steeply in uneven and unhappy descents.

The great hill-top or headland on which etruscan "Volterra,"
25   *Velathri, Vlathri*, once stood spreads out jaggedly, with deep-cleft
valleys in between, more or less in view, spreading two or three
miles away. It is something like a hand, the bluff steep of the palm
sweeping in a great curve on the east and south, to seawards, the
peninsulas or fingers running jaggedly inland. And the great wall of
30   the etruscan city swept round the south and eastern bluff, on the
crest of steeps and cliffs, turned north and crossed the first finger,
or peninsula, then started up hill and down dale, over the fingers
and into the declivities, a wild and fierce sort of way, hemming in
the great crest. The modern town merely occupies the highest bit
35   of the etruscan city-site.

The walls themselves are not much to look at, when you climb
down. They are only fragments, now, huge fragments of
embankment, rather than wall, built of uncemented square
masonry, in the grim, sad sort of stone. One only feels, for some
40   reason, depressed. And it is pleasant to look at the lover and his lass

going along the top of the ramparts, which are now olive orchards, away from the town. At least they are alive and cheerful and quick.

On from Santa Chiara the road takes us through the grim and depressing little suburb-hamlet of San Giusto, a black street that emerges upon the waste open place where the church* of San Giusto 5 rises like a huge and astonishing barn. It is so tall, the interior should be impressive. But no! It is merely nothing. The architects have achieved nothing, with all that tallness. The children play around with loud yells and ferocity. It is Sunday evening, near sundown, and cold. 10

Beyond this monument of christian dreariness we come to the etruscan walls again, and what was evidently once an etruscan gate: a dip in the wall-bank, with the groove of an old road running to it.

Here we sit on the ancient heaps of masonry and look into weird yawning gulfs, like vast quarries. The swallows, turning their blue 15 backs, skim away from the ancient lips and over the really dizzy depths, in the yellow light of evening, catching the upward gusts of wind, and flickering aside like lost fragments of life, truly frightening above those ghastly hollows. The lower depths are dark-grey, ashy in colour, and in part wet, and the whole thing looks new, as if it were 20 some enormous quarry all slipping down.

This place is called *Le Balze*—the cliffs. Apparently the waters which fall on the heights of Volterra collect in part underneath the deep hill and wear away at some places the lower strata, so that the earth falls in immense collapses. Across the gulf, away from the 25 town, stands a big, old, picturesque, isolated building, the Badia or Monastery of the Camaldolesi, sad-looking, destined at last to be devoured by Le Balze, its old walls already splitting and yielding.

From time to time, going up to the town homewards, we come to the edge of the walls and look out into the vast glow of gold, which is 30 sunset, marvellous, the steep ravines sinking in darkness, the further valley silently, greenly gold, with hills breathing luminously up, passing out into the pure, sheer gold gleam of the far-off sea, in which a shadow, perhaps an island, moves like a mote of life. And like great guardians the Carrara mountains jut forward, naked in the 35 pure light like flesh, with their crests portentous: so that they seem to be advancing on us: while all the vast concavity of the west roars with gold liquescence, as if the last hour had come, and the gods were smelting us all back into yellow transmuted oneness.

But nothing is being transmuted. We turn our faces, a little 40 frightened, from the vast blaze of gold, and in the dark, hard streets the town band is just chirping up, brassily out of tune as usual, and the populace, with some maidens in white, are streaming in crowds towards the piazza. And like the band, the populace also is out of 5 tune, buzzing with the inevitable suppressed jeering. But they are going to form a procession.

When we come to the square in front of the hotel, and look out from the edge into the hollow world of the west, the light is sunk red, redness gleams up from the far-off sea below, pure and fierce, and 10 the hollow places in between are dark. Over all the world is a low red glint. But only the town, with its narrow streets and electric light, is impervious.

The banquet, apparently, was not till nine o'clock, and all was hubbub. B. and I dined alone soon after seven, like two orphans 15 whom the waiters managed to remember in between-whiles. They were so thrilled getting all the glasses and goblets and decanters, hundreds of them, it seemed, out of the big chiffonnier cupboard that occupied the back of the dining-room, and whirling them away, stacks of glittering glass, to the banquet room: while out-of-work 20 young men would poke their heads in through the doorway, black hats on, overcoats hung over one shoulder, and gaze with bright enquiry through the room, as though they expected to see Lazarus risen,* and not seeing him, would depart again to the nowhere whence they came.—A banquet is a banquet, even if it is given to the 25 devil himself; and the new podestà may be an angel of light.

Outside was cold and dark. In the distance the town band tooted spasmodically, as if it were short-winded this chilly Sunday evening. And we, not being bidden to the feast, went to bed. To be wakened occasionally by sudden and roaring noises—perhaps applause—and 30 the loud and unmistakeable howling of a child, well after midnight.

Morning was cold and grey again, with a chilly and forbidding country yawning and gaping and lapsing away beneath us. The sea was invisible. We walked the narrow cold streets, whose high, cold, dark stone walls seemed almost to press together, and we looked in at 35 the alabaster work-shops, where workmen, in Monday-morning gloom and half-awakenedness, were turning the soft alabaster, or cutting it out, or polishing it.

Everybody knows Volterra marble—so-called—nowadays, because of the translucent bowls of it which hang under the electric lights, as 40 shades, in half the hotels of the world. It is nearly as transparent as alum, and nearly as soft. They peel it down as if it were soap, and tint it pink or amber or blue, and turn it into all those things one does not want: tinted alabaster lamp-shades, light-bowls, statues, tinted or untinted, vases, bowls with doves on the rim, or vine-leaves around, and similar curios. The trade seems to be going strong. Perhaps it is 5 the electric light demand: perhaps there is a revival of interest in "statuary." Anyhow there is no love lost between a Volterra alabaster-worker and the lump of pale Volterran earth he turns into marketable form. Alas for the goddess of sculptured form, she has gone from here also. 10

But it is the old alabaster jars we want to see, not the new. As we hurry down the stony street, the rain, icy cold, begins to fall. We flee through the glass doors of the museum,* which has just opened, and which seems as if the alabaster inside had to be kept at a low temperature, for the place is dead cold as a refrigerator. 15

Cold, silent, empty, unhappy the museum seems. But at last an old and dazed man arrives, in uniform, and asks us quite scared what we want.—Why, to see the museum! *Ah! Ah! Ah si—si!* It just dawns on him that the museum is there to be looked at. Ah sì, si Signori!

We pay our tickets, and start in. It is really a very attractive and 20 pleasant museum, but we had struck such a bitter cold April morning, with icy rain falling in the courtyard, that I felt as near to being in the tomb as I have ever done. Yet very soon, in the rooms with all those hundreds of little sarcophagi, ash-coffins, or urns, as they are called, the strength of the old life began to warm one up. 25

Urn is not a good word, because it suggests, to me at least, a vase, an amphora, a round and shapely jar: perhaps through association with Keats' "Ode on a Grecian Urn"—which vessel no doubt wasn't an urn at all, but a wine-jar—and with the "tea-urn" of children's parties. These Volterran urns, though correctly enough used for 30 storing the ashes of the dead, are not round, they are not jars, they are small alabaster sarcophagi. And they are a peculiarity of Volterra. Probably because the Volterrans had the alabaster to hand.

Anyhow here you have them in hundreds, and they are curiously alive and attractive. They are not considered very highly as "art." 35 One of the latest Italian writers on etruscan things, Ducati, says: If they have small interest from the artistic point of view, they are extremely valuable for the scenes they represent, either mythological or relative to the beliefs in the after-life.—*

George Dennis, however, though he too does not find much "art" 40

in etruscan things, says of the Volterran ash-chests:—"the touches
of Nature on these etruscan urns, so simply but eloquently
expressed, must appeal to the sympathies of all—they are chords to
which every heart must respond; and I envy not the man who can
5   walk through this museum unmoved, without feeling a tear rise to his
eye,

> 'And recognising ever and anon
> The breeze of Nature stirring in his soul.'"—*

     The breeze of Nature no longer shakes dewdrops from our eyes, at
10   least so readily, but Dennis is more alive than Ducati to that which is
alive. What men mean nowadays by "art" it would be hard to say.
Even Dennis said that the Etruscans never approached the pure, the
sublime, the perfect beauty which Flaxman reached. Today, this
makes us laugh: the greekified illustrator of Pope's Homer!* But the
15   same instinct lies at the back of our idea of "art" still. Art is still to
us something which has been well cooked—like a plate of spaghetti.
An ear of wheat is not yet "art." Wait, wait till it has been turned into
pure, into perfect macaroni.

     For me, I get more real pleasure out of these Volterran ash-chests
20   than out of—I had almost said, the Parthenon frieze.* One wearies of
the aesthetic quality—a quality which takes the edge off everything,
and makes it seem "boiled down." A great deal of pure Greek beauty
has this boiled-down effect. It is too much cooked in the artistic
consciousness.

25   In Dennis' day, a broken Greek or Greekish amphora would fetch
thousands of crowns in the market, if it was the right "period" etc.*
These Volterran urns fetched hardly anything. Which is a mercy, or
they would be scattered to the ends of the earth.

     As it is, they are fascinating like an open book of life, and one has
30   no sense of weariness with them, though there are so many. They
warm one up, like being in the midst of life.

     The downstairs rooms of ash-chests contain those urns repre-
senting "etruscan" subjects: those of sea-monsters, the sea-man
with fish tail, and with wings, the sea-woman the same: or the man
35   with serpent legs, and wings, or the woman the same. It was etruscan
to give these creatures wings, not Greek.

     If we remember that in the old world, the centre of all power was at
the depths of the earth, and at the depths of the sea, while the sun
was only a moving subsidiary body: and that the serpent represented

the vivid powers of the inner earth, not only such powers as volcanic and earthquake, but the quick powers that run up the roots of plants and establish the great body of the tree, the tree of life, and run up the feet and legs of man, to establish the heart: while the fish was the symbol of the depths of the waters, whence even light is born: we shall see the ancient power these symbols had over the imagination of the Volterrans. They were a people faced with the sea, and living in a volcanic country.

Then the powers of the earth and the powers of the sea take life as they give life. They have their terrific as well as their prolific aspect.

Someone says the wings of the water deities represent evaporation towards the sun, and the curving tail of the dolphin represent torrents. This is part of the great and controlling ancient idea of the come-and-go of the life-powers, the surging up, in a flutter of leaves and a radiation of wings, and the surging back, in torrents and waves and the eternal down-pour of death.

Other common symbolic animals in Volterra are the beaked gryphons, the creatures of the powers that tear asunder, and at the same time, are guardians of the treasure. They are lion and eagle combined, of the sky and of the earth with caverns. They do not allow the treasure of life, the gold, which we should perhaps translate as consciousness, to be stolen by thieves of life. They are guardians of the treasure: and then, they are the tearers-asunder of those who must depart from life.

It is these creatures, creatures of the elements, which carry man away into death, over the borders between the elements. So is the dolphin, sometimes: and so the hippocampus, the sea-horse; and so the centaur.

The horse is always the symbol of the strong animal life of man: and sometimes he rises, a sea-horse, from the ocean: and sometimes he is a land creature, and half-man. And so he occurs on the tombs, as the passion in man returning into the sea, the soul retreating into the death-world at the depths of the waters: or sometimes he is a centaur, sometimes a female centaur, sometimes clothed in a lion-skin, to show his dread aspect, bearing the soul back, away, off into the otherworld.

It would be very interesting to know if there were a definite connection between the scene on the ash-chest, and the dead whose ashes it contained. When the fish-tailed sea-god entangles a man to bear him off, does it mean drowning at sea? And when a man is

caught in the writhing serpent-legs of the Medusa, or of the winged snake-power, does it mean a fall to earth?—a death from the earth, in some manner; as a fall, or the dropping of a rock, or the bite of a snake? And the soul carried off by a winged centaur: is it a man dead
5 of some passion that carried him away.

But more interesting even than the symbolic scenes, are those scenes from actual life, such as boar-hunts, circus games, processions, departures in covered wagons, ships sailing away, city gates being stormed, sacrifices being performed, girls with open scrolls, as
10 if reading at school; many banquets with man and woman on the banqueting couch, and slaves playing music, and children around; then so many really tender fare-well scenes, the dead saying goodbye to his wife, as he goes on the journey, or as the chariot bears him off, or the horse waits; then the soul alone, with the death-dealing spirits
15 standing by with their hammers that gave the blow. It is as Dennis says, the breeze of Nature stirs one's soul. I asked the gentle old man if he knew anything about the urns. But no! no! he knew nothing at all. He had only just come. He counted for nothing.—So he protested. He was one of those gentle, shy Italians too diffident even
20 to look at the chests he was guarding. But when I told him what I thought some of the scenes meant, he was fascinated like a child, full of wonder, almost breathless. And I thought again, how much more etruscan than Roman the Italian of today is: sensitive, diffident, craving really for symbols and mysteries, able to be delighted with
25 true delight over small things, violent in spasms, and altogether without sternness or natural will-to-power.* The will-to-power is a secondary thing in an Italian, reflected on to him from the Germanic races that have almost engulfed him.

The boar-hunt is still a favourite Italian sport, the grandest sport
30 of Italy. And the Etruscans must have loved it, for they represented it again and again, on the tombs. It is difficult to know what exactly the boar symbolised to them. He occupies often the centre of the scene, where the one who dies should be: and where the bull of sacrifice is. And often he is attacked, not by men, but by young winged boys, or
35 by spirits. The dogs climb in the trees around him, the double axe is swinging to come down on him, he lifts up his tusks in a fierce wild pathos. The archaeologists say that it is Meleager and the boar of Calydon, or Hercules and the fierce brute of Erymanthus.* But this is not enough. It is a symbolic scene: and it seems as if the boar were
40 himself the victim this time, the wild, fierce fatherly life hunted down by dogs and adversaries. For it is obviously the boar who must die: he

is not, like the lions and gryphons, the attacker. He is the father of
life running free in the forest, and he must die.—They say too he
represents winter: when the feasts for the dead were held. But on the
very oldest archaic vases, the lion and the boar are facing each other,
again and again, in symbolic opposition.

Fascinating are the scenes of departures, journeyings in covered
wagons drawn by two or more horses, accompanied by the driver on
foot and friend on horseback, and dogs, and met by other horsemen
coming down the road. Under the arched tarpaulin tilt of the wagon
reclines a man, or a woman, or a whole family: and all moves forward
along the highway with wonderful slow surge. And the wagon, as far
as I saw, is always drawn by horses, not by oxen.

This is surely the journey of the soul. It is said to represent even
the funeral procession, the ash-chest being borne away to the
cemetery, to be laid in the tomb. But the *memory* in the scene seems
much deeper than that. It gives so strongly the feeling of a people
who have trekked in wagons, like the Boers, or the Mormons,* from
one land to another.

They say these covered-wagon journeys are peculiar to Volterra,
found represented in no other etruscan places. Altogether the
feeling of the Volterran scenes is peculiar. There is a great sense of
journeying: as of a people which remembers its migrations, by sea as
well as land. And there is a curious restlessness, unlike the dancing
surety of southern Etruria; a touch of the Gothic.

In the upstairs rooms there are many more ash-chests, but mostly
representing Greek subjects: so-called.—Helen and the Dioscuri,
Pelops, Minotaur, Jason, Medea fleeing from Corinth, Oedipus and
the Sphinx, Ulysses and the Sirens, Eteocles and Polynices, Centaurs and Lapithae, the Sacrifice of Iphigenia*—all are there, just
recognisable. There are so many Greek subjects, that one archaeologist suggested that these urns must have been made by a Greek
colony planted there in Volterra after the Roman conquest.

One might almost as well say that *Timon of Athens* was written by a
Greek colonist planted in England after the overthrow of the Catholic
Church. These "Greek" ash-chests are about as Grecian as *Timon of
Athens* is. The Greeks would have done them so much "better."

No, the "Greek" scenes are innumerable, but it is only just
recognisable, what they mean. Whoever carved these chests knew
very little of the fables they were handling: and fables they were,
to the etruscan artificers of that day, as they would be to the
Italians of this. The story was just used as a peg upon which the

native Volterran hung his fancy, as the Elizabethans in England used
Greek stories for their poems. Perhaps also the alabaster-cutters
were working from old models, or the memory of them. Anyhow, the
scenes show nothing of Hellas.

5   Most curious these "classic" subjects: so un-classic! To me they
hint at the Gothic which lay unborn in the future, far more than at
the Hellenistic past of the Volterran Etruscan. For of course, all
these alabaster urns are considered late in period, after the fourth
century B.C. The christian sarcophagi of the fifth century A.D.
10   seem much more nearly kin to these ash-chests of Volterra, than do
contemporary Roman chests: as if christianity really rose, in Italy,
out of etruscan soil, rather than out of Graeco-Roman. And the first
glimmering of that early, glad sort of christian art, the free touch of
Gothic within the classic, seems evident in the etruscan scenes. The
15   Greek and Roman "boiled" sort of form gives way to a raggedness of
edge and a certain wildness of light and shade which promises the
later Gothic, but which is still held down by the heavy mysticism
from the east.

Very early Volterran urns were probably plain stone or terra-cotta.
20   But no doubt Volterra was a city long before the Etruscans penetrated into it, and probably it never changed character profoundly. To
the end, the Volterrans burned their dead: there are practically no
long sarcophagi of Lucumones. And here most of all one feels that
the *people* of Volterra, or Velathri, were not oriental, not the same as
25   those who made most *show* at Tarquinii. This was surely another
tribe, wilder, cruder, and far less influenced by the old Aegean
influences. In Caere and Tarquinii the aborigines were deeply
overlaid by incoming influences from the east. Here not! Here the
wild and untameable Ligurian* was neighbour, and perhaps kin, and
30   the town of wind and stone kept and still keeps its northern quality.

So there the ash-chests are, an open book for anyone to read who
will, according to his own fancy. They are not more than two feet
long, or thereabouts, so the figure on the lid is queer and stunted.
The classic Greek or Asiatic could not have borne that. It is a sign of
35   barbarism in itself. Here the northern spirit was too strong for the
Hellenic or oriental or ancient Mediterranean instinct. The Lucumo
and his lady had to submit to being stunted, in their death effigy. The
head is nearly life-size. The body is squashed small.

But there it is, a portrait effigy. Very often, the lid and the chest
40   don't seem to belong together at all. It is suggested that the lid was

made during the lifetime of the subject, with an attempt at real portraiture: while the chest was bought ready-made, and apart. It may be so. Perhaps in etruscan days, there were the alabaster workshops as there are today, only with rows of ash-chests portraying all the vivid scenes we still can see: and perhaps you chose the one you wished your ashes to lie in. But more probably, the work-shops were there, the carved ash-chests were there, but you did not select your own chest, since you did not know what death you would die. Probably you only had your portrait carved on the lid, and left the rest to the survivors.

Or maybe, and most probably, the mourning relatives hurriedly *ordered* the lid with the portrait bust, after the death of the near one, and then chose the most appropriate ash-chest. Be it as it may, the two parts are often oddly assorted: and so they were found, with the ashes inside them.

But we must believe that the figure on the lid, grotesquely shortened, is an attempt at a portrait. There is none of the distinction of the southern etruscan figures. The heads are given the "imperious" tilt of the Lucumones, but here it becomes almost grotesque. The dead nobleman may be wearing the necklace of office and holding the sacred patera or libation dish in his hand; but he will not, in the southern way, be represented ritualistically as naked to below the navel; his shirt will come up to his neck; and he may just as well be holding the tippling wine-cup in his hand, as the sacred patera; he may even have a wine-jug in his other hand, in full carousal. Altogether the peculiar "sacredness," the inveterate symbolism of the southern Etruscans is here gone. The religious power is broken.

It is very evident in the ladies: and so many of the figures are ladies. They are decked up in all their splendour, but the ancient mystical formality is lacking. They hold in their hands wine-cups or fans or mirrors, pomegranates or perfume-boxes, or the queer little books which perhaps were the wax tablets for writing upon. They may even have the old sexual and death symbol of the pine-cone. But the *power* of the symbol has almost vanished. The Gothic actuality and idealism begins to supplant the profound *physical* religion of the southern Etruscans, the true ancient world.

In the museum there are jars and bits of bronze, and the pateras with the hollow knob in the middle. You may put your two middle fingers in the patera, and hold it ready to make the last libation of life, the first libation of death, in the correct etruscan fashion. But you

will not, as so many of the men on these ash-chests do, hold the symbolic dish upside-down, with the two fingers thrust into the "mundus." The torch upside-down means the flame has gone below, to the underworld. But the patera upside-down is somehow
5 shocking. One feels the Volterrans, or men of Vlathri, were slack in the ancient mysteries.

At last the rain stopped crashing down icily in the silent inner courtyard; at last there was a ray of sun. And we had seen all we could look at for one day. So we went out, to try and get warmed by a kinder
10 heaven.

There are one or two tombs still open, especially two outside the Porta a Selci. But I believe, not having seen them, they are of small importance. Nearly all the tombs that have been opened in Volterra, their contents removed, have been filled in again, so as not to lose
15 two yards of the precious cultivable land of the peasants. There were many tumuli: but most of them are levelled. And under some were curious round tombs built of unsquared stones, unlike anything in southern Etruria. But then, Volterra is altogether unlike southern Etruria.
20 One tomb has been removed bodily to the garden of the Archaeo-logical Museum in Florence: at least its contents have. There it is built up again as it was when discovered in Volterra in 1861, and all the ash-chests are said to be replaced as they stood originally. It is called the Inghirami Tomb,* from the famous Volterran archae-
25 ologist Inghirami.

A few steps lead down into the one circular chamber of the tomb, which is supported in the centre by a square pillar, apparently supposed to be left in the rock. On the low stone bed that encircles the tomb stand the ash-chests, a double row of them, in a great ring
30 encircling the shadow.

The tomb belongs all to one family, and there must be sixty ash-chests, of alabaster, carved with the well-known scenes. So that if this tomb is really arranged as it was originally, and the ash-chests progress from the oldest to the latest counter-clockwise, as is said,
35 one ought to be able to see certainly a century or two of development in the Volterran urns.

But one is filled with doubt and misgiving. Why oh why wasn't the tomb left intact as it was found, where it was found? The garden of the Florence museum is vastly instructive, if you want object-lessons
40 about the Etruscans. But who wants object-lessons about vanished

races? What one wants is a contact. The Etruscans are not a theory or a thesis. If they are anything, they are an *experience*.

And the experience is always spoilt. Museums, museums, museums, object-lessons rigged out to illustrate the unsound theories of archaeologists, crazy attempts to co-ordinate and get into a fixed order that which has no fixed order and will not be co-ordinated! It is sickening? Why must all experience be systematised? Why must even the vanished Etruscans be reduced to a system? They never will be. You break all the eggs, and produce an omelette which is neither etruscan nor Roman nor Italic nor Hittite, nor anything else, but just a systematised mess. Why can't incompatible things be left incompatible? If you make an omelette out of a hen's egg, a plover's, and an ostrich's, you won't have a grand amalgam or unification of hen and plover and ostrich into something we may call "oviparity." You'll have that formless object, an omelette.

So it is here. If you try to make a grand amalgam of Cerveteri and Tarquinia, Vulci, Vetulonia, Volterra, Chiusi,* Veio, then you won't get the essential *Etruscan* as a result, but a cooked-up mess which has no life-meaning at all. A museum is not a first-hand contact: it is an illustrated lecture. And what one wants is the actual vital touch. I don't want to be "instructed"; nor do many other people.

They could take the more homeless objects for the museums; and still leave those that *have* a place in their own place: the Inghirami Tomb here at Volterra.

But it is useless. We walk up the hill and out of the Florence gate, into the shelter under the walls of the huge mediaeval castle which is now a state prison.* There is a promenade below the ponderous walls, and a scrap of sun, and shelter from the biting wind. A few citizens are promenading even now. And beyond, the bare green country rises up in waves and sharp points, but it is like looking at the choppy sea from the prow of a tall ship, here in Volterra we ride above all.

And behind us, in the black fortress, are the prisoners. There is a man, an old man now, who has written an opera inside those walls. He had a passion for the piano: and for thirty years his wife nagged him when he played. So one day he silently and suddenly killed her. So, the nagging of thirty years silenced, he got thirty years of prison, and *still* is not allowed to play the piano. It is curious.

There were also two men who escaped. Silently and secretly they carved marvellous likenesses of themselves out of the huge loaves of hard bread the prisoners get. Hair and all, they made their own effigies life-like. Then they laid them in the bed, so that when the warder's light flashed on them he should say to himself: There they lie sleeping, the dogs!

And so they worked, and they got away. It cost the governor, who
5   loved his houseful of malefactors, his job. He was kicked out. It is curious. He should have been rewarded, for having such clever children, sculptors in bread.

VII.

THE FLORENCE MUSEUM

VII.

The Florence Museum

It would perhaps be easier to go to the Archaeological Museum in Florence,* to look at the etruscan collection, if we decided once and for all that there never were any Etruscans. Because, in the cut-and-dried museum sense, there never were.

The Etruscans were not a race, that is obvious. And they were not a nation. They were not even as much of a people as the Romans of the Augustan age* were: and a Roman of the Augustan age might be a Latin, an Etruscan, a Sabine, a Samnite, an Umbrian,* a Celt, a Greek, a Jew, or almost anything else of the world of that day. He might come from any tribe or race, almost, and still be first and foremost a Roman. "I am a Roman."

What makes a civilised people is not blood, but some dominant culture-principle. Certain blood-streams give rise to, or are sympathetic to, certain culture principles. The handful of original Romans in Latium contained the germ of the civilising principle of Rome, that was all.

But there was not even an original handful of original Etruscans. In Etruria there is no starting-point. Just as there is no starting-point for England, once we have the courage to look beyond Julius Caesar and 55 B.C.* Britain was active and awake and alive long before Caesar saw it. Nor was it a country of blue-painted savages in bear-skins. It had an old culture of its own, older than the little hill of Romulus.

But then the historical invasions started. Romans, Jutes, Angles, Saxons, Danes, Normans, Jews, French: after all, what is England? What does the word England mean, even? What clue would it give to the rise of the English, should all our history be lost? About as good a clue as Tusci or Tyrrheni* give to the make-up of the Etruscan.

Etruria is a parallel case to England. In the dim British days before Julius Caesar, there were dim Italian days too, and endless restless Italian tribes and peoples with their own speech and customs and religious practices. They were not just brutes, nor cave-men,

because they lived in the days before Homer.* They were men, alive
and alert, having their own complex forms of expression.

And in those dim days where history does not exist—not because
men, intelligent men did not then exist, but because one culture
5   wipes out another as completely as possible; in those dim days, there
were invasions, invasion after invasion no doubt, from the wild north
on foot, from the old, cultured Aegean basin, in ships. Men kept on
coming, and kept on coming: strangers.

But there were two deep emotions or culture-rhythms which
10   persisted in all the confusion: and one was some old, old Italian
rhythm of life, belonging to the soil, which invaded every invader;
and the other was the old cosmic consciousness, or culture principle,
of the prehistoric Mediterranean, particularly of the eastern
Mediterranean. Man is *always* trying to be conscious of the cosmos,
15   the cosmos of life and passion and feeling, desire and death and
despair, as well as of physical phenomena. And there are still
millions of undreamed-of ways of becoming aware of the cosmos.
Which is to say, there are millions of worlds, whole cosmic worlds, to
us yet unborn.

20   Every religion, every philosophy, and science itself, each has a
clue to the cosmos, to the becoming aware of the cosmos. Each clue
leads to its own goal of consciousness, then is exhausted. So religions
exhaust themselves, so science exhausts itself, once the human
consciousness reaches its own limit. The infinite of the human
25   consciousness lies in an infinite number of different starts to an
infinite number of different goals; which somehow, we know when
we get there, is one goal. But the new start is from a point in the
hitherto unknown.

What we have to realise in looking at etruscan things is that they
30   reveal the last glimpses of a human cosmic consciousness—or
human attempt at cosmic consciousness—different from our own.
The idea that our history emerged out of caves and savage lake-
dwellings is puerile. Our history emerges out of the closing of a
previous great phase of human history, a phase as great as our own. It
35   is much more likely the monkey is descended from us, than we from
the monkey.

What we see, in the etruscan remains, is the fag end of the
revelation of another form of cosmic consciousness: and also, that
salt of the earth, the revelation of the human existence of people who
40   lived and who *were*, in a way somewhat different from our way of

living and being. There are two separate things: the artistic or impulsive or culture-expression, and the religious or scientific or civilisation expression of a group of people. The first is based on emotion; the second on concepts.

The Etruscans consisted of all sorts of tribes and distinct peoples: that is obvious: and they did not intermingle. Velathri (Volterra) and Tarquinii were two quite distinct peoples, racially. No doubt they spoke different languages, vulgarly. The thing they had in common was the remains of an old cosmic consciousness, an old religion, an old attempt on man's part to understand, or at least to interpret to himself, the cosmos as he knew it. That was the civilising principle.

Civilisations rise in waves, and pass away in waves. And not till science, or art, tries to catch the ultimate meaning of the symbols that float on the last waves of the prehistoric period; that is, the period before our own; shall we be able to get ourselves into right relation with man as man is and has been and will always be.

In the days before Homer, men in Europe were *not* mere brutes and savages and prognathous monsters: neither were they simple-minded children. Men are always men, and though intelligence takes different forms, men are always intelligent: they are not empty brutes, or dumb-bells *en masse.**

The symbols that come down to us on the last waves of prehistoric culture are the remnants of a vast old attempt made by humanity to form a conception of the universe. The conception was shattered and diminished even by the time it rose to new life, in Egypt. It rose up again, in ancient China and India, in Babylonia and in Asia Minor, in the Druid, in the Teuton, in the Aztec and in the Maya of America, in the very negroes. But each time it rose in a smaller, dying wave, as one tide of consciousness slowly changed to another tide, full of cross-currents. Now our own tide of consciousness is on the ebb, so we can catch the ripples of the tide that ebbed as we arose, and we may read their meaning.

There is no unified and homogeneous etruscan people. There is no Etruscan, pure and simple, and never was: any more than, today, there is one absolute American. There are etruscan characteristics, that is all.

And the real *etruscan* characteristics are the religious symbols. As far as *art* goes, there is no etruscan art. It is an art of all sorts, dominated by an old religious idea.

The religious idea came presumably from the Aegean, the ancient eastern Mediterranean. It was an ebb from an old wider consciousness. If we look at our world today, as far as *culture* goes, it has one culture: the christian-scientific. Whether it be Pekin or Dahomey* or
5   New York or Paris, it is more or less the same conception of life and the cosmos, nowadays.

And so it must have been before. The pyramid builders of America must have had some old idea, remnant of an idea, in common with the Egyptian and the Etruscan. And the Celt, the
10 Gaul, the Druid, must have had some lingering idea of the ancient cosmic meaning of the waters, of the leaping fish, of the undying, ever re-born dead, shadowily sharing it with the ancient Italic peoples, as well as with the Hittites or the Lydians.

There are no Etruscans out-and-out, and there never were any.
15 There were different prehistoric tribes stimulated by contact with different peoples from the eastern Mediterranean, and lifted on the last wave of a dying conception of the living cosmos.

That is what one feels. If it is wrong it is wrong. But few things, *that are felt*, are either absolutely wrong or absolutely right. Things
20 absolutely wrong are not felt, they do not arise from contact. They arise from prejudice and pre-conceived notions. As for things absolutely right, they too cannot be felt. Whatever can be felt is capable of many different forms of expression, forms often contradictory, as far as logic or reason goes.

25 But in the bewildering experience of searching for the Etruscans there is the one steady clue that we can follow: or rather, there are two clues. The first is the peculiar physical or *bodily*, lively quality of all the art. And this, I take it, is Italian, the result of the Italian soil itself. The Romans got a great deal of their power from *resisting*
30 this curious Italian physical expressiveness: and for the same reason, in the Roman the salt soon lost its savour,* in the true Etruscan, never.

The second clue is the more concrete, because more ideal presence of the symbols. Symbols are at least *half* ideas: and so they
35 are half fixed. Emotion and the robust physical gesture are always fluid and changing, never fixed.

So we have the two clues, that of the dominant idea, or half-idea, in the religious symbols; and that of the dominant *feeling*, in the peculiar physical freeness and exuberance and spontaneity. It is the
40 spontaneity of the flesh itself.

These are the two clues to the Etruscan. And they lead from beginning to end, from the point where the Etruscan emerges out of the Oriental, Lydian or Hittite or whatever he may be, till the last days when he is swamped by the Roman and the Greek.

ITALIAN ESSAYS, 1919–27

Note on the texts

The base-texts used for this volume are as follows:

'David': corrected carbon typescript (TCCI), 7 pages, located at UCB.

'Looking Down on the City': corrected carbon typescript (TCC), 5 pages, located at UCLA.

'Europe Versus America': *Laughing Horse* (Per).

'Fireworks': *Nation & Athenæum* (Per1), emended occasionally from MS.

'The Nightingale': manuscript (MS), 8 pages, located at YU, emended from *Forum* (Per1).

'Man is a Hunter': manuscript (MS), 4 pages, located at UT, emended from the corrected carbon typescript (TCCI), 3 pages, located at UNM.

'Flowery Tuscany' I–III: manuscript (MS), 31 pages, in the collection of Mr George Lazarus, emended from *New Criterion* (Per1).

'Flowery Tuscany' IV: carbon typescript (TCCI), 8 pages, located at UCB, emended from *Phoenix* (A1).

'Germans and English': *Phoenix II* (E1).

The apparatus records all textual variants, except for the following silent emendations which have only been recorded when they form part of another variant:

1 Incomplete quotation marks and missing full stops at the end of sentences have been supplied.

2 DHL often followed a full stop, question mark or exclamation mark with a dash before beginning the next sentence with capital letter, e.g. 'nightingale.—But' at 214:8 of 'The Nightingale'. The dash occasionally omitted by the typist has been restored in this edition.

3 Clearly inadvertent errors made by DHL or by the typist, e.g. 'ethis' instead of 'ethic' at 250:27 of 'Germans and English', have not been recorded.

4 Omitted or misplaced apostrophes have been corrected.

5 Italicised punctuation variants have only been recorded when they form part of another variant.

6 Some typescripts and the printed versions house-styled '-is-' to '-iz-'; DHL's practice has been retained in this edition (but the base-text is followed in 'David' and 'Looking Down on the City').

7 Inconsistencies with the placing of quotation marks for a single word or short sentence before, over or after the punctuation have been regularised according to DHL's preferred practice, i.e. quotation marks appear after the punctuation.

8 The titles of the essays have all been standardised to DHL's practice of upper and lower case, including those where no MS survives and the base-text has all capitals.

DAVID

David*

Perpetual sound of water. The Arno, having risen with rain, is swirling brown: café-au-lait. It was a green river, suggesting olive trees and the hills. It is a rushing mass of café-au-lait, and it has already eaten one great slice from the flight of black steps. Café-au-lait is not respectful. But a world of women has brought us to it.

Morning in Florence. Dark, grey, and raining, with a perpetual sound of water. Over the bridge, carriages trotting under great ragged umbrellas. Two white bullocks urged from beneath a bright green umbrella, shambling into a trot as the whip-thong flickers between their soft shanks. Two men arm in arm under one umbrella, going nimbly. Midday from San Miniato—and cannon-shots.* Why cannon shots?—Innumerable umbrellas over the bridge, "like flowers of infernal moly."*

David in the Piazza livid with rain. Unforgettable, now I am safe in my upper room* again. Livid—unnatural. He is made so natural that he is against nature, there in his corpse-whiteness in the rain. The Florentines say that a hot excitement, an anticipatory orgasm, possesses him at midnight of the New Year.* Once told, impossible to forget. A year's waiting. It will happen to him, this orgasm, this further exposure of his nakedness. Uncomfortable. The Neptune, the Bandinelli statues, great stone creatures,* do not matter. Water trickles over their flanks and down between their thighs, without effect. But David—always so sensitive. Corpse-white and sensitive. The water sinks into him, cold, diluting his stagnant springs. And yet he waits with that tense anticipation. As if to clutch the moment. Livid! The Florentine.

Perpetual sound of water. When the sun shines, it shines with grand brilliance, and then the Arno creeps underneath like a cat, like a green-eyed cat in a strange garden. We scarcely observe. We seem to hear the sun clapping in the air, noiseless and brilliant. The aerial and inaudible music of all the sun-shaken ether, inaudible, yet surely

like chimes of glass. What is a river then, but a green thread fluttering? And now!—And particularly last night—Last night* the river churned and challenged with strange noises. Not a Florentine walked by the parapet. Last night enormous cat-swirls breathed
5 hoarse beyond the bank, the weir was a fighting flurry of waters. Like enormous cats interlocked in fight, uttering strange noises. Weight of dark, recoiling water. How is this Italy?

Florence—she puts up no fight. Who hears the river in Turin?* Turin camps flat in defiance. Great snowy Alps, like inquisitive gods
10 from the North, encircle her. She sticks a brandished statue* at the end of the street, full in the vista of glistening, peering snow. She pokes her finger in the eye of the gods. But Florence, the Lily-town* among her hills! Her hills, her hovering waters. She can be hot, brilliant, burnt dry. But look at David! What's the matter with him?
15 Not sun, but cold rain. Children of the South, exposing themselves to the rain. Savonarola, like a hot coal quenched. The South, the North: the fire, the wet downfall.* Once there was a pure equilibrium, and the Lily blossomed. But the Lily now—livid! David, livid, almost quenched, yet still strained and waiting, tense for that
20 orgasm. Crowds will gather at New Year's midnight.

The Lily, the flower of adolescence. Water-born. You cannot dry a lily-bulb. Take away its watery preponderance, surcharge and excess of water, and it is finished. Its flesh is dead. Ask a gardener. A water-blossom dripped from the North. How it blossomed here in
25 the flowery town. Obviously Northerners must love Florence. Here is their last point, their most southerly. The extreme south of the lily's flowering. It is said the fruits are best at their extremity of climate. The southern apple is sweetest at his most northerly limit. The lily, the water-born, most dazzling nearest the sun. Florence,
30 the flower-town. David!

Michelangelo's David is the presiding genius of Florence. Not a shadow of a doubt about it. Once and for all, Florence. So young: sixteen, they say. So big: and stark naked. Revealed. Too big, too naked, too exposed. Livid, under today's sky. The Florentine! The
35 Tuscan pose—half self-conscious all the time. Adolescent.* Waiting. The tense look. No escape. The Lily. Lily or iris, what does it matter? Whitman's Calamus,* too.

Does he listen? Does he, with his young troubled brow, listen? What does he hear? Weep of waters? Even on bluest, hottest day, the
40 same tension. Listen! The weep of waters. The wintry North. The

naked exposure. Stripped so bare, the very kernel of youth. Stripped even to the adolescent orgasm of New Year's night—at midwinter. Unbearable.

Dionysus and Christ of Florence. A clouded Dionysus, a refractory Christ. Dionysus, brightness of sky and moistness of earth: so they tell us is the meaning. Giver of riches. Riches of transport, the vine.* Nymphs and Hamadryads, Silenus, Pan and the Fauns and Satyrs: clue to all these Dionysus, Iacchos, Dithyrambus.* David?— Dionysus, source of reed-music, water-born melody. "The Crocus and the Hyacinth in deep grass",*—lily-flowers. Then wine. Dew and fire, as Pater says. Eleutherios, the Deliverer.* What did he deliver? Michelangelo asked himself that; and left us the answer. Dreams, transports. Dreams, brilliant consciousness, vivid self-realization. Michelangelo's Dionysus, and Michelangelo's David— what is the difference? The cloud on David. The four months of winter were sacred to Dionysus:* months of wine and dreams and transport of self-realization. Months of the inner fire. The vine. Fire which even now, at New Year's night, comes up in David. To have no issue. A cloud is on him.

Semele, scarred with lightning, gave birth prematurely to her child. The Cinquecento. Too fierce a mating, too fiery and potent a sire. The child was sewn again into the thigh of Zeus, re-entered into the loins of the lightning. So the brief fire-brand. It was fire overwhelming, over-weening, briefly married to the dew, that begot this child.* The South to the North. Married! The child, the fire-dew, Iacchos, David.

Fire-dew, yet still too fiery. Plunge him further into the dew. Dithyrambus, the twice-born, born first of fire then of dew. Dionysus leaping into the mists of the North, to escape his foes. David, by the Arno.

So Florence, this Lily. Here David trembled to his first perfection, on the brink of the dews. Here his soul found its perfect embodiment, in the trembling union of southern flame and northern waters. David, Dithyrambus: the adolescent. The shimmer, the instant of unstable combination, the soul for one moment perfectly embodied. Fire and dew, they call it. David, the Lily-flame, the Florentine.

The soul that held the fire and the dew clipped together in one lily-flame, where is it? David. Where is he? Cinquecento, a fleeting moment of adolescence. In that one moment the two eternal elements were held in consummation, forming the perfect

embodiment of the human soul. And then gone. David, the Lily, the
Florentine—Venus of the Scallop-Shell—Leonardo's John the
Baptist. The moment of adolescence—gone. The subtle evanescent
lily-soul. They are wistful, all of them: Botticelli's women,* Leo-
5 nardo's, Michelangelo's men: wistful, knowing the loss even in the
very moment of perfection. A day-lily, the Florentine. David
frowning, Mona Lisa sadly, subtly smiling, beyond bitterness,
Botticelli getting rapture out of sadness, his Venus wistfully Victrix.
Fire and dew for one moment proportionate, immediately falling
10 into disproportion.

They all knew. They knew the quenching of the flame, the
breaking of the lily-balance, the passing of perfection and the pure
pride of life, the inestimable loss. It had to be. They knew the mists
of the North damping down. Born of the fire, they had still to be born
15 of the mist. Christ, with his submission, universal humility, finding
one level, like mist settling, like water. A new flood. Savonarola
smokily quenched. The fire put out, or at least overwhelmed. Then
Luther and the North.

Michelangelo, Leonardo, Botticelli, how well they knew, artisti-
20 cally, what was coming. The magnificent pride of life and perfection
granted only to bud. The transient lily. Adam, David, Venus on her
shell, the Madonna of the Rocks:* they listen, all of them. What do
they hear? Perpetual sound of waters. The level sweep of waters,
waters overwhelming. Morality, chastity—another world drowned:
25 equality, democracy, the masses, like drops of water in one sea,
overwhelming all outstanding loveliness of the individual soul.
Quenching of all flame, in the great watery passivity which bears
down at last so ponderous. Christ-like submissiveness which, once it
bursts its bounds, floods the face of the earth with such devastation.
30 Pride of life! The perfect soul erect, holding the eternal elements
consummate in itself. Thus for one moment the young lily David.
For one moment Dionysus touched the hand of the Crucified: for
one moment, and then was dragged down. Meekness flooded the
soul of Dithyrambus, mist overwhelmed him. The elements super-
35 vene in the human soul, men become nature-worshippers; light,
landscape and mists—these take the place of human individuality.
Dionysus pale and corpse-like, there in the Piazza della Signoria.
David, Venus, Saint John, all overcome with mist and surrender of
the soul.
40 Yet no final surrender. Leonardo laughs last, even at the Cruci-

fied. David with his knitted brow and full limbs, is unvanquished. Livid, may be, corpse-coloured, quenched with innumerable rains of morality and democracy. Yet deep fountains of fire lurk within him. Must do. Witness the Florentines gathered at New Year's night to watch that fiery fruitless orgasm. They laugh, but it is Leonardo's 5 laugh. The fire is not ridiculous. It surges recurrent. Never to be quenched. Stubborn. The Florentine.

One day David finishes his adolescence. One day he reaps his mates.* It is a throbbing through the centuries of unquenchable fire, that will still leap out to consummation. The pride of life. The pride 10 of the fulfilled self. The bud is not nipped, it awaits its maturity. Not the frail lily. Not even the clinging purple vine. But the full tree of life in blossom.

LOOKING DOWN ON THE CITY

Supplementary note on the text

The text, taken from a carbon typescript (TCC) with autograph revisions, has not
been published previously. The Textual apparatus records all the deletions and
corrections made by DHL.

Looking Down on the City

I find I cannot force myself to look at the things one is supposed to look at. There stands the Bargello, the Medici Chapel, the Pitti Palace, Santa Croce.*—I get as far as the door, when a revulsion overcomes me—I go away. I don't want to *see* things any more: particularly the great works of man. They seem fixed at a point from which I want to get away. The Uffizi,* of course, is wonderful—but ten minutes is enough. These Christian-pagan pictures, with their yearnings and aspirations and personalities and self-consciousness: really I can stand no more. The war has worn out all the emotional tissue with which I cared and aspired. Now I no longer aspire: leave me alone and let me be myself.

It is easy still to deal out a certain intellectual-aesthetic appreciation for established works. But it is all a stunt. Even Lippo Lippi* does not touch me. I *see* his beauty: but I can't react. For a moment the pearl-like, air-and-sea-clean purity of Botticelli's Venus*—very lovely in the original, never seen in reproductions—enchants me. It reminds me that Florence is still the world-centre of the pearl-trade:* a fact I am told but don't pretend to vouch for. Some people can touch coral, and *know* it physically, in the grain. The Florentines seem to have the touch of pearls—the quick of the sea. All this probably is in a line with their curious adolescent interest in personalities.

But in my tissue I am weary of personality. I can't see it. I can't even hear it any more. Ach, the weariness of the personal! All that trend of self-conscious self-realization which the Renaissance initiates—how it aches me! All the pearly accretion of personality in mankind—what a disease it has become. Stubborn pagan indifference and sufficiency in the self: where can one find it? Certainly not in Florence.

Inside the town, the Piazza della Signoria alone goes below one's superficiality of vision. The great block of the Palazzo Vecchio, with

193

its hawk-head in heaven: and the uncouth Perseus: and that sheer
pearl of self-conscious adolescence, David.* The attainment of
personality—self-conscious self-realization—there he stands. It is
Narcissus, but with how vast a power inside him, how amazing a
5   potentiality. David is the clue. For that reason one really looks at
him. Perseus gives the show away, and so one keeps an eye on him
too. For the rest—ah, well!

And then—what else in Florence? Don't ask me, I am no Ruskin.
One thing moved me curiously. It is quite commonplace—I mean,
10   quite *de rigueur*, to go up to the Piazzale Michelangelo* and look
down upon the town. Every single tourist does it. Yet each time I
stand by the parapet and look down, I am moved by a strange deep
feeling which I cannot fathom: a kind of far-off emotion, like the
sound of surf in the distance, heavy. Who knows what it is.

15   The town lies below and very near. The river winds beneath one,
under four bridges, disappearing in a curve on the left. And the
brown-red town* spreads out so thick, so intense, so far. One could
almost stroke it with the hand. The Duomo—the naked tower of
Giotto*—the hawk-neck of the Palazzo Vecchio—a few other
20   churches—rising above the ruffled brown roofs, all level, far-
spreading, and the hills half encircling—a strange sight. One has
looked down on many cities—Turin* on her plain with the Alps
flashing beyond—London in her smoke—Edinburgh. But Florence
is different, quite different: not worldly.

25   "The Blessed Damosel looked down
         From the gold bar of Heaven—"*

Well, the bar is not gold, it is painted iron scratched with names. If
one could say:
"The Blessed Damosel looked down from the iron bar of
30   Heaven—" it would give something of the feeling. Florence—the
flowery town*—there is something tender and exposed about it. How
well one realizes that the Florentines love their city! It is hard to think
of fighting and dying for London; but one would fight and die for
Florence, even now.

35   A far-off sadness, an emotion deeper than the natural planes of
emotion, unrealizable, lying in the sub-stratum of one's being.
Florence! Beautiful, tender, naked as a flower—and why the grief?
Something of the same feeling comes to me from Leonardo's
*Madonna of the Rocks,** in our National Gallery—a sadness so deep

that it has hardly yet begun to be felt: root of all our modern nostalgia and neurasthenia. Leonardo's *Madonna of the Rocks* is the only picture I have seen which touches these roots.

It must be, I think, the pain which overcomes a man when he eats of the fruit of the Tree of Knowledge.* At the Renaissance mankind, and Florence perfectly, took a new apple, and opened a new field of consciousness, a new era. With it came the sense of sin and despair, as well as of delirious triumph. We have lived through this triumph, and began to feel the despair that was in the beginning. "Cursed is the earth in thy works," said God to Adam. Florence, the flower-town: clean, smokeless, with no factories—"cursed is the earth in thy works"?

In some scientific work I remember the stressed assertion *Nature abhors consciousness.** Yet what drives us into consciousness, except nature? They bit the apple, the Florentines, and entered upon the great era of modern civilization. Joy, and a misery inside the joy. Joy of the great gain in consciousness and power, enclosing a misery in the loss of spontaneity, the misery of becoming responsible for one's own reactions and reflexes, a hopelessly deliberate being: a conscious, self-conscious personality. Such a triumph with such a poison in it. The illusion and disillusion of Florence: David frowning. Leonardo unspeakably smiling.*

One must go right through with consciousness. Forward is the only direction. Sufficient consciousness liberates us to spontaneity again; a double freedom. Fata volentem ducunt, nolentem trahunt.* When we know enough we shall be perfectly willing. There is faith still in Florence.

In adolescence one seeks oneself. After adolescence comes maturity, where the self finds its own *aplomb* and powerful rich indifference.

But the Florentines still seek. And seeking, where will they not go? In our square by the river, on Saturday night, a fizzing torch, leaning against the rails of the monument, flaming on the darkness: a group of dark figures stooping, lifting: a tilted handcart standing aside. Instinct makes me go on without looking further. But after a few minutes a rattling behind me in the dark lane—a young man trotting holding aloft a torch—and the covered hand-cart pushed by two young men—a swathed body lying under the tilt—two more men trotting alongside. Gone in a moment, the torch running ahead in the narrow stone lane of the city.

Again in the night a great crowd near the Post Office—crowds of
men, all wildly talking—waiters running out from restaurants—men
eagerly reading the political notices stuck up on the wall. What
notices? I can't see; it is too dark. I can only see a faded "Viva Lenin,"
5 which dates from the election. Crowds of dark men,—a bomb
thrown in Gabrino's, I hear,—I wander through the groups,—
suddenly at my feet a long black pool of blood on the pavement.—
Why should I see, why should I hear? Only this I know: there is no
real danger, no real animosity: no virus in the crowd.

10 And then, next morning, music at an English friend's house over
the river. The beautiful old palace—a room in red damask and old
mirrors, with bluey-red rugs, and dark blue jars, shadowy in a
corner—a tall old rich-coloured room. The strings quivering in a
quintette—ah, how perfect! And then a Florentine girl playing a
15 violin concerto—her father's music: beautifully played, and causing
a pain of too-intense feeling. The old Florentine poignancy—all the
glamour, and besides, the hurt which is now almost surgical, as if our
tissue were being vivisected to give us consciousness. Afterwards,
the music-haunted eyes of the people—the curious, impressive
20 eye-brows of the girl, the rich old culture of the surroundings—the
violins laid down—the snatches of conversation in different languages.*

EUROPE VERSUS AMERICA

Europe Versus America

A young American said to me: "I am not very keen on Europe, but should like to see it, and have done with it." He is an ass. How can one "see" Europe and have done with it. One might as well say: I want to see the moon next week and have done with it. If one doesn't want to see the moon, he doesn't look. And if he doesn't want to see Europe, he doesn't look either. But neither of 'em will go away because he's not looking.

There's no "having done with it." Europe is here, and will be here, long after he has added a bit of dust to America. To me, I simply don't see the point of that American trick of saying one is "through with a thing," when the thing is a good deal bigger than oneself.

I can hear that young man saying: "Oh, I'm through with the moon, she's played out. She's a dead old planet anyhow, and was never more than a side issue." So was Eve, only a side issue. But when a man is through with her, he's through with most of his life.

It's the same with Europe. One may be sick of certain aspects of European civilisation. But they're in ourselves, rather than in Europe. As a matter of fact, coming back to Europe,* I realise how much more *tense* the European civilisation is, in the Americans, than in the Europeans. The Europeans still have a vague idea that the universe is greater than they are, and isn't going to change very radically, not for all the telling of all men put together. But the Americans are tense, somewhere inside themselves, as if they felt that once they slackened, the world would really collapse. It wouldn't. If the American tension snapped tomorrow, only that bit of the world which is tense and American would come to an end. Nothing more.

How could I say: I am through with America? America is a great continent; it won't suddenly cease to be. Some part of me will always be conscious of America. But probably some part greater still in me will always be conscious of Europe, since I am a European.

As for Europe's being old, I find it much younger than America. Even these countries of the Mediterranean, which have known quite a bit of history, seem to me much, much younger even than Taos, not to mention Long Island, or Coney Island.*

5   In the people here there is still, at the bottom, the old, young insouciance. It isn't that the young *don't care*: it is merely that, at the bottom of them there *isn't* care. Instead there is a sort of bubbling-in of life. It isn't till we grow old that we grip the very sources of our life with care, and strangle them.

10   And that seems to me the rough distinction between an American and a European. They are both of the same civilisation, and all that. But the American grips himself, at the very sources of his consciousness, in a grip of care: and then, to so much of the rest of life, is indifferent. Whereas, the European hasn't got so much care in him, 15 so he cares much more for life and living.

    That phrase again of wanting to see Europe and have done with it, shows that strangle-hold so many Americans have got on themselves. Why don't they say: I'd like to see Europe, and then, if it means something to me, good! and if it doesn't mean much to me, so 20 much the worse for both of us. Vogue la galère!*

    I've been a fool myself, saying: Europe is finished for me.—It wasn't Europe at all, it was myself, keeping a strangle-hold on myself. And that strangle-hold I carried over to America; as many a man, and woman worse still, has done before me.

25   Now, back in Europe, I feel a real relief. The past is too big, and too intimate, for one generation of men to get a strangle-hold on it. Europe is squeezing the life out of herself, with her mental education and her fixed ideas. But she hasn't got her hands round her own throat not half so far as America has hers; here the grip is already 30 falling slack; and if the system collapses, it'll only be another system collapsed, of which there have been plenty. But in America, where men grip themselves so much more intensely and suicidally—the women worse—the system has its hold on the very sources of consciousness, so God knows what would happen, if the system 35 broke.

    No, it's a relief to be by the Mediterranean, and gradually let the tight coils inside oneself come slack. There is much more life in a deep insouciance, which really is the clue to faith, than in this frenzied, keyed-up care, which is characteristic of our civilisation, 40 but which is at its worst, or at least its intensest, in America.

FIREWORKS

Supplementary note on the text

See Note on the texts, p. 182. The Textual apparatus only records Per1 and Per2. MS is recorded in a few cases when its reading has been preferred in order to emend accidental variants when a word or expression in Per1 matches MS exactly.

An additional silent emendation is Per2's use of the American spellings 'color' and 'colored'.

Fireworks

Yesterday being the twenty-fourth of June, and St. John's day; and
St. John's day being also the day of midsummer festival, when there
must be fiery celebration of some sort; St. John moreover being the
patron saint of Florence; for these various reasons Florence was lit
up last night, and there was a show of fireworks from the Piazzale.

The illuminations were rather scanty. The Palazzo Vecchio* had
little frames of electric bulbs round the windows, very meagre. But
above these, all along the battlements of the square roof, and in the
arches of the thin-necked tower, and between the battlements at the
top of the tower, the flames were orange-ruddy, and wavering. They
danced the night-long witch-night dance, midsummer's eve; a
hundred or two ruddy little dancements among the black, hard
battlements, and round the lofty, unrelenting square crown of the
building.

This was mediaeval and fascinating, in the soft, hot, moonlit night.
The Palazzo Vecchio has come down to our day, but not to our level.
It lifts its long slim neck, and is like a hawk looking round; in the
darkness its battlements ruffle their silhouette-like black feathers.
Like an old fierce bird from the Middle Ages it lifts its head over the
level town, eagle with notched plumes.

It is a wonder the modern spirit hasn't given it a knock over the
head, as it stands there so elegant in fierce old haughtiness.

But the modern spirit, this Midsummer's Eve, has only got as high
as the windows on the hard façade, fixing itself in stupid little electric
bulbs. Electric bulbs are stupid because they are fixed, unwinking,
unalive, giving off a flat, lifeless light. They are like brass nail-heads
on furniture, just about as midsummerish and frisky.

Above, where the black battlements ruffle like pinion-tips upon
the blond sky, and the darknecked tower suddenly shoots up, the
modern spirit has not yet reached. There the illuminations must be
the old, oil flare-lamps, like little torches. Because the flames have

203

living quick little bodies, that dance perpetually in the warm bland
air, and keep up the night; like the creative witches, or Shiva dancing
her dance of creation, the dance of the myriad movements.*

All this alive dancement is very encouraging, upon the severe old
5 building, that holds its fire-crested head in the sky, and ignores the
page-button electric bulbs on its breast below.

How dreary things are when they never flicker and waver and
change, when they keep on going on being the dreary same, and
never rise on tiptoe, nor shake their fingers and become different,
10 but pride themselves on their dead-head fixity. How stupid man has
been, craving for permanency and machine-made perfection, when
the only truly permanent things are those that are always quivering
and departing, like fire and like water. After all, the sunrays and the
rain have already wiped away a good deal of the Pyramids, which are
15 so stupid and pretentiously everlasting. Who on earth wants to be a
Pyramid, when we are all made up of little flames and rain-drops?

People were streaming out of the piazza, all in one direction; and
all having that queer little lively crowded look, under the high
buildings, that you see in the street-scenes of old pictures. Throngs
20 and groups of striding and standing and streaming little humans, that
still have a charm of alert life. And all diminutive, because of the
large buildings that rise around them.

Not that the Palazzo Vecchio or the Uffizi palace are really tall, in
terms of the Woolworth Tower.* But there again, the effect is all
25 different. Look down on the street from the twenty-second storey in
New York, and you see people creeping with the quick, mechanical
repulsiveness of ants. It is all a question of proportion.

The people are all flowing towards the dark mouth of the Uffizi,
towards the river. As they pass, the fountain continues to shoot up its
30 long and leaning stem of water, unheeded, only Bandinelli's thick,
naked marble man glistens all over in a gleaming wetness that gives
him an elemental life of his own. Michelangelo's David, untouched
by the fountain,* trails his foot with perpetual self-consciousness,
and hopes the crowd will look at him. They do not; they pass under
35 him and never think of him. Probably they do not like him, the
over-life-size, smirking, self-conscious young man who looks like
the beginning of all modern fatuity, with his big head. Anyhow, it is a
curious thing that his name is utterly unknown to the ordinary
Italians of the neighbourhood. Tell them your name is David, and
40 they stare at you with blank, stupefied incomprehension. They have

never heard the name. It might as well be tiddlywink. Yet there that great, realistic statue has stood, all this time, in the square where all the farmers meet every Friday to talk prices.* You would think they would know its name. They do not, though.

On the Lungarno* the crowd is solid. There is no wheel traffic. The whole length of the riverside has become one long theatre-pit, where the whole populace of the city is assembled to see the fireworks. In countless numbers, they stand and wait, yet you would hardly know they are there, they are so quiet.

The fireworks will go off from the Piazzale Michelangelo, which hangs like a platform or a natural terrace over the left bank of the Arno. So the crowd solidly lines the right bank of the river, and the whole town is there.

In the sky a little to the south, the fair, warm moon, almost full, lingers in a fleece of iridescent cloud, as if also wanting to look on, but from an immeasurable distance. There is no crowding near, on the moon's part.

The crowd is subdued and well behaved, without excitement and quite without exuberance. There is none of the usual exuberant holiday spirit. A man hawks half-a-dozen toy balloons, but nobody seems to buy them. Away down beyond the Ponte alle Grazie* there is a flare-lit little stall, and a man baking those small aniseed waffles,* which also nobody seems to buy. Only the vendors who silently walk through the crowd with little tubs of ice-cream, do a trade. But everything is curiously hushed.

It seems long to wait. Down on the grass and gravel of the still-full river, under the embankment, are silent throngs of people. And even the boats used in the daytime for loading gravel, are crowded. In the obscurity it is like a scene from Dante's noiseless underworld.

Still we must wait. The young men, wearing no hats now the summer is here, stroll winding through the groups of immovable citizens and wives, and nobody has anything to do. Easiest thing is to sit in the motor-car by the kerb, and look at the moon.

Near the car stand two women with a police-dog on a chain. The dog, of course, being a police-dog, is unhappy at the crowd. He crouches back against the car-wheel, rises again, turns round, looks at his mistresses, crouches again restlessly. *Bang*! up goes the first rocket, like a golden tadpole wiggling in the sky, emitting finally a shower of red and green sparks. And the dog winces almost out of his skin, tries to get under the running-board, and is pulled away.

Bang! Bang! Crackle! More rockets, more showers of sparks and
fizzes of aster-petal light in the sky. The dog working in agony on his
chain, the mistresses are divided between the showy heavens and
him. In the sky, the moon draws further and further off, while still
5 watching aloof. She is now at an immense distance, in another world
of time. And near at hand, in the tallish sky, there is a rolling and
fuming of smoke, a whistling of rockets, a spangling and splashing of
coloured lights, and most impressive of all, a continuous crepitation
and explosion within the air itself, the high air bursting in explosions
10 from within itself, in continual shocks. It is more like an air-raid,
than anything else.

So, the soul has two sets of impressions: that through hearing,
dark and sinister, an impression of air-raids and war; that
through vision, a sparkling and glitter of coloured lights in
15 heaven. One is holiday and entrancement, the other is menace
and depression.

The fool dog, of course, is in a pitiable state. He tries to hide
himself on the face of the earth, and cannot. At every extra bang and
crackle, he has to look, and he shivers mortally as the great lights
20 burst out on the night. *Bish!* the sky-asters open one beyond the
other, in a delayed fusillade. The dog shivers like a glass cup that is
going to shatter. The mistresses are more thrilled by his terror than
by the fireworks. It gives them a sense of strength, as they try to
comfort him. He puts his paws over his ears, and buries his nose. But
25 a fresh explosion shocks him out again, and he sits erect, like a
bronze statue of pure nervous suffering. Then he curls upon himself
again, as if he were his own only refuge. While the high sky bursts
and reverberates, wiggles with tadpoles of golden fire, plunges into
splashes of light, trembles downwards with spangles of fire, and is all
30 frazzled and broken as if someone from above threw down continual
stones into the sensitive ether.

The crowd watches in silence. Lounging young men wander by,
and in the subdued tone of mockery usual to the Italians, they say:
bello! bello! bellezza!*—But it is pure irony. As the light flares out,
35 you see dark trees and cypresses, Dantesque on the sky-line. And
down below, you see townspeople standing with uplifted faces,
motionless. Also you see a young man with his arm round the waist of
his white-clad girl, caressing her and making public love to her.
Love-making, like everything else, is now a public proceeding. The
40 stag goes into the depths of the forest. But the young city buck likes

the light to flare up and reveal his arm round the shoulders of his
girl, his hand stroking her neck.

Up on the Piazzale, they are letting off the figure-pieces:
wheels that turn round showerily in red and green and white fire,
fuming dense smoke, that moves curiously slow, in volumes, all   5
interpenetrated with colour. Then there is a red piece: and on top
of the old water-tower a column of red fire. It looks like a city
flaming and fuming in the distance, burnt by the enemy. And
again rattles the fusillade of a raid, while the smoke rolls ponderously, and the colour dies out, only the iridescence of the far,   10
unreachable moon nakedly tinges the low fume.

More rockets! There are lovely ones that lean down in the sky
like great spider-lilies, with long out-curving petals of soft light,
and at the end of each petal, a sudden drop of pure green fire, as
it were dew. But some strange hand of evanescence brushes the   15
blossom away, and it is gone, leaving the next rocket to burst and
show all the smoke-threads still stretching in the sky, the ghost of
the gone lily. The grey threads crumble like wild clematis fronds
in autumn, as the succeeding brilliance blots them out.

And all the time, in another, more real world, the explosions   20
and percussions continue, penetrating through the ear into the
soul, with a sense of fear. The dog in vain has tried to get used to
it. By now he is a numb nervous wreck.

There is a great spangling and puffing and trailing of long fires
in the sky, long sprays of white fire-blossoms puff out, other   25
many-petalled flowers curve their petals downwards like a grasping hand. Ah! Ah! at last it is all happening at once!

And as the eye is dazzled and thrilled, thinking how marvellous
man is, the ear almost ceases to hear. Yet the moment the sky
empties, it is the percussion of explosions that remains imprinted   30
on the hidden memory, the eye forgets almost instantly.

So, it is over! That was the *finale*. The chauffeur is gabbling
that it is shorter than last year. The crowd disperses quickly and
silently, diving into the outlets from the Lungarno, as if they were
running away. And you feel they are all mocking quietly at the   35
spectacle. *Panem et circenses** is all very well, but when the crowd
starts quietly jeering at your circus, you are left a bit at a loss.

And as you drive home again, into the silent countryside smelling faintly of vine-flowers, and you see the high moon filling the
sky with her soft presence, you are so glad that she does not spin   40

round and shed sparks, and make horrible explosions out of herself, but is still, and soft, and all-permeating.

THE NIGHTINGALE

Supplementary note on the text

See Note on the texts, p. 182. In MS a new paragraph always follows the quotations with one exception, whereas the printed versions often begin the new line without indentation; DHL's practice has been adopted throughout the essay.

MS – without the revisions found in Per1 – was published in Frieda Lawrence's memoir (A2); its variants and those of its setting-copy (TS) are recorded, but not the indented quotations which A2 printed in italics (except 211:28–9).

The Nightingale

Tuscany is full of nightingales, and in spring and summer they sing all the time, save in the middle of the night and the middle of the day. In the little leafy woods that hang on the steep of the hill towards the streamlet, as maidenhair hangs on a rock, you hear them piping up again in the wanness of dawn, about four o'clock in the morning: Hello! Hello! Hello! It is the brightest sound in the world: a nightingale piping up. Every time you hear it, you feel wonder and, it must be said, a thrill, because the sound is so bright, so glittering, it has so much power behind it.

"There goes the nightingale!" you say to yourself. It sounds in the half-dawn as if the stars were darting up from the little thicket and leaping away into the vast vagueness of the sky, to be hidden and gone. But the song rings on after sunrise, and each time you listen again, startled, you wonder: "Now *why* do they say he is a sad bird?"

He is the noisiest, most inconsiderate, most obstreperous and jaunty bird in the whole kingdom of birds. How John Keats managed to begin his *Ode to a Nightingale* with "My heart aches, and a drowsy numbness pains my senses——"* is a mystery to anybody acquainted with the actual song. You hear the nightingale silverily shouting: "What? What? What John?—Heart aches and a drowsy numbness pains?—tra-la-la!-tri-li-lilylilyly."

And why the Greeks said he—or she—was sobbing in a bush for a lost lover,* again I don't know. Jug-jug-jug! say the mediaeval writers,* to represent the rolling of the little balls of lightning in the nightingale's throat. A wild rich sound, richer than the eyes in a peacock's tail.—

> "And the bright brown nightingale, amorous
> Is half assuaged for Itylus——"*

They say, with that jug! jug! jug!—that she is sobbing. How they hear it, is a mystery. How anyone who didn't have his ears on upside

211

down ever heard the nightingale "sobbing," I don't know.

Anyhow, it's a male sound, a most intensely and undilutedly male sound. A pure assertion. There is not a hint nor a shadow of echo and hollow recall. Nothing at all like a hollow low bell. Nothing in the
5 world so unforlorn.

Perhaps that is what made Keats straightway feel forlorn.

> "Forlorn! the very word is like a bell
> To toll me back from thee to my sole self!"

Perhaps that is the reason of it: why they all hear sobs in the bush,
10 when the nightingale sings, while any honest-to-God listening person hears the ringing shouts of small cherubim. Perhaps because of the discrepancy.

Because in sober fact the nightingale sings with a ringing, punching vividness and a pristine assertiveness that makes a mere
15 man stand still. A kind of brilliant calling and interweaving of glittering exclamation such as must have been heard on the first day of creation, when the angels suddenly found themselves created, and shouting aloud before they knew it. Then there must have been a to-do of angels in the thickets of heaven! Hello! Hello! Behold!
20 Behold! Behold! It is I! It is I! What a mar-mar-marvellous occurrence! What?

For the pure splendidness of vocal assertion: *Lo! It is I!**—you have to listen to the nightingale. Perhaps for the visual perfection of the same assertion, you have to look at a peacock shaking all his eyes.
25 Among all the creatures created in final splendour, these two are perhaps the most finally perfect: the one is invisible, triumphing sound, the other is voiceless visibility. The nightingale is a quite undistinguished grey-brown bird, if you do see him: although he's got that tender, hopping mystery about him, of a thing that is rich
30 alive inside. Just as the peacock, when he does make himself heard, is awful, but still impressive: such a fearful shout from out of the menacing jungle. You can actually see him, in Ceylon,* yell from a high bough, then stream away past the monkeys, into the impenetrable jungle that seethes and is dark.

35 And perhaps, for this reason: the reason, that is, of pure angel-keen or demon-keen assertion of true self; the nightingale makes a man feel sad, and the peacock often makes him angry. It is a sadness that is half envy. The birds are so triumphantly positive in their created selves, eternally new from the hand of the rich bright God,

and perfect. The nightingale ripples with his own perfection. And
the peacock arches all his bronze and purple eyes with assuredness.

This,—this rippling assertion of a perfect bit of creation,—this
green shimmer of a perfect beauty in a bird, makes men angry or
melancholy, according as it assails the eye or the ear. The ear is   5
much less cunning than the eye. You can say to somebody: I like you
awfully: you look so beautiful this morning! and she will believe it
utterly, though your voice may really be vibrating with mortal hatred.
The ear is so stupid, it will accept any amount of false money in
words. But let one tiny gleam of the mortal hatred come into your   10
eye, or across your face, and it is detected immediately. The eye is so
shrewd and rapid.

For this reason, we get the peacock at once, in all his showy male
self-assertion: and we say, rather sneeringly: Fine feathers make fine
birds!* But when we hear the nightingale, we don't know what we   15
hear, we only know we feel sad: forlorn! And so we say it is the
nightingale that is sad.

The nightingale, let us repeat, is the most unsad thing in the
world: even more unsad than the peacock full of gleam. He has
nothing to be sad about. He feels perfect with life. It isn't conceit. He   20
just feels life-perfect, and he trills it out, shouts, jugs, gurgles, trills,
gives long, mock-plaintive calls, makes declarations, assertions, and
triumphs, but he never reflects. It is pure music, in so far as you
could never put words to it. But there are words for the feelings
aroused in us by the song. No! even that is not true. There are no   25
words to tell what one really feels, hearing the nightingale. It is
something so much purer than words, which are all tainted. Yet we
can say, it is some sort of feeling of triumph in one's own life-
perfection.

> " 'Tis not through envy of thy happy lot,   30
>   But being too happy in thine happiness,—
>   That thou, light-winged Dryad of the trees,
>   In some melodious plot
>   Of beechen green, and shadows numberless,
>   Singest of summer in full-throated ease.—"   35

Poor Keats, he has to be "too happy" in the nightingale's happiness, not being very happy in himself at all. So he wants to drink the
blushful Hippocrene* and fade away with the nightingale into the
forest dim.

> "Fade far away, dissolve, and quite forget
>   What thou among the leaves hast never known,
>   The weariness, the fever, and the fret—"

It is such sad, beautiful poetry of the human male. Yet the next
line strikes me as a bit ridiculous.

> "Here, where men sit and hear each other groan;
>   Where palsy shakes a few, sad, last grey hairs—" etc.

This is Keats, not at all the nightingale.—But the sad human male
still tries to break away, and get over into the nightingale world. Wine
will not take him across. Yet he will go.

> "Away! away! for I will fly to thee
>   Not charioted by Bacchus and his pards,
>   But on the viewless wings of Poesy—"

He doesn't succeed, however. The viewless wings of Poesy carry
him only into the bushes, not into the nightingale world. He is still
outside.

> "Darkling I listen: and, for many a time
>   I have been half in love with easeful Death,—"

The nightingale never made any man in love with easeful
death—except by contrast. The contrast between the bright flame of
positive pure self-aliveness, in the bird, and the uneasy flickering of
yearning selflessness, forever yearning for something outside
himself, which is Keats:

> "To cease upon the midnight with no pain,
>   While thou art pouring forth thy soul abroad
>   In such an ecstasy!
>   Still wouldst thou sing, and I have ears in vain—
>   To thy high requiem become a sod."—

How astonished the nightingale would be if he could be made to
realise what sort of answer the poet was answering to his song! He
would fall off the bough with amazement.

Because a nightingale, when you answer him back, only shouts
and sings louder. Suppose a few other nightingales pipe up in
neighbouring bushes—as they always do—then the blue-white
sparks of sound go dazzling up to heaven. And suppose you, mere

mortal, happen to be sitting on the shady bank having an altercation with the mistress of your heart, hammer and tongues, then the chief nightingale swells and goes at it like Caruso* in the third act, simply a brilliant, bursting frenzy of music, singing you down: till you simply can't hear yourself speak to quarrel. 5

There was, in fact, something very like a nightingale in Caruso, that bird-like bursting miraculous energy of song, and fullness of himself, and self-luxuriance.

> "Thou wast not born for death, immortal Bird!
> No hungry generations tread thee down;" 10

Not yet in Tuscany, anyhow. They are twenty to the dozen. Whereas the cuckoo seems remote and low-voiced, calling his low, half-secretive call as he flies past.—Perhaps it really is different in England.

> "The voice I hear this passing night was heard 15
> In ancient days by emperor and clown:
> Perhaps the self-same song that found a path
> Through the sad heart of Ruth, when, sick for home
> She stood in tears amid the alien corn;"—

And why in tears? Always tears. Did Diocletian, I wonder, among 20 the emperors, burst into tears when he heard the nightingale, and Aesop among the clowns? And Ruth,* really? Myself, I strongly suspect that young lady of setting the nightingale singing, like the nice damsel in Boccaccio's story, who went to sleep with the lively bird in her hand: *"tua figliuola è stata sì vaga dell' usignuolo, ch'ella l'ha* 25 *preso e tienlosi in mano."**

And what does the hen nightingale think of it all, as she mildly sits upon the eggs and hears milord giving himself forth? Probably she likes it for she goes on breeding him as jaunty as ever. Probably she prefers his high cockalorum to the poet's humble moan: 30

> "Now more than ever seems it rich to die,
> To cease upon the midnight with no pain—"

That wouldn't be much use to the hen nightingale. And one sympathises with Keats's Fanny,* and understands why she wasn't having any. Much good such a midnight would have been to *her*! 35 Perhaps, when all's said and done, the female of the species gets more out of life when the male isn't wanting to cease upon the midnight, with or without pain. There are better uses for midnights. And a bird that sings because he's full of his own bright life, and leaves her to keep the eggs cosy, is perhaps preferable to one who moans, even with love of her.

5   Of course, the nightingale is utterly unconscious of the little dim hen while he sings. And he never mentions her name. But *she* knows well enough that the song is half her; just as she knows the eggs are half him. And just as she doesn't want him coming in and putting a heavy foot down on her little bunch of eggs, he doesn't want her poking into his song, and fussing over it, and mussing it up. Every man to his trade, and every woman to hers.

> "Adieu! Adieu! thy plaintive anthem fades—"

It never was a plaintive anthem, it was Caruso at his jauntiest. But don't try to argue with a poet.

MAN IS A HUNTER

Man is a Hunter

It is a very nice law which forbids shooting in England on Sundays. Here in Italy, on the contrary, you would think there was a law ordering every Italian to let off a gun as often as possible. Before the eyelids of dawn have come apart, long before the bells of the tiny church* jangle to announce daybreak, there is a sputter and crackle as of irritating fireworks, scattering from the olive gardens and from the woods. You sigh in your bed. The Holy Day has started: the huntsmen are abroad: they will keep at it till heaven sends the night, and the little birds are no more.

The very word *cacciatore*, which means hunter, stirs one's bile. Oh Nimrod, Oh Bahram, put by your arrows!

> "And Bahram, the great hunter; the wild ass
> Stamps o'er his head, and cannot wake his sleep."*

Here, an infinite number of tame asses shoot over my head, if I happen to walk in the wood, to look at the arbutus berries, and they never fail to rouse my ire, no matter how fast asleep it may have been.

Man is a hunter! *L'uomo è cacciatore*! The Italians are rather fond of saying it. It sounds so virile. One sees Nimrod surging through the underbrush, with his spear, in the wake of a bleeding lion.—And if it is a question of a man who has got a girl into trouble: *l'uomo è cacciatore*! man is a hunter! what can you expect? It behoves the "game" to look out for itself. Man is a hunter!

There used to be a vulgar song: "If the Missis wants to go, for a row, let 'er go!"* Here it should be: "If the master wants to run, with a gun, let him run!"—For the pine-wood is full of them, as a dog's back with fleas in summer. They crouch, they lurk, they stand erect, motionless as virile statues, with gun on the alert. Then bang! they have shot something, with an astonishing amount of noise! And then they run, with fierce and predatory strides, to the spot.

There is nothing there! Nothing! The game! La caccia!* where is

it? If they had been shooting at the ghost of Hamlet's father, there could not be a blanker and more spooky emptiness. One expects to see a wounded elephant lying on its side writhing its trunk; at the very least, a wild boar ploughing the earth in his death-agony. But
5 no! There is nothing, just nothing at all! Man, being a hunter, is, fortunately for the rest of creation, a very bad shot.

Nimrod, in velveteen corduroys, bandolier, cartridges, game bag over his shoulder and gun in hand, stands with feet apart, virilissimo, on the spot where the wild boar should be, and gazes downwards at
10 some imaginary point in underworld space. So! Man is a hunter. He casts a furtive glance around, under the arbutus bush, and a tail of his eye in my direction, knowing I am looking on in raillery. Then he hitches his game bag more determinedly over his shoulder, grips his gun, and strides off uphill, large strides, virile as Hector. Perhaps
15 even he is a Hector, Italianised into Ettore. Anyhow, he's going to be the death of something or somebody, if only he can shoot straight.

A Tuscan pine-wood is by no means a jungle. The trees are umbrella pines, with the umbrellas open, and bare handles. They are rather parsimoniously scattered. The undergrowth, moreover, is
20 allowed to grow only for a couple of years or so, then it is most assiduously reaped, gleaned, gathered, cleaned up clean as a lawn, for cooking Nimrod's macaroni. So that, in a *pineta*,* you have a piney roof over your head, and for the rest, a pretty clear run for your money. So where can the game lurk? There is hardly cover for a
25 bumble bee. Where can the game be, that is worth all this powder? the lions and wolves and boars that must prowl perilously round all these Nimrods?

You will never know. Or not until you are going home, between the olive trees. The hunters have been burning powder in the open,
30 as well as in the wood: a proper fusillade. Then, on the path between the olives, you may pick up a warm, dead bull-finch, with a bit of blood on it. The little grey bird lies on its side, with its frail feet closed, and its red breast ruffled. Nimrod, having hit for once, has failed to find his quarry.
35 Or you will know better when the servant comes excitedly and asks: "Signore, do you want any game?"—Game! splendid idea! a couple of partridges? a hare? even a wild rabbit? Why of course! So she arrives in triumph with a knotted red handkerchief, and the not very bulky game inside it. Untie the knots! Aha!—Alas! There, in a
40 little heap on the table, three robins, two finches, four hedge-

sparrows, and two starlings, in a fluffy, coloured, feathery little heap, all the small heads rolling limp. "Take them away!" you say. "We don't eat little birds."—"But these," she says, tipping up the starlings roughly, "these are big ones!"—"Not these either do we eat."—"No?" she exclaims, in a tone which means: *more fools you*! 5 And disgusted, disappointed at not having sold the goods, she departs with the game.

You will know best of all if you go to the market, and see whole yard-lengths of robins, like coral and onyx necklaces, and strings of bull-finches, gold-finches, larks, sparrows, nightingales, starlings, 10 temptingly offered along with strings of sausages, these last looking like the strings of pearls in the show. If one bought the birds to wear as ornament, barbaric necklaces, it would be more conceivable. You can get quite a string of different coloured ones for tenpence. But imagine the small mouthful of little bones each of these tiny carcases 15 must make!

But after all, a partridge and a pheasant are only a bit bigger than a sparrow and a finch. And compared to a flea, a robin is big game. It is all a question of dimensions. Man is a hunter. "If the master wants to hunt, don't you grunt, let him hunt!" 20

FLOWERY TUSCANY

Supplementary note on the text

See Note on the texts, p. 182. Additional silent emendations are the following:

'Flowery Tuscany', I–III: Per2 dropped the part numbers and breaks and used the American spelling for 'color'.

'Flowery Tuscany', IV: A1 printed *'Wandervögel'*, whereas the typescripts read 'Wandervogel' in the adjectival form, and 'Wandervögeln' in the substantive, plural. In this edition, the plural forms of the word have been corrected according to A1, whereas DHL's practice has been preserved in the adjectival form; the words are not italicised, following DHL's practice.

Flowery Tuscany

I

Each country has its own flowers, that shine out specially there. In England it is daisies and buttercups, hawthorn and cowslips. In America it is golden rod, star-grass, June daisies, and maple and asters, that we call michaelmas daisies. In India, hibiscus and dattura and champa flowers, and in Australia mimosa, that they call wattle, and sharp-tongued strange heath-flowers. In Mexico it is cactus flowers, that they call roses of the desert, lovely and crystalline among many thorns; and also the dangling yard-long clusters of the cream bells of the yucca, like drooping froth.

But by the Mediterranean, now as in the days of the Argosy,* and, we hope, for ever, it is narcissus and anemone, asphodel and myrtle. Narcissus and anemone, asphodel, crocus, myrtle and parsley, they leave their sheer significance only by the Mediterranean. There are daisies in Italy too: at Paestum* there are white little carpets of daisies, in March, and Tuscany is spangled with celandine. But for all that, the daisy and the celandine are English flowers, their best significance is for us and for the north.

The Mediterranean has narcissus and anemone, myrtle and asphodel and grape hyacinth. These are the flowers that speak and are understood, in the sun round the Middle Sea.

Tuscany is especially flowery, being wetter than Sicily and more homely than the Roman hills. Tuscany manages to remain so remote, and secretly smiling to itself in its many sleeves. There are so many hills popping up, and they take no notice of one another. There are so many little deep valleys with streams that seem to go their own little way entirely, regardless of river or sea. There are thousands, millions of utterly secluded little nooks, though the land has been under cultivation these thousands of years. But the intensive culture of vine and olive and wheat, by the ceaseless industry of naked human hands and winter-shod feet, and slow-stepping, soft-eyed

225

oxen does not devastate a country, does not denude it, does not lay it
bare, does not uncover its nakedness, does not drive away either
Pan* or his children. The streams run and rattle over wild rocks of
secret places, and murmur through blackthorn thickets where the
5   nightingales sing all together, unruffled and undaunted.

It is queer that a country so perfectly cultivated as Tuscany, where
half the produce of five acres of land will have to support ten human
mouths, still has so much room for the wild flowers and the
nightingale. When little hills heave themselves suddenly up, and
10 shake themselves free of neighbours, man has to build his garden
and his vineyard, and sculpt his landscape. Talk of hanging gardens
of Babylon,* all Italy, apart from the plains, is a hanging garden. For
centuries upon centuries man has been patiently modelling the
surface of the Mediterranean countries, gently rounding the hills,
15 and graduating the big slopes and the little slopes into the almost
invisible levels of terraces. Thousands of square miles of Italy have
been lifted in human hands, piled and laid back in tiny little flats,
held up by the drystone walls, whose stones came from the lifted
earth. It is a work of many, many centuries. It is the gentle, sensitive
20 sculpture of all the landscape. And it is the achieving of the peculiar
Italian beauty which is so exquisitely natural because man, feeling his
way sensitively to the fruitfulness of the earth, has moulded the earth
to his necessity without violating it.

Which shows that it *can* be done. Man *can* live on the earth and by
25 the earth without disfiguring the earth. It has been done here, on all
these sculptured hills and softly, sensitively terraced slopes.

But of course, you can't drive a steam plough on terraces four
yards wide, terraces that dwindle and broaden and sink and rise a
little, all according to the pitch and the breaking outline of the
30 mother hill. Corn has got to grow on these little shelves of earth,
where already the grey olive stands semi-invisible, and the grape-
vine twists upon its own scars. If oxen can step with that lovely pause
at every little stride, they can plough the narrow field. But they will
have to leave a tiny fringe, a grassy lip over the dry-stone wall below.
35 And if the terraces are too narrow to plough, the peasant digging
them will still leave the grassy lip, because it helps to hold the
surface, in the rains.

And here the flowers take refuge. Over and over and over and over
has this soil been turned, twice a year, sometimes three times a year,
40 for several thousands of years. Yet the flowers have never been

driven out. There is a very rigorous digging and sifting, the little
bulbs and tubers are flung away into perdition, not a weed shall
remain.

Yet spring returns, and on the terrace tips, and in the stony nooks
between terraces, up rise the aconites, the crocuses, the narcissus 5
and the asphodel, the inextinguishable wild tulips. There they are,
forever hanging on the precarious brink of an existence, but forever
triumphant, never quite losing their footing. In England, in America,
the flowers get rooted out, driven back. They become fugitive. But in
the intensive cultivation of ancient Italian terraces, they dance round 10
and hold their own.

Spring begins with the first narcissus, rather cold and shy and
wintry. They are the little bunchy, creamy narcissus with the yellow
cup like the yolk of the flower. The natives call these flowers
"tazzette," little cups. They grow on the grassy banks rather sparse, 15
or push up among thorns.

To me they are winter flowers, and their scent is winter. Spring
starts in February, with the winter aconite. Some icy day, when the
wind is down from the snow of the mountains, early in February, you
will notice on a bit of fallow land, under the olive trees, tight, 20
pale-gold little balls, clenched tight as nuts, and resting on round
ruffs of green near the ground. It is the winter aconite suddenly
come.

The winter aconite is one of the most charming flowers. Like all
the early blossoms, once her little flower emerges it is quite naked. 25
No shutting a little green sheath over herself, like the daisy or the
dandelion. Her bubble of frail, pale, pure gold rests on the round frill
of her green collar, with the snowy wind trying to blow it away.

But without success. The tramontana* ceases, comes a day of wild
February sunshine. The clenched little nuggets of the aconite puff 30
out, they become light bubbles like small balloons, on a green base.
The sun blazes on, with February splendour. And by noon, all under
the olives are wide-open little suns, the aconites spreading all their
rays; and there is an exquisitely sweet scent, honey-sweet, not narcissus frosty; and there is a February humming of little brown bees. 35

Till afternoon, when the sun slopes, and the touch of snow comes
back into the air.

But at evening, under the lamp on the table, the aconites are wide
and excited, and there is a perfume of sweet spring that makes one
almost start humming and trying to be a bee. 40

Aconites don't last very long. But they turn up in all odd places—on clods of dug earth, and in land where the broad-beans are thrusting up, and along the lips of terraces. But they like best land left fallow for one winter. There they throng, showing how 5 quick they are to seize on an opportunity to live and shine forth.

In a fortnight, before February is over, the yellow bubbles of the aconite are crumpling to nothingness. But already in a cosy nook the violets are dark purple, and there is a new little perfume on the air.

Like the débris of winter stands the hellebore, in all the wild 10 places, and the butcher's broom is flaunting its last bright red berry. Hellebore is Christmas roses, but in Tuscany the flowers never come white. They emerge out of the grass towards the end of December, flowers wintry of winter, and they are delicately pale green, and of a lovely shape, with yellowish stamens. They have a 15 peculiar wintry quality of invisibility, so lonely rising from the sere grass, and pallid green, held up like a little hand-mirror that reflects nothing. At first they are single upon a stem, short, and lonely, and very wintry-beautiful, with a will not to be touched, not to be noticed. One instinctively leaves them alone. But as January draws towards 20 February, these hellebores, these greenish Christmas roses become more assertive. Their pallid water-green becomes yellower, pale sulphur-yellow-green, and they rise up, they are in tufts, in throngs, in veritable bushes of greenish open flowers, assertive, bowing their faces with a hellebore assertiveness. In some places they throng 25 among the bushes and above the water of the stream, giving the peculiar pale glimmer almost of primroses, as you walk among them. Almost of primroses, yet with a coarse hellebore leaf, and an uprearing hellebore assertiveness, like snakes of winter.

And as one walks among them, one brushes the last scarlet balls 30 off the butcher's broom. This low little shrub is the Christmas holly of Tuscany, only a foot or so high, with a vivid red berry stuck on in the middle of its sharp, hard leaf. In February the last red ball rolls off the prickly plume, and winter rolls with it. The violets already are emerging from the moisture.

35 But before the violets make any show, there are the crocuses. If you walk up through the pinewood that lifts its umbrellas of pine so high, up till you come to the brow of the hill at the top, you can look south, due south, and see snow on the Apennines, and on a blue afternoon, seven layers of blue-hilled distance.

40 Then you sit down on that southern slope, out of the wind, and

there it is warm, whether it be January or February, tramontana or not. There the earth has been baked by innumerable suns, baked and baked again: moistened by many rains, but never wetted for long. Because it is rocky, and full to the south, and sheering steep in the slope.

And there, in February, in the funny baked desert of that crumbly slope, you will find the first crocuses. On the sheer aridity of crumbled stone you see a queer, alert little star, very sharp, and quite small. It has opened out rather flat, and looks like a tiny single freesia flower, creamy, with a smear of yellow yolk. It has no stem, seems to have been just lightly dropped on the crumbled, baked rock. It is the first hill-crocus.

II

North of the Alps, the everlasting winter is interrupted by summers that struggle and soon yield. South of the Alps, the everlasting summer is interrupted by spasmodic and spiteful winters that never get a real hold, but that are mean and dogged. North of the Alps, you may have a pure winter's day, in June. South of the Alps, you may have a midsummer day in December or January or even February. The in-between, in either case, is just as it may be. But the lands of the sun are south of the Alps, even now, and the lands of greyness are north of the Alps, forever.

Yet things, the flowers especially, that belong to both sides of the Alps, are not much earlier south than north of the mountains. Through all the winter there are roses in the garden, lovely creamy roses, more pure and mysterious than those of summer, leaning perfect from the stem. And the narcissus in the garden are out by the end of January, and the little single hyacinths early in February.

But out in the fields, the flowers are hardly any sooner than English flowers. It is mid-February before the first violets, the first crocus, the first primrose. And in mid-February one may find a violet, a primrose, a crocus in England, in the hedgerows and the garden corner.

And still here is a difference. There are several kinds of wild crocus in this region of Tuscany: tiny little spiky mauve ones, and spiky little creamy ones, that grow among the pine-trees of the bare slopes. But the beautiful ones are those of a meadow in the corner of the woods, the low hollow meadow below the steep, shadowy pine-slopes, the secretive grassy dip where the water seeps through the turf all winter, where the stream runs between thick bushes, where the nightingale sings his mightiest, in May, and where the wild thyme is rosy and full of bees, in summer.

Here the lavender crocuses are most at home—here sticking out
5   of the deep grass, in a hollow like a cup, a bowl of grass, come the lilac-coloured crocuses, like an innumerable encampment. You may see them at twilight, with all the buds shut, in the mysterious stillness of the grassy underworld, palely glimmering like myriad folded tents. So the Apaches still camp, and close their teepees, in the hollows of
10 the great hills of the west, at night.

But in the morning, it is quite different. Then the sun shines strong on the horizontal green cloud-puffs of the pines, the sky is clear and full of life, the water runs hastily, still browned by the last juice of crushed olives.* And then the earth's bowl of crocuses is
15 amazing. You cannot believe that the flowers are really still. They are open with such delight, and their pistil-thrust is so red-orange, and they are so many, all reaching out wide and marvellous, that it suggests a perfect ecstasy of radiant, thronging movement, lit-up violet and orange, and surging in some invisible rhythm of concer-
20 ted, delightful movement. You cannot believe they do not move, and make some sort of crystalline sound of delight. If you sit still and watch, you begin to move with them, like moving with the stars, and you feel the sound of their radiance. All the little cells of the flowers must be leaping with flowery life and utterance.

25 And the small brown honey-bees hop from flower to flower, dive down, try, and off again. The flowers have been already rifled, most of them. Only sometimes a bee stands on his head, kicking slowly inside the flower, for some time. He has found something. And all the bees have little loaves of pollen, bee-bread, in their elbow joints.

30 The crocuses last in their beauty for a week or so, and as they begin to lower their tents and abandon camp, the violets begin to thicken. It is already March. The violets have been showing like tiny dark hounds for some weeks. But now the whole pack comes forth, among the grass and the tangle of wild thyme, till the air all sways
35 subtly scented with violets, and the banks above where the crocuses had their tents are now swarming brilliant purple with violets. They are the sweet violets of early spring, but numbers have made them bold, for they flaunt and ruffle till the slopes are a bright, blue-purple blaze of them, full in the sun. With an odd late crocus still standing
40 wondering and erect amongst them.

And now that it is March, there is a rush of flowers. Down by the other stream, which turns sideways to the sun and has tangles of briar and bramble, down where the hellebore has stood so wan and dignified all winter, there are now white tufts of primroses, suddenly come. Among the tangle and near the water-lip, tufts and bunches of primroses, in abundance. Yet they look more wan, more pallid, more flimsy than English primroses. They lack some of the full wonder of the northern flowers. One tends to overlook them, to turn to the great, solemn-faced purple violets that rear up from the bank, and above all, to the wonderful little towers of the grape-hyacinth.

I know no flower that is more fascinating, when it first appears, than the blue grape-hyacinth. And yet, because it lasts so long, and keeps on coming so repeatedly, for at least two months, one tends later on to ignore it, even to despise it a little. Yet that is very unjust.

The first grape-hyacinths are towers of blue, thick and rich and meaningful, above the unrenewed grass. The upper buds are pure blue, shut tight; round balls of pure, perfect warm blue, blue, blue; while the lower bells are darkish blue-purple, with the spark of white at the mouth. As yet, none of the lower bells has withered, to leave the greenish, separate sparseness of fruiting that spoils the grape hyacinth later on, and makes it seem naked and functional. All hyacinths are like that, in their seeding.

But at first, you have only a compact tower of night-blue clearing to dawn, and extremely beautiful. If we were tiny as fairies, and lived only a summer, how lovely these great trees of bells would be to us, towers of night and dawn-blue globes. They would rise above us thick and succulent, and the purple globes would push the blue ones up, with white sparks of nipples, and we should see a god in them.

As a matter of fact, someone once told me they were the flowers of the many-breasted Artemis; and it is true, the Cybele of Ephesus, with her clustered breasts,* was like a grape-hyacinth at the bosom.

This is the time, in March, when the sloe is white and misty in the hedge-tangle by the stream, and on the slope of land the peach tree stands pink and alone. The almond blossom, silvery pink, is passing, but the peach, deep-toned, bluey, not at all ethereal, this reveals itself like flesh, and the trees are like isolated individuals: the peach and the apricot.

A man said this spring: "Oh, I *don't* care for peach blossom! It is such a vulgar pink!" One wonders what anybody means by a "vulgar" pink. I think pink flannelette is rather vulgar. But probably

it's the flannelette's fault, not the pink. And peach-blossom has a beautiful sensual pink, far from vulgar, most rare and private. And pink is so beautiful in a landscape: pink houses, pink almond, pink peach and purply apricot, pink asphodels. It is so conspicuous and so
5   individual, that pink among the coming green of spring.

Because the first flowers that emerge from winter seem always white or yellow or purple. Now the celandines are out, and along the edges of the podere,* the big, sturdy, black-purple anemones, with black hearts.

10   They are curious, these great, dark-violet anemones. You may pass them on a grey day, or at evening or early morning, and never see them. But as you come along in the full sunshine, they seem to be baying at you with all their throats, baying deep purple into the air. It is because they are hot and wide open now, gulping the sun. Whereas
15   when they are shut, they have a silkiness and a curved head, like the curve of an umbrella handle, and a peculiar outward colourlessness, that makes them quite invisible. They may be under your feet, and you will not see them.

Altogether anemones are odd flowers. On these last hills above
20   the plain, we have only the big black-purple ones, in tufts here and there, not many. But two hills away, the young green corn is blue with the lilac-blue kind, still the broad petalled sort with the darker heart. But these flowers are smaller than our dark-purple, and frailer, more silky. Ours are substantial, thickly vegetable flowers,
25   and not abundant. The others are lovely and silky-delicate, and the whole corn is blue with them. And they have a sweet, sweet scent, when they are warm.

Then on the priest's podere there are the scarlet, Adonis-blood anemones:* only in one place, in one long fringe under a terrace, and
30   then by a path below. These flowers above all you will never find unless you look for them in the sun. Their silver silk outside makes them quite invisible, when they are shut up.

Yet if you are passing in the sun, a sudden scarlet faces on to the air, one of the loveliest scarlet apparitions in the world. The inner
35   surface of the Adonis-blood anemone is as fine as velvet, and yet there is no suggestion of pile, not as much as on a velvet rose. And from this inner smoothness issues the red colour, perfectly pure and unknown of earth, no earthiness, and yet solid, not transparent. How a colour manages to be perfectly strong and impervious, yet of a
40   purity that suggests condensed light, yet not luminous, at least, not

transparent, is a problem. The poppy in her radiance is translucent, and the tulip in her utter redness has a touch of opaque earth. But the Adonis-blood anemone is neither translucent nor opaque. It is just pure, condensed red, of a velvetiness without velvet, and a scarlet without glow.   5

This red seems to me the perfect premonition of summer—like the red on the outside of apple-blossom—and later, the red of the apple. It is the premonition in redness of summer and of autumn.

The red flowers are coming now. The wild tulips are in bud, hanging their grey leaves like flags. They come up in myriads,   10 wherever they get a chance. But they are holding back their redness till the last days of March, the early days of April.

Still, the year is warming up. By the high ditch the common magenta anemone is hanging its silky tassels, or opening its great magenta daisy-shape to the hot sun. It is much nearer to red than the   15 big-petalled anemones are: except the Adonis-blood. They say these anemones sprang from the tears of Venus, which fell as she went looking for Adonis. At that rate, how the poor lady must have wept, for these anemones by the Mediterranean are common as daisies in England.   20

The daisies are out here too, in sheets, and they too are red-mouthed. The first ones are big and handsome. But as March goes on, they dwindle to bright little things, like tiny buttons, clouds of them together. That means summer is nearly here.

The red tulips open in the corn like poppies, only with a heavier   25 red. And they pass quickly, without repeating themselves. There is little lingering in a tulip.

In some places there are odd yellow tulips, slender, spiky and Chinese-looking. They are very lovely, pricking out their dulled yellow in slim spikes. But they too soon lean, expand beyond   30 themselves, and are gone like an illusion.

And when the tulips are gone, there is a moment's pause, before summer. Summer is the next move.

III

In the pause towards the end of April, when the flowers seem to   35 hesitate, the leaves make up their minds to come out. For some time, at the very ends of the bare boughs of fig-trees, spurts of pure green have been burning like little cloven tongues of green fire vivid on the tips of the candelabrum. Now these spurts of green spread out, and

begin to take the shape of hands, feeling for the air of summer. And
tiny green figs are below them, like glands on the throat of a goat.

For some time, the long stiff whips of the vine have had knobby
pink buds, like flower buds. Now these pink buds begin to unfold
5 into greenish, half-shut fans of leaves with red in the veins, and tiny
spikes of flower, like seed-pearls. Then, in all its down and pinky
dawn, the vine-rosette has a frail, delicious scent of a new year.

Now the aspens on the hill are all remarkable with the translucent
membranes of blood-veined leaves. They are gold-brown, but not
10 like autumn, rather like the thin wings of bats when like birds—call
them birds—they wheel in clouds against the setting sun, and the
sun glows through the stretched membrane of their wings, as
through thin, brown-red stained glass. This is the red sap of
summer, not the red dust of autumn. And in the distance the aspens
15 have the tender, panting glow of living membrane just come awake.
This is the beauty of the frailty of spring.

The cherry tree is something the same, but more sturdy. Now, in
the last week of April, the cherry-blossom is still white, but waning
and passing away: it is late this year: and the leaves are clustering
20 thick and softly copper in their dark, blood-filled glow. It is queer
about fruit-trees in this district. The pear and the peach were out
together. But now the pear-tree is a lovely thick softness of new and
glossy green, vivid with a tender fulness of apple-green leaves,
gleaming among all the other greens of the landscape, the half-high
25 wheat, emerald, and the grey olive, half-invisible, the browning
green of the dark cypress, the black of the evergreen oak, the rolling,
heavy green puffs of the stone pines, the flimsy green of small peach
and almond trees, the sturdy young green of horse-chestnut. So
many greens, all in flakes and shelves and tilted tables and round
30 shoulders and plumes and shaggles* and uprisen bushes, of greens
and greens, sometimes blindingly brilliant, at evening, when the
landscape looks as if it were on fire from inside, with greenness and
with gold.

The pear is perhaps the greenest thing in the landscape. The
35 wheat may shine lit-up yellow, or glow bluish, but the pear-tree is
green in itself. The cherry has white, half-absorbed flowers, so has
the apple. But the plum is rough with her new foliage, and
inconspicuous, inconspicuous as the almond, the peach, the apricot,
which one can no longer find in the landscape, though twenty days
40 ago they were the distinguished pink individuals of the whole

countryside. Now they are gone. It is the time of green, pre-eminent green, in ruffles and flakes and slabs.

In the wood, the scrub-oak is only just coming uncrumpled, and the pines keep their hold on winter. They are wintry things, stone-pines. At Christmas, their heavy green clouds are richly beautiful, when the cypresses raise their tall and naked bodies of dark green, and the osiers are vivid red-orange, on the still blue air, and the land is lavender. Then, in mid-winter, the landscape is most beautiful in colour, surging with colour.

But now, when the nightingale is still drawing out his long, wistful, yearning, teasing plaint-note, and following it up with a rich and joyful burble, the pines and the cypresses seem hard and rusty, and the wood has lost its subtlety and its mysteriousness. It still seems wintry, in spite of the yellowing young oaks, and the heath in flower. But hard, dull pines above, and hard, dull tall heath below, all stiff and resistant, this is out of the mood of spring.

In spite of the fact that the stone-white heath is in full flower, and very lovely when you look at it. But it does not, casually, give the impression of blossom. More the impression of having its tips and crests all dipped in hoar-frost; or in whitish dust. It has a peculiar ghostly colourlessness amid the darkish colourlessness of the wood altogether, which completely takes away the sense of spring.

Yet the tall white heath is very lovely, in its invisibility. It grows sometimes as tall as a man, lifting up its spires and its shadowy-white fingers with a ghostly fulness, amid the dark, rusty green of its lower bushiness; and it gives off a sweet honied scent in the sun, and a cloud of fine white stone-dust, if you touch it. Looked at closely, its little bells are most beautiful, delicate and white, with the brown-purple inner eye and the dainty pin-head of the pistil. And out in the sun, at the edge of the wood, where the heath grows tall and thrusts up its spires of dim white next a brilliant, yellow-flowering vetch-bush, under a blue sky, the effect has a real magic.

And yet, in spite of all, the dim whiteness of all the flowering heath-fingers only adds to the hoariness and out-of-date quality of the pine-woods, now in the pause between spring and summer. It is the ghost of the interval.

Not that this week is flowerless. But the flowers are little, lonely things, here and there: the early purple orchid, ruddy and very much alive, you come across occasionally, then the little groups of bee-orchid, with their ragged, conceited indifference to their appear-

ance. Also there are the huge bud-spikes of the stout, thick-flowering pink orchid, huge buds like fat ears of wheat, hard-purple and splendid. But already odd grains of the wheat-ear are open, and out of the purple hangs the delicate pink rag of a floweret. Also there
5   are very lovely and choice cream-coloured orchids, with brown spots on the long and delicate lip. These grow in the more moist places, and have exotic tender spikes, very rare-seeming. Another orchid is a little, pretty yellow one.

But orchids, somehow, do not make a summer. They are too aloof
10 and individual. The little slate-blue scabious is out, but not enough to raise an appearance. Later on, under the real hot sun, he will bob into notice. And by the edges of the paths there are odd rosy cushions of wild-thyme. Yet these, too, are rather samples than the genuine thing. Wait another month, for wild thyme.
15 The same with the irises. Here and there, in fringes along the upper edge of terraces, and in odd bunches among the stones, the dark-purple iris sticks up. It is beautiful, but it hardly counts. There is not enough of it, and it is torn and buffeted by too many winds. First the wind blows with all its might from the Mediterranean, not
20 cold, but infinitely wearying, with its rude and insistent pushing. Then, after a moment of calm, back comes a hard wind from the Adriatic, cold, and disheartening. Between the two of them, the dark-purple iris flutters and tatters and curls as if it were burnt: while the little yellow rock-rose streams at the end of its thin stalk, and
25 wishes it had not been in such a hurry to come out.

There is really no hurry. By May, the great winds will drop, and the great sun will shake off his harassments. Then the nightingale will sing an unbroken song, and the discreet, barely-audible Tuscan cuckoo will be a little more audible. Then the lovely pale-lilac irises
30 will come out in all their showering abundance of tender, proud, spiky bloom, till the air will gleam with mauve, and a new crystalline lightness will be everywhere.

The iris is half-wild, half-cultivated. The peasants sometimes dig up the roots, iris root, orris root, orris powder, the perfume that is
35 still used. So, in May, you will find ledges and terraces, fields just lit up with the mauve light of irises, and so much scent in the air, you do not notice it, you do not even know it. It is all the flowers of iris, before the olive invisibly blooms.

There will be tufts of iris everywhere, rising up proud and tender.
40 When the rose-coloured wild gladiolus is mingled in the corn, and

the love-in-the-mist opens blue: in May and June, before the corn is cut.

But as yet it is neither May nor June, but end of April, the pause between spring and summer, the nightingale singing interruptedly, the bean-flowers dying in the bean-fields, the bean-perfume passing with spring, the little birds hatching in the nests, the olives pruned, and the vines, the last bit of late ploughing finished, and not much work to hand, now, not until the peas are ready to pick, in another two weeks or so. Then all the peasants will be crouching between the pea-rows, endlessly, endlessly gathering peas, in the long pea-harvest which lasts two months.

So the change, the endless and rapid change. In the sunny countries, the change seems more vivid, and more complete, than in the grey countries. In the grey countries, there is a grey or dark permanency, over whose surface passes change ephemeral, leaving no real mark. In England, winters and summers shadowily give place to one another. But underneath lies the grey substratum, the permanency of cold, dark reality where bulbs live, and reality is bulbous, a thing of endurance and stored-up, starchy energy.

But in the sunny countries, change is the reality, and permanence is artificial and a condition of imprisonment. In the north, man tends instinctively to imagine, to conceive that the sun is lighted like a candle, in an everlasting darkness, and that one day, the candle will go out, the sun will be exhausted, and the everlasting dark will resume uninterrupted sway. Hence, to the northerner, the phenomenal world is essentially tragical, because it is temporal, and must cease to exist. Its very existence implies ceasing to exist, and this is the root of the feeling of tragedy.

But to the southerner, the sun is so dominant that, if every phenomenal body disappeared out of the universe, nothing would remain but bright luminousness, sunniness. The absolute is sunniness; and shadow, or dark, is only merely relative: merely the result of something getting between one and the sun.

This is the instinctive feeling of the ordinary southerner. Of course, if you start to *reason*, you may argue that the sun is a phenomenal body, therefore it came into existence, therefore it will pass out of existence, therefore the very sun is tragic in its nature.

But this is just argument. We think, because we have to light a candle in the dark, therefore some First Cause had to kindle the sun in the infinite darkness of the beginning.

The argument is entirely short-sighted and specious. We do not know in the least whether the sun ever came into existence, and we have not the slightest possible ground for conjecturing that the sun will ever pass out of existence. All that we do know, by actual experience, is that shadow comes into being when some material object intervenes between us and the sun, and that shadow ceases to exist when the intervening object is removed. So that, of all temporal or transitory or bound-to-cease things that haunt our existence, shadow, or darkness, is the one which is purely and simply temporal. We can think of death, if we like, as of something permanently intervening between us and the sun: and this is at the root of the southern, underworld idea of death. But this doesn't alter the sun at all. As far as experience goes, in the human race, the one thing that is always there is the shining sun, and dark, shadow is an accident of intervention.

Hence, strictly, there is no tragedy. The universe contains no tragedy, and man is only tragical because he is afraid of death. For my part, if the sun always shines, and always will shine, in spite of millions of clouds of words, then death, somehow, does not have many terrors. In the sunshine, even death is sunny. And there is no end to the sunshine.

That is why the rapid change of the Tuscan spring is utterly free, for me, of any sense of tragedy. "Where are the snows of yes-teryear?"* Why, precisely where they ought to be. Where are the little yellow aconites of eight weeks ago? I neither know nor care. They were sunny, and the sun shines, and sunniness means change, and petals passing and coming. The winter aconites sunnily came, and sunnily went. What more? The sun always shines. It is our fault if we don't think so.

IV

It is already summer in Tuscany, the sun is hot, the earth is baked hard, and the soul has changed her rhythm. The nightingales sing all day and all night—not at all sadly, but brightly, vividly, impudently, with a trilling power of assertion quite disproportionate to the size of the shy bird. Why the Greeks should have heard the nightingale weeping or sobbing* is more than I can understand. Anyhow, perhaps the Greeks were looking for the tragic, rather than the rhapsodic consummation to life. They were pre-disposed.

To-morrow, however, is the first of May, and already summer is here. Yesterday, in the flood of sunshine on the Arno at evening, I saw two German boys steering out of the Por Santa Maria on to the Ponte Vecchio* in Florence. They were dark-haired, not blondes, but otherwise the true Wandervogel* type, in shirts and short trousers and thick boots, hatless, coat slung in the rucksack, shirt-sleeves rolled back, above the brown muscular arms, shirt-breast open from the brown, scorched breast and the face and neck glowing sun-darkened as they strode into the flood of evening sunshine, out of the narrow street. They were talking loudly to one another in German, as if oblivious of their surroundings, in that thronged crossing of the Ponte Vecchio. And they strode with strong strides, heedless, marching past the Italians as if the Italians were but shadows. Strong, heedless, travelling intently, bent a little forward from the rucksacks in the plunge of determination to travel onwards, looking neither to right nor left, conversing in strong voices only with one another, where were they going, in the last golden light of the sun-flooded evening, over the Arno? Were they leaving town, at this hour? Were they pressing on, to get out of the Porta Romana* before nightfall, going southwards?

In spite of the fact that one is used to these German youths, in Florence especially, in summer, still the mind calls a halt, each time they appear and pass by. If swans, or wild geese flew honking, low over the Arno in the evening light, moving with that wedge-shaped intent, unswerving progress that is so impressive, they would create the same impression on one. They would bring that sense of remote, far-off lands which these Germans bring, and that sense of mysterious, unfathomable purpose.

Now no one knows better than myself that Munich or Frankfurt-am-Main are not far off, remote, lonely lands: on the contrary: and that these boys are not mysteriously migrating from one unknown to another. They are just wandering for wandering's sake, and moving instinctively, perhaps, towards the sun, and towards Rome, the old centre-point. There is really nothing more remarkable in it than in the English and Americans sauntering diffidently and, as it were, obscurely along the Lungarno.* The English in particular seem to move under a sort of Tarnhelm,* having a certain power of invisibility. They manage most of the time to efface themselves, deliberately, from the atmosphere. And the Americans, who don't try to efface themselves, give the impression of not being really there. They have left their real selves way off in the United States, in

Europe they are like rather void Doppelgänger. I am speaking, of course, of the impression of the streets. Inside the hotels, the trains, the tea-rooms and the restaurants, it is another affair. There you may have a little England, very insular, or a little America, very
5   money-rich democratic, or a little Germany, assertive, or a little Scandinavia, domestic. But I am not speaking of indoor impressions. Merely of the streets.

And in the streets of Florence or Rome, the Wandervögel make a startling impression, whereas the rest of the foreigners impress
10 one rather negatively. When I am in Germany, then Germany seems to me very much like anywhere else, especially England or America.

And when I see the Wandervögel pushing at evening out of the Por Santa Maria, across the blaze of sun and into the Ponte Vecchio,
15 then Germany becomes again to me what it was to the Romans: the mysterious, half-dark land of the north, bristling with gloomy forests, resounding to the cry of wild geese and of swans, the land of the stork and the bear and the Drachen and the Greifen.*

I know it is not so. Yet the impression comes back over me, as I see
20 the youths pressing heedlessly past. And I know it is the same with the Italians. They see, as their ancestors saw in the Goths and the Vandals, *i barbari*, the barbarians. That is what the little policeman with his staff and his peaked cap thinks, as the boys from the north go by: *i barbari*! Not with dislike or contempt: not at all: but with the old,
25 weird wonder. So he might look up at wild swans flying over the Ponte Vecchio: wild strangers from the north.

So strong is the impression the Wandervögel make on the imagination! It is not that I am particularly impressionable. I know the Italians feel very much as I do.

30 And when one sees English people with rucksacks and shirt-sleeves rolled back and hob-nailed boots, as one does sometimes, even in Tuscany, one notices them, but they make very little impression. They are rather odd than extraordinary. They are just *gli escursionisti*,* quite comprehensible: part of the fresh-air movement.
35 The Italians will laugh at them, but they know just what to think about them.

Whereas about the Wandervögel they do not quite know what to think, nor even what to feel: since we even only feel the things we know how to feel. And we do not know what to feel about these
40 Wandervogel boys. They bring with them such a strong feeling of

somewhere else, of an unknown country, an unknown race, a powerful, still unknown northland.

How wonderful it must have been, at the end of the old Roman Empire, for the Roman citizens to see the big, bare-limbed Goths, with their insolent-indifferent blue eyes, stand looking on at the market-places! They were there like a vision. *Non angli sed angeli*, as we were told the first great Pope said of the British slaves.* Creatures from the beyond, presaging another world of men.

So it was then. So it is, to a certain extent, even now. Strange wanderers towards the sun, forerunners of another world of men. That is how one still feels, as one sees the Wandervögel cross the Ponte Vecchio. They carry with them another world, another air, another meaning of life. The meaning is not explicit, not as much as it is even in storks or wild geese. But there it lies, implicit.

Curious how different it is with the well-dressed Germans. They are very often quite domesticated, and in the sense that Ibsen's people are ridiculous, just a little ridiculous. They are *so* bourgeois, so much more a product of civilisation than the producers of civilisation. They are *so* much buttoned up inside their waistcoats, and stuck inside their trousers, and encircled in their starched collars. They are not so grotesquely self-conscious and physically withered or non-existent as the equivalent English bourgeois tourist. And they are never quite so utterly domesticated as the equivalent Scandinavian. But they have so often the unsure look of children who have been turned out in their best clothes by their mama, and told to go and enjoy themselves: Now enjoy yourselves! that is a little absurd.

The Italians, whatever they are, are what they are. So you know them, you feel that they have developed themselves into an expression of themselves, as far as they go. With the English, weird fish as they are very often, you feel the same: whatever they are, they are what they are, they can't be much different, poor dears. But with the Germans abroad, you feel: These people ought really to be something else. They are not themselves, in their Sunday clothes. They are being something they are not.

And one has the feeling even stronger, with many Russians. One feels: These people are not themselves at all. They are the roaring echoes of other people, older races, other languages. Even the things they say aren't really Russian things: they're all sorts of half-translations from Latin or French or English or God-knows-what.

Some of this feeling one has about the Germans one meets abroad: as if they were talking in translation: as if the ideas, however original, always had a faint sound of translations. As if they were never *quite* themselves.

5 Then, when one sees the Wandervögel, comes the shock of realisation, and one thinks: There they go, the real Germans, seeking the sun! They have really nothing to say. They are roving, roving, roving, seeking themselves. That is it, with these "barbarians." They are still seeking themselves. And they have not yet 10 found themselves. They are turning to the sun again, in the great adventure of seeking themselves.

Man does not start ready-made. He is a weird creature that slowly evolves himself through the ages. He need never stop evolving himself, for a human being who was completely himself has never 15 even been conceived. The great Goethe was half-born, Shakespeare the same, Napoleon only a third-born. And most people are hardly born at all, into individual consciousness.

But with the Italians and the French, the mass consciousness which governs the individual is really derived from the individual. 20 Whereas with the German and the Russian, it seems to me not so. The mass-consciousness has been *taken over*, by great minds like Goethe or Frederick,* from other people, and does not spring inherent from the Teutonic race itself. In short, the Teutonic mind, young, powerful, active, is always thinking in terms of 25 somebody else's experience, and almost never in terms of its own experience.

Then comes a great unrest. It seems to show so plainly in the Wandervögel. Thinking in terms of somebody else's experience at last becomes utterly unsatisfactory. Then thought altogether falls 30 into chaos—and then into discredit. The young don't choose to think any more. Blindly, they turn to the sun.

Because the sun is anti-thought. Thought is of the shade. In bright sunshine no man thinks. So the Wandervögel turn instinctively to the sun, which melts thoughts away, and sets the blood 35 running with another, non-mental consciousness.

And this is why, at times of great change, the northern nations turn to the sun. And this is why, when revolutions come, they often come in May. It is the sun making the blood revolt against old conceptions. And this is why the nations of the sun do not live the life of thought, 40 therefore they are more "themselves." In the grey shadow the northern nations mould themselves according to a few ideas, until their whole life is buttoned and choked up. Then comes a revulsion. They cast off the clothes and turn to the sun, as the Wandervögel do, strange harbingers.

GERMANS AND ENGLISH

Germans and English*

Yesterday, in Florence, in the flood of sunshine on the Arno at evening, I saw two German boys steering out of the Por Santa Maria, on to the Ponte Vecchio, passing for a moment in the bright sun, then gone again in shadow. The glimpse made a strong impression on me. They were dark-haired, not blond, but otherwise the true Wandervogel type: thick boots, heavy rucksack, hatless, with shirt-sleeves rolled back above brown, muscular arms, and shirt-breast open from the scorched breast, and face and neck glowing sun-darkened as they strode into the flood of evening sunshine, out of the dark gulf of the street. They were talking loudly to one another in German, as if oblivious of their surroundings, in the thronged crossing of the Ponte Vecchio. And they leaned forward in the surge of travel, marching with long strides, heedless, past the Italians, as if the Italians were but shadows. Travelling so intently, bent a little forward from the rucksacks in the plunge of determination to urge onwards, looking neither to right nor left, conversing in strong voices only with one another, as if the world around were unreal, where were they going, in the last golden sun-flood of evening, over the Arno? Were they leaving town, at this hour? Were they pressing on, to get out of the Porta Romana before nightfall, going south?

In spite of the fact that one is used to these German boys, in Florence especially, in summer, still the mind calls a halt, each time they appear and pass by. If swans, or wild geese flew low, honking over the Arno in the evening light, moving with that wedge-shaped, intent, unswerving progress that is so impressive, they would create something of the same impression on one. They would bring that sense of remote, northern lands, and the mystery of strange, blind, instinctive purpose in migration, which these Germans give.

Now no one knows better than I do that Munich and Frankfurt and Berlin are heavily civilised cities; they are not at all remote and lonely homes of the wild swan; and that these boys are not

247

mysteriously migrating, they are only just wandering out of restlessness and need to move. Perhaps an instinct carries them south,
once more to Rome, the old centre point. But in absolute fact, the
Wandervogel is not very different from any other tourist.

5   Then why does he create such a strong and almost startling
impression, here in the streets of Florence, or in Rome? There are
Englishmen who go with knapsacks and sleeves rolled up; there are
even Italians. But they look just what they are, men taking a walking
tour. Whereas when I see the Wandervogel pushing at evening out of
10   the Por Santa Maria, across the blaze of sun and into the Ponte
Vecchio, then Germany becomes again to me what it was to the
Romans: the mysterious, half-dark land of the north, bristling with
gloomy forests, resounding to the cry of the wild geese and swans,
the land of the bear and the stork, the Drachen and the Greifen.

15   I know it is not so. I know Germany is the land of steel and of
ordered civilisation. Yet the old impression comes over me, as I see
the youths pressing heedlessly past. And I know the Italians have
something of the same feeling. They see again the Goths and the
Vandals passing with loud and guttural speech, *i barbari*. That is the
20   look in the eyes of the little policeman in his peaked cap and belt, as
he watches the boys from the north go by: *i barbari*! Not a look of
dislike or contempt; on the contrary. It is the old weird wonder. So
he might look up at wild swans flying over the bridge: strangers!

There are English strangers too, of course, and American and
25   Swedish and all sorts. They are all a bit fantastic to the Italian policeman. All nations find all other nations ridiculous. That is not the
point. The point is, that though the English and American and Swede
may be ridiculous to the Italian policeman, they are all, as it were,
compatible, they are all part of the show, and we must expect them.

30   Whereas the Wandervogel is incompatible, you can't expect him,
he is strictly not in the game. He has got a game of his own up his
sleeve, like a predative old Goth in the sixth century. And he brings
with him such a strong feeling of somewhere else, somewhere *outside*
our common circle. That was the impression the Russians used to
35   give so vividly: the impression of another country, outside the group.
The impression of a land still unknown and unencircled, large and
outside. Now the Russians have disappeared, or have lost their
dynamic vibration. And now it is the Wandervögel alone who trail
with them the feeling of a far country, outside the group, a northland
40   still unknown. The impression is there in spite of facts.

How wonderful it must have been, at the end of the Roman Empire, to see the big, bare-limbed Goths with their insolent-indifferent blue eyes, pass through the Roman market-place, or stand looking on, with the little Germanic laugh, part derision, part admiration and wonder, part uneasy, at the doings of the little, fussy natives! They were like a vision. *Non angli sed angeli*, we are told the first great Pope said of the British slave-children in the slave-market. Creatures from the beyond, presaging another world of men.—

Coming home, I found books from Germany, and among them: *Zeit und Stunde*, by Karl Scheffler. The first essay, called *Der Einsame Deutsche*, at once brought back to me the Wandervögel, and reminded me of the problem: Where are they going? What are they making for? And there on the first page of Scheffler's book, there is the answer: "Weil sie—eine Welt der reinen Idee brauchen."*

Was that why those boys were steering so intent out of town, in the evening? Was it that they were seeking for a world of the pure idea? Or, which amounts to the same thing, as Scheffler says, because they were steering impatiently away from all forms that have already been developed, all the ideas that have already been made explicit? Were they rushing towards what shall be, in their queer haste at nightfall? Or were they rushing away from all that is?

It looked much like the latter. They seemed to be rushing away from Germany, much more positively than rushing to Rome. Perhaps they want to touch the centre stone,* there in the Roman Forum, to see if there is still virtue in it. Probably they'll find it dead, like a dead heart. As the German boy said to me, in the tombs at Tarquinia, speaking of his travels in Italy and Tunis: It's all *mehr Schrei wie Wert*.* If not something much worse. One day, as Scheffler says, the German desire for a world of pure idea led the Germans to invent militarism; the next day, it was industrialism. If that isn't enough to cure any man of wanting a world of pure idea, I don't know what is.

Herr Scheffler advises the Germans to accept their race-destiny as the heaviest of all destinies. "Die Einsamkeit in der Welt und im eigenen Volk ertragen lernen: das ist der Sieg. Schwindelfrei, wie die Geflügelte Göttin auf der Kugel, das Ganze überschauen, den Graus der Geschichte mit derselben Gefasstheit und ehrfürchtigen Neugier erleben, wie er in besseren Zeiten nur gedacht worden ist, an die Weltmission deutscher Problematik, an die höhere Sittlichkeit scheinbarer Charakterlosigkeit, an die Kraft in der Schwäche glauben, und alles das tätig tun, jeden Tag für verloren halten, an dem nicht irgend etwas getan worden ist: das ist, das sei das irdische Glück des in der Welt und im eigenen Land einsamen Deutschen."*

That sounds fine and heoric, especially the Goddess on the globe,
5 but to a mere outsider and Englishman, a little unnecessary. Those boys crossing the Ponte Vecchio, I am sure had no need to learn all those difficult things. It seemed to me, they had really learned intuitively what they had to learn, already. They had such a look of bolting away from Germany to escape any further coil of "pure
10 ideas," that it seemed to me they were all right.

What has ruined Europe, but especially northern Europe, is this very "pure idea." Would to God the "Ideal" had never been invented. But now it's got its claws in us, and we must struggle free. The beast we have to fight and to kill is the Ideal. It is the worm, the
15 foul serpent of our epoch, in whose coils we are strangled.

But this very German unrest that seems so lamentable is just a healthy instinct fighting off the coils of the beast. The Germans are more frantically entangled up in the folds of the serpent of the Ideal than any people; except, perhaps, the Russian intelligents. But also,
20 the Germans are much more lusty, fighting the beast. The German has a strong primitive nature still, unexploited by civilisation. And this primitive nature has an intuitive wisdom of its own, an intuitive ethic also, much deeper than the ideal ethic. When the German learns to trust his own intuitive wisdom, and his own intuitive ethic,
25 then he will have slain the ideal dragon, for the rest of Europe as well as for himself. But it needs a very high sense of responsibility and a deep courage, to depend on the intuitive wisdom and ethic, instead of on the ideal formula.

This is the point that Herr Scheffler makes in the very interesting
30 essay: "Warum Wir den Krieg Verloren Haben."* He links together instinct, intuition, and imagination a little confusingly. But it certainly was for lack of these three things that Germany lost the war; and for lack of the same three things, in the other nations, there was a war at all. It is not only Germany, it is our whole civilisation that is
35 damned by the "Ideal," and by the lack of trust in the intuitive, instinctive, imaginative consciousness in ourselves.

Herr Scheffler's essay on the Englishman is also very amusing. And possibly, from the outside, it is quite true. That is obviously how the Englishman *looks* to any foreigner who only sees him from the
40 outside. But from the inside, the story is a different one.

The clue to the Englishman is the curious radical isolation, or instinct of isolation, which every born native of my country has at the core of him. We are little islands, each one of us is a tiny island to himself, and the immutable sea washes between us all. That is the clue to the Englishman. He is born alone. He is proud of the fact. And he is proud of the fact that he belongs to a nation of isolated individuals. He is proud of being one island in the great archipelago of his nation.

But it is the fact of his own consciousness of isolation that makes the Englishman such a good citizen. He wants no one to touch him, and he wants not to touch anybody. Hence the endless little private houses of England, and the fierce preservation of the privacy.

The Englishman, however, is not bourgeois. Myself, I could never understand what *bourgeois* meant, till I went abroad, and saw Germans and Frenchmen and Italians. They have a bourgeoisie, because they have had bourgs for centuries. In England, there are no bourgs.

So the Englishman is not bourgeois. But he is hopelessly civilly disciplined, with a discipline he has imposed on himself. He is an islander, an individualist. What has carried the Englishman abroad, what has made him "imperial"—though the word means very little to an Englishman—is his fatal individualism. The Englishman, [*ab ovo*],* is fatally and fantastically individualistic. That is, he is aware of his own isolation almost to excrucation. So he disciplines himself almost to extinction, and is the most perfect civilian on earth. But scratch one of these civilian, made-to-pattern Englishmen, and you will find him fantastic, almost a caricature. Hence his endless forbearing, and at the same time, his absolute resistance to tyranny. He is an island to himself.

Perhaps it was the mixture of Germanic with celtic British blood that produced this Hamletish-Falstaffian sense of being distinct from the body of mankind, which is the glory and the torture of the Englishman. The Englishman *cannot not* be alone. He is essentially always apart. For this reason he seems a hypocrite. His nature is so private to him, that he leaves it out in most of his social dealings. He expects other people to do the same, and it seems to him a lack of breeding when the others don't do it.

But nowadays, the Englishman has so disciplined himself to the social ideals, that he has almost killed himself. He is almost a walking pillar of society, as dead and stiff as a pillar. He has crucified himself on the social ideal most effectively, and has a terrible moment ahead of him, when he cries *consummatum est*,* and the life goes out of him. There is something spectral about the British people.

Cut off! That is the inner tragedy of the English. They are cut off
5 from the flow of life. Nowhere are the classes so absolutely cut off from touch, from living contact, as in England. It is inhuman, it is almost ghoulish.

As for the English not being revolutionary—they made the first great European revolution,* and it is highly probable that among
10 them is preparing the last. The English will bear anything, till the sense of injustice really enters into them. And then nothing will stop them. But it needs that fatal sense of injustice. Only that can make them see red, and blind them to that fetish of theirs, "the other fellow's point of view."

15 So it is. We all have our own Völkerschicksale.* At the same time, we are all men, and we can all have some glimpse of realisation of one another, if we use imagination and intuition and *all* our instincts, instead of just one or two. And the fate of all nations in Europe hangs together. We have our separate Völkerschicksale. But there is over
20 and above a human destiny, and a European destiny.

APPENDIX I

SKETCHES OF ETRUSCAN PLACES

THE PAINTED TOMBS OF TARQUINIA, FIRST VERSION

Note on the text

The text is taken from DHL's autograph manuscript, 26 pages, at UT; it has not been published previously.

The Textual apparatus records all the deletions and corrections contained in MS.

Sketches of Etruscan Places

III.
The Painted Tombs of Tarquinia

We arranged for the guide to take us to the painted tombs, which are the real fame of Tarquinia. After lunch we set out, climbing to the top of the town, and passing out through the south-east gate, on the level hill-crest. Looking back, the wall of the town, mediaeval, with a bit of more ancient black wall lower down, stands blank. Just outside the gate are one or two forlorn new houses, then ahead, the long, running tableland of the hill, with the white highway dipping and going on to Viterbo, inland.

"All this hill in front," said the guide, "is tombs! All tombs! The city of the dead."

So! Then this hill is the necropolis hill! The Etruscans never buried their dead within the city walls. And the modern cemetery and the first etruscan tombs lie almost close up to the present city gate. Therefore, if the ancient city of Tarquinia lay on this hill, it can have occupied no more space, hardly, than the present little town of a few thousand people. Which seems impossible. Far more probably, the city itself lay on that opposite hill there, which lies splendid and unsullied, running parallel to us.

We walk across the wild bit of hill-top, where the stones crop out, and the first rock-rose flutters, and the asphodels stick up. This is the necropolis. But there is no sign of any tombs: no tumulus, nothing but the bare hill-crest, with stones and short grass and flowers, the sea gleaming away to the right, under the sun, and the soft land inland glowing very green and pure.

But we see a little bit of wall, built perhaps to cover a water-trough. Our guide goes straight towards it. He is a fat, good-natured young man, who doesn't look as if he would be interested in tombs. We are mistaken, however. He knows a good deal, and has a quick, sensitive interest, absolutely unobtrusive, and turns out to be as pleasant a companion for such a visit as one could wish to have.

The bit of wall we see is a little hood of masonry with an iron gate, covering a little flight of steps leading down into the ground. One comes upon it all at once, in the nothingness of the hillside. The guide kneels down to light his acetylene lamp, and his old terrier lies down resignedly in the sun, in the breeze which rushes persistently from the south-west, over these long, exposed hilltops.

5 The lamp begins to shine and smell, then to shine without smelling: the guide opens the iron gate, and we descend the steep steps down into the tomb. It seems a dark little hole underground: a dark little hole, after the sun of the upper world! But the guide's lamp begins to flare up, and we find ourselves in a little chamber in the rock, just a small, bare little cell of a room that some anchorite 10 might have lived in. It is so small and bare and familiar, quite unlike the rather splendid spacious tombs at Cerveteri.

But the lamp flares bright, we get used to the change of light, and see the paintings on the little walls. It is the tomb of hunting and fishing, so-called from the pictures on the walls, and it is supposed to 15 date from the sixth century B.C. The little room is frescoed all round with sea and sky, birds and fishes, and little men hunting, fishing, rowing in boats. The lower part of the wall is all a blue-green of sea with a silhouette surface that ripples all round the room. From the sea rises a tall rock, off which a naked man is beautifully and cleanly 20 diving into the sea, while a companion climbs up the rock after him, and on the water a boat waits with rested oars, in it three men watching the diver, the middle man standing up naked, holding out his arms. Meanwhile a great dolphin leaps behind the boat, a flight of birds soars upwards to pass the rock, in the clear air, while from the 25 bands of colour that border the wall at the top hang the regular loops of garlands, garlands of flowers and leaves and buds and berries, garlands which belong to maidens and to women, and which represent the flowery circle of the female life and sex. The top border of the wall is horizontal stripes of colour that go all round the 30 room, red and black and dull gold and green and blue, and these are the colours that occur invariably. Men are nearly always painted a darkish red, which is the colour of many Italians when they go naked in the sun, as the Etruscans went. Women are coloured paler, because women did not go naked in the sun.

35 At the end of the room, where there is a recess in the wall, is painted another rock rising from the sea, and on it a man with a sling is taking aim at the birds which rise scattering this way and that. A boat with a big paddle oar is holding off from the rock, a naked man amidships is giving a queer salute to the slinger, a man kneels over 40 the bows with his back to the others, and is letting down a net. The

prow of the boat has a beautifully painted eye, so the vessel shall see
where it is going. In Syracuse you will see many a two-eyed boat
today come swimming in to quay. One dolphin is diving down into
the sea, one is leaping out. The birds fly, and the garlands hang from
the border.   5

It is all small and gay and quick with life, spontaneous as only
young life can be. If you want to be impressed, awed, thrilled,
uplifted, don't look, because you'll be disappointed. But if you are
content with just a sense of the quick ripple of life, then here it is.

If it helps at all to know that, to the ancients, to the old Etruscans   10
certainly, all things had a life and a soul of their own, since the
universe was a great body of life: and secondly, that everything had a
symbolical meaning, derived from its own nature; then you can look
for second meanings even in these natural and childish pictures. But
if you are a real modern, and bored by anything having any meaning   15
at all, you can glance and say: Pretty nursery pictures!—and have
done.

I am of the opinion that, painting tombs, the Etruscans never
forgot they were painting tombs: just as, carving the ash-chests and
the sarcophagi with all the wealth of sculptured pictures, they never   20
forgot that it was the death-chest they were carving.

To the Etruscans, the sea or the great waters were the deeps from
which all life emerges, and to which it returns. Therefore the womb
itself was the depth within the waters: and the dolphin, diving into
the water and re-emerging, could be the symbol either of the male   25
organ of procreation, diving into the living waters so that new life
shall leap out; or of the soul diving into the sea of death to re-emerge
in a new life. The fish is that which swims animate but apart, in
another world, the world of the deeps of the beginning and the end
of life and existence. So in the first Christian centuries even Jesus   30
was represented as a fish, having all these three meanings. According
to the same meanings, in these pictures, we have the man diving into
the deeps of death, and the dolphin leaping in and out.

Birds, on the other hand, played a large part in the etruscan
religion, the religious science of augury being divination from the   35
flight of birds. And just as a fish could represent that part of a man
which dives into the deeps, either in sex or death, so the winged bird
could represent that part of a man which soars into the sky, the ether,
the upper regions. In one aspect, birds were spirits driven across the
sky in the flight of the divine will, and the priests, the augurs who   40

watched, would read the divine will from their flight. In the picture, the slinger [who] is about to bring down one of these flying birds, is about to bring down a spirit. He will sling the stone of death. And if we knew anything of the science of augury, then in the disposition of
5   the dark birds, the grey birds, and the white birds in their flight, we should know how to read the signs of the soul of the dead man. And the movements of the goose would tell still another story.

But whoever likes may reject all that, and take the paintings of this tomb just as nursery pictures of hunting and fishing.
10   In the triangle of the end wall, above the hunting scenes, the space is filled in with one of the frequent banqueting scenes of the dead. The dead man, looking very much alive, reclines upon his banqueting couch with his flat wine-dish in his hand, resting on his elbow, and beside him, also half risen, lies a handsome and jewelled lady in
15   fine robes, resting her left hand on the naked breast of the man, and in her right holding up the garland to him, the garland of the female offering. Behind the man stands a naked slave-boy, perhaps with music, and on the wall hangs a seven-stringed lyre, while another naked slave-man is just filling a wine-pitcher from one of the big,
20   splendid wine-jars. Behind the woman stands a maiden playing on the flute, apparently. A thing like a bird-cage hangs on the wall; and two maidens with garlands, sit, one of them turned round to watch the banqueting pair, the other with her back to it all. In the corner of the maidens are more garlands, and two ducks or birds.—The
25   garlands, of course, you can take to mean the circle of eternity, but they are not the same as the crown or wreath, which is small and firm and round. The garland or necklace is long and flexible, and is placed over the head for love, and is really that eternity which the woman alone can offer to a man.
30   In this tomb, everything is gay and naïve and full of life! But the Etruscans really believed in a gay death, they went down to no gloomy Homeric afterworld, in the imagination. So all the creatures about them seem alive and pleased. The naked slave-men are by no means humble and down-trodden menials. There is a certain dance
35   in their movement, they are part of the show, part of the natural intimacy, included in the flow of the master's life. The masters were luxurious, and the slaves enjoyed their share in the luxury. That is obvious in many a tomb, even if some Roman hadn't said so. The maidens too seem alert and full of the fresh spring of life: it is always
40   the same, down to the dogs and cats. All seem to live in the throb of

quick, bright life, which flows from the masters and embraces all, slaves and animals too.

And this is where the Etruscans differ most from the brutal, uneasy, moral and immoral Romans. To the Roman, a slave was either a valuable possession, an object of prostitution, a herd of useful cattle, or a piece of living carrion. Whatever Rome has left behind weighs on one and has an element of depression in it, with its lack of true humanity. Whereas this little tomb of hunting and fishing is as gay as out-of-doors in June, and as natural: neither moral nor immoral, any more than out-of-doors in June is moral or immoral. To produce it must have required a degree of culture in life itself, of which we are now utterly incapable, and of which even the vaunting, overweening Greeks were incapable: that tolerance which is quite dignified, sure of itself, able to control its own *ambiente*,* and yet driving with a perfectly easy rein, in easy, living contact with everything, down to the slave and the dog. To have sufficient inborn pride and strength of control to be able to accept each living thing according to its own nature—that must have been the quality of the etruscan Lucumo at his best. And he must have had a perfect response from the people. And in this he must have been the opposite of the Roman.

Which leads one to believe, that if the Roman was typically Italic, then the Etruscan was not Italic. It leads one to conclude, much further, that the Italian people of today is on the whole not Italic—in that Roman sense—but much more near to the Etruscan. Which leads one further to suppose that the Latins may have been some extraneous stock, the basic Italian stock being really different in its eternal vibration.

But that is one way of putting it. Possibly we lay far too much stress on race and extraction, Indo-European or not Indo-European, Italic or non-Italic, long-skulls or short-skulls. It seems to me, especially when one comes closer to the mystery and confusion of races in early Europe, at the dawn of history, that it is not so much the race that matters, as the sort of spark of new consciousness that comes awake in people. Who knows what was in those old Latins of the Tiber plains, weird farmers in huts, before Rome was thought of? Many things, many potentialities were in them. But perhaps it was their very poverty and struggle which determined for ever their ruthless natures, just as the easier circumstances of their etruscan neighbours, only twenty miles away, determined their easier, more human

characters. Man's nature is formed to a large extent by the obstacles he has to overcome. Overcoming his obstacles fixes his own rhythm, and he goes on and on, overcoming obstacles that don't exist, conquering where there is no need for conquest, driven on by his
5 own momentum, in the direction of the first blind necessity, on to the ultimate destruction.

The so-called etruscan tribes, better situated, naturally received earlier and more easily the sparks of culture from Crete or Cyprus, or Lydia or Cilicia* or wherever it may be, in the ancient, pre-
10 Hellenic world. And naturally they developed more harmoniously, softly fanning the flames of their new feelings, new consciousness: for that is what it all amounts to, the flame of new consciousness, new *awareness* physical and mental, sensual and spiritual, that springs up in a people and makes it a people. Given a new flame of
15 consciousness, long skulls may gradually turn into round ones, and a race, mixing itself in the eternal mixture of races, may fuse and produce a people entirely new, like the English, like the northern Italian, like the modern Frenchman or the modern German or the American.

20 But it is inevitable that the harmoniously-developing race will get smashed when an inharmoniously-developed race gets started with a rush. It is like letting the pigs in the garden. They produce a desert, and the gardening has to begin all over again.

Romans and Etruscans, Sabines, Samnites and Umbrians were
25 probably not much different, to start with, from one another or from any other of the European tribes of the bronze age. But they lived under diverse circumstances, and the tide of energy rising in the world caught them at different levels of consciousness, and roused some to a dogged fight with their surroundings, others to a con-
30 tinuous harmonious moulding of their surroundings to their own tastes. And so different races emerged, at different levels of consciousness, and with different opportunities at hand. The cul- tured race nearly always provides weapons for its own destruction at the hands of a race less cultured, whose energy is crude instead of
35 being delicately unfolded. Is there really more energy in a slug than in a sprouting oak-tree? Not at all! The energy is only more crude, more voracious, a blind mouth instead of a sensitive complication and development.

Yet in spite of all, slugs have not devoured all oak trees, and roses
40 blossom in spite of myriads of chewing mouths. And Italy is still

here, long after Rome has fallen under the weight of her own obtuseness.

We come up the steps into the upper world, the sea-breeze and the sun. The old dog shambles to his feet, the guide blows out his lamp and locks the gate, we set off again, the dog trundling apathetic at his master's heels, the master speaking to him with that soft Italian familiarity which seems so very different from the spirit of Rome, the strong-willed Latin.

The guide steers across the hill-top, in the clear afternoon sun, towards another little hood of masonry. And one notices there is quite a number of these little gateways, built by the government to cover the steps that lead down to the separate small tombs. It is utterly unlike Cerveteri, though the two places are not forty miles apart. Here there is no stately tumulus city, with its highroad between the tombs, and inside, rather noble, many-roomed houses of the dead. Here the little one-room tombs seem scattered at random on the hill-top, here and there: though probably, if excavations were fully carried out, here also we should find a regular city of the dead, with its streets and crossways. But it would not be like Cerveteri even then. As it is, there are scattered little one-room tombs, and we dive down into them just like rabbits popping down a hole. It is quite amusing.

It is interesting to find it so different from Cerveteri. The Etruscans carried out perfectly what seems to be the Italian instinct: to have single, independent cities, with a certain surrounding territory, each district speaking its own dialect and feeling at home in its own little capital, yet the whole confederacy of city states loosely linked together by a common religion and a more-or-less common interest. Even today, Lucca is very different from Ferrara, and the language is hardly the same. In ancient Etruria, this isolation of cities developing according to their own idiosyncrasy, within the loose union of a so-called nation, must have been complete. The contact between the plebs, the mass of the people, of Caere and Tarquinii must have been almost null. They were, no doubt, foreigners to one another. Only the Lucumones, the ruling sacred magistrates of noble family, the priests and the other nobles, and the merchants, must have kept up an intercommunion, speaking "correct" etruscan, while the people, no doubt, spoke dialects varying so widely as to be different languages. To get any idea of the pre-Roman past, we must break up the conception [of] oneness* and uniformity, and see an endless confusion of differences.

We are diving down into another tomb, called, says the guide, the
Tomb of the Leopards. Every tomb has been given a name, to
distinguish it from its neighbours. The tomb of the Leopards has two
spotted leopards in the triangle of the end wall, between the
5 roof-slopes. Hence its name.

The Tomb of the Leopards is a charming, cosy little room, and
the paintings on the walls have not been so very much damaged. All
the tombs are ruined to some degree by weather and vulgar
vandalism, having been left and neglected like common holes, when
10 they had been broken open again and rifled to the last gasp.

But still the paintings are fresh and alive, the ochre reds and
yellows, the blacks and blues and blue-greens are curiously harmonious and alive. The ceiling is painted chequer-board, with pale
and dark squares of black and red and yellow-white. The leopards
15 are putting out their tongues and lifting their paws on either side the
little tree, in the triangle above the banqueting scene, a naked
wine-bearer is lifting up his pitcher in the centre, to show it is empty,
while on the banqueting couch lie two couples, a man and a woman
in each, the women with startling pale-yellow hair. Because of their
20 pale yellow hair they are called Hetaerae, courtesans of the upper
class: and perhaps so they are, for they have a knowing sort of look.
Their mantles fall in elegant folds, with wide, rich borders, as they
turn, along with the second man, to look towards the most important
man, the one at the end on the right. All three, two blonde women
25 and the swarthy man, turn their faces in profile to look at him who
has lifted his hand and is holding up, between his thumb and
forefinger of the right hand, an egg. In his left hand he holds a very
big wine-cup, the libation cup, the patera containing the wine of life.

But they seem, the three others, to be looking at the egg which the
30 man holds up so distinctly. He is the dead man of the tomb, and that
egg is the egg of his resurrection. It means to say, the tomb is but an
egg, from which the soul hatches out again. And that egg is precisely
the same as our Easter egg. On Easter Sunday we hold up the Easter
egg just as this Etruscan does in the tomb, for the same reason.

35 The second couple, man and woman, are making a very familiar
gesture, lifting the right hand and curving it over, towards the man
with the egg. The gesture is a little exaggerated. Probably it means
the salute to death, the grief salute. The man in the boat in the Tomb
of Hunting and Fishing makes it to the slinger who is about to hurl
40 the stone.

On the side walls, there are the most beautiful frescoes of dancers and musicians, about half life size. The drawing is beautiful, exquisite, full of life and verve and impulse, absolutely real in its archaic style. It looks so simple and somehow natural, that one would think it must be easy. But try to copy these paintings. It is curiously 5 difficult to get them. Greek things are much easier. Here, the mass seems heavy, but isn't, it is most alert, while the outline seems almost crude, till you try to get it, and then you find it has a power and a freedom very hard to seize.

Very lovely is the young man alone, dancing and playing on a 10 double flute, in front of a little tree with berries on—perhaps an olive. He is dark red, and naked save for his scarf of fine white linen with a rich border, which has dropped from his shoulder and hangs round him from his arms. Drawn in silhouette, he might be Greek, save for a certain thickness and vital, vigorous substantialness which 15 is truly etruscan, and which conveys the modern Italian *bodily* vitality. On the damaged wall are birds—naïve and alert and fresh, drawn according to their own nature.

But this is a tomb of the dance, dating, they say, from the fifth century B.C. The dancers wear laced sandals, not the etruscan long 20 shoes. But we see here as usual the hands and feet exaggerated in length, rather than diminished.

If one once starts looking, there is much to see. But if one glances only, there is nothing but a little pathetic room with rock walls thinly stuccoed and frescoed with unimposing figures a good deal damaged 25 by damp and rough usage.

There are many tombs. As soon as we have seen one, up we go, a little bewildered, into the afternoon sun, across a tract of hill, then down again to the underground, like rabbits. And gradually the underground world of the Etruscans becomes more real than the 30 above day. One begins to live with the painted dancers and feasters and mourners.

A very lovely dance tomb is the *Tomba del Convito*, the Tomb of the Feast. Here men and women dance round the walls, large figures, in an almost bacchic abandon. They wear the long low boots, but not 35 with turned-up toes, and their long, curiously-exaggerated hands carry the dance into the very finger-tips.

It is very interesting to compare, in F. Weege's *Etruskische Malerei* (Leipzig. 20 M), the drawings made from this tomb, many years ago, with the photographs made more recently. Weege gives many 40

interesting things besides just reproductions of photographs, and the complete reproduction of the drawings made from the Tomba del Convito show us, for one thing, details which have now disappeared, owing to damp and damage. There is a fascinating little cat curling
5 peeping round the trunk of a thin tree, and just prepared to dart up. It is so etruscan—one might almost say Italian—that one laments its so recent loss. But other little animals remain, alert little dogs and birds, to make the dance perfectly natural.

Most curious, however, comparing the drawing with the photo-
10 graphs, is to see where the artist failed. The drawing looks at a glance excellent—and really is good. But examine closely, and time after time you find a divergence, a foot wrongly placed, wrongly modelled, a line "beautified" and spoilt, a gesture just missed: the fine edge of the vitality and the fresh strong movement just lost, the whole effect
15 just dulled and banalised. Yet the drawing is the work of a conscientious and skilful artist.

But it is difficult to copy these etruscan figures, and to get the original spirit.

The most ridiculous reproductions in Weege's book are those
20 made about a hundred years ago, in the Flaxman and Canova spirit. They are Greekish as Flaxman and Canova* are Greekish, and beside the original, they are so perfectly ridiculous and macaroni, that it should teach one forever to beware of "improving" or "beautifying"or "Greekifying" a lively and naïve work of art.

25 Not that the paintings in the Tarquinian tombs are amateur. They are most highly skilled, and must have been done by trained artists. In some tombs, looking closely, one can see where the whole outline has been changed, sometimes quite a lot, to bring the painting to the artist's desire. And these changes, these "alterations" have the same
30 freshness and earnest carelessness as if they had been done yester- day. The etruscan artist must have been intense and earnest as a child, and inwardly insouciant as a child. None of that Michelangelo sweating-blood business, nor of Leonardo's painful pedgilling.* An intense temporary earnestness, coupled with a complete *inward*
35 freedom, seems characteristic of the etruscan artist.

Another fascinating tomb is the Tomb of the Lionesses, so called from the two lionesses with bell-like udders, on the end wall under the roof angle. They are guarding, with one paw lifted, a sort of altar. The two Leopards of the other tomb heraldically faced a little tree.
40 The altar is much more usual.

But this is a constant motive over a door, or over an urn or sarcophagus, in etruscan tombs: the two heraldic beasts, leopards, lions, lionesses, griffins, even bulls, facing each other over a tree, an altar, an animal. They are the beasts of brute force, of elemental physical life, guarding the gateways of life and death; and ready to tear asunder the *individual* life or soul, which must die and be reduced back to its elements. The life which comes and goes is guarded jealously by these powerful and life-representing beasts of the blood-stream, which are the mothers of the soul, and the devourers of the soul, both: according as the soul is coming or going. In the tombs, the soul is departing. But the Capitoline wolf suckles the young souls. And these lionesses with their udders remind one strongly of the famous bronze Capitoline wolf that suckles Romulus and Remus, and which surely was made by etruscan artists.

The tomb of the Lionesses is an old tomb—they say the VI century, but perhaps earlier. It has an ancient, somewhat oriental character—that is, the orient of the Aegean. The fascinating dancing figures go round in a frieze at the top of the wall, and some have the long shoes with turned-up toes, that belong to the Minoan art of ancient Crete; also to the Hittites. Under the lionesses is a great urn painted, the urn of the dead soul-treasure, and guarding it are two musicians, again like two heraldic creatures, one playing the double flute, the other the lyre. Then, splendid and strong, with thick but vivid limbs, the dancers go round the room, men and women, in all the archaic earnestness of insouciance.

Under the dancers is a dado suggesting the old eastern lotus pattern, and below that again, very charming, all the way round go the dolphins, all leaping in a live curve down into the greenish, wavy sea, all the way round the tomb, most fresh and fascinating.

The lions and leopards and lionesses of the Etruscan must have come from over the sea—there are none in Italy. And the women-dancers especially, in this tomb, either almost nude, or wearing the swinging, dark-lined mantle over a transparent robe, suggest the east. And still the whole thing has a vivacious, thick-limbed, natural quality that is surely etruscan, and surely, essentially Italian, in a line with the Italian painters from Giotto onwards.

One visits tomb after tomb, some very much damaged, some fresh and surprisingly alive still. In all cases but one, as far as I remember, the walls have been lightly stuccoed and the painting done on the stucco. In one case, the painting is done on the bare rock, and here

APPENDIX II
SKETCHES OF ETRUSCAN PLACES
HISTORICAL OUTLINE

HISTORICAL OUTLINE

9th–7th century BC (early Iron Age)	Etruscan pre-history. Villanovan culture in Italy, which spread from the centres on the Tyrrhenian coast and in southern Etruria (Cerveteri, Tarquinia, Vulci, Vetulonia, Populonia, Veio).
7th century BC	The League of the Twelve city-states in the region between the Arno and the Tiber. Appearance of Etruscan script.
End of 7th century–end of 6th century BC	Etruscan colonisation and expansion in Campania, down to the Gulf of Salerno. Rome governed by Etruscan kings (Tarquinius Priscus, Servius Tullius, Tarquinius Superbus).
6th century BC	Etruscan colonisation in the Po valley and extension of their trading links beyond the Alps; Etruria reaches the peak of its economic and cultural power.
540 BC	Naval victory of the allied Etruscan and Carthaginian forces against the Phocaeans on the Sardinian Sea. The Greeks are expelled from Corsica; nevertheless, Etruscan domination of the sea begins to weaken.
End of 6th century BC	The Etruscan kings are expelled from Rome, and Rome becomes a Republic.
504 BC	King Porsenna of Chiusi temporarily conquers Rome; his army is then defeated by the Greeks and the Latins at Cumae, and the Etruscans are forced to leave Latium, also losing their access to Campania by land.
482 BC	The wars between Rome and Veio start; in 474 BC a thirty-year truce is signed.
480 BC	Etruscan, Carthaginian and Persian allied forces defeated at Himera by the Greeks from Syracuse led by Gelon.

474 BC	Naval battle near Cumae: the Etruscans are defeated by the Greeks from Syracuse led by Hiero I and lose control of the Tyrrhenian Sea; their economic power also begins to decline.
453 BC	The Greeks from Syracuse appear close to the Etruscan coast, sack Corsica and occupy the isle of Elba temporarily.
423 BC	Capua is conquered by the Samnites; the Etruscans lose Campania completely; their naval power ends.
413 BC	Defeat of the Etruscans and the Greeks from Athens in the naval expedition against Syracuse.
396 BC	Veio destroyed by the Romans.
390–389 BC	Tarquinia attacks the Roman fortresses of Nepi and Sutri.
Beginning of 4th century BC	Gallic invasion of Italy.
386 BC	An uneasy alliance between Rome and Cerveteri, united against the Gallic threat despite the previous tension between the two cities. In 387–386 BC the Romans are defeated by the Gauls who occupy Rome temporarily and then retreat towards northern Italy, settling in the Po valley. Northern Etruria is definitively lost.
358 BC	Cerveteri and Tarquinia united against Rome.
354 BC	Tarquinia defeated by Rome. The truce, signed between the two cities in 351 BC, is renewed in 308 BC.
340 BC	Southern Etruria under the Roman power.
310 BC	A thirty-year truce signed between Rome and Perugia, Cortona and Arezzo.
308 BC	Peace between Rome and Volsinii (Orvieto).
300–299 BC	New Gallic invasion of Italy.
299–290 BC	War between the Romans and the allied forces of Etruscans, Gauls, Samnites and Lucanians.
298 BC	Conquest of Volterra.
295 BC	Roman victory near Sentinum. Conquest of Perugia.
294 BC	Conquest of Roselle.
*293 [or 273] BC	Conquest of Cerveteri.

285–282 BC	Etruscans and Gauls allied again against the Romans; Roman victory.
*281 [or 280 or 278] BC	Defeat of Volsinii and Vulci.
280 BC	Conquest of Tarquinia and of Pisa; usually taken as the completion of the military conquest of Etruria.
265 BC	Volsinii destroyed after the Roman intervention to put down the rebellion of the serfs. End of Etruscan political autonomy.
225 BC	Final victory of the Romans over the Gauls near Talamone.
218–202 BC	Second Punic War: the Etruscan cities support Rome against Hannibal.
89 BC	The Etruscans gain the right to Roman citizenship.
79 BC	Silla conquers Populonia and Volterra.
27 BC	Etruria becomes the seventh region in the administrative division of Roman Italy devised by Augustus.

* Some sources give 273 BC for the conquest of Cerveteri, 280 or 278 for that of Vulci and Volsinii.

APPENDIX III
SKETCHES OF ETRUSCAN PLACES
PHOTOGRAPHS

PHOTOGRAPHS

The forty-three extant *Sketches of Etruscan Places* photographs in the Lawrence collection at UCB, together with two others, are printed in this edition, following the order of Lawrence's narrative. Thirty-five of the UCB photographs came from Alinari, six from Brogi (Florence) and two from Moscioni (Rome).

There are three additional photographs in the UCB collection which are not included in this edition. One of a peasant and a mule with hills in the background has on its verso the stamp of the photographic firm 'Giuseppe Cacopardo Zagari – Taormina', and the title 'Hills of Sicily' and 'Phot. Cacopardo Zagari' in Lawrence's hand. The other two are of a bronze relief panel from a chariot and an Etruscan bronze chariot, and were printed with the 'Tarquinia' essay in *Travel*; they were not collected by Lawrence, do not have captions in his hand and do not appear in his list of photographs (see below). They were almost certainly sent to Lawrence when his photographs were returned by *Travel*, as is indicated by a letter of 3 August 1928 from Nancy Pearn in response to his concern (*Letters*, vi. 266): 'Herewith the photographs you were so kind as to lend "Travel" for reproduction in connection with your ETRUSCAN sketches. I think you will find they have added some prints of their own as well' (UT). She noted that she was sending, under separate cover, seventy photographs.

In his Memorandum notebook (NWU), Lawrence made a list dated 14 June 1927 of the photographs he had collected for each essay: forty-one in all. The top half of the last page has the heading of 'Vulci' and blank space, thus indicating that at the time he was still hoping to obtain photographs for that essay – which he never did. The list gives the titles in Italian – except for no. 10, in this edition – (although he did not always exactly repeat their printed captions), the printed number and the name of the firm. This list matches the UCB photographs with four exceptions. One of the original 'Cerveteri' photographs is now missing (i.e. it is not in the UCB collection): described as '7. Sarcofago di Caere (dettaglio) Villa Giulia. terracotta—heads of man & wife 41089' from Alinari, it was published in E1 (and reproduced on the dust-jacket) and A1. It is included here as no. 7. Three of the UCB photographs, with titles on the verso in Lawrence's hand, do not appear in the list; Lawrence probably acquired them after he had compiled it (one is published in E1); they are published as nos. 9, 28 and 30. The order in his list was 'Cerveteri' 1, 2, 6, 3, 5, 4, 7, 8; 'Tarquinia' 10–12, 14, 45, 13; 'The Painted Tombs of Tarquinia' 1. 22, 23, 19–21, 17, 18, 15, 16; 'The Painted Tombs of Tarquinia' 2. 24–7, 31, 29; 'Volterra' 33, 35, 34, 44, 36, 39, 38, 40, 37, 42, 43, 41.

Travel printed ten illustrations – some drawings, some photographs – in each of the first three sketches and eleven in the fourth; the photographs were not all taken from those Lawrence had sent. Those from the UCB, in the sequence in which they appeared, were 7, 1, 3, 5 in 'The City of the Dead at Cerveteri'; 12, 9, 11, 14 (partial) in 'The Ancient Metropolis of the Etruscans'; 10, 17, 18, 15, 16, 31, 24, 20, 22 in 'The Painted Tombs of Tarquinia'; and 37, 34, 35, 33, 42, 38, 43, 44 in 'The Wind-Swept Stronghold of Volterra'. The *World Today* printed three photographs in the last essay, 'Volterra', only one of which (no. 33) was taken from those Lawrence collected (another was a different view of the Porta all'Arco, no. 34). E1 included twenty pictures (see chart).

The autograph captions were written on the verso of the photographs. Lawrence's practice has been followed, even where it is inconsistent. Someone corrected his spelling on no. 4 from 'u' to 'o' in 'Regolini-Galassi'. No. 21 had no caption, and the editor has provided one in square brackets, following Lawrence's most usual practice.

Lawrence had a struggle to find some photographs, notably for the chapter on Vulci. He wrote to Earl Brewster on 14 June 1927 that 'I am in rather a fix for some photographs for my Etruscan essays. I can get some, very good, from Alinari and Brogi here [in Florence]: but some they haven't done ... I know Moscioni has done two *Tomba della Caccia e Pesca* at Tarquinia, and I want that very much ... Also I want *very much* a photograph of Vulci (Volci): *The Ponte dell'Abbadia*, and any tomb that has been photographed' (vi. 85); see above, p. xxxiii. He expressed to Brewster his pleasure at getting the Moscioni photographs and his 'despair' about 'nothing' for Vulci (vi. 90, 93). He asked Millicent Beveridge to investigate the British Museum and then told Martin Secker on 22 July: 'The best thing is to get from the Brit Museum Print Room Plate 35—of *Forty Drawings by British Artists*—a view of the Ponte and Castello at Vulci—very nice—and very necessary' (vi. 105 and n. 2). Secker apparently did not attempt to locate *Forty Drawings of Roman Scenes by British Artists (1715–1850) from Originals in the British Museum* (1911);

Plate XXXV is *Ponte della Badia, Vulci* (dated 1842) by Samuel James Ainsley (fl. 1820–74), etcher and lithographer who travelled in Etruria, 1842–3, with George Dennis. The Ainsley drawing is reproduced here (no. 32).

In the list in the Memorandum notebook, Lawrence specified that the ash-jars in no. 45 are kept in the Archaeological Museum of Florence. At that time he had not yet written 'The Florence Museum', so he included this illustration in the group of photographs to be published with 'Tarquinia'. Since the order of the illustrations follows the narrative of the sketches when possible, the editor has considered it appropriate to place this photograph last.

Short caption	*CUP no.*	*DHL's order*	*UCB*	*Travel*	*E1 order*
Cerveteri necropolis	1	1	+	+	–
Chamber tombs	2	2	+	–	2
Grotta Bella	3	4	+	+	4
Regolini-Galassi Tomb	4	6	+	–	6
Tomb of the Saracophagi	5	5	+	+	3
Tomb of the Alcove	6	3	+	–	–
Terracotta heads	7	7	–	+	5
Bronze centre of shield	8	8	+	–	–
View of Tarquinia	9	–	+	+	–
S. Maria in Castello	10	9	+	+	1
Sarcophagus of a Magistrate	11	10	+	+	–
End view of a sarcophagus	12	11	+	+	–
Bronzes and terra-cottas	13	14	+	–	8
Greek vases	14	12	+	+	7
Tomb of Hunting and Fishing 1.	15	22	+	+	9
Tomb of Hunting and Fishing 2.	16	23	+	+	–
Tomb of the Leopards 1.	17	20	+	+	11
Tomb of the Leopards 2.	18	21	+	+	10
Tomb of the Feast 1.	19	17	+	–	12
Tomb of the Feast 2.	20	18	+	+	13
Tomb of the Feast 3.	21	19	+	–	–
Tomb of the Lionesses 1.	22	15	+	+	–
Tomb of the Lionesses 2.	23	16	+	–	14
Tomb of the Bulls	24	24	+	+	15
Tomb of the Augurs (1)	25	25	+	–	–
Tomb of the Augurs (2)	26	26	+	–	–
Tomb of the Augurs (3)	27	27	+	–	–
Tomb of the Baron (1)	28	–	+	–	16
Tomb of the Baron (2)	29	29	+	–	–
Tomb of Typhon	30	–	+	–	–
Tomb of Orcus	31	28	+	+	–
Vulci	32	–	–	–	–
View of Volterra	33	30	+	+*	–
Porta dell'Arco	34	32	+	+	17
Alabaster workers	35	31	+	+	–
Ash-chest (boar-hunt)	36	34	+	–	18

Short caption	CUP no.	DHL's order	UCB	Travel	E1 order
Ash-chest (farewell scene)	37	38	+	+	19
Ash-chest (underworld)	38	36	+	+	–
Ash-chest (attack on woman)	39	35	+	–	–
Ash-chest (Paris)	40	37	+	–	–
Ash-chest (Acteon and dogs)	41	41	+	–	20
Ash-chest (attack on city)	42	39	+	+	–
Ash-chest (barbarians)	43	40	+	+	–
Inghirami Tomb	44	33	+	+	–
Ash-jars	45	13	+	–	–

* Also printed in *World Today*.

APPENDIX IV
MAPS

1   Lawrence's Italy

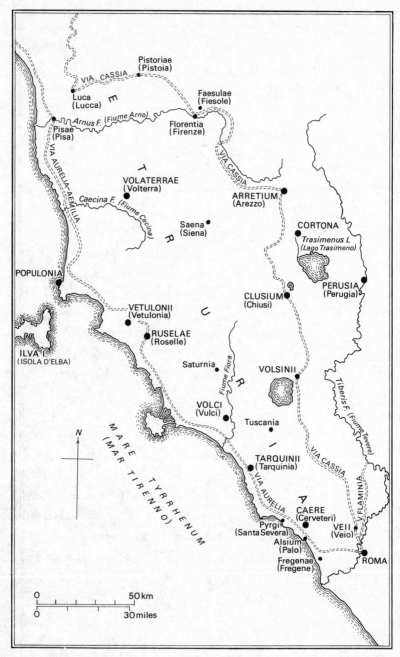

2 Etruria

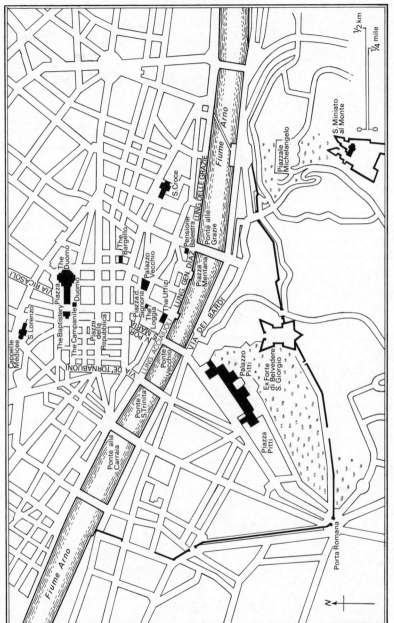

3 Florence

APPENDIX V

Fireworks
[Fireworks in Florence]

Note on the text

The text is taken from DHL's autograph manuscript, 8 pages, located at UT, and variants in TCC, 10 pages, also at UT, and A1 are recorded.

Fireworks

[Fireworks in Florence]

Yesterday being St. John's day, the 24th. June; and St. John being the patron saint of Florence; his day being also the day of midsummer festival, when, in the north, you jump through the flames; for all these reasons Florence was lit up, and there was a show of fireworks from the Piazzale. There must be fire of some sort, on midsummer day: so let it be fireworks.

The illuminations were rather scanty. The Palazzo Vecchio had frames of little electric bulbs round the windows. But above that, all along the battlements of the square roof, and in the arches of the thin-necked tower, and between the battlements at the top of the tower, the flames were orange-ruddy, and they danced about in one midsummer witch-night dance, a hundred or two little ruddy dancements among the black, hard battlements, and round the lofty, unrelenting square crown of the old building. It was at once mediaeval and fascinating, in the soft, hot, moonlit night. The Palazzo Vecchio has come down to our day, but it hasn't yet quite come down to us. It lifts its long slim neck like a hawk rearing up to look around, and in the darkness its battlements in silhouette look like black feathers. Like an alert fierce bird from the Middle Ages it lifts its head over the level town, eagle with serrated plumes. And one feels it is a wonder that the modern spirit hasn't given it a knock over the head, it is so silently fierce and haughty and severe with splendour.

On midsummer night the modern spirit had only fixed itself, like so many obstinate insects, in the squares of paltry electric bulb-lights on the hard façade. Stupid, staring, unwinking, unalive, unchanging beads of electric lights! As if there could be anything festive or midsummerish about them, in their idiotic fixity like bright colourless brass nail-heads nailed on the night.

Thus far had the modern spirit nailed itself on the old Palazzo.

But above, where the battlements ruffled like pinion-tips upon the blond sky, and the darknecked tower suddenly shot up, the modern spirit unexplainedly ceased, and the Middle Ages flourished. There the illuminations must have been oil flare-lamps, old oil torch-
5 lamps, because the flames were like living bodies, so warm and alive, and they danced about perpetually in the warm bland air of night, like Shiva dancing her myriad-movement dance. And all this alive dancement the severe old building carried calmly, with pride and dignity, its neck in the sky. As for the rows of electric bulbs below,
10 like buttons on the breast of a page-boy, they didn't exist.

If anything is detestable, it is hard, stupid fixity, that doesn't know how to flicker and waver and be alive, but must keep on going on being the same, like the buttons on a coat; the coat wears out, but the idiotic buttons are the same as ever.

15 The people were streaming out of the piazza, all in one direction, and all quiet, and all seeming small and alive under the tall buildings. Of course the Palazzo Vecchio and the Uffizi aren't really tall: in terms of the Woolworth Tower, that is, or the Flatiron Building.* But underneath their walls people move diminished, in small, alert, lively
20 throngs, just as in the street-scenes of the old pictures; throngs and groups of striding and standing and streaming people who are quick and alive, and still have a certain alert human dignity, in spite of their being so diminished. And that again is different from the effect of looking down from the top of the Flatiron Building, let us say. Then
25 you see people little and scurrying and insect-like, rather repulsive, like the thick mechanical hurrying of ants.

Out of the Piazza Signoria the people were all flowing in one direction, towards the dark mouth of the Uffizi, towards the river. The fountain was shooting up a long, leaning stem of water, and the
30 rather stupid thick Bandinelli statue below glistened all over, in his thick nakedness; but not unpleasant, really. Michelangelo's David, in the dry dimness, continued to smirk and trail his foot self-consciously, the incarnation of the modern self-conscious young man, and very objectionable.

35 But the crowd streamed on, towards the Lungarno, under the big-headed David, unheeding.—It is a curious thing, that in spite of that extremely obtrusive nude statue of David which stands and has stood for so long a time there in the Piazza where every Friday the farmers from the country throng to discuss prices, still the name
40 *David* is practically unknown among the ordinary people. They have never heard it. It is meaningless sound to them. It might as well be

Popocatepetl. Tell them your name is Theophrastus,* and they have
it in an instant. Tell them your name is David, and they remain
utterly impervious and blank. You cannot bring them to utter it.

On the Lungarno the crowd is solid. There is no traffic. The
whole length of the riverside has become one long theatre-pit, where   5
the whole populace of Florence waits to see the fireworks. In
countless numbers, they stand and wait, the whole city, yet quiet
almost as mice.

The fireworks will go off from the Piazzale Michelangelo, which is
like a platform, a little plateau away above the left bank of the river. 10
So the crowd solidly lines the right bank, the whole city.

In the sky a little to the south, the fair, warm moon, almost full,
lingers in a fleece of iridescent cloud, as if also wanting to look on,
but from an immeasurable distance. There is no drawing near, on
the moon's part.   15

The crowd is quiet, and perfectly well behaved. No excitement,
and absolutely no exuberance. In a sense, there is no holiday spirit at
all. A man hawks half-a-dozen toy balloons, but nobody buys them.
There is a little flare-lit stall, where they cook those little aniseed
waffles. And nobody seems to buy them. Only the men who silently   20
walk through the throng with little tubs of ice-cream, do a trade. But
almost without a sound.

It seems long to wait. Down on the grass by the still-full river,
under the embankment, are throngs of people. Even those boats in
which during the day one sees men getting gravel, are full of   25
spectators. But you wouldn't know, unless you looked over the
rampart. They are so still. In the river's underworld.

It is weary to wait. The young men, all wearing no hats, stroll
winding among the throng of immovable citizens and wives. There is
nothing to see. Best sit in the motor-car by the kerb.   30

By the car stand two women with a police-dog on a chain. The dog,
alert, nervous, uneasy, crouches and then rises restlessly. *Bang!* up
goes the first rocket, like a golden tadpole wiggling up in the sky,
then a burst of red and green sparks. The dog winces, and crouches
under the running-board of the car. *Bang! Bang! Crackle!* More   35
rockets, more showers of stars and fizzes of aster-petal light in the
sky. The dog whimpers, the mistresses divide their attention
between the heavens and him. In the sky, the moon draws further
and further off, while still watching palely. At an immense distance,
the moon, pallid far. Nearer, in the high sky, a rolling and fuming of   40

smoke, a whistling of rockets, a spangling and splashing of fragments of coloured lights, and, most impressive of all, the continuous explosions, crepitation within the air itself, the high air bursting outwards from within itself, in continual shocks. It is more like an
5 air-raid, than anything. And perhaps the deepest impression made on the psyche, is that of a raid in the air.

The dog suffers and suffers more. He tries to hide away, not to look at all. But there is an extra bang and a fusillade! he has to look! *bish*! the sky-asters burst one beyond the other! He cannot bear it.
10 He shivers like a glass cup that is going to shatter. His mistresses try to comfort him. They want to look at the fireworks, but their interest in the dog is more real. And he, he wants to cover his ears, and bury his head, but at every new bang! he starts afresh and rises, and turns round. Sometimes he sits like a statue of pure distress, still as
15 bronze. Then he curls away upon himself again, curling to get away. While the high sky bursts and reverberates, wiggles with tadpoles of golden fire, and plunges with splashes of light, spangles of colour, as if someone had thrown a stone into the ether from above, and then pelted the ether with stones.
20 The crowd watches in silence. Young men wander by, and in the subdued tone of mocking irony common to the Italians, they say: bello! bello! bellezza! But it pure irony. As the light goes up, you see the dark trees and cypresses standing tall and black, like Dantesque spectators, on the sky-line. And down below, you see the townspeo-
25 ple standing motionless with uplifted faces. Also, rather frequently, a young man with his arm round his white-dressed sweetheart, caressing her and making public love to her. Love-making, it seems, like everything else, must be public nowadays. The stag goes into the depths of the forest. But the young city buck likes the light to flare up
30 and reveal his arm round the shoulders of his girl, his hand stroking her neck.

Up on the Piazzale, they are letting off the figure-pieces: wheels that turn round showerily in red and green and white fire, fuming dense smoke, that moves in curious slow volumes, all penetrated
35 with colour. Now there is a red piece: and on top of the old water-tower a column of red fire and reddish smoke. It looks as if a city in the distance were being burnt by the enemy. And again the fusillade of a raid, while the smoke rolls ponderously, the colour dies out, only the iridescence of the far, unreachable naked moon tinges
40 the low fume.

In heaven are more rockets. There are lovely ones that lean down in the sky like great spider-lilies, with long out-curving petals of soft light, and at the end of each petal, a sudden drop of pure green, ready to fall like dew. But some strange hand of evanescence brushes it away, and it is gone, and the next rocket bursting shows all the 5 smoke-threads still stretching, like the spectre of the great fire-lily, up in the sky: like the greyness of wild clematis fronds in autumn, crumbling together, as the succeeding rocket bursts in brilliance.

Meanwhile, in another world, and a world more real, the explosions and percussions and fusillades keep up, and penetrate into the 10 soul with a sense of fear. The dog, reduced and shattered, tries to get used to it, but can't succeed.

There is a great spangling and sparkling and trailing of long lights in the sky, and long sprays of whitish, successively-bursting fireblossoms, and other big many-petalled flowers curving their petals 15 downwards like a grasping hand. Ah, at last, it is all happening at once!

And as the eye is thrilled and dazzled, the ear almost ceases to hear. Yet the moment the sky empties, it is the percussion of explosions on the heart that one feels. 20

It is quickly all over. The chauffeur is gabbling *sotto voce* that it is shorter than last year. The crowd is dispersing so quickly and silently, as if they were running away. And you feel they are all mocking quietly at the spectacle. *Panem et circenses* is all very well, but when the great crowd quietly jeers at your circus, it leaves you at a 25 loss.

The cathedral dome, the top of Giotto's tower, like a lily stem, and the straight lines of the top of the Baptistery* are outlined with rather sparse electric bulbs. It looks very unfinished. Yet, with that light above illuminating the pale and coloured marbles ghostly, and the 30 red tiles of the dome, in the night sky, and the abrupt end of the lily-stem without a flower, and the old hard lines of the Baptistery's top, there is a lovely ethereal quality to the great cathedral group, and you think again of the lily of Florence.—"The lily of Florence shall become the cauliflower of Rovezzano,"* somebody said. 35

But not yet, anyhow.

EXPLANATORY NOTES

EXPLANATORY NOTES

Sketches of Etruscan Places

9:2 **Cerveteri** From Caere Vetus, Ancient Cere (Cere Antica). Its Etruscan name was probably Chaire or Cheri; the Latin name was Caere while the Greek was Agylla (cf. Virgil, *Aeneid*, VIII, v. 478 and ff.). The legend about the origin of the name is reported in Dennis: 'when the Lydian or Etruscan colonists were about to attack the city, they hailed it and inquired its name; whereon, a soldier from the ramparts, not understanding their motives or language, replied with a salutation – χαῖρε – "hail!" which they receiving as a good omen, on the capture of the city applied to it as its name' (i. 231).

Cerveteri is about 45 km. n. of Rome. The Etruscan city lies on a plateau above the modern Cerveteri; it is first recorded as a 9th–8th century BC Iron Age settlement during the Villanovan period (see note on 27:15). The Villanovan tombs are like little wells or graves excavated in the porous rock (tufa). The 7th century BC is generally called the Orientalising period, when Cerveteri reached a very important cultural position and traded with the East. To this period belongs the necropolis of the Banditaccia with its round-shaped tumuli (see note on 14:24), while the square-shaped tumuli belong to the 6th century BC. The more modest tombs (14:20–3), simply hollowed out in the rock, belong to the period of decline of the 5th and 4th centuries BC.

9:6 **The Etruscans [9:3]…a very big R.** The Etruscans, whose early culture has been recently identified with the Villanovan culture (see note on 27:15), settled in central Italy between the Arno (Tuscany) and the Tiber (Latium), *c.* 900 BC. In the 6th and 5th centuries BC their civilisation and culture became highly developed, and they expanded their dominion northward, in the Po valley, and southward, towards Campania, forming a confederation of politically independent city-states. In the 4th century BC their power began to decline, as a consequence of the Tarquin's banishment from Rome and of several military defeats which subjected them to the Roman empire. They were gradually absorbed by Roman civilisation, until their national identity completely disappeared.

9:8 **etruscan** For the use of the lower case initial letter, see Introduction, pp. xlviii–xlix and Note on the text.

9:10 **the inevitable result…the Romans.** The conquest of central Italy was the first stage of Roman expansion, which culminated in the constitution of the Roman empire when Octavian (63 BC–AD 14), Caesar's adoptive son, assumed the name of Augustus and the title of Emperor (27 BC). Rome easily defeated the Etruscan cities in the 3rd century BC, profiting by weaknesses (due to internal conflicts) within the confederation of the Etruscan city-states; the battle of Sentinum (295 BC) marked the decisive Roman victory against a coalition of

Etruscans, Samnites, Lucanians (inhabitants of central and s. Italy) and Gauls (see note on 13:22 and 'Historical outline').

9:12 **we know nothing...Latin writers.** No Etruscan literature survives, and even some of the inscriptions found in the tombs have still to be deciphered (see note on 18:19). Information about Etruscan history and culture can be found in Latin and Greek writers such as Polybius, Herodotus, Statius, Silvius Italicus, Thucydides, Virgil, Livy, Dionysius of Halicarnassus, Horace, Ovid, Seneca and Pliny the Elder.

9:17 **the first time...at Perugia,** On 25 March 1926 (see Introduction, p. xxv). Perugia is the main town in Umbria, in central Italy. The Etruscan arch bears witness to its pre-Roman culture, and the Etruscan–Roman Museum houses one of the most important collections of pre-historic and Etruscan remains, including a sarcophagus, *cippi* (cf. 20:5–11 and note) and Roman gravestones, a great number of urns, generally with the person's name inscribed, and a famous document of the Etruscan language – the Perugia cippus – a boundary stone with a long inscription (46 lines and 130 words) mentioning the two families of Velthina and Afuna. There is also a rich collection of terracotta vases (*buccheri*) (see note on 38:18), bronzes, mirrors and weapons.

9:22 **Mommsen** See Introduction, pp. xxvii–xxviii.

9:30 **the Etruscans were vicious...said so.** See 'Cypresses' in *Birds, Beasts and Flowers*: 'men of Etruria,/ Whom Rome called vicious...Evil-yclept Etruscan?/ For as to the evil/ We have only Roman word for it' (*The Complete Poems of D. H. Lawrence*, ed. Vivian de Sola Pinto and Warren Roberts), 1964, i. 297, ll. 34–5, 54–6; see also Introduction, pp. xxiii–xxiv).

9:33 **the late war...A la bonne heure!** World War I...'That's right!' or 'Well done!' or 'Good idea!' (The French expression is sarcastic.)

10:1 **Messalina and Heliogabalus** Messalina (*c.* 25–48), third wife of the emperor Claudius and Heliogabalus (204–22), Roman emperor, were both notorious for their depravity and dissoluteness.

10:3 *basta!* **Quand...se tait.** 'Enough!' or 'That will do!' (Italian). 'When the master speaks, everybody shuts up' (French).

10:8 **To the Puritan...somebody says.** Cf. Titus i. 15 ['To the pure all things are pure', Revised Version].

10:14 **On a sunny April morning...From Rome...to Pisa.** 6 April 1927 (see Introduction, p. xxx)...DHL and Earl Brewster (the 'B.' of 13:7) visited the Villa Giulia Museum in Rome...Pisa, one of the main towns in Tuscany, was also one of the most important Etruscan cities.

10:26 **The inestimable big Italian railway-guide...Palo...post omnibus.** Probably the *Guida Ferroviaria* annually published by the Italian railways, containing the train timetable for the whole of Italy...Palo, Alsium in Latin, near Ladispoli, used to be one of the three ports for the sea trade of Cerveteri, the other two being Pyrgi (Santa Severa) (28:15) and Punicum (Santa Marinella). In 384 BC they were all destroyed by a violent attack of the Syracusans; in 247 BC the Romans re-established Pyrgi, Alsium and Fregenae as colonies in the territory taken from Caere...Motor omnibus which also carried mail.

10:29 **Ladispoli.** 'City of Ladislao', a small village founded by Prince Ladislao Odescalchi, *c.* 1830.

11:13 **an ugly big grey building:** The old Orsini (later Ruspoli) castle stands in the main square and dates from the 16th century; it was donated in 1967 as a museum (Museo Nazionale di Cerveteri) (see also 12:33 and 13:13). Dennis says: 'The village, and the land for some miles round it, are the property of Prince Ruspoli, whose palace forms a conspicuous object in the scene' (i. 229).

11:18 **the fall of the Roman empire** 5th century.

11:24 *Vini e Cucina,* The cheapest and most informal eating places in Italy.

11:37 **so-called sheep's cheese...Calabria** DHL gave his impressions of Sardinia in *Sea and Sardinia* (see Introduction, p. xxii), and mentioned the cheese in a description of the Cagliari market (chap. III)...Calabria is a region in s. Italy.

12:2 **shaggy-legged faun.** Mythological Roman deity of the woods, represented as a man with horns and goat's legs (see also note on 187:8).

12:14 **straight-nosed face** In 'Cypresses', DHL makes the same comment: 'Is it the secret of the long-nosed Etruscans?/ The long-nosed, sensitive-footed, subtly-smiling Etruscans,/ Who made so little noise outside the cypress groves?' (*Complete Poems of D. H. Lawrence*, ed. Pinto and Roberts, i. 296, ll. 14–16).

12:28 **maremma** Alluvial plain on the coast of central Italy, mainly in Tuscany, which used to be a marsh; its reclamation was completed in 1924 (see 140:16–32).

12:29 **Cerevetus, the old Cere.** DHL is translating the Latin name which is, in fact, Caere Vetus (cf. note on 9:2); his spelling mistake has not been emended because at 10:20 he uses the two forms as possible alternatives.

12:31 **the acropolis,** The high and fortified place of Greek towns, called 'arx' in Etruscan cities. Arx, arcis (Latin) has a figurative meaning of a safe place, a refuge (see also 13:15–18 and cf. note on 20:25).

13:5 **cotton together,** I.e. '"get on" together or with each other; to suit each other' (*OED*).

13:12 **pack-mules arrived, as in Mexico.** In *Mornings in Mexico*, DHL describes mules arriving at a Mexican market in 'Market Day'. Cf. 14:27–32 and the description of the landscape in 'Walk to Huayapa', in *Mornings in Mexico*.

13:22 **Ionia...Gauls...Vestal Virgins** Ancient name for a coastal region in Asia Minor, which included a confederation of twelve cities. Those Greeks coming from Ionia, the Phocaeans, were defeated by the allied Etruscan and Phoenician forces (*c.* 540 BC). On the other hand, it was in this period (second half of the 6th century BC) that cultural influences from the Hellenic world were particularly strong in the development of the figurative arts in Cerveteri. In the 2nd century BC Ionia was conquered by Rome...The Gauls, a Celtic people who settled in western Europe (modern France) in very ancient times, conquered the Po valley (5th century BC), Rome (387 BC) and Asia Minor (3rd century BC) but were later completely defeated by Caesar (58–51 BC)...The Vestal Virgins were the priestesses of Vesta. Virgins from the Roman patrician families, they were charged with keeping the goddess's sacred fire alight in the Temple and were buried alive if they broke their vow of chastity. The Roman Senate, unable to stop the invasion of the Gauls and fearful that they might desecrate the sacred hearth-fire, ordered the Vestal Virgins to take refuge at Cerveteri.

14:24 **Banditaccia** The principal necropolis of Cerveteri. Dennis comments: 'The name is simply indicative of the proprietorship of the land, which once belonging to the *comune*, or corporation of Cervet[e]ri, was *terra bandita* – "set apart;" or "forbidden" to the public, and, as it was uncultivated and broken ground, the termination descriptive of its ugliness was added – *banditaccia*. It retains the name, though it has passed into the hands of Prince Ruspoli' (i. 238).

14:40 **a great feature** See Textual apparatus. The MS reading (p. 11) comes from an incomplete revision: '⟨such⟩ ⌐a great⌐ a feature'. This is also true of 35:15 where MS (p. 19) reads: 'urns, ⟨however,⟩ are'. (⟨ ⟩ indicates a deletion; ⌐ ⌐ an addition.)

15:13 **having stood on the rocks in Sicily,** DHL's home was in Taormina (March 1920–February 1922).

15:23 **Etna,** The highest active volcano in Europe (3263 m.), in n.e. Sicily, not far from Taormina.

16:7 **the million-dollar cemetery in New Orleans. Absit omen!** It is not possible to say whether DHL had in mind a particular cemetery; however, New Orleans has a number of large cemeteries such as the Providence Memorial Park cemetery and the Garden of Memories Memorial Cemetery in the w. end; the major cemeteries are in the central area (Lakelawn Park Cemetery, Greenwood Cemetery, Masonic Cemetery) whereas the ancient cemeteries are towards the e. end (St Louis Cemetery, St Rock Cemetery). 'Absit omen!' is 'May there be no ill omen!' (Latin).

16:22 **the weirdness of** [16:19]...**the south;** DHL refers to the places where he had visited remains of past civilisations; Teotihuácan and Cholula are near Mexico City, and Mitla is further s., not far from Oaxaca where DHL stayed (November 1924–February 1925).

17:16 **Lucumones,** The highest political, judicial and religious authority in each city was a priest-king, called *lauchme* ('Chief' or 'Lord') in Etruscan, or *lucumo* in Latin; he was chosen from among the oldest and most distinguished families (see also 37:16–17, 33–38, 47:12–13, 116:5–25).

17:30 **the little bronze...other world,** Cf. DHL's poem 'The Ship of Death' (August–October 1929): 'Oh build your ship of death, your little ark/ and furnish it with food, with little cakes, and wine/ for the dark flight down oblivion' (*Complete Poems of D. H. Lawrence*, ed. Pinto and Roberts, ii. 718, ll. 38–40; cf. also ll. 53–5 and 105–7, p. 718 and p. 720).

17:36 **death.** DHL added to the paragraph in TSa (p. 16) and then deleted: '—But now nothing is left. Only in one tomb'.

17:38   **Tomb of the Tarquins...early Rome.**   Tarquinius Priscus and Tarquinius Superbus were the fifth and seventh kings of Rome in 6th century BC. After the coup d'etat (509 BC) which deposed Tarquinius Superbus, he and two of his sons are said to have gone into exile at Cerveteri. The Tomb of the Tarquins, discovered in 1845, contained the inscription in Etruscan at 18:11, Tarchnas being an Etruscan form of Tarquin (cf. 17:39; cf. also Dennis, i. 242–5).

18:19   **in Caesar's day...language is entirely lost.**   Gaius Julius Caesar (102–44 BC)...Over thirteen thousand Etruscan inscriptions are known today but most of them are only a few words long, and the total vocabulary is only about five hundred words. Some Etruscologists believe that the so-called 'mystery' of the Etruscan language will never be totally revealed since the language does not belong to any defined family of languages. (At 18:18 DHL must have meant 'west-central' since both Rome and Cerveteri are in west-central Italy.)

18:21   *Grotta Bella*   'Beautiful cave' (Italian). Also called the Tomb of the Stuccoes or of the Reliefs, 4th century BC, it was discovered in 1850 during the excavations made by the Marquis G. P. Campana.

18:31   **the sacred drinking bowl [18:26]...and the End.**   All these symbols recur in Etruscan art (see also the essays on the painted tombs).

19:27   **the Shiva lingam at Benares!**   The lingam is a phallic stone worshipped by the Hindus as a symbol of the god Shiva (see note on 204:3). Benares is the ancient Hindu holy city, on the Ganges river, n.e. India.

20:5   **cippus—cippi.**   Latin (singular, plural). Nowadays, in the necropolis of Cerveteri there are many fewer phallic stones than in 1927.

20:25   **the Ark, the arx [20:21]...the manna and the mysteries.**   The vessel in which Noah, along with his family and animal creation, was saved during the Flood has also the metaphorical sense of a place of refuge (Genesis vi. 9–22, vii. 1–24). In Jewish history the Ark of the Covenant, or the Ark of Testimony, made according to instructions given by God to Moses (Exodus xxv. 10–22), contained the tablets of stone on which were inscribed the Ten Commandments (1 Kings viii. 9)...Manna was the nourishment sent from Heaven to the Hebrews during the forty years spent in the desert with Moses (Exodus xvi. 14–15); as spiritual nourishment in a wider sense, it refers to Holy Communion. Arx (see note on 12:31) is connected with the pregnant womb (high, pointed place; safe place for refuge); in *The Rainbow* Will compares the pregnant Anna, after she has danced naked 'to her unseen Lord', to the ark: 'She was the ark, and the rest of the world was flood. The only tangible, secure thing was the woman' (ed. Mark Kinkead-Weekes, Cambridge, 1989, 173:21–2).

20:39   **dance gaily to the double flute,**   Dancing figures and flute-players are often represented on the painted walls of the Tarquinian tombs (cf. pp. 45–55 *passim*).

21:1   **Delenda est Cartago.**   'Carthage must be destroyed' (Latin); originally from Plutarch, *Life of Cato*.

22:6   **the Regolini–Galassi tomb.**   In 1836 archpriest Alessandro Regolini and General Vincenzo Galassi excavated the necropolis to the s.w. of Cerveteri.

Archaeologists have dated this tomb, usually called the 'royal tomb', to the first half of the 7th century BC, indicating the year 670 BC as the possible date.

22:19   beautiful frail…years ago.   The revision from the MS reading (see Textual apparatus) might be due to DHL's discovering later that the woman first believed to be the warrior's wife could have been the queen of Cerveteri, whose tomb was guarded by the warrior (see following note).

22:25   On two of [22:21]…a lady—??   A silver table service of eleven pieces, each engraved with the name Larthia, was found at the feet of the woman in the tomb, but doubts remain about the name. Some scholars think that it and the rich and abundant jewellery must have belonged to a high priest, or to some man of rank; others believe that Larthia is a woman, perhaps a queen of Cerveteri. Since in the 7th century BC certain city-states were probably ruled by monarchs, and the woman in the Etruscan world was held in much higher esteem than in Greek or Roman culture, it is feasible that Lady Larthia was a queen who deserved this splendid 'royal' tomb.

25:2   Tarquinia   The Etruscans' main city, Tarquinii, was on a plateau 150 m. high. In the Middle Ages the little town of Corneto (Corgnetum, Cornietum) was founded on a neighbouring hill by the people who had left Tarquinia after the barbarian invasion, and flourished during the Renaissance when the Palazzo Vitelleschi was built (see note on 31:15). In 1872 the city was called Corneto Tarquinia, but in 1922 the Fascist régime restored the Roman form of Tarquinia (see 30:32–9; cf. also Dennis, i. 424). The Latin name comes from Tarchon, brother or son of Tyrrhenus, who led the Etruscans in their migration from Lydia (Asia Minor) and founded Tarquinii (cf. Dennis, i. 417).

The first settlement, which was to become the city of Tarquinia, can be dated to the beginning of the Iron Age (9th century BC); the tombs of this period are little cylindrical wells dug into the ground, covered by a slab of stone. In the 9th and the 8th centuries BC Tarquinii enjoyed a cultural and political predominance among the Etruscan centres. The fame of the city is particularly due to the painted walls of its tombs, associated with an artistic tradition from the middle of the 6th century to the 2nd century BC. About 150 painted tombs have been discovered; about 60 are still preserved today.

25:4   Città Vecchia.   A town on the coast of Latium, n. of Rome, originally a port called Centumcellae whose construction was ordered by the emperor Trajan (98–117). In 889, it was called *Civitas Vetula* which, in the Middle Ages, became *Civitas Vetus*. In the 17th century the Latin form was Italianised into *Città Vecchia*; this lost the accent mark after the 18th century and by the end of the 19th century the town had taken the present name of *Civitavecchia*.

25:34   Sicily of the Greek tyrants;   In the 8th century BC, e. Sicily was colonised by the Greeks, whereas the w. of the island was taken over by the Phoenicians. In the 5th century BC, Syracuse was governed by two tyrants: Gelon and Hiero, who succeeded his brother in 478 (see *Letters*, iii. 518 and n. 3; see also 'Historical outline').

26:9   Lydians, or Hittites   The Lydians were the inhabitants of Lydia, the ancient region in Asia Minor which was the seat of a powerful dynasty founded by Gyges in 716 BC, whose successors extended the empire to nearly all Asia Minor.

The Hittites were an Indo-European people who occupied Asia Minor in the second millennium BC, defeating Ramses II; later they conquered Babylon, extending their empire and civilisation throughout Mesopotamia and Syria. The Hittite empire was broken up by subsequent invasions (*c.* 1180 BC).

26:27 in Prince Charlie's day,   Charles Edward Stuart (1720–88), the Young Pretender.

26:35 However that may…already here: The origin of the Etruscans is a problem which has not yet been solved. The most credited theory is that small culturally homogeneous groups arrived in Italy, and, being superior in military strength, they were able to impose their languages, without disturbing the gradual cultural development of the peninsula. The Etruscans are then believed to be a product of events which took place between the Bronze and the Iron Age in the Italian peninsula.

27:4 Pelasgian…Minoan…Carian,   Pelasgian is an ancient name attributed to a people believed to have inhabited Greece and the e. Mediterranean basin before the Hellenes. The Pelasgians are famous for their great fortifications constructed of large rocks, called pelasgic or cyclopean walls…The Minoan or Aegean civilisation started before Hellenic civilisation in the third millennium BC on the island of Crete. It is generally divided into three periods: ancient (*c.* 2500–2000 BC); middle or the so-called Cretan or Minoan (*c.* 2000–1500 BC); late or Mycenaenan (*c.* 1500–1100 BC) so called from Mycenae, an ancient Greek city in the Argive plain. Minoan art is considered to be the most outstanding phenomenon of proto-historic culture in the Mediterranean world, possibly of formative influence on Greek figurative art (see 121:1 and 265:19–20)…Caria was an ancient region in the s.w. of Asiatic Turkey, inhabited by peoples of Asiatic origin. Greek colonies flourished on the Carian coast.

27:15 Villanovans,   The Villanovan or Umbran culture (9th–8th centuries BC), is so named after the village of Villanova near Bologna where archaeologists found the first evidence of the use of iron in a large cemetery (1853–5). This culture spread from n. Italy through Tuscany down to Latium; further s. similar evidence was found in Salerno.

27:25 a great league   The Etruscan league, also called the League of Twelve, was founded by Tarchon who first founded twelve cities in the n. of Italy; then he crossed the Apennines and founded the city of Mantua, and later he is said to have founded another eleven cities which were united in a league called by the Latins *duodecim populi Etruriae* (cf. 137:6–7). Tarquinii was the most ancient of the twelve city-states; the other eleven were: Vulci, Vetulonia, Cerveteri, Arezzo, Chiusi, Roselle, Volterra, Cortona, Perugia, Volsini and Populonia. (The twelfth city was at first Veio but after its destruction in 396 BC, Populonia entered the confederation; see Ducati, i. 134–5).

27:29 The etruscan alphabet…the Chalcidians of Cumae   A number of hypothesis about the Chalcidians and their language as a source for the Etruscan alphabet are discussed in R. A. L. Fell, *Etruria and Rome* (Cambridge, 1924); see Introduction, p. xxviii. The Chalcidians originally came from the Greek port of Chalcis, in Euboea. Before the 8th century BC they traded with Etruria from their base at Pithekoussai on the Island of Ischia. In the 8th century BC the Chalcidians founded Cumae, an important colony in Magna Graecia, the region now called Campania, with Naples as its principal city. In fact, Naples was founded by colonisers from Cumae.

28:9 in the days of Solomon...of Abraham. Solomon (960–927 BC) king of Israel, son of David and Bathsheba, celebrated for his wisdom...Abraham, first patriarch of the Hebrew people.

28:26 Hellas or from [28:17]...tyrant of Syracuse. Hellas is the ancient name of Greece; Magna Graecia was the name given to the Greek colonies which were founded in s. Italy and Sicily during the 8th–6th centuries BC. The mainland part of Magna Graecia came under Roman domination between 280 and 265 BC, Sicily in 241 BC. Tyre and Sidon were the two most important Phoenician cities, and rivals in trade. Livy (59 BC–AD 17), in *The War with Hannibal* relates the contribution made by the Etruscan cities to Scipio's campaign: 'Caere offered grain from the crews and supplies of all sorts; Populonium promised iron; Tarquinii sail-cloth; Volaterrae grain and timber for keels and garboards; ...' (XXVIII, 45). Livy also wrote *History of Rome* (see 63:3 and note).

For the first defeats, see note on 25:34; later, when Athens decided on a naval expedition to Sicily against Syracuse, the Etruscans allied themselves with the Greeks against their ancient enemies but were defeated again (414–413 BC).

28:35 Ostia, The seaside resort on the Tyrrhenian coast, 4 km. s.w. of Ostia Antica, the ancient town, which is situated 23 km. to the n.e. of Rome. Ostia is also called Lido di Roma or Lido di Ostia ('Lido' means 'beach').

30:9 a very interesting museum in Città Vecchia, The National Archaeological Museum contains a number of Roman sculptures among which is a famous statue of Apollo from the times of Emperor Hadrian (76–138).

30:12 the present régime The fascist movement assumed power in Italy after the march on Rome (28 October 1922) and the elections in 1923. Its leader, Benito Mussolini (1883–1945), became dictator in 1925 and aimed to restore the ancient greatness and power of the Roman empire.

30:18 the soft answer to turn away wrath, Cf. Proverbs xv. 1: 'A soft answer turneth away wrath'.

31:15 a beautiful stone palazzo The Palazzo Vitelleschi (33:11), a Renaissance building in the central square of Tarquinia, built by Cardinal Giovanni Vitelleschi (1436–9). In 1924 it was chosen to house the National Archaeological Museum, and it contains one of the most important collections of Etruscan antiquities and Greek pottery in Italy (see also note on 35:3).

31:16 Dazio, The town customs (see 115:6–14), still in existence in a number of Italian towns during DHL's tour, were finally abolished in March 1930.

31:37 *Teh! Lina!* [31:34]...Eh!...Fai presto!...È pronto!...Ecco!" 'Teh!' is a colloquial interjection in northern-central Italy, used by Albertino to call Lina who answers 'Eh!', i.e. 'Yes?' or 'What?'...'Hurry up!'...'It is ready!'...'There you are!'

34:9 salute us...alla Romana...all'etrusca! To salute in the Roman manner ...in the Etruscan manner. The Fascists restored the Roman salute, the right arm raised and the hand kept open. The Romans used to accompany this gesture with the words 'Ave Caesar!' ('Hail Caesar!'). The Etruscan salute was believed by DHL to be the gesture in a painting of the Tombs of the Leopards which is described at 49:1–2 (see also photograph no. 17). A different gesture is described at 116:18, as being more similar to the Roman salute, mentioned at 158:33.

34:34 only things [34:14]**…a million** The typist skipped MS p. 17; see Introduction, p. xli.

35:3 cortile 'Courtyard' (Italian). Palazzo Vitelleschi has an internal courtyard surrounded by a loggia with a well in the middle, and with columns and Gothic arches set on two levels.

35:27 the sides were lined See Textual apparatus. The revision is allowed because although DHL noticed the mistyping of 'buried' for MS 'lined' (p. 19), in TSc (p. 17) it is clear from the alignment of the words that he corrected to 'lined' and *then* altered 'frequently' to 'the sides were' which has been deemed a re-thinking, rather than a response to error.

36:18 And in the beginning…a chirrup. Cf. John i. 1: 'In the beginning was the Word, and the Word was with God, and the Word was God' (see also 122:37 and 131:1); cf. also the opening of 'Foreword to *Sons and Lovers*'.

36:35 the sacred patera, or mundum, A round flat saucer, made of clay or metal. 'Mundum' is 'world', 'universe' (Latin); 'mundus', the masculine form, was more common (see 170:3).

38:2 the Sarcophagus of the Magistrate, with his written scroll Sarcophagus of Laris Pulena, from one of the noble families of Tarquinii, dated *c.* 180 BC. The scroll has one of the longest Etruscan inscriptions known, about sixty words, listing Pulena's forefathers and the dignities they held.

38:18 bucchero, Glossy black pottery known as bucchero ware, which started being produced during the second half of the 7th century BC.

38:37 Already in…etruscan tombs: DHL probably refers to the opinion reported by Dennis, that the rifling of the tombs 'took place in the time of Julius Caesar, when the painted vases were much prized' (i. 390).

38:38 the *sigilla Tyrrhena* 'Sigilla' are small figures or statuettes (Latin); Tyrrhenus, in its adjectival form, meant Etruscan. The correct Latin form is *Tyrrhena sigilla*. DHL echoes Ducati's 'little bronzes…so much liked by the Roman connoisseurs of the Augustan age' (ii. 55).

39:5 "still-unravished brides of quietness," Keats, 'Ode on a Grecian Urn,' l. 1 ('Thou still unravish'd bride of quietness') (see also 145:3 and note).

43:4 the painted tombs, The tombs described in this and in the following essay, were constructed between the 6th and the 2nd century BC: *6th century BC* – the Bulls, the Lionesses, Hunting and Fishing, Painted Vases, the Old Man, the Dead Man, the Inscriptions, the Baron, the Augurs, the Bacchanti; *5th century BC* – the Feast, the Leopards, the Chariots, the Maiden, Francesca Giustiniani; *4th century BC* – the Orcus, the Shields; *2nd century BC* – the Typhon. Dennis proposed a general classification of the tombs of Tarquinia: the Archaic, or purely Etruscan; the Graeco-Etruscan; and the Roman-Etruscan (i. 380).

43:11 Viterbo, One of the five main cities in the region of Latium, n.w. of Tarquinia.

44:15 the Tomb of Hunting and Fishing, The *Tomba della Caccia e della Pesca*, 520–500 BC, discovered in 1873, comprises two chambers; it belongs to the most ancient group of painted funeral chambers which were influenced in style by the Ionic artistic movement that spread throughout Etruria from the Greek centres on the w. coast of Asia Minor.

46:15 They are by...they will. After the abolition of the monarchy (late 6th century BC) the cities were controlled by a wealthy nobility. Though not slaves on the Greek and Roman model the lower classes felt themselves increasingly bound to rich merchants and landowners, thus creating a sort of vassalage.

47:6 Lucca...Ferrara, Founded by the Ligurians and occupied by the Etruscans in the 5th century BC; now one of the nine main cities in the region of Tuscany...One of the eight principal cities in the region of Emilia-Romagna in n. Italy, was an Etruscan dominion.

47:20 the Tomb of the Leopards. The *Tomba dei Leopardi*, 480–460 BC, discovered in 1875 or 1833. Its paintings reflect the artistic movement imported from Athens and the rest of mainland Greece.

48:10 *chlamys...subulo* 'A short mantle or cloak worn by men in ancient Greece' (*OED*), usually fastened with a clasp in front or at the right shoulder...'Flute-player'.

48:30 hetaerae, Feminine plural of the Latin word derived from Greek εταίρα, 'companion'; 'a mistress, concubine; a courtesan' (*OED*).

49:14 the leopards or panthers of the underworld Bacchus, Bacchus (in Greek, Dionysus) went down to hell to recover his mother, covered with the skin of a panther, which therefore became sacred to him (see notes on 51:35 and 187:8).

49:30 the *Tomba del Triclinio*, 480–460 BC, discovered in 1830; its frescoes are preserved in the museum at Tarquinia (see Dennis, i. 318–25).

50:4 the bacchic woman The votaries of Bacchus were well-known for the uninhibited frenzy with which they behaved.

50:31 the old dictum...with the gods. Primitive civilisations believed in the 'anima', the soul (Latin) as a vital principle, which was sometimes identified with organs or parts of the human body; Indo-European pre-Christian philosophical doctrines never considered the soul as something separate from the body whereas Christians conceived man to be the result of two principles: the material, the body, and the spiritual, the anima. Plato (427–347 BC) was the first philosopher who formulated explicitly the dualistic conception of man (see also 55:1–4).

50:31 You may meet them so, in the streets of the American towns. DHL's main home, 1922–5, was near Taos, New Mexico, where one of the most ancient American-Indian Pueblo tribes still live; he would have seen them with their bodies and faces smeared with red paint. They still paint themselves during celebrations and festivals (see also note on 200:4).

50:38 *minium.* 'Native cinnabar, red lead' (OED).

51:2 And Ezekiel...their nativity.— The Biblical passage reads: 'she saw ...vermilion, Girded with girdles upon their loins, exceeding in dyed attire upon their heads, all...nativity:' (AV).

51:20 The Etruscans shared [51:16]...in a chair. In early Roman times women were not only barred from participating in banquets, but as Pliny says 'it was not lawful for women to drink wine'; in Greece only 'courtesans' would lie on a couch with men at a banquet, and the only respectable public career for Greek and Roman women was as a priestess; whereas in Etruria women appear to have been highly regarded and enjoyed social equality. Greek writers like Timaeus of Taormina and Theopompus depicted Etruscan women as depraved and free from any sexual restraint (see note on 131:2).

51:28 *alabastron,* A little jar for perfumes, generally made of alabaster (Greek). See also Dennis, i. 319.

51:35 the ivy of the underworld Bacchus, Dennis commented on this part of the painting:
> The known relation of the panther to Bacchus is suggestive of a funeral signification of the two over the doorway, and the same may be said of the ivy which surrounds the room in a broad band above the heads of the figures...Did not the archaic character of the paintings in this and similar tombs of Tarquinii, forbid us to assign to them so recent a date, the frequent occurrence of Bacchic emblems might lead to the supposition that these festive scenes represent the Dionysia, which were imported from Greece into Etruria about two hundred years before Christ, and thence introduced into Rome. (i. 324)

52:4 Fritz Weege's book *Etruskische Malerei,* See Introduction, pp. xxviii and xxxii. The reproduction is among the illustrations in sepia at the end of the book (see also 263:33–264:8).

52:13 Flaxmanised John Flaxman (1755–1826) neo-classical sculptor and draughtsman, whose drawings and models formalise the qualities of Greek design. See also 164:13–14 and note.

52:18 the Tomb of the Bacchanti 510–500 BC, discovered in 1874; it consists of one small chamber where the frescoes are considerably faded: only a few isolated figures, dancing or playing, and small trees can still be seen.

52:36 the *Tomba del Morto,* 520–510 BC, discovered in 1832; the subject of the old dead man described by DHL from the principal scene painted on the left-hand wall is unusual. There was also a banquet scene but only the figures of two men drinking can still be seen (see Dennis, i. 325–7).

53:9 the *Tomba delle Leonesse,* 520–510 BC, discovered in 1877; its paintings show the influence of Ionic art. The Tomb of the Lionesses was named so by mistake: the two wild beasts painted in the pediment on the back wall are panthers.

53:29 **The *Tomba della Pulcella*,** 470–430 BC, the time when Etruscan artistic production began to decline, discovered in 1837 or 1865. It shows a banquet scene with four couples; to their left are a slave and a pretty girl with curly hair (the Pulcella); there are also the figures of two players and a Medusa head (see Dennis, i. 313–15).

53:31 **the key pattern,** An ornamental frieze running along the walls, generally under the main painting (see also 63:26).

53:32 **The *Tomba dei Vasi Dipinti*,** 530–500 BC, discovered 1864–7; its paintings are examples of the archaic style of Etruscan art. The banquet scene on the back wall and two men and a woman dancing on the left-hand wall can still be seen. DHL does not mention a boy and a girl, who sit to the left of the couple, and who are embracing each other with fraternal affection; they are vividly described by Dennis (i. 358–62), but probably the painting, already rather indistinct then, was hardly visible when DHL was there about eighty years later (128:21–2).

54:21 **the *Tomba del Vecchio*,** 510–500 BC, discovered 1864–7; this tomb shows an Ionic elegance similar to that in the Tomb of the Painted Vases to which it bears 'a close resemblance in form, size, decoration, and style of art' (Dennis, i. 356). According to Dennis, 'everything betrays the primitive Etruscan style, before it had been modified and improved by the influence of Hellenic art' (i. 357). DHL did not describe this tomb in detail, and so missed an opportunity to celebrate authentic Etruscan art at the expense of Greek, but the reason probably lies in the considerable degree of damage that the paintings had suffered.

54:23 **her hair...of the east,** A conical headdress, a sort of embroidered bonnet called *tutulus* which men and women wore after the Oriental fashion.

55:13 **the *Tomba delle Iscrizioni*,** 540–520 BC, discovered in 1826–7; the tomb is so named for the Etruscan inscriptions on its walls. See Dennis, i. 364–8.

56:28 **Yet in...of them.** DHL refers here to the 5th–4th centuries BC.

57:29 **The cosmos [57:2]...rushing apart.** DHL echoes the theories of Heraclitus of Ephesus (550–480 *c*. BC). From 1915, DHL read J. Burnet's *Early Greek Philosophy* (2nd edn, 1908) several times, and Burnet explains Heraclitus' theory of the origin of the world through the words of Diogenes:
> He called change the upward and the downward path, and held that the world comes into being in virtue of this. When fire is condensed it becomes moist, and when compressed it turns to water; water being congealed turns to earth, and this he calls the downward path. And, again, the earth is in turn liquefied, and from it water arises, and from that everything else; for he refers almost everything to the evaporation from the sea. This is the path upwards. (p. 164; see also pp. 164–9)

57:33 **Babylonia,** Historic region in s. Mesopotamia, centre of one of the major ancient civilisations in the 7th and 6th centuries BC. In the 7th century BC it was conquered by the Assyrians who ruled until the death of King Ashurbanipal (669–626 BC); Belshazzar was the last king, killed in the sack of Babylon by Cyrus in 538 BC (see 58:6).

58:7 or Tarquin; or, in The typist typed 'or Tarquin;' above 'Ashiburnipal or, in' (p. 22), and DHL marked for insertion differently in TSa and TSc (see Textual apparatus).

58:11 It was even…a personal god. This idea is central to his play *David* where DHL suggests that, before David, religion was an unknown living cosmos and the Lord an indefinable entity called by various, impersonal names (Almighty, Flame, Thunderer, Wind, etc.); after David religion became more rational and the Lord was identified with and represented according to an anthropomorphic vision of the cosmos.

58:22 Nineveh, Ancient capital of Assyria on the Tigris; it flourished in the 7th century BC but after the sack of 612 BC never recovered its former glory.

59:11 Any more is fatal [59:4]…dangerous thing. In this passage DHL is interpreting Etruscan social history in terms of his idea of 'natural aristocracy', expressed in his 'leadership novels' and in most of the essays written from 1920 to 1925, where he suggests that the masses should accept that a few chosen men bear the burden of power and knowledge on behalf of everybody. Cf. A. Pope, *An Essay on Criticism* (1711), l. 215 ('A little learning is a dang'rous thing').

59:23 There is none of the priest-work of Egypt. DHL apparently considers Egyptian funeral art to be the expression solely of an aristocratic culture dominated by its priesthood.

60:31 the same goose…the night. The geese of the Capitol were sacred to the temple of Jupiter, because they are said to have saved the city from the nocturnal assault of the Gauls, by awakening the Roman defenders with their cackling (390 BC).

62:14 the haruspex, Priests who divined the future by scrutinising the entrails of the sacrificial victims; the name derived from the Chaldean word 'har', liver.

62:19 stream of consciousness The typist, probably DHL, typed 'conscious stream' (p. 27) and then crossed out the first word using 'x's on the typewriter, and DHL added the last two words by hand.

63:4 It is amazing…the Republic. 'Augury and the augural priesthood received so much honour that thereafter nothing was ever done in war or peace unless the auspices had first been taken' (Livy, *History of Rome*, i. 36. 6). DHL might also have had in mind the famous story about the decision, taken by augury, that Romulus and not Remus should be sole ruler of Rome (*ibid.*, i. 7).

63:36 So even Jesus is the lamb. John i. 29. The lamb is one of the 'gentle' creatures (63:31) associated with fertility; thus even Jesus, the lamb of God, is a symbol of reproduction, the 'endless gendering' of which DHL proceeds to write.

63:37 endless endless…cattle, DHL added a comma after the first 'endless' ('endless, endless') in TSa and after 'cattle' in TSc: they come at the end of successive lines (p. 29). It seems likely that he meant to add only one comma; therefore the base-text reading (TSc) is accepted.

64:6 the wolf…first Romans; According to legend, the she-wolf suckled Romulus and his brother Remus who had been abandoned on the bank of the

Tiber to escape pursuit of Amulio, the usurper of the throne of Alba Longa belonging to Romulus' grandfather. Romulus is the mythical founder of Rome (753 BC) and its first king. The she-wolf has been the sacred animal of Rome since earliest times.

64:18 **Sargent,** John Singer Sargent (1856–1925), American portrait painter whose work DHL had always considered 'cold' (see *The Letters of D. H. Lawrence*, ed. Boulton, i. 113).

116:10 **his beard...oriental style,** In Etruscan paintings men are often represented with a pointed beard, curving at the end, reminiscent of Oriental hair-styles and shoes (see note on 54:23).

117:15 **c'è—"** 'There is' (Italian).

117:40 **ecco! pane!...si capisce!...*vino*!** 'Here it is!—bread!...that's the word!'...'wine!' (Italian).

119:11 **he has been sinned against...to drink.** 'I am a man/ More sinn'd against than sinning' (*Lear* III. ii. 59–60)...Cf. Matthew xxvii. 48.

119:19 ***mehr Schrei wie Wert...nicht viel Wert***; 'All show and little substance' (literally 'more shout than value')...'not worth much' (German).

119:32 **anything—** MS punctuation (p. 36) is the result of an incomplete deletion: '*anything*, ⟨" in good American⟩—'.

120:24 **the Tomb of the Bulls...*di pornografico*!** The *Tomba dei Tori*, 540 BC, discovered in 1892, is the most ancient painted tomb of Tarquinia and the only one with a mythological subject; taken from Greek mythology, it depicts the trap set by Achilles for Troilus, during the Trojan war. On the back wall there is an inscription indicating the name of the noble family to whom the tomb belonged...'a touch of pornography!' (Italian). DHL refers to two scenes, in the register above the Achilles and Troilus fresco, depicting the erotic activity of a threesome (two men and one woman) and of two men. The scene relates to an Etruscan version of the Achilles/Troilus myth in which Achilles rapes Troilus before killing him.

120:40 **Cyprus,** Conquered by the king of Egypt (6th century BC), later annexed to Persia (525 BC), then to Egypt (295–258 BC), and finally to the Roman empire.

121:11 **the long, pointed boots of the east:** Etruscan leather shoes, *calcei repandi*, were high at the back and turned up at the front (see 265:19).

122:1 **On the [121:35]...proper Chimaera.** The Chimaera of Arezzo is a bronze representing the mythical monster which was killed by Bellerophon with the aid of the winged horse Pegasus (see 122:12–17). It dates back to the end of the 5th century BC and was found in 1553. Two of its legs had been broken and were restored by Benvenuto Cellini (1500–71); it is now in the Archaeological Museum of Florence.

For a discussion of TSa p. 31 see Introduction, p. xlvi.

123:35 **the Francesco Giustiniani,** 470–450 BC, discovered in 1833, and also called the Tomb of the Two Chariots. The correct name is 'Francesca Giustiniani'; DHL's misspelling in MS was reproduced in subsequent texts and has not been emended because this (wrong) form of the name also appears in some Italian guide-books. It, as Dennis explains, derives from a young lady who was present at the opening of the tomb (i. 371–2). The paintings represent a man and a woman dancing to the sound of the double-flute, on the back wall, with a woman and a man in a chariot at their side, and a second man 'on foot, with the crook in his hand,' who, 'has nothing but a blue *chlamys* or shawl over his shoulders' (Dennis, i. 371–2); game and dance scenes on the left and right walls are only partially visible.

124:7   **the late Tomb of Typhon**   The *Tomba del Tifone*, *c.* 150 BC, discovered in 1832; its paintings are the latest Etruscan paintings known and the Roman pictorial style is already evident. The pillar has a long Latin inscription of about thirty-five words (see Dennis, i. 327–36; see also 128:9–36).

124:28   **but in** [124:12] **...the horn of fertility;**   The revisions typed onto p. 34 are present in the deletion of the original typing of this passage on p. 35 (originally, p. 34) in TSa (except for the changes of colon to semi-colons in ll. 17, 25–7). Variants in TSc are 124:13 'emotionally, or vitally,'; 124:19 'travel, and with the passionate movement and menace of the blood'; 124:21 'In those days' instead of 'Then also,'; 124:28 'the horns of fertility'. TSb follows TSa except 124:19 and 21 where it matches TSc, and 124:28 where it reads 'its horn of fertility'.

   At 124:17 DHL altered TSa only from 'nag:' to 'nag;', and it was then retyped with the semicolon, which has been accepted.

125:14   **admiration in the Latin sense**   'Admiratio' means both 'wonder' and 'admiration'.

125:39   **The Tomb of the Augurs**   The *Tomba degli Auguri*, 530–520 BC, discovered in 1878. In the painting, the man holding the leash (126:20) is masked, with a pointed cap (*tutulus*) and a very long beard; called *phersu* in an inscription, corresponding to the Latin *persona*, mask.

126:38   **the Tomb of the Chariots;**   The *Tomba delle Bighe*, *c.* 490 BC, discovered in 1827. Its paintings, now in Palazzo Vitelleschi, represent a banquet scene with men who recline in pairs on three couches, a dance scene including figures of both sexes distinguished by their colour (the men are reddish-brown, the women white according to the Etruscan convention) and a number of chariots preparing for the race and sport scenes: see Dennis, i. 373–6.

127:15   **the Sarcophagus of the painted Amazons,**   340–330 BC, discovered in 1869; it has battle scenes between Greeks and Amazons painted on the sides.

127:22   **Actaeon and his dogs.**   Famous huntsman who, in one version of the myth, boasted that he was a better hunter than Artemis, or, in another, saw her bathing: for his offence he was changed into a stag by the goddess, torn to pieces and devoured by his own dogs.

127:23   **the Tomb of the Baron,**   The *Tomba del Barone*, 510–500 BC, discovered in 1827. On the back wall a bearded man embraces a boy who plays the double-flute, while with his left hand the man holds up a cup to a richly dressed noble lady with raised arms, perhaps his wife; two men on horseback frame the group. On the left-hand wall there is a second family scene with the same characters: the woman talks to the two young men, now dismounted. The tomb seems to have been built and painted for the woman, who probably died before the other members of the family (see Dennis, i. 368–70).

127:28 **Rosa Bonheur or Rubens or even Velasquez,** Marie Rosalie ('Rosa') Bonheur (1822–99), French artist who often painted horses: e.g. *Chevaux à l'abreuvoir* (Horses at the Drinking-Trough), 1843, and *Le marché aux chevaux* (The Horse Market), 1853. Peter Paul Rubens (1577–1640) and Diego Rodríguez de Silva y Velázquez (1599–1660), respectively Flemish and Spanish painters, were both masters in the genre of equestrian portraits.

128:4 **What is** [127:30]**...external form.** The idea of camera vision as opposed to real and human 'seeing' is discussed in 'Art and Morality', in *Study of Thomas Hardy and Other Essays*, ed. Bruce Steele (Cambridge, 1985), pp. 164–6.

128:10 **a big tomb,** The *Tomba del Tifone*: see note on 124:7.

128:19 **rather Pompeian** The styles of Roman wall painting prevalent especially at Pompeii (destroyed in 79). A particular tone of red is the dominant colour, known as Pompeian red. See also 129:9 and apparatus to 128:17; see Dennis: 'these frescoes are so like those of Pompeii, that they might be pronounced Greek' (i. 334).

128:22 **Dennis who...archaic dancers.** Dennis made several tours of Etruria in 1842–7 (the 1st edn of his study appeared in 1848); since many new discoveries were made afterwards, he returned to Etruria (2nd revised edn, 1878). Describing the Typhon Dennis says: 'The attitude of the body – the outspread wings – the dark massy coils of the serpent-limbs – the wild twisting of the serpent-locks – the countenance uplifted with an expression of unutterable woe, as he supports the cornice with his hands – make this figure imposing, mysterious, sublime. In conception, the artist was the Michael Angelo of Etruria' (i. 330).

128:33 **Veii,** Now Veio, the southernmost Etruscan city and closest to Rome, had been conquered and destroyed (396 BC) after a ten-year war. Archaic terracottas were found in Veio in 1916, including an Apollo, a statue of painted terracotta (510–500 BC), generally considered the finest extant example of early Etruscan sculpture, now in the Villa Giulia Museum.

129:1 **the Tomb of Orcus, or Hell,** The *Tomba dell'Orco*, or *dell'Inferno*, 400–375 BC, discovered in 1868. See 130:11–16 and 131:3–11. Its wall paintings show banquet scenes taking place in the underworld in the presence of monstrous demons, according to the pessimistic religious conception of this period. In the corner of the right wall is the beautiful profile of a woman lying on the banquet couch by her husband (see 131:4–5); her name, Velcha in Etruscan and Velia in Latin, is indicated by an inscription, and next to her stands Charon (Charun in Etruscan), the messenger and herald of death. On the walls of the second chamber, the underworld is represented with Hades and Persephone seated on their thrones; Homeric heroes are painted on the left wall, and Theseus is on the right wall. The third chamber contains a large painting on the back wall representing the killing of Polyphemus.

129:10 **free** A strange revision from the MS reading 'stiff' (p. 51), since DHL often emphasises the freedom of the paintings in the old tombs; however, p. 42 of all three typescripts was retyped because of the many revisions and it is therefore impossible to establish if the word 'free' was his change or is a typist's mistake. The phrase 'at the same time' might suggest that DHL wished to draw a distinction between the genuine Etruscan freedom (129:8) and the merely technical freedom of drawing found in this late work.

129:22 **Aztec and Maya** The Aztec population lived in s. Mexico, the Maya in central America (Yucatan and Guatemala). Their religion was polytheistic and also required human sacrifice. In Babylonia, Egypt and Assyria (see notes on 57:33 and 58:22) the king had absolute power, being the political, religious and military leader.

129:34 **Giotto and the early sculptors** Giotto di Bondone (?1267–1337), Florentine painter and architect (see also 265:36). Among the early sculptors DHL probably had in mind was Nicola Pisano (?1210/15–1278/84) because in Ducati's book (ii. 123) the spirit of Etruscan art is said to have flourished again in Tuscany in the 15th century thanks to the paintings of Giotto and the sculptures of Nicola Pisano.

129:38 **the Tomb of the Shields** The *Tomba degli Scudi*, 350–340 BC, discovered in 1870; its paintings exemplify the decadence of Etruscan art. Dennis describes the couple in an utterly different way: 'the man reclines with his right hand on his companion's shoulder, holding a *phiala* in the other. He regards her fondly, but she casts her large black eyes into space, and clasps her hands before her, as if in deep thought' (i. 337). There are a great number of inscriptions; fourteen shields are painted in the second room.

131:2 **Theopompus collected [130:38]…is enough.** Theopompus of Chios (4th century BC), Greek historian, wrote *Hellenic Histories*, covering the period 410–394 BC, a continuation of *The History of the Peloponnesian War* by Thucydides (460–396 BC), a work in eight books covering the period up to 411 BC. Theopompus also wrote *Philippic Histories*; in book 43 of that work he states that an Etruscan law allows men to share women, who, moreover, often strip themselves naked in the presence of men, do not share their banquet couch with their husbands but with any man taking part in the banquet, drink a great deal and readily make love with anyone who asks them (see Ducati, i. 172). Dennis, describing the Tomb of the Feast, comments: 'It is worthy of remark that all the women in this tomb, even the slave who is waiting on the banqueters, are decently robed. So it is in the other tombs; and this tends to belie the charge brought against the Etruscans by the Greeks, that the men were waited on by naked handmaids' (i. 321).

132:6 **"fattorie."** 'Farms' (Italian).

132:40 **playing *morra*,** Also 'mora' (in Italian and English), an ancient and popular game in which two players both quickly hold out the fingers of one hand and, trying to guess the total number of fingers shown by both players, shout out simultaneously a figure between two and ten. DHL refers to it in 'Il Duro', in *Twilight in Italy* (1916).

133:23 **Norman adventurers, or Barbary pirates** The Normans, sailors and pirates of Scandinavian origin, founded kingdoms in several parts of Europe and in

Italy in the 9th century. The Barbary pirates, from n.w. Africa, derived their name from that of its Berber inhabitants. North African piracy had very ancient origins but it reached its climax during the 17th century.

133:27 **a town like Bologna...chimney-stacks** Bologna, chief city in the region of Emilia-Romagna in the n. of Italy; in mediaeval times noble families competed with each other by erecting tall towers to satisfy their pride...Pittsburgh, Pennsylvania, is famous for its many tall chimneys, the city being once the site of one of the world's largest steel industries.

137:2 **Vulci** Velx in Etruscan, Volci in Latin. Its ruins and necropolises are situated in an uninhabited area between the two villages of Montalto di Castro and Canino, in the Maremma. The remains of the city do not pre-date the 4th century BC whereas the necropolises – first excavated in 1828 – range from the beginning of the 8th century BC to the 1st century AD. They are to be found in two extensive areas, on the banks of the river Fiora. Only a few of the tombs are tumuli; the oldest tombs (9th century BC) are mostly wells within which smaller holes were dug where the remains of the dead were buried; later tombs (8th–5th centuries BC) are larger, but generally have only one small chamber, and often stone-sculptures were put at the entrance of the corridor leading to the tomb or by the sides of the door of the chamber. Dennis says that at least fifteen thousand tombs had been excavated when he visited Vulci (about 1845). DHL seems to have been misled by the spelling 'Volci' found in Fell's *Etruria and Rome* as occasionally he refers to this form as the modern name (see Note on the text).

137:14 **wiped out...the Saracens.** A topographic index with essential information about the history, geography and art of the Etruscan cities is included in Ducati's work; under 'Vulci': 'Fallen into decline during the Roman empire, the city was destroyed by the Saracens and never rose again' (ii. 136).

137:17 **Vetulonia, Populonia.** Cities of n. Etruria situated on the Tyrrhenian coast opposite the island of Elba. Vetulonia, which is a little way inland, has tombs in the shape of round wells (8th century BC) and tumuli and wells dating from the 7th century BC. Populonia, the only great Etruscan city situated on the coast itself, became an important trade centre and a centre for an iron industry. Its necropolises include well and chamber tombs belonging to the 8th century BC and tumuli dating from the 7th–6th centuries BC.

137:23 **and Saturday.** 9 April 1927.

137:33 **the Ponte della Badia:** On the Fiora, not far from the castle (144:1–2 and note on 143:17), to the n.; first built by the Etruscans (4th–3rd centuries BC) and then reinforced by the Romans (1st century BC), it has three arches: two small ones on the sides and a 20 m. wide arch in the centre. The bridge was strengthened and restored in 1931.

138:11 **no barroccino, no carretto?** Light carts generally used for the transport of goods; the 'barroccino' can have two or four wheels; the 'carretto' usually has only two wheels.

139:14 **finocchio** 'Fennel' (Italian).

139:34 **Via Aurelia.** The Roman road, probably constructed between the 3rd and the 2nd century BC, built by a member of the Aurelia family, connects Rome to

Ventimiglia, on the present-day French frontier, following the Tyrrhenian coastline and passing through Latium, Tuscany and Liguria.

139:38 **sparse,** This word – though printed correctly in PP (p. 145) – had been questioned in setting-copy (TSa p. 5) and was altered for E1 to 'spare'. This also happened to 'gryphons' at 165:18 (TSa p. 16).

141:18 **the Grand-duke Leopold of Tuscany** Leopold II (1797–1870) became Grand-Duke of Tuscany in 1824; he abdicated in 1859, shortly before Tuscany joined the new kingdom of Italy. The reclamation decree was signed on 27 November 1828.

141:34 **Luigi,** Originally 'Bruno' here and at 142:1 and 142:8 in MS (pp. 11–12); however, from 142:33 on DHL wrote 'Luigi' only.

141:37 **men who have always lived** MS (p. 12) originally read 'men who live' and in deleting 'live' and adding 'have always', DHL forgot to replace the verb; the typist (p. 9) added 'lived' which is accepted.

At 168:9–10 DHL wrote in MS (p. 27): 'century ⟨after Christ⟩ ⌐A.D.⌐ ⟨seem curiously⟩ ⌐much more nearly⌐ kin'. He failed to replace the verb which the typist realised and typed 'seem' interlinearly (TSa p. 21).

143:17 **the ruin…a castle** Also called the Monastery (137:34) or the Badia (144:12), it now contains a small museum. It was destroyed by the Saracens and rebuilt by Cistercian Monks between the 12th and the 13th centuries.

144:14 **Lucien Bonaparte,** Lucien Bonaparte (1775–1840) supported his brother Napoleon and became his Minister of Internal Affairs in 1799; he then moved to Madrid as ambassador (1800–2) and then to Italy where as Prince of Canino he owned a large tract of land near Vulci. During the four months that followed the accidental discovery of an Etruscan tomb in 1828 (see 144:18), Lucien Bonaparte dug up more than two thousand authentic Etruscan pieces (144:39) and became an ardent collector. His collection of Greek vases was later dispersed to form the bulk of the collections in Munich, London and Paris.

145:3 **In 1828** [144:18]**...much ravished.** DHL paraphrases Dennis's account of the discovery and of the excavations carried out by Lucien Bonaparte (cf. Dennis, i. 447–50). Keats's 'Ode on a Grecian Urn' had recently been published (1820): hence the reference to 'the hey-day of the "Grecian urn"' (144:21). The first line of the poem is recalled at 145:3 in a bitterly ironical sense (see also 39:5 and 163:28).

The word 'cyclix' at 144:36 means 'a shallow cup with a tall stem' (*OED*).

145:20 *dispensa* 'Pantry' (Italian).

147:5 **maremmano** Native of the Maremma.

147:36 **Coccumella and Coccumelletta** More commonly known as Cuccumella and Cuccumelletta, they are among the few tombs constructed in the tumuli form at Vulci. The Cuccumella was opened by the Prince of Canino in 1828 (see 150:11–151:10; see also note on 151:2); it is extraordinarily big (about 18 m. high and 65 m. wide) and unusual. In the centre, at the end of a long corridor, is an open area, excavated into the rock; at the sides are two small openings with false roofs, and at the end are two chambers with benches. A steep staircase connects the last chamber and the centre of the tumulus where complicated underground tunnels are excavated, which are probably the labyrinth-like passages mentioned below (p. 150). The Cuccumelletta is also an example of the monumental sepulchral architecture that appears in the 7th century BC, showing an Oriental influence. Dennis explains the etymology of the names:

> Cucumella – probably *a cacumine* – is a term commonly applied in Central Italy to a mound, hillock, or barrow. This Vulcian *tumulus* is called the Cucumella, *par excellence*, as there is no other on this site to rival it...Southward from this is a much smaller mound, called 'La Cucumelletta,' because it is a miniature of the other. It was opened by the Prince in 1832, and was found to contain five chambers. (i. 452 n. 2, 455)

147:36 **the river tombs.** The big necropolises of Cavalupo (9th–8th centuries BC) and Ponte Rotto (4th century BC) are on the left bank of the Fiora.

150:3 **the famous François Tomb** An elaborately constructed tomb, 450–440 BC, with eight chambers, only two of which were painted. The paintings – in the Torlonia museum, Villa Albani, in Rome – depict six couples, among which are the owners of the tomb, members of a noble family; an Etruscan in the act of killing a Roman; mythological figures and scenes from Etruscan history and Greek legends. The tomb was discovered by the Florentine archaeologist Alessandro François (1796–1857), already known for his discovery of 'the all-famous but rather boring François vase' (apparatus for 150:4), a painted Attic mixing bowl found in 1844 near Chiusi, now in the Archaeological Museum of Florence.

151:2 **But Dennis [150:36]...no doubt collapsed.**

> In the heart of the mound were unearthed two towers, one square, the other conical...of horizontal, uncemented masonry, but extremely rude and irregular...it seems probable that they served no more practical purpose than to support the figures with which the monument was crowned.
>
> At the foot of these towers...were found two small chambers...They were approached by a long passage, leading directly into the heart of the tumulus; and here on the ground lay fragments of bronze and gold plates...Two stone sphinxes stood guardians at the entrance of the passage, and sundry other quaint effigies of lions and griffons were also found within this tumulus. (Dennis, i. 452–3)

151:3 **burrowing** All texts have 'being burrowing' (see Textual apparatus) which arose from DHL first writing 'being' and then adding the more vivid 'burrowing', without cancelling his original choice.

151:28 **"*Tu pure, no?*"** DHL's account suggests that Luigi is not fat. The woman's retort means: 'You too, eh?', but may be ironical. In Italian, the use of 'no' after 'pure' can only be a tag-question, and not syntactic; DHL appears to have misconstrued the words he heard, so his punctuation has been emended (see Textual apparatus). The Italian for '*You* haven't though!' (l. 27) would be 'Tu, invece, no!', i.e. 'You, on the other hand, have not!'

151:38 **Once this...itself crumbling.**

the water flowing from the table-land of the necropolis, charged with tartaric matter, in its passage through the aqueduct had oozed out of its channel, and by the precipitation of the earthy matter it held in solution, had formed this petrified drapery to the bridge. The stalactites stand out six or seven feet from the wall, and depend to a depth of fifteen or twenty feet...The aqueduct...I take to be Roman...The enormous masses of stalactite which drape the bridge seem to indicate a high antiquity for the whole structure...(Dennis, i. 440, 443)

152:35 **Tomb of Isis,** The *Tomba di Iside*, in the necropolis of Polledrara, on the e. bank of the Fiora, from the first decades of the 6th century BC, discovered in 1839; many objects were found in the tomb, including an alabaster statuette (88 cm. high) of a richly dressed woman, with her forearms raised and a strange long-horned animal clutched in her left hand; this is believed to be a very important example of primitive Greek sculpture (580–570 BC). DHL misrepresents Dennis (152:35–6) who only said that the contents of the tomb had an 'Egyptian or oriental character'; in fact, he says that the tomb was for 'two Etruscan ladies' and describes the two effigies of 'this fair Etruscan' and 'this Etruscan Lesbia' (i. 457, 459, 460).

153:6 **site...was** The plural verb (see Textual apparatus) was the result of an incomplete revision: MS's original 'tombs' was changed to 'site' without altering the verb (p. 33).

157:2 **Volterra** Velathri in Etruscan, Volaterrae in Latin; it flourished between the 4th and the 1st centuries BC. In 298 BC the town yielded without resistance to the Romans and maintained a major role amongst the centres of n. Etruria up to the 1st century BC. Various necropolises surround the hill of Volterra, with well-tombs and chamber-tombs dating from the 7th century BC. However, the majority of tombs and objects originate from three or four centuries later. Excavations started in 1728. Volterra is perched upon cliffs called Le Balze (161:22) which slope down to the valley; they were caused by a huge landslide which also engulfed a large part of the Etruscan necropolis of the archaic period (see note on 161:5).

157:8 **the Cecina...mountains of Carrara,** A Tuscan river in the hills between Livorno (Leghorn) and Siena...The Tuscan area of Carrara is famous for its marble industry.

157:17 *Saline di Volterra*...**salt-works** About 6 km. s.w. of the town, and still in use.

158:8 *podestà* Power, authority, magistrate (Italian, from the Latin 'potestas'). During the Fascist régime the *podestà*, a town governor, was appointed by the national government and carried out the same functions as a Mayor.

158:30 **she has...Florentine yoke.** In the 14th century, Volterra became involved in the struggle for supremacy in Tuscany, along with Florence, Pisa, Siena, Lucca and San Gimignano; in 1361, finally defeated by Florence, it became part of the Florentine Republic; in 1472, a war between the two cities ended with the sack of Volterra which regained its independence only partly in 1513; it was not until 1530 that attempts to regain independence finally came to an end.

158:40 *Lenin*...**long enough dead,** Lenin had died three years before, in 1924.

159:3 **Some are...upon them.** Cf. *Twelfth Night* II. v. 158: 'Some men are born great...'

159:16 mediaeval piazza...the Palazzo Pubblico...the cold cathedral, The Piazza dei Priori, the centre of Volterra, is completely surrounded by 13th century buildings all constructed out of the same grey stone. Among them, the Palazzo Pubblico, also called the Palazzo dei Priori (1208–54), the exterior of which is adorned with mediaeval coats of arms; seat of the town council...The roman-esque cathedral (13th century) stands behind the Palazzo dei Priori in the Piazza del Duomo.

159:22 the Porta all'Arco, The s. gateway to the town, probably of the 4th century BC; it was badly damaged by a fire and restored in the 1st century BC. The three heads on the arch are in a poor state of preservation; at 159:34–5, DHL mentions the legend as it is reported by Ducati: 'Three heads of dark peperino stone decorate the front of the gateway; they have now lost their features, but are still a reminder of the savage habit of cutting off the head of the enemy and exhibiting it as a trophy on the city gates' (ii. 91). More probably the heads were images of deities and protectors of the town (see also Dennis, ii. 140–7). (All quotations from Italian texts are by the editor.)

160:2 Strange, dark [159:32]...merely mediaeval. Although this passage was cut from TSc (and thus Per1), some of the information was used to describe the accompanying photograph in Per1 (p. 28):

THE OLD ETRUSCAN GATE AT VOLTERRA

From the *Porta all'Arco*, the famous old Etruscan gateway, three dark heads, now worn featureless, reach out curiously and inquiringly, one from the keystone of the arch and one from each arch base. According to some authorities they represent the heads of slain enemies, according to others they were Etruscan city deities of some sort. Archeologists say that only the doorposts of the outer arch and the inner wall are Etruscan work. The Romans probably restored the arch, and the wall above the arch is said to be medieval.

160:12 the city wall, Volterra was protected by city walls which were built to enclose the acropolis (5th century BC) and were later enlarged (4th century BC) to include the necropolis. The circumference was about 7 km. long; only 2.6 km. remain. Two main gates allowed access into the town: the Porta Diana, or Portone (the Great Gate) in the northern section of the walls, and the Porta all'Arco (see also 160:29–39).

161:5 suburb-hamlet of San Giusto...the church 1 km. n. of Volterra, with an 18th century church, famous for its site, Le Balze (see 161:19–25). Erosion takes place continually and over two centuries two churches and a cemetery have disappeared over Le Balze. The nearby Badia (161:26–7) had to be abandoned in 1861 because of the danger of collapse.

162:23 Lazarus risen, John xi. 11–44.

163:13 the museum, The Guarnacci Museum of Volterra, founded in 1739, contains an important Etruscan collection particularly of urns (see 163:23ff.). Made of tufa, terracotta and especially alabaster, their reliefs represent rosettes, Etruscan symbolic figures such as gryphons or sea-monsters, funerary scenes of the death-journey and episodes from Greek mythology.

163:39 Ducati, says...after-life.— DHL is not quoting from Ducati whose observations on their 'small interest from the artistic point of view' (l. 37) are expressed in two extended paragraphs, and are much more extreme:

These ash-chests, somewhat tedious in their monotonous continuity…have a twofold importance both for the sculpture figure of the dead person on the lid, with features portrayed in a true likeness, and for the scenes in relief, on the three sides of the ash-chest, with scenes of a funerary nature or of local character. However, what predominates are scenes taken from Greek legends, especially the Theban and the Trojan cycles, often with arbitrary intrusions and mistaken interpretations…Only a few ash-chest reliefs are remarkable for their careful execution and noble expression, whereas the great majority are mediocre, careless, and banal. (ii. 110)

164:8 **"the touches [164:1]…in his soul."**— Dennis, ii. 184–5 which ends with Wordsworth's *Excursion* (1814), iv. 599–600.

164:14 **Flaxman…the greekified illustrator of Pope's Homer!** Flaxman is particularly well-known for his engravings of 1793 for Pope's translations of the *Iliad* and the *Odyssey*.

164:20 **the Parthenon frieze.** The Parthenon temple dedicated to Athena was built on the acropolis of Athens in 447–432 BC. The Ionic frieze, now in the British Museum, 1 m. high and 160 m. long, represents the Panathenaic procession which took place during the national festival of Athens, the Great Panathenaea, held in honour of Athena every five years.

164:26 **In Dennis's day…"period" etc.** DHL probably refers to Dennis's account of the excavations at Vulci, when pottery of no pecuniary value was destroyed in order to protect the market-price of pottery of the 'right period' (see note on 145:3).

166:26 **will-to-power.** A concept central to the ideas of Friederich Nietzsche (1844–1900).

166:38 **Meleager and…of Erymanthus.** In Greek mythology, when Meleager was a young man, his father, the king of Calydon, neglected his sacrifice to Artemis who sent a great boar to take revenge on Calydon; Meleager attacked it with a band of heroes and destroyed it…Hercules, in one of his legendary twelve labours, had to catch the Boar of the Arcadian mountain Erymanthus alive, so he drove it into a snowfield, tired it out and caught it in a net; according to a different tradition he killed it.

167:17 **the Boers, or the Mormons,** The Boers, the original Dutch colonists who settled in South Africa; in 1836–7 they migrated towards unexplored lands ('the great trek'). The Mormons, a protestant American sect founded by Joseph Smith Jr. in 1830 at Manchester, New York, migrated towards the Far West: 143 men, 3 women and 2 children set off on 73 wagons on 7 April 1847.

167:29 **Helen and…of Iphigenia** In Greek mythology, the Dioscuri, the twins Castor and Pollux, rescued their young sister Helen when she was carried off by Theseus…Pelops was killed by his father Tantalus when he was a child and his flesh was served to the gods, but they recognised what they were eating and restored Pelops to life; Tantalus was punished in Hades…The Minotaur, half-bull and half-man, was kept in the Labyrinth by Minos, king of Crete, and fed with youths and maidens sent by Athens until Theseus destroyed it…Jason sailed with the Argonauts in the ship Argo to Colchis to recover the golden fleece of the winged ram...Medea fled from Corinth after killing the king of the town and his daughter, who was about to marry her former husband, Jason; in vengeance against Jason's desertion she killed her own children, partly in order to make Jason childless...Oedipus, son of Laius, king of Thebes, and of Jocasta, solved the riddle of the Sphinx and was rewarded with the crown of Thebes and Jocasta's hand...Ulysses escaped the spell of the Sirens' song by filling the ears of his men with wax, and by having himself tied to the mast of his ship...Eteocles and Polynices, sons of Oedipus and Jocasta, agreed to share rule by alternating every year; Eteocles refused to leave the throne after his first year was over, and Polynices attacked Thebes; the two brothers killed each other...The Centaurs, half-horse and half-men, were invited to the wedding of Hippodamia and Pirithous, king of the Lapithae; they tried to carry off the bride and other women but were defeated...Iphigenia was chosen as a sacrifice to Artemis in order to ensure the Greek fleet a safe voyage to Troy, but Artemis saved her carrying her away to Taurus (Modern Crimea), and substituting a deer for her at the altar.

Dennis remarks that the Etruscan urns form 'a series of the most celebrated deeds of the mythical cycle, from Cadmus to Ulysses' (ii. 164) and describes a number of them in detail (see ii. 164–70).

168:29 **the wild and untameable Ligurian** A very ancient people of uncertain origin, who settled between the Po river, the Maritime Alps and the Tyrrhenian sea, the boundaries of modern Liguria.

170:24 **the Inghirami Tomb,** One of the most famous later Etruscan tombs, it belongs to the ancient Inghirami family of Volterra, who owned the land where the tomb was discovered, and who include among their ancestors the Etruscologist Francesco Inghirami (1772–1846), author of a ten volume work on Etruscan monuments.

171:17 **Chiusi,** In n. Etruria, not far from Lake Trasimene, Chiusi, Clusium in Latin, flourished during the 6th–4th centuries BC; during the following two centuries, the city was absorbed into Roman territory, maintaining autonomous laws and culture up to the 1st century BC.

171:27 **the huge...state prison.** A Medici fortress built in 1472 in the e. part of the town, at its highest point, one of the most impressive examples of Renaissance military architecture.

175:4 **the Archaeological Museum in Florence,** The original nucleus was the Egyptian collection; in 1872 the museum was enlarged by the addition of the Etruscan Museum which formed part of the Medici and Lorraine collections in the Uffizi Gallery, and which included such famous works as the Chimaera, the Orator (Arringatore), the Minerva and the François vase.

175:9 **the Augustan age** Term generally used to describe the flourishing state of Latin literature under the Emperor Augustus (27 BC–AD 14), with particular reference to the works of Virgil, Horace and Ovid (see also note on 9:10).

175:10 **a Sabine, a Samnite, an Umbrian,** The Sabines, an ancient people living in central Italy; after the legendary rape of their women, they were conquered and merged into the Roman people, obtaining Roman citizenship after the battle of

Sentinum (295 BC). The Samnites, ancient inhabitants of part of the Abruzzi and of e. Campania, tried to expand southwards but were defeated by the Romans after the three Samnite Wars (343–341 BC, 327–304 BC, 298–290 BC). The Umbrians occupied the territory n. of the Tiber as far as Etruria and Emilia; they were defeated by the Romans at the battle of Sentinum.

175:22 **Julius Caesar and 55 B.C.** The Roman invasion of Britain.

175:30 **Tusci or Tyrrheni** The Etruscans were also called Tusci after the name Tuscia given to Etruria around 377 BC and later extended to Umbria, and Tyrrheni after their mythical leader.

176:1 **in the days before Homer.** The Greek poet lived sometime before the 7th century BC (probably between the 10th and the 9th centuries BC). Cf. 175:7–176:8 with 259:29–260:32.

177:22 *en masse.* DHL discusses Whitman's use of this phrase in the opening lines of *Leaves of Grass* in 'Democracy' (*Reflections on the Death of a Porcupine and Other Essays*, ed. Michael Herbert, Cambridge, 1988, p. 74).

178:4 **Dahomey** West African state on the Gulf of Guinea.

178:31 **the salt…savour,** Matthew v. 13.

Italian Essays, 1919–27

David

185:1 **David** The statue of the biblical king by Michelangelo (1475–1564), sculpted, 1501–4, as a symbol of the liberty of the Florentine Republic, and placed in front of the Palazzo Vecchio (see note on 203:7) in the Piazza della Signoria (185:15; see also note on 194:2) on 8 June 1504. In 1873 it was moved into the Galleria dell'Accademia in via Ricasoli in order to prevent weather damage, and a copy replaced it in the Piazza. For dating of the essay (185:1–11), see Introduction, p. lv.

185:12 **San Miniato—and cannon-shots.** The Romanesque church of San Miniato al Monte, founded in 1018 and its inner structures completed in 1063 (the basilica and bell tower were finished in 1207), stands on a hill overlooking the Piazzale Michelangelo (see note on 194:10). Until World War II, its bells rang at noon and cannon shots were fired from the Forte Belvedere, an ancient fortress just to the n.w. of the church.

185:14 **"like flowers of infernal moly."** In mythology moly was 'a fabulous herb having a white flower and a black root, endowed with magic properties, and said by Homer to have been given by Hermes to Odysseus as a charm against the sorceries of Circe' (*OED*). The quotation is unidentified.

185:16 **in my upper room** In November 1919 DHL was at the Pensione Balestra, 5 Piazza Mentana, just off the Lungarno and most probably he could see the river from his window (see Introduction, p. lv). In his letters, he often mentioned his 'nice room over the Arno' (*Letters*, iii. 423; see also pp. 419–22). The Pensione Balestra was renamed 'Nardini' in *Aaron's Rod* 206.

185:19 **The Florentines...New Year.** No evidence of this tradition remains.

185:22 **The Neptune...stone creatures,** *Neptune* (1563–75) by Bartolomeo Ammannati (1511–92), a huge, rather graceless statue commonly known as 'il Biancone' (the Big White Fellow), placed in the middle of a fountain in the Piazza della Signoria; the fountain edges are adorned with elegant bronze figures representing sea-gods and satyrs. The marble *Hercules and Cacus* (1534) by Baccio Bandinelli (1488–1560), represents the mythical hero in the act of killing the giant who, according to the legend, had robbed him of his oxen. Both of these sculptures reveal Michelangelo's influence, especially in the adoption of gigantic proportions. The Bandinelli group is on *David*'s left-hand side, at the entrance of the Palazzo Vecchio; the *Neptune* is a little further away, on the right, beyond the Palazzo Vecchio, in line with the two other statues (see also note on 204:33).

186:2 **Last night** This reference cannot be precisely dated, but DHL complains about heavy rain in a number of letters (see Introduction, p. lv).

186:8 **the river in Turin?** Turin, the main city in Piedmont, is situated on one bank only of the Po.

186:10 **She sticks a brandished statue** DHL probably refers to the equestrian monument (1838) by Carlo Marocchetti (1805–67), sculpted in honour of Emanuele Filiberto of Savoy and placed in the middle of the large Piazza San Carlo. The Duke of Savoy is represented in the act of drawing his sword.

186:12 **Florence, the Lily-town** The lily is the symbol on the coat of arms of Florence. It is said to have been bestowed on the city by Charlemagne; according to other legends, the name of Florence ('Florentia' in Latin, i.e. 'the City of Flowers') was derived from the abundance of flowers in the town and the lily, as the noblest flower, was chosen to be its symbol. The Florentine lily is an iris rather than a proper lily, divided into three leaves and called in botany *ireos florentina* (see 186:36).

186:17 **Savonarola...wet downfall.** Girolamo Savonarola (1452–98), Dominican friar who preached asceticism against the paganising spirit of the Renaissance. When the Medici were banished from Florence in 1494, he became the leader of the Florentine Republic. In 1497, after his violent attack against Pope Alexander VI, Savonarola was excommunicated; he was then tried as a heretic, and hanged and burnt at the stake. DHL refers to Savonarola's religious fervour ('hot coal') as representing the southern, passionate spirit 'quenched' by the deadly spirit of the North (see also 188:16–18). Savonarola is discussed at length by DHL in *Movements in European History*, ed. Philip Crumpton (Cambridge, 1989), pp. 153–7.

186:35 **Michelangelo's David...time. Adolescent.** A very similar description of the statue recurs in *Aaron's Rod*: 'But the David in the Piazza della Signoria...standing forward stripped and exposed and eternally half-shrinking, half-wishing to expose himself, he is the genius of Florence. The adolescent, the

white, self-conscious, physical adolescent' (211:33–7; see also 'David' 188:30–
189:7 and Introduction, p. lv). In 'Study of Thomas Hardy' the statue had been
described in different terms: 'the David, young, but with too much body for a
young figure, the physique exaggerated, the clear, outward-leaping, essential spirit
of the young man smothered over, the real maleness cloaked, so that the statue is
almost a falsity' (*Study of Thomas Hardy and Other Essays*, ed. Steele, 74:2–5).
David's age at the time of his anointing is not mentioned in the Bible, but several
references are made to his youth (1 Samuel xvii. 14, 33, 42, 58).

186:37 **Whitman's Calamus,** 'Calamus', a sequence of 45 poems by Walt
Whitman (1819–92), was first published in the third edition of *Leaves of Grass*
(1860); its theme is homosexual love. The calamus is a reed, a cane which in
Whitman's poetry becomes a symbol of comradeship. DHL refers to the 'Calamus'
section at length, in his essay on Whitman in *Studies in Classic American Literature*
(1923). In mythology, Calamus is a son of the river Meander and in this acceptation
it probably hints at adolescence; it is also connected with the myth of Pan (see note
on 187:10).

187:7 **Dionysus and Christ** [187:4]**...transport, the vine.** DHL presents
the figure of David, like the image of the lily, as the symbol of Florence, summing
up Dionysus's vitality and the mortifying aspects of Christ in the Christian
tradition. A similar interpretation of the biblical king is proposed by DHL in his
play *David* (1926). Dionysus is the Greek god of the fertility of nature; god of wine
whose worship is characterised by wild dances and music; a suffering god who dies
and comes to life again (see also notes on 187:8, 187:16 and 187:25).

187:8 **Nymphs and Hamadryads...Dithyrambus.** The Nymphs are semi-
divine creatures generally represented as young and beautiful virgins, fond of
music and dancing, who inhabit the sea, rivers, hills, woods and trees; the
Hamadryads are wood-nymphs...Silenus, a demi-god, a Satyr who was preceptor
and companion of Dionysus, is usually represented as a fat and cheerful old man,
riding on an ass with a crown of flowers and always intoxicated...Pan is the Greek
god of woods and mountains, represented as half-man and half-goat; the mythical
figure is particularly dear to DHL as the symbol of nature's fertility; in the first part
of his essay 'Pan in America' (written in May 1924), DHL mentions the god as the
'father of fauns, and nymphs, satyrs and dryads and naiads' (see *Phoenix* 22; see
also 'The Overtone' and 'St. Mawr', in *St. Mawr and Other Stories*, ed. Brian
Finney, Cambridge, 1983, pp. 13–17 and p. 65)...The Fauns are Roman rural
deities (see note on 12:2), represented as men with horns and the tail and legs of a
goat, renowned for their lustful character, like the Satyrs who are Greek woodland
deities, with a similar half human, half bestial aspect...Iacchus and Bacchus are the
Roman names for the god of wine...Dithyrambus is one of Dionysus's epithets and
the name of a choric hymn in honour of him; its etymology is very uncertain: it
might refer to a Sanskrit word meaning 'impetuous', or it might mean 'twice-born'
hinting at the legend of Dionysus' birth (see also note on 187:25).

    All these deities resemble Dionysus, both in their physical aspect (Dionysus is
sometimes represented as a goat) and in their sensual and natural character, all
being mostly woodland deities.

187:10 **source of reed-music...deep grass",** A myth which is usually believed to refer to Pan who fell in love with the nymph Syrinx and chased her until, at her own request, she was turned into a reed which Pan then wrought into a flute…Crocus was a beautiful youth in love with the nymph Smilax, but he was impatient and his passion too great, so he was changed into a flower while she was turned into a yew tree (cf. Ovid, *Metamorphoses*, IV. v. 283). Hyacinth, also a beautiful youth, was loved by Apollo and killed by the jealous Zephyrus who struck him dead by blowing a quoit thrown by Apollo, as the two youths were playing; from his blood sprang a flower. The quotation is unidentified.

187:11 **Dew and fire…the Deliverer.** DHL probably refers to the essay 'The Poetry of Michelangelo' (1871) included in *The Renaissance* (1873) by Walter Pater (1839–94). Pater discusses Michelangelo's love poems written for Vittoria Colonna (1490–1547) where 'frost and fire are almost the only images – the refining fire of the goldsmith; once or twice the phoenix; ice melting at fire; fire struck from the rock which it afterwards consumes.' The opposition of fire and water, or sun and dew is also reminiscent of Heraclitus (see Burnet, *Early Greek Philosophy*, pp. 164–9; see also note on 57:29). Eleutherios is one of the names of Zeus 'as protector of political freedom' (*OED*).

187:16 **The four months…to Dionysus:** Probably refers to the Athenian festivals in honour of Dionysus: the Rustic Dionysia, held in December, consisted of a burlesque procession in the rural districts with dramatic performances; the Lēnaea, in January, was the feast of the wine-vats, with a procession; the Anthēsteria, in February, with the opening of the barrels and the tasting of wine, lasted three days; the Great or Urban Dionysia, in March, was celebrated with a procession in which the statue of Dionysus was carried on a chariot, and with dramatic performances. Another festival called Oschophoria was held in October, and consisted of a race where young men carried vine-branches with clusters and grapes.

187:25 **Semele, scarred [187:20]…this child.** DHL was influenced by Gilbert Murray's 1904 translation of *The Bacchae* by Euripides (480–406 BC) where the myth of Dionysus's birth is given: 'I am Dionysus, the son of Zeus/ …My mother was Cadmus' daughter, Semele by name,/ midwived by fire, delivered by the lightning's blast' (ll. 1, 3–4); then the Chorus continues the narration: '– Zeus it was who saved his son;/ with speed outrunning mortal eye,/ bore him to a private place/ bound the boy with clasps of gold;/ in his thigh as in a womb,/ concealed his son' (ll. 94–9). As for the marriage of fire and dew that begot Dionysus, the Chorus explains: '– O Dirce, holy river,/ child of Achelous' water,/ yours the springs that welcomed once/ divinity, the son of Zeus!/ For Zeus his father snatched his son/ from deathless flame, crying:/ *Dithyrambus, come!/ Enter my male womb./ I name you Bacchus and to Thebes/ proclaim you by that name*' (ll. 520–9).
The 16th century, the 'Cinquecento', was the great period of the Florentine Renaissance, which DHL identifies with the myth of Dionysus's birth associated with fire and dew.

188:4 **Venus of…Boticelli's women,** Sandro Botticelli (1445–1510) painted *La nascita di Venere* (*The Birth of Venus, c.* 1485) for Lorenzo dei Medici; it depicts Venus emerging from the sea in a huge scallop-shell and being blown towards the land (at the Uffizi Gallery; see note on 193:7). Venus was the Roman goddess of beauty, love and reproduction (Greek Aphrodite). In one legend she sprang from the sea-foam (see *Letters*, iii. 39 and n. 3)...Leonardo da Vinci (1452–1519) painted *San Giovanni Battista* when he was in Rome (1513–17).

In his essays 'Sandro Botticelli' (1870) and 'Leonardo da Vinci' (1869), Walter Pater describes Botticelli's *Venus* as 'a more direct inlet into the Greek temper than the works of the Greeks themselves'; and Leonardo's *Saint John* as 'one of the few naked figures Leonardo painted – whose delicate brown flesh and woman's hair no one would go out into the wilderness to seek, and whose treacherous smile would have us understand something far beyond the outward gesture or circum-stance...we are no longer surprised by Saint John's strange likeness to the *Bacchus* which hangs near it' (a painting by Cesare da Sesto also kept in the Louvre Museum).

For 'Botticelli's women' see apparatus at 129:12.

188:22   **Adam...Madonna of the Rocks:**   Adam's creation, the subject of one of the nine fresco panels by Michelangelo on the vault of the Sistine Chapel (1508–12) representing the history of creation, has God holding out his right hand, nearly touching Adam's hand with his forefinger as if to infuse life into him who is still languidly lying on a rock, his face turned towards his creator. This image of Adam is strongly reminiscent of the features of the statue of David. Walter Pater, in his essay 'The Poetry of Michelangelo', describes Adam: 'In that languid figure there is something rude and satyr-like, something akin to the rugged hillside on which it lies. His whole form is gathered in an expression of mere expectancy and reception; he has hardly strength enough to lift his finger to touch the finger of his creator; yet a touch of the finger-tips will suffice' (see apparatus at 129:12)...Leo-nardo painted *La vergine delle rocce* (1483–6) while he was in Milan at the court of Ludovico il Moro. It shows a young woman in a black cloak, her right hand delicately touching the shoulder of a baby kneeling by her; another woman in a red cloak and a baby are sitting on her left-hand side, in the foreground; in the background are brown rocks with some small openings where the light comes through. This painting is at the Louvre in Paris; the painting at the National Gallery in London is believed by critics to be a later version painted by Giovanni Ambrogio De Predis (*c.* 1455–1508), who worked with Leonardo during the realisation of the *Virgin of the Rocks*.

189:9   **One day he reaps his mates.**   Despite the editor's conviction that this word – meaningless in context – was typed in error, DHL did not correct it; neither did the typist of TCCII question it nor did Edward McDonald alter it for A1.

Looking Down on the City

193:4   **the Bargello...Santa Croce.**   The Bargello, or Palazzo del Podestà, was started in 1255 and continued 1345–67. In 1857–65 it was restored and converted into a National Museum, and houses one of the most important collections of Renaissance sculpture in Florence, including Donatello's *David* and Michel-angelo's *Drunken Bacchus*. The Medici Chapels, built as a mausoleum for the Medici by Michelangelo in 1520–4, are annexed to the church of San Lorenzo. The Pitti Palace, begun in 1458 on a project by Filippo Brunelleschi (1377–1446), was later (1558–77) enlarged and completed by Bartolomeo Ammannati (see note on 185:22); in 1549 it was purchased by Duke Cosimo I and henceforward belonged to the rulers of the city; now it houses a large picture gallery. Santa Croce, originally a small Franciscan church (1228), was later rebuilt (1295–1320) and is now the largest Franciscan church in Italy: the façade (1858–63) and the bell tower (1847) are in neo-gothic style; at the back of the cloisters is the Cappella dei Pazzi (1430) by Brunelleschi; Dante, Machiavelli, Galileo, Michelangelo and other artists are buried there.

193:7 **The Uffizi,** Begun in 1560 by Giorgio Vasari (1511–74) and completed in 1580 by Bernardo Buontalenti (1536–1608), with a Loggia in the upper part and a portico below it, it was the seat of the administrative office of the Medici duke-dom; today it houses the chief gallery of Italian paintings and the State Archives.

193:14 **Lippo Lippi** Filippo Lippi, Florentine painter (*c.* 1406–69) who painted a number of very moving and melancholy Madonnas.

193:16 **Botticelli's Venus** See note on 188:4.

193:19 **world-centre of the pearl-trade:** Florence is famous for its jewel-lery, but particularly for mother of pearl, rather than for the pearl trade.

194:2 **the Piazza della Signoria** [193:31]...**David.** The Piazza della Signo-ria, the old centre of civic life, contains the Palazzo Vecchio (see note on 203:7), the statues of *David*, *Neptune* and *Hercules* (see notes on 185:1 and 185:22), and the Loggia dei Lanzi (1376–82), a vaulted portico which houses several sculptures, including the bronze *Perseus* (1546–54) by Benvenuto Cellini (1500–71). See also *Aaron's Rod* 211:14–212:32.

194:10 **the Piazzale Michelangelo** Named after Michelangelo because in 1530 he made the top of the hill, overlooking the Piazzale, into a fortress by surrounding it with a star-shaped bastion. The Piazzale itself was realised in 1869 as part of the project for the enlargement of the city carried out by the architect Giuseppe Poggi (1811–1901); from it there is a wide view of Florence. A group of bronze reproductions of Michelangelo's statues, foremost among them the *David*, was placed there in 1875.

194:17 **four bridges...the brown-red town** The bridges over the Arno which can be seen from the Piazzale are the Ponte alla Carraia, the Ponte Santa Trinita, the Ponte Vecchio and the Ponte alle Grazie...Light brown is the colour of Florence houses, red that of their roof tiles.

194:19 **The Duomo...of Giotto** Built on the original church of Santa Reparata during the 14th century, the cathedral assumed its present name of Santa Maria del Fiore in 1421, when it was completed. Artists such as Francesco Talenti (14th century) and Filippo Brunelleschi contributed to its construction at different periods; the façade is in neogothic style (1875–87); the cathedral is built of horizontal layers of green and white marble. The Campanile, a square bell-tower, was designed by Giotto (see note on 129:34) in 1334, continued by Andrea Pisano (*c.* 1295–1349) and by Francesco Talenti, and completed in 1387.

194:22 **Turin** See Introduction, p. lvi, 186:8–12 and note.

194:26 **"The Blessed...of Heaven—"** The first two lines ['The Blessed Damozel leaned out'] of Dante Gabriel Rossetti's (1828–82) poem 'The Blessed

Damozel' (1850). DHL misquoted it also in *Aaron's Rod* 235; see also *The White Peacock*, ed. Andrew Robertson (Cambridge, 1983), p. 85.

194:31 **the flowery town** See 186:12 and note.

194:39 *Madonna of the Rocks,* See note on 188:22.

195:5 **the Tree of Knowledge.** The tree of knowledge of good and evil, in the Garden of Eden (Genesis ii. 9, 17). 'Cursed is...thy works' (ll. 9–10) is unidentified.

195:14 *Nature abhors consciousness.* It is possible that DHL was making up a saying from 'Nature abhors a vacuum' ('Natura abhorret vacuum', Plutarch, *De Placitis Philosophorum*, i. 18), or 'Nature abhors annihilation' ('Ab interitu naturam abhorrere', Cicero, *De Finibus*, V. xi. xxxi).

195:22 **David...smiling.** Michelangelo's *David* has knitted brows; Leonardo's *Mona Lisa* is famous for her smile.

195:25 **Fata...trahunt.** 'The fates lead the willing and drag the unwilling' (Seneca, *Epistolae ad Lucilium*, CVII).

196:22 **In our square** [195:32]...**different languages.** These last three paragraphs echo episodes narrated in *Aaron's Rod* (see Introduction, p. lvii and n. 9).

The 'faded' inscription on the wall (196:4) could refer to various elections: political national elections were held on 16 November 1919 and 15 May 1921; local elections took place in Florence on 7 November 1920.

Gabrino's (196:6) is probably meant to be 'Gambrinus', a café in Piazza Vittorio – now Piazza della Repubblica – frequented by artists and intellectuals. There are no records of bombs thrown into the café in those years; however, bombs were thrown during a political demonstration in via Tornabuoni, not far from the Gambrinus, in February 1920.

Europe Versus America

199:19 **coming back to Europe,** DHL returned to Europe at the end of September 1925. Before moving to Italy, he was in England until the end of October and in Germany until 12 November. He wrote this essay when he was at Spotorno, on the Ligurian Riviera (200:36); see also Introduction, pp. lvii–lviii.

200:4 **Taos...Long Island, or Coney Island.** See note on 50:31. DHL refers to Taos as one of the most ancient American places he could compare with Europe...Long Island, part of New York City central business district, and Coney Island, famous amusement park, are mentioned as symbols of American modern life.

200:20 **Vogue la galère!** 'Let's chance it, here goes, come what may!' (French).

Fireworks

203:7 **the Piazzale...The Palazzo Vecchio** See 205:10 and note on 194:10...'The Old Palace', in the Piazza della Signoria, a castle-like edifice built

1298–1314, later remodelled inside (1454 and 1495) and successively extended at the back (1548–93) by Giorgio Vasari (1511–74) and Bernardo Buontalenti (1536–1608); various artists, including Michelangelo, Vasari and Bandinelli, decorated it. Named the Palazzo dei Priori, since the 15th century it has also been called the Palazzo Vecchio or the Palazzo della Signoria. With the Piazza it formed the political centre of Florence; since 1872 it has been the seat of the Town Hall. Its battlements have an unusual pointed design which may have suggested the image of a bird (203:21).

204:3 **like the creative witches...myriad movements.** In post-Vedic mythology Shiva is the Merciful God of the Indian Trinity, together with Brahma the Creator and Vishnu the Preserver. He is usually portrayed with one or five heads and with four hands holding symbols such as a trident, a bow and a drum. Shiva is not only the principle of death and destruction, symbolised by his dance which represents the end of the world, but also of rebirth and of the everlasting renewal of nature. He is also the god of procreation adored through the symbols of the phallus (Liṅga; see note on 19:27). DHL's references to the god by the feminine pronoun here and at 288:7 have not been emended because he may have mistaken the god for a feminine divinity, given his creative function.

204:24 **the Uffizi palace...the Woolworth Tower.** See note on 193:7... The Woolworth Tower, built 1911–13, the world's tallest building (cf. *Letters*, v. 307).

204:33 **the fountain continues [204:29]...by the fountain,** The fountain (see note on 185:22) is on *David*'s right-hand side, so perhaps he seems untouched by it because he turns his head away. For Bandinelli's statue see note on 185:22.

205:3 **in the square...to talk prices.** The farmers still meet, on Fridays, at the same corner in the Piazza della Signoria to talk business and negotiate (there is no market and no goods are sold).

205:5 **the Lungarno** A street running along the river on either side, which takes different names after the various mansions of the ancient Florentine families and the bridges crossing the Arno. DHL probably refers to Lungarno Acciaiuoli (coming from the Piazza della Signoria, through Via Por Santa Maria towards the Ponte Vecchio) and to the Lungarno Generale Diaz (coming from the Piazza della Signoria through the Uffizi Palace).

205:21 **the Ponte alle Grazie** Built in 1237, the bridge is named after the Chiesa delle Grazie, on the Lungarno delle Grazie. 'Ponte alle' means the bridge leading 'to' the Chiesa (church) delle Grazie; DHL probably got confused with the name of the church (see Textual apparatus).

205:22 **aniseed waffles,** Tuscan waffles called 'brigidini'. Originally from Lamporecchio (Pisa), they are generally baked and sold in the streets during fairs, in markets, etc.

206:34 **bello! bello! bellezza!** 'Beautiful, beautiful, wonderful!' (Italian); it should be 'bello! bello! che bellezza!'

207:36 *Panem et circenses* 'Bread and circus-games' (Latin), organised by imperial Rome to content the plebs with food and entertainment (Juvenal, *Satires*, X. 81).

The Nightingale

211:19 **"My heart...my senses—"** Lines 1–2. The following quotations from Keats's poem (1819) refer to lines 71–2 (212:7–8), 5–10 (213:30–5), 21–3 (214:1–3), 24–5 (214:6–7), 31–3 (214:11–13), 51–2 (214:17–18), 56–60 (214:24–8), 61–2 (215:9–10), 63–7 (215:15–19), 55–6 (215:31–2), 75 (216:12); see also note on 213:38.

211:24 **why the Greeks...lost lover,** In Greek mythology, Aedon, wife of Zethus king of Thebes, was changed by gods into a nightingale for the bitter pain she suffered after killing her own son Itylus by mistake, during her attempt to kill the children of her sister-in-law Niobe. Philomela underwent a similar metamorphoses after she was raped by her brother-in-law Tereus, king of Thrace, and left in the woods with her tongue cut out. Her sister Procne released her and revenged her by killing her own son Itys and serving up his flesh to Tereus. He tried to kill the two sisters but was changed into a hoopoe, Procne into a swallow and Philomela into a nightingale (see Ovid, *Metamorphoses*, VI. 424–674).

211:25 **Jug-jug-jug! say the mediaeval writers,** John Skelton (*c.* 1460–1529), 'To Maystres Isabell Pennell', *The Garlande of Laurell* (1523), ll. 25–8: 'To here this nightingale/ Among the byrdes smale,/ Warbelynge in the vale:/ Dug, dug, jug, jug' (*Poems*, ed. R. S. Kinsman, Oxford, 1969, p. 131).

211:29 **"And the bright...for Itylus—"** From *Atalanta in Calydon* (1865) by Algernon Charles Swinburne (1837–1909), ll. 69–70 ['the brown bright nightingale amorous...'].

212:22 *Lo! It is I!* In 1908 DHL read the *Nature Book*, a fortnightly magazine later collected in six volumes, where it is said that the sound of the Common Bunting can be rendered by the words 'See-see-see-I-I—I'm he-r-r-re' (Maurice C. H. Bird, 'How to Know the Birds: The Finches', i. 146). That early reading may have surfaced years later and, although not associated with the nightingale, DHL may have retained the idea of a bird song being interpreted by words and applied it to the nightingale. It is also possible that DHL misremembered with which bird that sound had been originally associated since he had probably read about the nightingale in another article by Bird in the same magazine (i. 80–2).

212:32 **in Ceylon,** DHL was in Kandy (Ceylon) in the spring of 1922. He does not mention peacocks in his letters from Kandy but he refers to the 'scraping and squeaking tropical creatures' and to 'the horrid noises of the birds and creatures' (*The Letters of D. H. Lawrence*, ed. Warren Roberts, James T. Boulton and Elizabeth Mansfield, Cambridge, 1987, iv. 218, 225).

213:15 **Fine feathers make fine birds!** Aesop (?620–560 BC), *Fables*, 'The Jay and the Peacock': 'It's not only fine feathers that make fine birds.'

213:38 **the blushful Hippocrene** 'Ode to a Nightingale', ll. 15–16: 'O for a beaker...the blushful Hippocrene'. Hippocrene, which literally means 'fountain of the horse', is 'the name of a fountain on Mount Helicon, sacred to the Muses; hence used allusively in reference to poetic or literary inspiration' (*OED*).

215:3 **hammer and tongues...Caruso** A play on 'hammer and tongs'...Enrico Caruso (1873–1921), Neapolitan tenor.

215:22 Diocletian...Ruth, Diocletian (245–313), Roman emperor (284–305)...Ruth, biblical character who was driven by famine from her native land and had to work in the field of her kinsman Boaz (Ruth ii. 2–23).

215:26 like the nice damsel...*in mano*." 'Your daughter has been so fond of the nightingale that she has caught it and holds it in her hand' (*Decameron*, fifth day, fourth story). The original reads: '...dell'usignolo, che ella è stata tanto alla posta che ella...' (the missing words mean 'and has so long lain in wait for it').

At 215:24–5 MS read: 'She too heard the nightingale in Tuscany:' (p. 7) which DHL deleted and revised to 'who went...her hand.' But he did not delete the colon after 'Tuscany', though he probably intended to keep it rather than the full stop after 'hand', which he might have written accidentally.

215:34 Keats's Fanny, Fanny Brawne for whom Keats wrote his 'Ode to Fanny' (1820).

Man is a Hunter

219:6 the tiny church DHL probably refers to the church of Scandicci, the small village near Florence where he lived at the time.

219:14 Nimrod, Oh Bahram...his sleep." Nimrod is described as a 'mighty hunter before the Lord' (Genesis x. 8–9). Bahram is the name of five Sassanid kings. The quotation is from *The Rubáiyát of Omar Khayyám* (12th century), trans. Edward Fitzgerald (1809–83) in 1859: 'And Bahram, that great Hunter – the Wild Ass/ Stamps o'er his Head, and he lies fast asleep' (xvii. 3–4).

219:25 "If the Missis...'er go!" A music hall song (1902), written, composed and sung by Phil Ray. The complete title is 'If the Missus Wants to Go (or Let Her Drown)'. The line quoted by DHL is the opening of the first chorus, which continues: 'If the Missis wants to row, let 'er row – let 'er row./ Ten to one she'll get upset,/ Then you watch her going down – / But don't interrupt her/ She might feel annoyed./ Let her drown; let her drown'.

219:31 La caccia! 'Hunting' (Italian); DHL probably meant to translate 'game', 'cacciagione'.

220:22 *pineta*, 'Pine-wood' (Italian).

Flowery Tuscany

225:12 the Argosy, In the 16th century the Argosy was a big merchant vessel, particularly of Ragusa (Sicily) and Venice. The word 'argosy' was derived from Ragusa (Ragusi in Venetian) which appeared in 16th-century English as Aragouse, Arragouese, Arragosa (cf. *OED*).

225:16 Paestum Near Salerno in Campania, famous for its Greek temples.

226:3 Pan See note on 187:8.

226:12 hanging gardens of Babylon, Probably built by Belshazzar (see note on 57:33), the gardens formed perhaps part of a great ziggurat, a pyramid-shaped temple with terraces.

227:29   **tramontana**   'North wind' (Italian).

230:14   **the water...crushed olives.**   The crushing takes place in November.

231:31   **the many-breasted...clustered breasts,**   Artemis, daughter of Zeus (Roman Diana), goddess of wild life, a virgin huntress attended by nymphs, and goddess of childbirth. In Ephesus, the centre of her cult, there was a famous statue representing her with many breasts; she was worshipped for her maternal character and as goddess of fertility. In *The Lost Girl* there is a similar reference: 'Everywhere little grape hyacinths hung their blue bells. It was a pity they reminded her of the many-breasted Artemis, a picture of whom, or of whose statue, she had seen somewhere' (ed. John Worthen, Cambridge, 1981, 333:25–8). Cybele, the Phrygian goddess of the Earth and of fecundity, was generally represented as a robust pregnant woman; she was also portrayed with many breasts symbolising the nutriment that all living creatures receive from the earth, and was worshipped as the Great Mother (Magna Mater) by the Romans from 204 BC (see Sir James Frazer, *The Golden Bough*, 1890–1915, Part IV, i. 263).

232:8   **podere,**   'Estate', 'farm' (Italian).

232:29   **Adonis-blood anemones:**   According to one legend, Adonis was killed by a boar while hunting, and the rose or the anemone sprang from his blood; according to another, Venus was in love with Adonis and from the tears she shed at his death sprang the anemone; a third legend maintains that Venus, after Adonis' death, changed his body into an anemone (see 233:16–18). DHL had already seen Adonis-blood anemones in Sicily (see 'Introduction to "Memoirs of the Foreign Legion"', *Phoenix II*, ed. Roberts and Moore, p. 328). In *The Lost Girl* DHL mentions many of the flowers he describes in 'Flowery Tuscany': wild narcissus, green hellebore, cyclamen, wild gladioli, irises (see *The Lost Girl*, ed. Worthen, pp. 331–5); and he also refers to anemones: 'She turned with thankfulness to the magenta anemones that were so gay. Someone told her that wherever Venus had shed a tear for Adonis, one of these flowers had sprung. They were not tear-like. And yet their red-purple silkiness had something pre-world about it, at last' (333:31–4).

234:30   **shaggles**   DHL's version of the dialect word 'shackles', meaning the stiff, upstanding stalks of stubble.

238:24   **"Where are...yesteryear?"**   'The Ballad of Dead Ladies' (l. 8), Dante Gabriel Rossetti's translation (1870) of 'Ballade des Dames du Temps Jadis', in *Le Grand Testament* (1461) by François Villon (?1431–63). The original version is 'Mais où sont les neiges d'antan?' (See also *Letters* i., ed. Boulton, p. 157 and *Study of Thomas Hardy*, ed. Steele, 11:2).

238:36   **Why the Greeks...sobbing**   See note on 211:24.

239:3   **the Por Santa Maria...the Ponte Vecchio**   The most ancient street in Florence, near the Piazza della Signoria, leading to the Ponte Vecchio. The name derives from that of the gate ('porta' in Italian) of the first city walls...The oldest bridge over the narrowest stretch of the Arno, known for its jewellery shops. In 1345 it was rebuilt and enlarged with two arcades where little butcher shops were located, but during the 16th century Cosimo I dei Medici, disliking the smell of meat, turned out the butchers, allowing only silversmiths and goldsmiths.

239:4 **Wandervogel** Literally, 'migratory bird' (German); 'wanderer' in a metaphorical sense.

239:18 **the Porta Romana** An old town gate leading out of the city, southwards, to Siena and Rome.

239:35 **Rome, the old centre-point…the Lungarno.** From the time of the Roman empire, Rome represented the centre of power and civilisation; hence the saying 'All roads lead to Rome'…See note on 205:5.

239:36 **a sort of Tarnhelm,** In the *Nibelungenlied*, the mediaeval German epic poem, the malignant gnome Alberich forges and wears a helmet called the Tarnhelm which makes him invisible and can transform his appearance; represented in the opera-cycle *Der Ring des Nibelungen* (1853–70), by Richard Wagner (1813–83).

240:18 **the Drachen and the Greifen.** 'The dragons and the gryphons' (German).

240:34 *gli escursionisti,* 'The excursionists' or 'the tourists' (Italian).

241:7 *Not angli sed angeli*…**of the British slaves.** 'Not Angles but angels' (Latin). The legend is that Gregory the Great (?540–?640) saw fair-haired Anglo-Saxon slaves being sold in the market of Rome and was so impressed by their beauty that he compared them to angels, afterwards sending a mission led by Augustine of Canterbury.

242:22 **Frederick,** Frederick II the Great (1712–86), king of Prussia (1740–86).

Germans and English

Note Annotation has not been supplied where the notes of 'Flowery Tuscany' IV provide the requisite information.

247:1 **Germans and English** For the title see Introduction, pp. lxx–lxxi.

249:14 *Zeit und Stunde*…**Idee brauchen."** Karl Scheffler (1869–1951) collected twenty-eight essays on various general topics (Leipzig, Insel-Verlag; 'Time and Hour'); the title of the first essay mentioned by DHL is 'The Lonely German' (pp. 5–7)…'Because they—need a world of pure Idea' (p. 5).

249:24 **the centre stone,** A reference to the *miliarium aureum*, the marble column erected by Augustus to mark the central point of the original city.

249:28 **As the German…***wie Wert.* Cf. *Sketches of Etruscan Places*, pp. 119–21 above, where the same German expression occurs at 119:16 (and see note on 119:19).

250:3 **'Die Einsamkeit [249:34]…einsamen Deutschen."**
To learn to bear loneliness in the world and in one's own people: this is victory. To overlook the whole, free from vertigo, like the winged goddess on the globe, to experience the horror of history with the same composure and respectful curiosity one had in better times, when one only imagined such horror, to believe in the world mission of the German problem, in the superior morality of an

apparent lack of character, in strength in weakness, and to do all this actively, considering each day wasted in which nothing has been done; this is—and it should be—the earthly happiness of the German solitary in the world and in his own country. (p. 7)

250:30 **"Warum Wir...Verloren Haben."** 'Why We Have Lost the War' (German), the fourth essay in *Zeit und Stunde*, pp. 14–18.

251:23 [*ab ovo*], 'From the egg, from the origin' (Latin). Horace (*Satires*, I. 3, 6) adopted this expression referring to the Roman habit of eating eggs as an appetizer for a meal. The complete expression – 'ab ovo usque ad mala' ('from the egg to the apples' referring to a Roman banquet) – means from the beginning to the end. TS has '*above*'; in an attempt to make sense of the sentence, E1 printed the equally inadequate and nonsensical '*alone*'. The reading '*ab ovo*' appeared in the German and Italian translations.

252:2 *consummatum est,* 'It is finished', Jesus's last words on the cross (John xix. 30). Cf. 'Return to Bestwood': 'When Jesus gave up the ghost, he cried: It is finished. Consummatum est! But was it? And if so, what? What was it that was consummate?' (*Phoenix II*, ed. Roberts and Moore, p. 261).

252:9 **the first great European revolution,** The Civil War (1642–9), which led to the beheading of Charles I and to Oliver Cromwell's republic.

252:15 **Völkerschicksale.** 'National destinies'(German).

The Painted Tombs of Tarquinia

Note Annotation has not been supplied where the notes on 'The Painted Tombs of Tarquinia' 1. provide the requisite information.

259:14 *ambiente,* 'Environment' (Italian).

260:9 **Cilicia** Ancient coastal region of Asia Minor, the peninsula which now constitutes the greater part of Turkey.

261:39 **conception [of] oneness** DHL omitted 'of' and the typist reproduced the mistake; the text was emended in proof (see 47:17 and apparatus).

264:21 **Canova** Antonio Canova (1757–1822), Italian sculptor whose art showed a neoclassical tendency especially in sculptures with mythological subjects such as *The Three Graces* and *Cupid and Psyche*.

264:33 **pedgilling.** Dialect word of the central Midlands, also spelt 'peggling'; 'struggling...plodding' (*English Dialect Dictionary*, ed. Joseph Wright, 6 vols (1898–1905); see also *The Letters of D. H. Lawrence*, ed. Boulton, i. 336).

Fireworks [Fireworks in Florence]

Note Annotation has not been supplied where the notes on 'Fireworks' provide the requisite information.

288:18 **the Flatiron Building.** D. H. Burnham's design for the Flatiron Building was realised by George Fuller in 1901. A steel structure clad in limestone, it was a landmark on the triangle where Broadway and 5th Avenue meet at 23th Street in New York.

289:1 **Popocatepetl...Theophrastus,** The highest volcano in central Mexico (Sierra Nevada), 5386 m...Greek philosopher (372–287 BC), Aristotle's successor as leader of the peripatetic school.

291:28 **The cathedral dome...the Baptistery** For the cathedral and Giotto's tower, see note on 194:19...St John's Baptistery, in front of the cathedral, an octagonal domed building, dating from the 7th or 8th century and probably enriched with its marble incrustations in the 11th century. These three religious monuments are set in the Piazza del Duomo, in the centre of Florence; they are all characterised by the same polychrome marbles – pink, green and white – arranged in geometric patterns.

291:35 **"The lily of Florence...of Rovezzano,"** For the lily of Florence, see note on 186:12...Rovezzano is a small suburb, s.e. of Florence, towards Arezzo, particularly famous for its agricultural produce. The sentence quoted by DHL might well be a popular saying, reflecting the Florentine country folk's typical irony towards the city folk. DHL's misspelling 'Rovenzano' might be due to the fact that he never saw the name written and misunderstood its pronunciation.

TEXTUAL APPARATUS

TEXTUAL APPARATUS

Sketches of Etruscan Places

The following symbols are used to distinguish states of texts:
  MS = Manuscript
  TSa, TSb, TSc = Typescripts (see Introduction, pp. xl–xliii)
    Per1 = First periodical publication (*Travel*)
    Per2 = Second periodical publication (*World Today*)
    PP = Page proofs
    E1 = First English edition

Whenever the *MS* reading is adopted, it is given within the square bracket with no symbol; other variants appear in the order given at the beginning of each essay below. In the absence of information to the contrary, the reader should assume that a variant recurs in all subsequent states. When the reading of *MS* corresponds to the reading of another text, their respective symbols are given within the square bracket.

The following symbols are used editorially:
  Ed. = Editor
  Om. = Omitted
    ~ = Repeated word in recording an accidental variant
  { } = Partial variant reading
    P = New paragraph
    / = Line or page break associated with hyphenation error or other error
    # = Internal division
    R = Revision by DHL; see Introduction, pp. xl–xlvii
    C = Correction by another person

In order to reduce the difficulty of tracing DHL's revisions and omissions in *Per1* and *Per2*, some passages are printed with variants internally recorded inside braces. When variants occur in revisions which replace these passages, they are indicated by the note '*see also entries to…*'.

Cerveteri

The sequence of the states of the text is: *MS, TSa, TSaR, TSaC, Per1, PP, E1*; *Per2* follows *TSaR* unless otherwise indicated.

9:14	go:] ~; *Per2*	9:31	vicious,] ~ *Per1*
9:18	sympathy, *MS, PP*] ~ *Per1*	9:32	detractors,] ~ *PP*
9:19	B.C. *MS, Per2*] B. C. *Per1*	9:32	A la bonne heure] *À la bonne*
	B.C. *PP*		*heure TSa À la bonne heure*
9:25	Romans. So] ~; so, *Per2*		*Per1 À la bonne heure Per2*

335

10:3 Quand le...se tait] *Quand le maître parle, tout le monde se tait TSa*

10:4 earth,] ~ *PP*

10:5 snow-flakes] snowflakes *TSa, PP* snow-/ flakes *Per1*

10:11 But] ~, *Per2*

10:13 bonnet. It] ~, it *Per2*

10:13 campagna] Campagna *TSa*

10:15 campagna] Campagna *Per2, PP*

10:17 narcissus] narcissi *Per2*

10:18 queer] green *TSa*

10:18 foam-white *TSaR, PP*] foam white *MS, Per1*

10:21 Agylla *PP*] Argylla *MS*

10:22 hovels:] ~ *Per2*

10:24 The inestimable...eight-and-a-half...post omnibus.] *Om. Per1* The inestimable...eight and a half...post omnibus. *PP* The inestimable...eight and a half...post-/ omnibus. *E1*

10:32 difficult!] ~, *Per2*

10:32 meaning] Meaning *PP*

10:33 help.—Is] ~. P Is *Per2* ~. Is *PP*

10:33 They *MS, PP*] —~ *Per1*

10:36 them. Because] ~, because *Per2*

10:39 holdall] hold-all *TSa, PP* hold-/ all *Per1*

11:5 umbrella pines] umbrella-pines *E1*

11:6 sea,] ~; *Per2*

11:7 oxen-wagon] oxen wagon *Per2*

11:8 distance] ~, *Per2*

11:8 tall *TSaR*] tall pink *MS*

11:11 wheat,] ~ *Per2*

11:12 hills,] ~ *Per2*

11:13 building: *MS, PP*] ~; *TSa*

11:15 Caere *TSaR, PP*] Cerveteri *MS, Per1, Per2*

11:18 empire] Empire *Per2, PP*

11:20 village,] ~ *Per2*

11:20 walls,] ~ *Per2*

11:22 lounging talking *MS, PP*] ~, ~, *Per1*

11:24 Wines and Kitchen] (Wines and Kitchen) *Per2* Wines and Kitchen *E1*

11:25 mule drivers] mule-drivers *PP*

11:28 street,] ~ *Per2, PP*

11:28 go, *TSaR*] ~ *MS*

11:31 it:] ~; *Per2*

11:32 broth:] ~; *Per2*

11:32 tripe:] ~; *Per2*

11:33 alas,] also, *Per1* alas! *PP*

11:34 meal—] ~!— *Per2*

11:35 cheese,] ~ *Per2*

11:39 cave *MS, Per2*] Cave *TSa* cavern *PP*

11:40 rusty-brown] rusty brown *PP*

11:40 goat's hair *Per2, PP*] goats-hair *MS* goat's-hair *Per1*

12:8 swirling,] ~ *Per2*

12:10 christian *Ed.*] Christian *MS*

12:11 You cannot hard-boil him. *TSaR, PP*] *Om. MS, Per1* You cannot hard boil him. *Per2*

12:12 me,] ~ *Per2, PP*

12:18 south] South *PP*

12:20 war:] ~; *Per2*

12:21 Anyway] ~, *Per2*

12:23 war-memories] war memories *Per2* war memories, *PP*

12:24 revived,] ~ *Per2*

12:24 go-ahead *TSaR*] modern *MS*

12:24 women-folk] women-/ folk *Per2* womenfolk *PP*

12:24 Probably,] ~ *PP*

12:25 south again,] South ~ *PP*

12:28 maremma] Maremma *TSa, Per2, PP* Mareumma *Per1*

12:28 shepherd!] ~. *Per2*

12:29 Cere *MS, Per1*] Caere *TSaC see notes*

12:31 the acropolis, *TSaR*] *Om. MS*

12:33 palace, or *MS, PP*] or *Per1*

12:34 and a *MS, PP*] *Om. Per1*

12:34 sort of *MS, PP*] *Om. Per1*

12:35 by] by a *Per2*

12:35 forlorn beyond words, *MS, PP*] forlorn, *Per1* forlorn beyond words; *Per2*

12:36 dead,] ~ *Per2*

12:36 still] ~, *Per2*

12:37 below *MS, PP*] *Om. Per1*

12:40 place,] ~ *PP*

13:4 with him *MS, PP*] *Om. Per1*

13:18 Agylla *PP*] Argylla *MS*

13:20 Caere,] ~ *PP*

13:20 place. About *MS, PP*] ~. P
About *Per1*

13:21 B.C.] B. C. *Per1* B.C. *Per2, PP*

13:24 rock. P And] ~. And *TSa*

13:26 Certainly it...hill-top...
Cerveteri. But the *TSaR*] The
MS, Per1, Per2 Certainly it...
hilltop... Cerveteri. But the
PP

13:29 wood,] ~; *Per2* ~— *PP*

13:30 temples,] ~— *PP*

13:32 like] the *TSa*

13:32 underground. P But] ~. But
TSa

13:38 outside,] ~ *PP*

13:40 opposite,] ~ *Per2, PP*

14:1 their necropolis] the
necropolis *TSa*

14:3 houses *TSa*] house *MS*

14:6 sea-plain] sea plain *Per2*

14:7 a mile or *TSaR, PP*] *Om. MS,
Per1, Per2*

14:8 heaves] leaves *TSa* leaves the
coast *TSaR*

14:8 low, crowned] low-crowned
TSa

14:13 linen. They...inwardness,
which...[14:19] out. P Up
MS, PP] linen. Up *Per1* linen.
They...inwardness
which...out. P Up *Per2*

14:19 side] ~, *Per2*

14:21 rock face] rock-face *E1*

14:24 No-one] No one *Per1, Per2*

14:25 cliff-face] cliff face *Per2*

14:30 distance; *TSaR*] ~, *MS*

14:36 dumb-bell *MS, PP*] dumbbell
Per1

14:36 It...flower!] "~...~!" *PP*

14:38 up *TSaR*] nearly up *MS*

14:39 a great *TSa*] a great a *MS see
notes*

14:40 landscape,] ~. *PP*

15:2 "È un fiore! Puzza!"—] "È un
fiore! Puzza!"— *TSa Om.
Per1* "É un fiore! Puzza!"—
Per2, PP

15:2 It is...stinks!— *MS, PP*] "~
~...~!" *Per1*

15:4 me:] ~, *Per2*

15:6 flowerets] flowers *TSa*

15:7 stripes. P Many *MS, PP*] ~.
Many *Per1*

15:9 It is true, the...[15:13] And
having *MS, PP*] Having *Per1*
It is true the...And having
Per2

15:15 pink] ~, *Per2*

15:19 One man...Greece? It...
[15:27] lent...[15:34] way
themselves.] *Om. Per1* One
man... Greece! It...lent...way
themselves. *Per2* One man...
Greece. It...Lent...way
themselves. *PP*

15:40 near,] ~ *PP*

16:2 touching the earth *TSaR*] the
big bases *MS*

16:5 between,] ~ *Per2*

16:7 Absit omen] *Absit omen TSa*

16:8 Between us...is gratuitous.
MS, PP] *Om. Per1*

16:12 just by, *TSaR*] *Om. MS*

16:16 an *MS, PP*] *Om. Per1*

16:16 the *MS, PP*] a *Per1*

16:18 queer stillness,] stillness *Per1*
queer stillness *Per2, PP*

16:18 a curious peaceful *MS, PP*]
Om. Per1

16:18 the *MS, PP*] *Om. Per1*

16:20 repellant] repellent *Per1, Per2*

16:21 campagna] Campagna *TSa*

16:21 the rather *MS, PP*] rather
Per1

16:22 Teotihuacán *Ed.*] Teotihuacan
MS

16:22 south; *TSaR*] ~, *MS*

16:23 amiably *TSa*] aimiably *MS*

16:38 to imitate *TSaR*] cut out of the
rock, like *MS*

16:38 home.] house. *TSa, Per2*
house, a home. *TSaR*

16:40 ante-chambers] antichambers
TSa antechambers *Per1, Per2*

17:2 presumably. Whereas *MS,
PP*] ~; whereas *Per2*

17:3 full-length] full length *Per2*

17:3 sometimes *TSaR, PP*] Om.
MS, Per1, Per2

17:4 sometimes...terra cotta,
TSaR] Om. *MS, Per1, Per2*
sometimes...terra-/ cotta, *PP*

17:4 But most often *TSaR, PP*] Or
perhaps sometimes *MS, Per1,
Per2*

17:6 now,] ~; *Per2*

17:8 large,] ~; *PP*

17:9 apparently *TSaR*] Om. *MS*

17:10 roof as] ~, ~ *Per2*

17:11 rock, sometimes...tier, *TSaR,
PP*] rock *MS, Per1, Per2*

17:12 laid,] ~ *Per2*

17:13 wood,] ~; *Per2*

17:13 armour, *MS, PP*] armor *Per1*

17:13 a woman] women *Per2*

17:15 necks,] ~ *Per2*

17:16 daughters, many...tomb.
TSaR, PP] daughters. *MS,
Per1, Per2*

17:19 thing] things *Per2*

17:19 Egypt; *TSaR*] ~, *MS*

17:22 It is...spiritual
consciousness...accustomed
to. *Per2, PP*] It is spiritual
Consciousness...accustomed
to. *MS* Om. *Per1*

17:28 the Lucumo and *TSaR, PP*]
Om. *MS, Per1, Per2*

17:30 of small] or small *Per2*

17:32 sometimes,] ~ *E1*

17:33 room,] ~ *E1*

17:34 combs] ~, *Per2*

17:35 silver *TSaR*] golden *MS*

17:37 Tomb *Ed.*] tomb *MS*

18:1 living-room *MS, PP*] living
room *Per1, Per2*

18:3 wall,] ~ *Per2*

18:4 long, double-tier *TSaR*] long

MS, Per1, Per2 long
double-tier *PP*

18:4 bed,] ~; *TSa*

18:5 or scratched...the finger,
TSaR, PP] Om. *MS, Per1,
Per2*

18:7 downwards *TSaR*] upwards
MS

18:10 them,] ~ *PP*

18:11 Avle—Tarchnas—Larthal—
Clan. *MS, Per1*]
Avle-Tarchnas—Larthal—
Clan. *TSa, PP*
"Avle-Tarchnas-Larthal-
Clan." *Per2*
*Avle—Tarchnas—Larthal—
Clan. E1*

18:12 enough. But] ~, but *Per2*

18:14 "Aule, son...so far. *TSaR*]
Om. *MS*

18:21 *Grotta Bella Ed.*] Grotta Bella
MS

18:21 low relief] low-relief *PP*

18:23 big] Om. *TSa*

18:26 noble:] ~; *Per2*

18:27 sceptre *MS, PP*] scepter *Per1*

18:29 triton,] ~ *Per2*

18:31 End *TSaR*] end *MS*

18:34 contained:] ~; *Per2*

18:35 tombs:] ~; *Per2*

18:36 tombs: and...the sea; *TSaR,
PP*] tombs: *MS, Per1* tombs,
Per2

19:2 them. It] ~; it *Per2*

19:4 unRomanised] un-Romanised
Per1, Per2 unromanized *PP*

19:6 spontaneity] ~, *PP*

19:7 spaces,] ~ *Per2*

19:9 no.] ~! *Per2*

19:11 life. Even] ~; even *Per2*

19:12 ease] easy *Per2*

19:16 wine] ~, *Per2*

19:24 cheerful. The] ~; the *Per2*

19:24 so *MS, PP*] Om. *Per1*

19:25 B., who...[21:2] vice
incarnate. *MS, Per2, PP*] B.
who...vice incarnate. *TSa* Om.
Per1 see also entries to 21:1

19:29	And that…[20:11] cut short.] *Om. Per2*
19:33	unmistakeable] unmistakable *E1*
20:3	born.—The] ~. *P* The *TSa*
20:4	tumuli] ~, *TSa*
20:5	cippus—cippi] *cippus, cippi TSa*
20:6	grave-stone] gravestone *TSa*
20:8	round] *Om. TSa*
20:10	decorative] decorated *TSa*
20:10	phallic, and] ~. And *TSa*
20:11	phallus] phallic *TSa*
20:20	boat-part] boat part *TSa*
20:21	arx] *arx E1*
20:22	creatures. The] ~; the *Per2*
20:23	arx] *arx E1*
20:23	refuge. The] ~; the *Per2*
20:27	perhaps] ~, *Per2*
20:31	conscious] conscience *Per2* consciousness *E1*
20:31	rooted,] ~ *PP*
20:31	blithely,] ~ *E1*
20:36	days,] ~ *PP*
20:38	ark,] ~ *Per2*
20:38	dominion and] ~, ~, *Per2* ~ ~, *PP*
20:39	flute,] ~ *Per2, PP*
21:1	Delenda est Cartago] *Delenda est Cartago TSa*
21:4	left. Most] ~; most *Per2*
21:4	must] *Om. TSa*
21:4	levelled *MS, PP*] leveled *Per1*
21:5	water:] ~; *Per2*
21:6	quarry-place *MS, PP*] quarry place *Per1, Per2*
21:9	earth; and…tumulus, it…[21:12] here all *TSaR*] earth. They are all, in this necropolis, *MS, Per1, Per2* earth, and…tumulus it…here all *PP*
21:14	most *TSaR, PP*] all *MS, Per1, Per2*
21:14	chambers,] ~ *Per2*
21:14	ante-chambers] antechambers *Per2, PP*
21:15	these tombs…high-way *TSaR*] of them *MS, Per1, Per2* these tombs…highway *PP*
21:15	would *TSaR*] would have *MS, Per2*
21:17	dead, with…the summit. *TSaR, PP*] dead. *MS, Per1, Per2*
21:19	necropolis, as…concerned, *TSaR, PP*] necropolis *MS, Per1, Per2*
21:21	empty. All] ~; all *Per2*
21:38	mounds, trees,] mounds; trees and *Per2* mounds; trees *PP*
21:39	graves,] ~; *PP*
22:1	ravaged, *MS, PP*] ~ *Per1*
22:4	town,] ~ *Per2*
22:4	discovered:] ~, *Per2*
22:5	Regolini *Per1, E1*] Regulini *MS, PP*
22:6	it:] ~, *Per2*
22:6	Regolini-Galassi *Per1, E1*] Regulini-Galassi *MS, PP*
22:7	interesting,] ~: *PP*
22:7	like a…and covered *TSaR, PP*] *Om. MS, Per1, Per2*
22:10	out] ~, *Per2*
22:12	gothic] Gothic *Per2, E1*
22:12	arch:] ~; *Per2*
22:14	the remains of *TSaR, PP*] *Om. MS, Per1, Per2*
22:14	warrior,] ~ *Per2*
22:16	sunk on his dust *TSaR, PP*] around him *MS, Per1, Per2*
22:16	beautiful frail…surely, of…years ago *TSaR*] lay a lady, surely his wife, with marvellous {marvelous *Per1*} gold and silver ornaments upon her *MS, Per1, Per2* beautiful, frail…surely of…years ago *PP*
22:22	Regolini-Galassi *MS, E1*] Regulini-Galassi *Per2, PP*
22:22	tomb,] ~ *Per1*
22:23	inscription—Mi Larthia—] ~, "~ ~." *Per2* ~—~ ~. *PP* ~—Mi Larthia. *E1*

22:24　anyhow? *TSaR*] ~. *MS* ~?—
　　　　Per1, Per2
22:24　"This is Larthia"—…lady—??
　　　　TSaR] *Om. MS* "This…lady?
　　　　Per1, PP "This is
　　　　Larthia."…lady? *Per2*

22:30　go,] ~ *Per2, PP*
22:33　post-automobile *MS, E1*] post
　　　　automobile *TSa*
22:40　the phallic knowledge and
　　　　MS, PP] *Om. Per1*

Tarquinia

The sequence of the texts is *MS, TSa, TSc, TSaR, TScR, TSaC, TScC, Per1, PP, E1*; *Per2* follows *TSaR* unless otherwise indicated.

25:3　In Cerveteri…[25:19] beat us.
　　　　MS, PP] *Om. TScC see also
　　　　entries to* 25:17
25:3　Cerveteri,] ~ *PP*
25:4　Città] Civita *Per2*
25:5　5.0] 5 *TSa* five *PP*
25:5　o'clock: *TSa*] oclock: *MS*
　　　　o'clock, *Per2*
25:5　nowhere:] ~, *Per2*
25:9　sea-side] seaside *Per2, PP*
25:12　wall,] ~ *PP*
25:16　only runs] runs only *PP*
25:17　road,] ~ *PP*
25:22　establishments,] ~; *PP*
25:23　bathers,] ~ *Per1*
25:24　was deserted,] ~ ~— *Per2*
25:27　sky, *TSaR*] sky spread *MS*
25:27　emitted *TSaR*] emitting *MS*
25:32　sea *MS, PP*] Sea *Per1*
25:34　Sicily,] ~— *Per2*
26:2　iron-ore] iron ore *PP*
26:4　B.C.] B. C. *Per1* B.C. *PP*
26:5　host] ~, *PP*
26:6　sparsely-peopled] sparsely
　　　　peopled *PP*
26:8　strange] ~, *Per2*
26:9　Lydians,] ~ *PP*
26:17　and earlier *TSaR*] or
　　　　thereabouts *MS*
26:20　two-eyed *TSaR*] *Om. MS*
26:23　Even before…here. And
　　　　TSaR] And that they were not
　　　　Latins, nor Umbrians, nor
　　　　Sabines, of that too we are
　　　　certain. But anyhow there they
　　　　were, and *MS*

26:25　probably; with *TSaR*]
　　　　probably. And no doubt they
　　　　had *MS*
26:25　grain, and flocks of *TSaR*]
　　　　corn, and *MS*
26:27　Hebrides *TSaR*] isles *MS*
26:29　sea *MS, PP*] Sea *Per1*
26:29　But by…[26:33] was built.
　　　　TSaR] *Om. MS see also entries
　　　　to* 26:33
26:29　etruscan *TSaR, PP*] Etruscan
　　　　TScC, Per2, E1
26:30　in Caere *TSaR*] *Om. TScR*
26:30　B.C. *TSaR*] B. C. *Per1* B.C. *PP*
26:30　there was certainly *TSaR*] no
　　　　doubt there was *TScR*
26:31　on the…of that *TSaR*] here at
　　　　Caere. There was a city, *TScR*
26:31　sure; *TSaR*] sure, of natives,
　　　　TScR
26:32　linen *TSaR, PP*] linens *Per1*
26:33　Regolini-Galassi *Per1, E1*]
　　　　Regulini-Galassi *TSaR*
　　　　Regulini-Galasai *Per2*
26:33　built. P However *TSaR, PP*]
　　　　~. However *Per1*
26:37　up:] ~, *Per2*
26:37　probably,] ~ *TSa*
26:37　arrived,] ~— *Per2* ~ *PP*
26:39　east,] East— *Per2*
27:5　one and *TSaR*] *Om. MS*
27:7　The *TSaR*] Looking at those
　　　　things that remain to us, from
　　　　the Etruscans, one is driven at
　　　　last to feel that the mass and
　　　　basis of the Etruscan

{etruscan *TSaR*} people were never Greek, and never Indo-European. The throb of some older world comes through; it seems the ancient world of the Mediterranean basin, not Indo-Germanic in the sense that we now apply to Indo-Germanic: that is, containing the germ of modern civilisation. {civilization. *TSa*} The *MS*

27:8 pre-historic] pre-/ historic *Per2* pehistoric *PP*

27:17 highly-developed] highly developed *Per1*

27:22 But it...colony, it was a slowly developed country. *TSaR, PP*] *Om. MS* But it...colony: it was a slowly developed country. *TScR* But it...colony: it was probably a country that took a good many years to develop. *Per1*

27:29 Greek *TSaR*] great Greek *MS*

27:34 prehistoric...prehistoric] pre-historic...pre-historic *Per2* ...

27:37 universe *MS, TScC*] Universe *TSa, PP*

28:8 Solomon,] ~— *E1*

28:11 sails. Then...them. *P* Just *TSaR*] sails. Just *MS see also entries to* 28:14

28:12 Phoenicians *TSaR, E1*] Phœnicians *Per2, PP*

28:13 of *TSaR*] about *TScR*

28:14 them. *P* Just *TSaR, PP*] their movements. *P* Just *TScR, Per2* their movements. Just *Per1*

28:17 Phoenician *TSa, E1*] Phœnician *MS, Per2, PP*

28:18 Carthage,] ~ *Per2*

28:25 Phoenicians *TSa*] Phœnicians *MS, Per2, PP*

28:26 that *TSaR*] that later, *MS*

28:26 Etruscans, all except those of Caere, *TSaR*] Etruscans *MS*

28:28 corsairs] Corsairs *Per2*

28:34 new] *Om. TSa*

28:34 coast-line] coast-/ line *PP*

28:34 bathing places] bathing-places *TSa*

28:35 sea-side] seaside *Per1, Per2*

28:39 dark-grey,] dark grey *E1*

28:40 peered-at] peered at *PP*

29:3 still *MS, PP*] *Om. Per1*

29:7 Città] Civita *Per2*

29:9 gave our...[30:24] enough, we *MS, PP*] *Om. TScC see also entries to* 30:24

29:24 papers—] ~. *Per2, PP*

29:26 half a pace] half-a-pace *PP*

29:31 us *TSaR*] one *MS*

29:37 B.'s *PP*] B's *MS*

30:2 half a dozen] half-a-dozen *PP*

30:4 half an hour] half-an-hour *PP*

30:6 Città] Civita *Per2*

30:6 *always*] always *TSa*

30:6 fools?—Even] ~—even *Per2* ~? Even *PP*

30:7 *could*] could *TSa*

30:7 doing!] ~? *TSa*

30:8 hotel-manager] hotel manager *PP*

30:9 Città] Civita *Per2*

30:10 —Ah!] ~! *Per2* "~!" *PP*

30:10 But all...at then.—] ~ ~ ~...~ ~. *Per2* "~ ~...~ ~." *PP*

30:12 régime] regime *Per2, PP*

30:13 —But...mean,] ~...~, *Per2* "~...~," *PP*

30:14 behaving like...to travel!] "~ ~...~ ~! *PP* "~ ~...~ ~!" *E1*

30:15 —Ah!] ~! *Per2* "~!" *PP*

30:15 It is...di Roma.—] ~ ~...~ ~. *Per2* "~ ~...~ ~." *PP*

30:19 Città] Civita *Per2*

30:22 eight o'clock *TSa*] eight oclock *MS* eight-o'clock *PP*

30:24 And] ~, *PP*

30:24 left *MS, PP*] left Città Vecchia the next morning *TScC*

30:24 eight o'clock *TSa*] eight oclock *MS* eight-o'clock *PP*

30:25 Città] Civita *Per2*

30:26 maremma] Maremma *PP*

30:31 league] League *PP*

30:32 re-birth] rebirth *PP*

30:35 remembrance,] ~ *PP*

30:36 Corneto-Tarquinia!] ~. *TSa*

30:37 régime] regime *Per2, PP*

30:38 Corneto,] ~; *Per2*

30:40 station,] ~ *PP*

30:40 letters] ~, *PP*

31:1 Tarquinia!] *Tarquinia. E1*

31:5 empire] Empire *TSa*

31:16 Dazio,…customs,] ~(…~) *Per2 Dazio, …~, E1*

31:18 says,] ~: *Per2, PP*

31:18 Do…sleep?— *TSaR*] ~…~? *MS* "~…~?"— *Per2* "~…~?" *PP*

31:22 half-asleep *MS, Per2*] half-/asleep *TSa* half asleep *TScC*

31:26 little lad in long trousers, *TSaR*] little, sturdy lad, *MS*

31:27 old] ~, *Per2*

31:31 on. He] ~. # P He *Per2*

31:31 us] *Om. Per2*

31:34 Teh! *Lina*] Toh! Lina *TSaC, Per2, PP,* Toh! Lina *Per1, E1*

31:35 Eh] *Eh E1*

31:36 Fai presto *MS, PP*] *Fai presto TScC, E1*

31:36 È pronto] È pronto *TSa È pronto TScC È pronto Per1, E1* E pronto *Per2* É pronto *PP*

31:37 Ecco *MS, PP*] Ecco *TScC, E1*

32:8 all.—] ~. *TSa* ~! *Per2*

32:12 travellers: *MS, PP*] travelers: *TScC* travellers, *Per2*

32:18 faintly gleaming *MS, PP*] faintly-gleaming *Per1*

32:18 seemed *TSaR*] was so near at hand, yet *MS*

32:22 forlorn] ~, *Per2*

32:22 lot,] ~ *PP*

32:26 where] when *TSa*

32:26 huge] ~, *Per2*

32:28 changing,] ~ *Per2, PP*

32:29 earth,] ~ *Per1, Per2*

32:35 freely-modelled, *TSaR*] freely

modelled, *MS, PP* freely modeled, *Per1* freely modelled *E1*

32:36 gay] ~, *Per2*

33:2 run,] ~ *Per2*

33:4 upon!] ~? *Per2, PP*

33:11 café *MS, PP*] Café *TSa* cafe *Per2*

33:16 garden,] ~ *Per2*

33:19 seen:] ~— *Per2*

33:20 wheat-green] wheat—green *TSa*

33:21 newness *TSaR*] wheat *MS*

33:25 peak,] ~ *Per2*

33:28 and *TSaR*] and in *MS*

33:33 ever-green] evergreen *Per1, Per2*

33:38 that, *MS, PP*] ~ *Per1*

34:2 sunny,] ~ *Per2*

34:3 sea. And] ~; and *Per2*

34:6 enough,] ~ *PP*

34:8 alla Romana. *MS, PP*] *alla Romana. Per1* alla Romana! *E1*

34:9 all'etrusca *MS, PP*] *all'etrusca TScC* all'Etrusca *Per2* all'Etrusca *E1*

34:10 on] *Om. TSa*

34:12 delightful, *MS, PP*] ~ *Per1, Per2*

34:14 and only…[34:20] etruscan…[34:34] a million *Ed.*] and only…Etruscan…a million *MS Om. TSa see note on* 34:34

35:3 entrance-room] entrance room *PP*

35:8 little round] ~, ~ *Per2*

35:12 discovered,] ~ *Per1* ~; *Per2*

35:14 unburned,] ~— *Per2*

35:15 urns *TSa*] ~, *MS see note on* 14:40

35:16 people,] ~ *TSa*

35:22 chamber tombs:] ~ ~, *TSa* chamber-tombs, *PP*

35:27 the sides were lined *TSaR*] frequently lined *MS* frequently buried *TSA see notes*

35:28 stone. *P* The] ~. The *TSa*
35:30 artizans] artisans *Per1*
35:33 burial place] burial-place *PP*
35:35 their] and their *PP*
35:35 vases] ~, *Per2*, *PP*
35:36 beautiful,] ~ *Per2*, *PP*
35:39 many, *MS*, *PP*] ~ *Per1*
35:40 Apparently] ~, *Per2*
36:2 Rome] ~, *PP*
36:3 flung. *P* It *MS*, *PP*] ~. It *Per1*
36:5 lives lives *MS*, *PP*] ~, ~ *Per1*
36:10 Napoleon *MS*, *PP*] ~, *TSa*
36:13 pyramids] Pyramids *PP*
36:13 moment,] ~ *PP*
36:15 oblivion,] ~ *PP*
36:16 still will] will still *Per2*
36:16 preaching] ~, *Per2*
36:17 teaching] ~, *Per2*
36:17 commanding] ~, *Per2*
36:23 pulse,] ~ *Per1*, *Per2*
36:23 Roman:] ~— *Per2*
36:25 corn,] ~ *Per2*
36:25 to revert] and revert *Per2*
36:30 for *MS*, *PP*] *Om. Per1*
36:31 whereas] ~, *Per2*
36:31 usually,] ~ *PP*
36:32 up] ~, *Per2*
36:35 patera] *patera E1*
36:35 mundum] *mundum E1*
36:38 which remains...end, the...all things, *TSaR*, *Per1*] *Om. MS* which remains...end, the...all things; *TScR* which remains... end—the...all things, *Per2*
37:2 earth: and...its own unfailing ...is what is symbolised... [37:9] germ central within the living plasm. *P* And this patera, this symbol, is *TSaR*] earth: the ever-dividing living cell. This is the symbol *MS* earth: and...its unfailing...is symbolised...germ within the plasm, central. *P* And this patera, this symbol, is *TScR* earth. The patera, this symbol, is *TScC see also entries to* 37:10
37:3 sea, and] sea, *Per2*

37:5 him,] ~; *Per2*
37:6 vivid] *Om. Per2*
37:7 And this] This *Per2*
37:7 patera] *patera E1*
37:7 made to flower] given petals *Per2*
37:8 a] the *Per2*
37:10 patera] *patera E1*
37:11 woman,] ~ *PP*
37:12 jewellery *MS*, *PP*] jewelery *TScC* jewelry *Per1*
37:13 mundum] *mundum E1*
37:16 families *MS*, *PP*] Etruscan families *Per1*
37:19 had *PP*] has *MS*
37:28 B.C., at...a people, *TSaR*] B.C. *MS* B. C., at...a people, *Per1* B.C. at...a people, *Per2* B.C., at...a people, *PP*
37:32 spoilt *TSaR*] feeble *MS*
37:33 Lucumones] *Lucumones E1*
37:34 prince-magistrates, *TSaR*] ~ *MS*
37:34 seers, governors in religion, then *TSaR*, *PP*] chieftains, religious lords, *MS* seers...religion; then *TScR*, *Per2*
37:35 magistrates; then princes *TSaR*] magistrates, nobles *MS*
37:36 germanic] Germanic *Per2*, *E1*
37:39 life-significance. *P* And *Ed.*] life-significance. / So *MS* life-significance. So *TSa* life-significance. And *TSaR* life significance. And *Per2*
38:1 even *TSaR*] *Om. MS*
38:1 Sarcophagus] sarcophagus *Per2*
38:1 Magistrate,] magistrate *Per2*
38:2 alert] ~, *Per2*
38:4 So he lies, in...at Tarquinia. *TSaR*, *PP*] *Om. MS* So he lies in...at Tarquinia. *Per1*
38:6 well, and...difficult. On *TSaR*] well. And on *MS*, *Per2*
38:7 sarcophagus,] ~ *PP*
38:12 mundum] *mundum E1*

38:12 dish,] ~; *Per2*
38:13 laws. As] ~, as *Per2*
38:14 Lucumo.—Though] ~.
       Though *TSa*
       Lucomo—though *Per2*
38:15 Lucumones] Lucomones *Per2*
38:16 vases,] ~ *Per2*
38:17 black ware *MS, PP*] blackware
       Per1
38:18 bucchero,] "~," *Per2* bucchero,
       E1
38:22 best,] ~ *Per2*
38:23 days,] ~ *TSa*
38:24 bowls, ...bowls,] ~ ...~ *Per2*
38:24 pitchers,] ~ *Per2*
38:25 wine cups, *Ed.*] wine cups like
       saucers, *MS* wine-cups like
       saucers, *TSa* wine-cups, *TSaR*
       wine-cups *Per2, PP*

38:26 times,] ~ *PP*
38:27 taking perhaps] ~, ~, *Per2*
38:29 jars,] ~ *Per2*
38:29 and perfumes] perfumes *PP*
38:32 then *MS, PP*] *Om. Per1*
38:33 thousand *MS, PP*] thousands
       Per1
38:33 vases. So] ~, so *Per2*
38:35 B.C.] B. C. *Per1* B.C. *PP*
38:40 just] *Om. TSa*
39:8   begin *MS, Per1*] begins *TSa*
39:8   flowers,] ~,— *Per2*
39:9   red-and-black *TSaR*] *Om.
       MS*
39:13 bold] ~, *PP*
39:17 uplift,] "~," *Per2*
39:17 gothic *MS, PP*] Gothic *Per1,
       Per2, E1*
39:18 Roman. But] ~; but *Per2*

The Painted Tombs of Tarquinia 1.

The sequence of the texts from 43:1 to 45:25 and 46:17 to 47:29 ('ochre reds') is
MS, TSa, TSc, TSaR, TScR, TScC, Per1, PP, E1; *Per2* follows *TSaR* unless
otherwise indicated, but if *TSaR* differs from *TScR* or *TScC*, *Per2* follows the latter.
For the rest of the essay (see Introduction, pp. xliv–xlv), *TSa* is the base-text, and
the first state to be recorded.

43:3   1. *Ed.*] *Om. MS* 1 *PP*
43:4   We arranged...to the *MS, PP*]
       The *TScC*
43:4   tombs, which *MS, PP*] tombs
       TScC
43:5   out, *MS, PP*] out to visit them,
       TScC
43:6   town,] ~ *Per2*
43:6   out] *Om. TSa*
43:6   south-west *Per2, PP*]
       south-east *MS* south-/ east
       TSa south-/ west *TSaR*
       southwest *Per1*
43:9   gate] gates *Per2*
43:10 tableland] table land *Per2*
43:22 hill-top] hilltop *TScC* hill-/
       top *Per2*
43:24 Once it...tombs. Now *TSaR*]
       But *MS*

43:26 rough *TSaR*] *Om. MS* rough,
       Per2
44:1   rough *TSaR*] *Om. MS*
44:4   south-west *MS, Per2, PP*]
       southwest *TScC*
44:4   hilltops *MS, TScC*] hill-tops
       TSa, Per2
44:8   hole,] ~ *Per2*
44:12 splendid ~, *Per2*
44:14 Tomb *E1*] tomb *MS*
44:14 Hunting and Fishing *TSa,
       Per2, E1*] hunting and fishing
       MS, PP
44:15 so-called] so-/ called *Per1* so
       called *Per2, PP*
44:16 B.C.] b.c. *PP*
44:16 But it...[44:23] fragmentary
       little *TScR*] The little room is
       frescoed all round with sea

and sky, birds and fishes, and
MS see also entries to 44:23

44:16 But it *TScR, Per2*] It *TSaR*

44:16 damaged. Pieces *TScR*] ~,
pieces *TSaR*

44:17 wall-face are shattered *TScR*]
wall have fallen *TSaR*

44:18 tempera *TScR*] Om. *TSaR*

44:18 but disappointment *TScR*]
Om. *TSaR*

44:19 dimness, as...light, *TScR*]
dimness *TSaR*

44:19 see *TScR*] perceive *TSaR*

44:20 rising from the sea *TScR*] Om.
TSaR

44:21 wings. And *TScR*] wings. And
as *TSaR* wings; and *Per2*

44:21 closer. The *TScR,*] closer, we
see the *TSaR* closer we see
the *PP*

44:21 was *TScR*] is *TSaR*

44:22 sea and sky of light, *TScR*]
hazy sky and sea, with *TSaR*

44:22 flying *TSaR, PP*] Om. *Per1*

44:23 fragmentary *TScR*] Om. *TSaR*

44:26 man, shadowy but still
distinct, *TSaR*] man *MS*

44:28 oars,] ~ *TSa*

44:28 it] ~, *TSa*

44:29 up] ~, *Per2*

44:31 air. Above all, *TSaR*] air, while
MS

44:35 sex. The] ~. P The *Per2*

44:36 formed of *TSaR*] Om. *MS*

44:36 or ribbands *TSaR, PP*] Om.
MS or ribands *Per1, E1*

44:37 dull-gold *TScR*] dull gold *MS,*
Per1

44:38 blue and primrose *TSaR*]
green and blue *MS*

45:5 rise] ~, *Per2*

45:8 bows] ~, *Per2*

45:15 only it...because of the young
liveliness of it. There is
nothing impressive or grand.
But *TScR*] you want to be
impressed, awed, thrilled,
uplifted, don't look, because

you'll be disappointed. But
MS only it...because here is
the real etruscan {Etruscan
E1} liveliness and naturalness.
It is not impressive or grand.
But *TSaR* only it...because of
the young...grand; but *Per2*

45:17 through the...men...still sees
TScR, Per2] if you are content
with just a sense of *MS*
through the...man...still sees
Per1

45:18 life here...Etruscans knew
TScR, Per2] life, then here it is
MS

45:20 The little...[45:25] this
necropolis. *TSaR*] If it helps at
all to know that, to the
ancients, to the old Etruscans
certainly, all things had a life
and a soul of their own, since
the universe was a great body
of life: and secondly, that
everything had a symbolical
meaning, derived from its own
nature; then you can look for
second meanings even in
these natural and childish
pictures. But if you are a real
modern, and bored by
anything having any meaning
at all, you can glance and say:
MS see also entries to 45:25

45:21 deep] Om. *Per2*

45:21 perhaps] perhaps the *Per2*

45:23 perhaps under...wall. And]
probably under the
banqueting scene of the inner
wall; and *Per2*

45:24 the older...necropolis]
Tarquinia *Per2*

45:31 jewelled *MS, PP*] jeweled
TScC

45:33 garland,] ~— *PP*

45:35 amphora or wine-jar] ~, ~ ~,
Per2

45:37 flute;] ~— *Per2* ~: *PP*

45:38 funerals;] ~— *Per2*

45:40   maidens] ~, *Per2*
45:40   corner] ~, *Per2*
46:14   slave-men] slave-/ men *PP*
46:19   gate,] ~; *Per2*
46:23   hill-top *MS, Per2*] hilltop
        TScC
46:25   government] Government *E1*
46:31   hill-top *MS, Per2*] hilltop
        TScC
46:31   there:] ~; *Per2*
46:31   though] ~, *Per2*
46:33   And probably...Anyhow, today
        TScR] But it would not be like
        Cerveteri even then. As it is,
        MS see also entries to 46:37
46:33   probably *TSaR*] perhaps *Per2*
46:34   above-ground *TSaR*] above
        ground *Per2*
46:35   tomb entrances. But *TScR*,
        E1] tomb-entrances. But
        TSaR tomb entrances; but,
        Per2
46:36   Cerveteri, from Caere: *TScR*]
        Cerveteri, from Caere; *TSaR*
        Cerveteri: *Per2*
46:37   small *TSaR*] tiny *Per2*
46:39   The place is a warren *TSaR*]
        It is quite amusing *MS*
47:4   city states] city-states *PP*
47:6   today,] to-/ day *Per1* to-day
        PP
47:7   Etruria,] ~ *PP*
47:8   idiosyncrasy *Per1*]
        idiosyncracy *MS*
47:11   null. They] ~; they *Per2*
47:13   family,] family, and *Per2*
47:13   merchants,] ~ *Per2*
47:14   Etruscan *Ed.*] etruscan *MS*
47:16   past,] ~ *PP*
47:17   conception of *Per1, Per2*]
        conception/ *MS*
47:21   Tomb *TSa*] tomb *MS*
47:29   But] But here *Per2*
47:29   alive, the] ~. The *Per1* ~: the
        PP
47:29   ochre reds] ochre-reds *PP*
47:29   and blacks *TSaR*] blacks *TSa*
47:36   Christ;] ~, *PP*

48:5   dark-red] dark red *PP*
48:6   all,] ~ *Per2*
48:8   men] ~, *Per2*
48:8   loose] ~, *Per2*
48:9   *chlamys*] chlamys *PP*
48:11   hands, *TSa, PP*] ~; *TScC,*
        Per2
48:12   seven-stringed *TSaR*] seven
        stringed *TSa*
48:12   lyre,] ~; *Per2*
48:13   right. And] ~; and *Per2*
48:14   long] ~, *Per2, PP*
48:14   sandalled *TSa, PP*] sandaled
        Per1
48:14   olive trees] olive-trees *PP*
48:19   wraps] ~, *Per2*
48:20   sea-light] sea light *Per2*
48:21   olive trees] olive-trees *PP*
48:25   dancers, but...wild moments.
        TSa, PP] dancers. *TScC*
48:30   hetaerae] *hetaerae PP*
48:31   favourite *Per2, PP*] favorite
        TSa
48:38   she *TSaR*] and *TSa*
49:2   they too] ~, ~, *Per2*
49:4   died] ~, *PP*
49:5   couple,] ~ *PP*
49:6   say,] ~ *Per1*
49:7   further] farther *PP*
49:17   goes] go *PP*
49:17   common-place] commonplace
        TScC, Per2
49:18   light. Yet] ~; yet, *Per2*
49:21   unimposing,] ~ *Per2*
49:26   hill-top *MS, Per2*] hilltop
        TScC
49:26   gradually,] ~ *PP*
49:27   above day] above-day *Per2*
49:29   mourners, *TSaR, Per2*] ~
        TScR
49:32   chamber,] ~ *PP*
49:33   15] fifteen *Per1, Per2*
49:33   11 feet] eleven feet *Per1, Per2*
        eleven *PP*
49:35   further] farther *PP*
49:36   rock floor] rock-floor *E1*
49:36   two *TSaR*] about two *TSa*
49:40   are! *TSaR*] ~. *TSa*

50:4   bacchic *TSa, PP*] Bacchic *Per1*

50:5   long] ~, *PP*

50:8   little trees *TScC*] littñe trees *TSa* littñe trees *Per2*

50:9   naïve *TScC*] naive *TSa*

50:13   anima *Ed.*] anima *TSa*

50:15   scarf] ~, *Per2*

50:17   Yet] ~, *Per1*

50:22   days,] ~ *Per1*

50:23   natures. The...[50:32] towns. P It *TSa, PP*] natures. It *TScC see also entries to* 50:30

50:25   selves,] ~ *PP*

50:25   their bodies *TSaR*] themselves *TSa*

50:26   serious or *TSaR*] great or *TSa* serious and *Per2*

50:28   today,] ~ *Per2* to-day, *PP*

50:29   true, *TSaR*] true, beyond lies, *TSa*

50:30   it in] it into *PP*

50:30   so,] ~ *Per2*

50:32   The red...see!—But] "~ ~...~!" But *TScC* "~ ~...~!"—but *Per2*

50:35   Apparently] And apparently *Per2*

50:36   Man all...his bodily godly self. *TSa, PP*] Om. *TScC* Man all...his bodily self. *Per2*

50:37   know] know that *Per2*

50:38   vermilion *TSaR*] ~, *TSa*

50:38   *minium*] minium *PP*

50:39   ch.] Om. *PP*

50:39   She] "~ *Per2, PP*

50:39   portrayed...portrayed *TSaR, TScC*] pourtrayed...pourtrayed *TSa, PP*

50:40   vermilion—] ~... *PP*

51:2   nativity.—] ~. *TScC* ~." *Per2, PP*

51:3   It is...[52:16] they are.] Om. *TScC see also entries to* 52:13

51:3   is then] ~, ~, *Per2*

51:4   red...a strong red *PP*] red...s strong red *TSa* strong red in colour *Per2*

51:7   beach,] ~ *PP*

51:7   of a lovely] Om. *Per2*

51:7   ruddy colour, dark...Indian.] ruddy in colour. *Per2*

51:8   good] great *Per2*

51:9   minium] *minium Per2*

51:12   narrow fringed]

51:12   narrow-fringed *Per2* ~, ~ *PP*

51:14   We see] One sees *Per2*

51:15   woman] women *Per2*

51:15   is dark-haired] are dark haired *Per2*

51:15   she] they *Per2*

51:15   a courtesan] courtesans *Per2*

51:17   Romans] the Romans *Per2*

51:17   period] time *Per2*

51:18   an honest woman] the women *Per2*

51:19   did, even...table. If] did. So, if *Per2*

51:19   woman] women *Per2*

51:20   straight,] stiff *Per2*

51:21   Here,] ~ ~ *Per2*

51:21   calmly] at ease *Per2*

51:21   and one shows] showing *Per2*

51:22   lecti] *lecti Per2, PP*

51:22   the couches] or couches *Per2*

51:23   delicate] delicate little *Per2*

51:26   No! *TSaR*] no *TSa* "No!" *Per2*

51:27   side] ~, *PP*

51:28   apparently *TScR*] perhaps *TSa* presumably *TSaR*

51:28   ointment jar] ointment-jar *PP*

51:38   sitting] ~, *Per2*

51:39   an *PP*] Om. *TSa* the *Per2*

52:4   book] ~, *Per2, PP*

52:5   water-colour] water-color *TScC* water-/ colour *Per2, PP*

52:6   yet] ~, *PP*

52:13   Greekified] ~; *PP*

52:20   strange,] ~ *PP*

52:23   maiden] ~, *Per2*

52:24   wonderful,] ~ *Per2*

52:27   Above the...[53:8] and significant. *TSa, PP*] Om. *TScC see also entries to* 53:3

52:29   them, ~ *PP*

52:29   lions] ~, *PP*
52:32   border] ~, *Per2*
53:2   —On *TSaR*] ~ *TSa, Per2, PP*
53:3   these etruscan legs, *TSaR*] the legs of this Etruscan, *TSa* these Etruscan legs, *Per2, E1*
53:3   they are *TSaR*] he is *TSa*
53:10   gable,] ~ *PP*
53:11   udders] ~, *Per2, PP*
53:12   flute player] flute-player *Per2, PP*
53:12   zither player] zither-player *PP*
53:16   room] ~, *PP*
53:19   head-dress] ~, *PP*
53:23   side. He] ~. *P* He *Per2*
53:26   or *E1*] of *TSa*
53:27   dandelion-stems *TSaR*] dandelion stems *TSa*
53:29   faded *TSa, PP*] ~, *Per1*
53:31   key pattern] key-pattern *PP*
53:31   mantles. *P* The *TSa, PP*] ~. The *TScC*
53:32   *Dipinti E1*] *Depinti TSa*
53:33   amphoras] amphorae *E1*
53:34   The amphoras…[54:30] all. *P* So we *TSa, PP*] The amphoras…[53:36] out. On…[53:38] the couch. In the *Tomba* [54:21]…[54:26] each time. *P* So we *TScC Om. Per1 see also entries to* 54:23
53:34   amphoras] amphoræ *PP* amphorae *E1*
53:37   slave boy] slave-boy *PP*
53:39   *cylix*] *cylix, PP* kylix, *E1*
53:39   wine-bowl] ~, *PP*
53:39   holds,] ~ *PP*
54:15   leopards] ~, *Per2*
54:18   another] ~, *Per2*
54:19   fish-tails] fish tails *Per2*
54:20   sea-board] seaboard *PP*
54:23   east] East *PP*
54:23   elegant] ~, *PP*
54:31   much,] ~ *PP*
54:34   wilfully!] ~. *PP*
54:36   away!— *TSaR*] ~. *TSa* ~! *Per1, Per2*
54:37   wine] ~, *PP*

55:1   For no…the gods.— *TSaR*] for ~…~ ~.— *TSa* For ~…~ ~. *Per1* "For ~…~ ~." *Per2, PP*
55:5   Which is…[56:10] tomorrow. # ——— # / There *Ed.*] Which is…tomorrow. # / *P* There *TSa* Which is…tomorrow. # ——— *P* There *TSaR P* There *Per1* Which is…to-morrow. *P* There *Per2* Which is…to-morrow. # *P* There *PP see also entries to* 55:36
55:16   door *TSaR*] wall *TSa*
55:18   right, *TSaR*] ~ *TSa*
55:19   dancers,] ~ *PP*
55:25   with their long tails, *TSaR*] *Om. TSa*
55:31   design: two *TSaR*] design of *TSa*
55:36   shrinking *TSaR*] wincing *TSa*
56:11   hippocampi:] ~; *PP*
56:17   egg! *TSaR*] ~. *TSa*
56:26   depths,] ~ *PP*
56:28   to life, self-assertion *TSaR*] *Om. TSa*
56:29   knew;] ~: *PP*
56:31   ugliness;] ~: *PP*
56:38   to the *TScC*] to/ *TSa*
56:40   Etruscan,] ~ *PP*
56:40   alive:] ~; *Per2, PP*
56:40   lived:] ~; *PP*
57:10   inspiration] inspirations *Per2*
57:11   anima] *anima Per2, PP*
57:13   stream] ~, *PP*
57:15   anima] *anima Per2, PP*
57:17   handful] ~, *PP*
57:26   myriad:] ~; *PP*
58:6   Pharaoh] ~, *PP*
58:6   Belshazzar] ~, *PP*
58:6   Ashurbanipal *E1*] Ashiburnipal *TSa*
58:6   or Tarquin; or, *TScR*] or, or Tarquin; *TSaR* or Tarquin; *PP see notes*
58:7   *de crescendo*] decrescendo *E1*
58:22   east] East *PP*

58:25 treasure house] treasure-/ house *Per2, PP*
58:26 their] their own *Per2*
58:30 are *TSaR*] were *TSa*
58:33 safe-guard] safeguard *Per2, PP*
59:16 religion. There] ~, there *Per2*
59:17 For they...high-born and the pure-bred. *TScR*] Om. *TSa* For they...high born, the pure bred. *TSaR* For they...high-born, the pure-bred. *Per2, PP*
59:22 So,] ~ *Per2*
59:22 simple,] ~ *Per2*
59:26 artizans] artisans *Per1, Per2*
59:28 east] East *PP*
59:32 But the...[59:35] priest-rule. *TSa, PP*] Om. *Per1*
59:37 Socrates,] ~ *Per2*
59:39 Then again...please themselves. *TSa, PP*] Om. *Per1*
60:5 death;] ~ *Per2*
60:9 In the...[64:12] the symbolism *TSa, PP*] Symbolism *Per1 see also entries to 64:10*
60:13 also, whose inwardness *TSaR*] like that *TSa*
60:14 womb] the womb *Per2*
60:15 are devoured back *TSaR*] return *TSa*
60:22 the dolphin] The ~ *PP*
60:24 He is...deeps of death.] Om. *Per2*
60:33 anima *Ed.*] anima *TSa*
60:35 christian *Ed.*] Christian *TSa*
60:37 anima] *anima Per2, PP*
60:38 pharaohs] Pharaohs *PP*
60:39 east] East *PP*
61:2 underwater] under water *PP*
61:5 phallus and] Om. *Per2*
61:8 maiden,] ~ *PP*
61:8 duck] ~, *PP*

61:11 consciousness] ~, *PP*
61:25 flight,] ~ *PP*
61:26 suddenly-roused *TSaR*] suddenly roused *TSa, PP*
61:26 birds] ~, *PP*
61:28 corresponded,] ~ *PP*
61:29 vice versa] *vice versa PP*
61:38 way,] ~ *PP*
61:40 you are] your are *Per2*
62:1 thing,] ~ *PP*
62:4 on,] ~ *PP*
62:7 upon,] ~ *PP*
62:12 was *PP*] were *TSa*
62:19 of consciousness *TSaR*] Om. *TSa*
62:19 him,] ~ *Per2*
62:20 death," *Per2, PP*] ~" *TSa* ~", *TSaR*
62:26 question. P It *Per2, PP*] ~./ It *TSa*
62:31 infallibility] ~, *E1*
62:38 attempt at *TSaR*] Om. *TSa*
62:38 research *TSaR*] thought *TSa*
63:17 conscious *TSaR*] Om. *TSa*
63:20 vividness,] ~ *PP*
63:23 the soul...not dual; *TSaR*] even the soul has its dual aspect; *TSa*
63:31 deer,] ~ *PP*
63:31 lamb,] ~ *PP*
63:34 and indicating *Per2, E1*] and indication *TSa*
63:34 beasts *TSaR*] lions *TSa*
63:36 endless endless *TSa, TSc*] endless, endless *TSaR* endless *Per2 see notes*
63:37 cattle, *TScR, Per2*] ~ *TSa*
64:2 death; *TSaR*] ~: *TSa, TSc, Per2*
64:4 deer] ~, *E1*
64:5 These too...These too] ~ ~, ...~ ~, *Per2* ~, ~, ...~, ~, *PP*
64:6 Romans;] ~: *PP*
64:10 in] in the *Per2*
64:16 emotion] emotions *Per2*
64:20 quail] ~, *Per1*

Photographs

The captions in *E1* have been collated with DHL's own. *E1* had a list in the preliminary pages, entitled 'LIST OF ILLUSTRATIONS', with the captions given in upper and lower case; those under the photographs were in small capitals (the latter is not recorded unless there is another variant). *E1* always began with the name of the Etruscan city followed by a full stop (e.g. 'Cerveteri.') and omitted the complete title of the essay and any associated numbers (e.g. no. 15 simply read 'Tarquinia.' in place of DHL's 'Sketches of Etruscan Places III. The Painted Tombs of Tarquinia (1)'). All further descriptions of the photograph were omitted in *E1* (e.g. no. 14 did not have 'The "eye"…bridegroom.'). None of these features is recorded. *Per1* had lengthy captions, some echoing the text and others including material cut from it – see Explanatory note to 160:2; none of these features is recorded. (The following entries are cited by illustration number of this edition.)

2 with etruscan inscriptions] *Om. E1*
3 (interior)] *Om. E1*
4 *Regolini-Galassi Tomb*] The Regolini-Galassi Tomb *E1* THE REGOLINI-GALESSI TOMB *E1* (*photo caption*)
5 (interior)] *Om. E1*
7 [Rome…Cerveteri]] Cerveteri. Terra-cotta Heads on Sarcophagus now in the Villa Giulia Museum, Rome *E1*
10 corner of city] Corner of the City *E1*
13 terra-cottas…period.] Terra-cottas of the Archaic Period *E1*
14 vases with…the head] Vases with Eye-pattern and Head *E1*
24 The] *Om. E1*
34 The] *Om. E1*
36 boar-hunt] Boar-hunt *E1*
37 Farewell scene &] *Om. E1*
37 departure…underworld] Departure by Boat for the Underworld *E1*
41 ash-chest] Ash-chest *E1*
41 dogs] Dogs *E1*

The Painted Tombs of Tarquinia 2.

The sequence of the states of the text is: *MS, TSa, TSb, TSc, TSaR, TSbR, TScR, TSaC*. *PP* follows *TSaR*, and *E1* follows *PP* unless otherwise indicated. For 123:13–124:28 and 128:6–131:2 (see Introduction, pp. xlv–xlvi), *TSa* is the base-text.

115:1 IV. *TScR*] *Om. MS* IV *TSaR*
115:3 2. *TSaR*] II *MS* II. *TSa* 2 *PP*
115:4 gate,] ~ *PP*
115:5 this] the *TSa*
115:6 gate,] ~ *PP*
115:7 Dazio] *Dazio E1*
115:9 brush-wood] brushwood *PP*
115:9 up,] ~ *PP*

115:12 other *TSbR*] many other *MS*, *TSc*
115:18 doubt] ~, *PP*
115:19 produce:] ~; *PP*
115:21 soil:] ~; *PP*
115:25 bodies:] ~; *PP*
115:26 linen:] ~; *PP*
115:27 pipes,] ~; *PP*

115:33 fronts, painted, *TSbR*] ~ ~ *MS, TSc*
115:33 terra cottas] terracottas *TSa* terra-cottas *PP*
115:36 white, *MS, PP*] ~ *TSa*
115:36 ghost-like] ghostlike *PP*
116:7 temple,] ~ *PP*
116:7 to perform...[116:21] said. Then *TScR*] and prepared to hear for a moment or two any plea from the free people, as he sat there proud and yet responsible in his chair within the chariot, as a nobleman and a sacred magistrate, his robe loosely draped, leaving bare his breast and his body. The naked peasant standing before him would humbly, but hotly urge his own case, and the Lucumo would listen in silence. Till {silence till *TSa*} the end— *MS see also entries to* 116:19
116:9 trimmed, *TScR*] ~ *TSaR*
116:9 oriental *TSaR*] Oriental *PP*
116:10 rich mantle *TSbR*] mantle, or wrap *TSaR* mantle or wrap *PP*
116:12 chair of *TSbR*] chair in *TSaR*
116:13 And the *TSbR*] The *TSaR*
116:14 forward a little *TSbR*] a little forward, *TSaR*
116:14 temple; *TScR, PP*] ~, *TSaR*
116:15 sitting *TSbR*] sitting erect *TSaR*
116:15 chair *TSaR, TScR*] ~, *TSbR*
116:15 in his chariot, *TScR*] in the chariot, *TSaR Om. TSbR*
116:15 would drop...shoulders and...and shoulders. *TScR*] and bare-shouldered and bare-breasted, wait {waits *PP*} for the people. *TSaR* would drop...shoulders, and...and shoulders. *TSbR*
116:17 fear *TSaR, TScR*] reverence *TSbR*
116:17 And *TSbR*] But *TSaR*

116:18 lift up his arms in the salute, and *TScR*] lift up his arms in salute, and *TSaR Om. TSbR*
116:19 state some difficulty or ask *TScR*] state his difficulty, or to plead *TSaR* make a complaint or to seek *TSbR*
116:19 Lucumo, seated...knowledge and...said. Then a *TScR*] Lucumo, seated...knowledge for the people, would listen till the end. Then a *TSaR* Lucumo would listen in silence, glowing within a different aura, like a mountain glowing in the distance, until he had heard all. Then he utters a brief *TSbR*
116:23 citizens *TSaR*] peasants *MS*
116:25 possible,] ~ *PP*
116:27 home] ~, *TSa*
116:28 living,] ~; *PP*
116:29 we *TSa*] were *MS*
116:30 Today,] To-day *PP*
116:34 the] a *PP*
116:34 altogether,] ~ *PP*
116:35 only feasible] feasible only *PP*
116:37 it] It *PP*
117:2 Japanese *TSaC, PP*] Japonese *MS*
117:4 government] Government *E1*
117:15 Er—c'è—] ~——~—— *PP* Er—c'è—— *E1*
117:15 he] He *PP*
117:16 Tzar] Tsar *PP*
117:16 off,] ~ *PP*
117:18 say—] ~, *PP*
117:19 Jerusalem.—] ~: *PP*
117:19 beefsteak—er—] ~—~ *PP*
117:20 potatoes—] ~. *PP*
117:23 Albertino—] ~, *PP*
117:24 by the Chinese,] "~ ~ ~," *PP*
117:24 whispers)—] ~), *PP*
117:24 but...frogs.] "~...~." *PP*
117:25 There are what?] "~ ~ ~?" *PP*
117:25 *Le rane TSbR*] Le rane *MS*,

TSc "Le rane PP "Le rane
E1

117:25 frogs!—] ~!" PP

117:25 What...frogs?—] "~...~?"
PP

117:25 I'll show you!—] "~ ~ ~!"
PP

117:27 frogs' TSbR, PP] frogs MS,
TSc

117:27 way,] ~ PP

117:32 word,] ~ PP

117:34 semi-colons] semicolons PP

117:35 book,—] ~— PP

117:36 table-cloth] tablecloth PP

117:38 ecco! pane!—pane!—si
capisce] ecco!
pane!—pane!—si capisce E1

117:39 book—] ~ PP

117:40 pane, e vino TSbR, E1] pane, e
vino MS, TSc

118:1 name] name TSa

118:1 Name! You] you TSa

118:2 Albertino!] ~. TSa

118:2 le rane] le rane E1

118:4 frogs' legs PP] frogs-legs MS

118:5 underneath,] ~ PP

118:9 postage-stamps] postage
stamps PP

118:12 —Er!] "~!" PP

118:12 But the...Chinese!—] "~
~...~!" PP

118:13 insist] insist that TSa

118:14 —Er!...Asia!—] "~!
...~!"— PP

118:22 Dazio PP] dazio MS Dazio E1

118:29 furthest] farthest PP

118:34 libeccio] libeccio PP

118:35 high-way] highway PP

118:38 mountain top] mountain-top
PP

119:5 while,] ~ PP

119:12 half mile] half-mile PP

119:16 Wert—] ~, PP

119:18 of—;] ~; PP

119:26 government] Government E1

119:31 stoical] ~, PP

119:31 not much...anything— PP] not
much...anything,— MS not

much worth—doesn't amount
to anything—E1 see notes

120:4 head-stones] headstones PP

120:4 and the...of the mediaeval
aqueduct...a dip, TSbR] Om.
MS and the...of a mediaeval
acqueduct {mediæval
aqueduct PP}...a dip, TSaR
and the...of the mediaeval
acqueduct...a dip, TScR and
the...of a mediaeval
aqueduct...a dip, E1

120:9 camomiles] camomile PP

120:9 mound] ~, PP

120:9 which was once a tumulus,
TSaR, TScR] Om. MS which
no doubt was once a tumulus,
TSbR

120:12 on] Om. TSa

120:12 wheat,] ~— PP

120:12 which still...all tumuli, TSaR]
Om. MS which still...all
tumuli— PP

120:23 un po' di pornografico! TSaR]
un po' di pornografico! MS un
po' di pornografico! TScR, PP

120:25 me] us TSa

120:28 there is...side walls, TSaR]
Om. MS

120:35 po' di pornografico] po' di
pornografico E1

120:36 bull TSbR] Om. MS

120:38 pornografico,"] ~" PP
pornografico" E1

120:40 east] East PP

120:40 Cyprus TSaR] Assyria MS

121:4 fountain head] fountain-head
TSa

121:11 east] East PP

121:14 What...means?—] "~...~?"
PP

121:14 Ach] "~ PP

121:15 drinking trough]
drinking-trough PP

121:16 more!—] ~!" PP

121:16 And...sword?—] "~...~?"
PP

121:16 Oh...enemy.—] "~...~." PP

121:17 And...lions?—] "~...~?" *PP*
121:17 Ach...fountain.—] "~...~." *PP*
121:20 so-called] so called *PP*
121:21 —And...symbol?—] "~...~?" *PP*
121:22 —Here no!] "~ ~!" *PP*
121:22 —Merely a decoration!] "~ ~ ~!" *PP*
121:23 —Which perhaps...cannot believe. *TScR*] *Om. MS see also entries to* 121:25
121:23 Which *TSaR*] which *PP*
121:23 perhaps is *TSbR*] is perhaps *TSaR*
121:23 artist *TSaR, TScR*] painter *TSbR*
121:24 more *TSaR, TScR*] *Om. TSbR*
121:24 idea of its being *TSbR*] feeling for it, as *TSaR*
121:24 than *TSaR, TScR*] any more than *TSbR*
121:24 an English *TSbR*] a modern *TSaR*
121:25 today *TScR*] *Om. TSaR*
121:25 we *TScR*] that we *TSaR*
121:25 believe *TSaR, TScR*] admit *TSbR*
121:27 —Can...it?] "~...~?" *PP*
121:29 —Do...means?] "~...~?" *PP*
121:30 Nobody knows.] "~ ~." *PP*
121:32 rams' *PP*] ram's *MS*
121:33 corners *PP*] corner *MS*
121:39 head,] ~ *E1*
121:40 So that this is the proper Chimaera.— *TScR*] *Om. MS* So this is the proper chimaera:— *TSaR* This is the old chimaera.— *TSbR* So this...Chimæra. *PP* So this...Chimaera. *E1*
122:3 What is...and neck?—] "~ ~...~ ~?" *PP*
122:5 Nothing!—] "~!" *PP*
122:5 It meant...facto meaningless.] It meant...nothing except the A.B.C. {A B C *PP*} of facts, means {facts means

PP}...meaning, it is ipso facto {meaning it is, *ipso facto PP*} meaningless. *TSa, TSc* The Germans seem to think that the Etruscans used the old east-Mediterranean symbols merely as decoration-patterns, as we still use the lotus or the key-pattern, knowing no more about the meaning of the chimaera or the man-faced bull than a modern house-painter knows about the egg-and-dart pattern. But then science always believes what it wants to believe. Scientists don't like symbols: they are far-fetched. Mommsen didn't like the thought of the Etruscans: they too were far-fetched. And that is enough for the scientist. Neither Etruscan nor symbol ever really existed. *TSbR see note on* 122:1
122:10 Chimaera *TSaR, E1*] Chimaera (so-called) *MS* Chimæra *PP*
122:14 serpent] ~, *E1*
122:15 lion,] ~ *E1*
122:15 back. *P* Though this...[122:22] cosmic religion. *TScR*] *Om. MS see also entries to* 122:19
122:15 back. *P* Though *TSaR, TScR*] back. And though *TSbR*
122:16 Chimaera, with...In fact, *TSaR, TScR, E1*] Chimaera of the Greek myth, with the two wounds, in hip and throat, given by Bellerophon, still it is not meaningless, just a fantastic imagination. *TSbR* Chimæra, with...In fact, *PP*
122:18 the *TScR*] *Om. TSaR*
122:19 certain very...gods are...cosmic religion. *TScR*] certain very...gods,

are...cosmic religion. *TSaR*
exact esoteric knowledge, the
Chimaera represents a precise
esoteric conception much
older than the myth of
Bellerophon. *TSbR*

122:23 arises] arise *E1*

122:25 was more or less aware of
TScR, PP] wished to convey
MS was more or less is aware
of *TSaR* more or less is aware
of *TSbR*

122:29 mundum] *mundum E1*

122:30 a *personal*] a personal *TSa* by a
personal *E1*

122:40 ram] a ram *E1*

123:4   became] becomes *TSa* might
become *TSaR*

123:5   interrupted *TSaR*] lost *MS*

123:6   blood stream] blood-stream
TSa

123:6   and some always *TSaR*] which
sometimes *MS*

123:9   modern *TSaR*] German *MS*

123:10 the obvious *TSaR*] ideas
MS

123:10 can have *TSbR*] have *MS* has
TSaR

123:14 them. They] ~; they *TSa*

123:20 altered. You] ~, you *TSa* ~:
you *PP*

123:22 the drawing *TSa*] his drawing
MS

123:26 india-rubber] indiarubber *PP*

123:30 want to...[123:40] "drawing."
It...[124:8] and shade. *PP*]
want to spy. *P* The stone bed
goes round the tomb, round
the inner chamber as well as
the outer, but no bier or
sarcophagus is left, nothing
but the walls with the artist's
successes and mistakes; and
sometimes, the sockets in the
rock, into which the legs of
the bier fitted. *MS* want to...
'drawing'. It...and shade. *TSa*
want to...Etruscan...[123:31]

Etruscan... "drawing."
It...Etruscan...and shade. *E1*

124:10 alive and...thing had a *TSa*]
as a looming vision, not
merely as a defined fact of the
mind; and where things had
MS

124:12 outline *TSa*] outlines *MS*

124:12 its *TSa*] their *MS* see note on
124:28

124:13 was *TSa*] were *MS*

124:13 or vitally *TSa*] Om. *MS*

124:16 In those days *TSa*] Then *MS*

124:17 nag; *TSaR*] ~: *MS* see note on
124:28

124:17 suave-skinned *TSa*] visionary
MS

124:19 travel, with...the blood, *TSa*]
menace or glowed with
promise, red, *MS*

124:21 weight *TSa*] wind *MS*

124:21 Then also, a *TSa*] A *MS*

124:25 force: *MS*] ~; *TSa*

124:25 the herd-lord, *TSa*] Om. *MS*

124:26 cows: *MS*] ~; *TSa*

124:27 milk: *MS*] ~; *TSa*

124:27 he who...of fertility; *TSa*] Om.
MS he who...symbolizing...of
fertility; *PP*

124:31 and self-consciousness, *TSbR*]
Om. *MS* and
self-consciousness *TSaR*

124:32 procreation *TSaR*] milk *MS*

124:36 lick up...hot tongue *TSaR*]
destroy *MS*

124:38 reeking *TSaR*] vast *MS*

125:1   potential *TSaR*] conscious *MS*

125:3   only] Om. *PP*

125:4   symbolically] only symbolically
PP

125:5   lion] ~, *PP*

125:5   divine *TSaR*] sacred *MS*

125:6   germ, the...God...it so.
TSbR] germ. *MS* germ,
the...god...it so. *TSaR*

125:11 unconsciously:] ~, *PP*

125:12 world,] ~ *PP*

125:13 fear,] ~ *PP*

125:15 meaning, *TSaR*] ~ *MS, TSb*
125:15 dread,] ~ *PP*
125:16 arose *TSaR*] came *MS*
125:18 inter-related] inter-/ related *TSa* interrelated *PP*
125:21 power,] ~ *PP*
125:22 true *TSaR*] Om. *MS*
125:23 Where they…truly adult…vice versa. *TSbR*] Om. *MS* Where they…true adults…*vice versa. TSaR* Where they…true adults…vice versa. *PP*
125:25 "pornografico" *Ed.*] '~' *MS* '*pornografico*' *E1*
125:25 Bulls *Ed.*] Bull *MS*
125:27 them,] ~ *PP*
125:28 the same…the panther. *TSbR*] and the meaning which is like a stone fallen into the consciousness, {into consciousness, *TSa*} sending its rings ebbing out and out, to the extremes. *MS* the same archaic innocence, accepting life, knowing all about it, and *feeling* the meaning, which is like a stone fallen into consciousness, sending its rings ebbing out and out, to the extremes. *TSaR*
125:32 They are…bull; not…the panther. *TScR*] The words moral and immoral have no force. *MS* They are…bull: not…the panther. *TSbR*
125:34 There is…man-faced bull *MS, TSb*] Some acts—what Dennis would call flagrant obscenity—the man-faced bull accepts them calmly {accepts calmly *PP*} lying down; against other acts, he {acts he *PP*} charges *TSaR*
125:36 milk and procreation *TScR*] milk *MS* milk and increase *TSbR*
125:38 far off] far-off *TSa*

126:1 doorway-to-a-tomb] doorway to a tomb *E1*
126:1 momentous, one hand to the brow. *TSaR, TScR*] momentous. *MS* momentous one…brow. *TSbR*
126:3 No!] "~!" *PP*
126:3 The…[126:6] mourning—] "~…~." *PP*
126:7 Then…doing?] "~…~?" *PP*
126:13 altar] ~, *PP*
126:14 hip. *TSaR*] hip. And milk-giving life will be torn in two between them, these two passions of Before and After, of Night and Day, of the two extremes, of the fiery and watery elements, of the upward and downward forces, of the blood-drinking powers, which can be also life-giving powers. *MS*
126:17 skin girdle] skin-girdle *PP*
126:21 big limbed] big-limbed *TSa*
126:29 augur *Ed.*] Augur *MS* augur, *PP*
126:32 tomb,] ~ *PP*
126:36 blind-folded] blindfolded *PP*
126:36 raging] ~, *PP*
126:37 sport,] ~ *PP*
126:39 so *real*] *so* real *TSa*
127:10 play."—But *Ed.*] ~"./ —But *MS* ~". / But *TSa* ~". *P* But *TSaR* ~." *P* But *PP*
127:13 the man *TSa*] man *MS*
127:14 painted] Painted *PP*
127:20 And the…turned by the Greeks into…his dogs. *TSbR*] Om. *MS* And the…turned in Greece into…his dogs. *TSaR*
127:24 around] round *PP*
127:27 horse-like] horselike *PP*
127:28 Velasquez] Velazquez *PP*
127:29 these; so *TSaR*] these, *MS, TSc*
127:30 what] —~ *PP*
127:31 who sees] ~ ~, *PP*

127:33 instantaneous *TSaR*]
momentaneous *MS, TSb*
127:35 shall *represent*] *shall* represent
TSa
127:36 We have...[128:4] external
form. *TScR*] That is why a
camera is so unsatisfactory: its
eye is flat, it sees only a tithe
of what the living eye sees; it
is, so to speak, wall-eyed. *MS*
That is...flat, it is related only
to a negative thing inside the
box: whereas inside our living
box there is a decided
positive. *TSaR see also entries to*
128:4
127:38 him *TScR*] his *TSbR*
127:39 experience *TScR*] knowledge
TSbR
127:39 him: *TScR*] ~; *TSbR*
127:40 frenzy, *TScR*] ~ *TSbR*
128:1 a *TScR*] the *TSbR*
128:2 and potent. But *TScR*] of
potency. And *TSbR*
128:2 in us *TScR*] Om. *TSbR*
128:3 pruned *TScR*] mutilated
TSbR
128:4 static *TScR*] Om. *TSbR*
128:7 We have...aqueduct...dip,
then...the cemetery *PP*] Then
MS We have...acqueduct...
dip then...the cemetery *TSa*
128:11 under-ground] underground
PP
128:12 in the centre a massive square
TSa] a *MS*
128:13 sea-man] seaman *PP*
128:13 snake legs] snake-legs *PP*
128:14 roof; two...the first. *TSa*]
roof. *MS*
128:17 cavern. The...[128:30] is
dead. *TSaR*] cavern, and the
typhon has not much
meaning, and he is painted in
a new manner, with deep
shade and modelling of the
flesh—rather like Pompei,
uninteresting. We go up, not

sorry to be in the air. *MS see
also entries to* 128:26
128:18 modelling, *TSaR, TScR*] ~
TSb
128:21 Dennis] ~, *TSbR, PP*
128:22 ago] ~, *TSbR, PP*
128:26 "roses," *PP*] '~,' *TSa*
128:26 "one" *PP*] '~' *TSa*
128:32 B.C.] B.C. *PP*
128:34 B.C. *MS*] B.C., *TSa* B.C., *PP*
128:35 B.C.] B.C. *PP*
128:37 supposed to be *TSa*] Om. *MS*
128:37 V] fifth *PP*
129:3 great, *MS*] ~ *TSa*
129:4 much damaged]
much-damaged *PP*
129:9 Pompei] Pompeian *PP*
129:10 free *TSa*] stiff *MS*
129:11 at the...is gone; *TSa*] Om. *MS*
129:12 them. There is...[129:40]
with a *TSa*] them. *P* One of
the secrets of the etruscan
charm in the tomb-paintings
is their conveying of a sense of
pleasant physical flow between
all the people and animals and
fishes and birds and even
plants. They are all *living*,
living together, and there is a
certain fecund contact or
unison of life between them.
In the delightful banqueting
scene of the Tomb of the
Painted Vases, one *feels* that
one is in the presence of a real
family, that glows with a fresh
unison of life. The wife
reclines with the husband on
the banqueting couch, in
fresh, natural intimacy: a thing
which could never have
happened in Greece or in
Rome at the same period, for
there women were never
allowed at the banquet—
except perhaps a courtesan—
and men were as little as
possible in the company of

their wives. In Etruria, it must have been different. The family must have banqueted gaily together, mother and father, boys and maidens, while the slaves skipped happily away to the wine-jars, or brought in food, or made music. Even the slaves, even the dogs and birds join in and are part of the scene, part of the warm life-flow. *P* And this is conveyed perfectly in the old tombs. It is what one would call the unison of touch: they are all naturally and vividly in touch with one another, there is no breach in the flow of natural contact, as there was always, apparently, in Rome, when slaves or women or children were present. Very rarely in art, even in modern art, is there any sense of touch between the painted people. In Michelangelo, the Lord touches Adam very gingerly, as one might touch a snail. And usually in art, figures are either alone, or they lay their arms on one another as if they were so many chair-backs, or they roll together like so many potatoes, or they lay hold of one another, but there is no real contact. A man like Botticelli can pose three women together, but they are no more in touch than if they were knives and forks. Giotto, with his clumsy figures, has the sense of touch: so has Piero della Francesco. But with the really clever ones, it is lacking entirely. The figures are just all stuck in a bunch— or apart—or rolling in heaps

—*P* But the one vivid quality, the rarest and most precious, and one that the Etruscans possess *par excellence* is the quality of touch. When this man banqueting delicately touches the woman beside him under the chin, it is a beautiful gesture of sensitive contact. The woman is really *with* him: not just stuck next to him. *P* This is entirely lost in the later tombs. In the Tomb of the Shields, of the third Century, the *MS see also entries to* 129:39

129:13 forms,] ~ *PP*
129:17 B.C.] B.C. *PP*
129:28 once,] ~ *PP*
129:32 B.C.] B.C. *PP*
129:37 life,] ~ *PP*
129:38 tomb—] ~, *PP*
129:38 Shields—*TSaR*] ~ *TSa* ~, *PP*
129:39 third century *PP*] Third Century *TSa*
130:1 taking *TSa*] is taking *MS*
130:4 all on...nothing inside *TSa*] modern, self-conscious *MS*
130:4 Yet they...today...child-like ...naïve...are empty. *Ed.*] They are really only aware of themselves, and the flow of contact, like a warm light, is gone, dead. *MS* Yet they... today...child-like...naive... are empty. *TSa* Yet they... to-day...childlike...naïve... are empty. *PP*
130:8 The egg...those men and women...gone cold. *Ed.*] *Om. MS* The egg...those men and woman...gone cold. *TSa* The egg...that man and woman...gone cold. *PP*
130:17 The old...[130:28] inadequate fiction. *TSa*] *Om. MS see also entries to* 130:27

130:26 religions, *TSa*] ~ *PP*
130:26 afterlife *TSa*] after-life *PP*
130:27 Idea, *TSa*] ~ *PP*
130:27 afterlife*TSa*] after-life *PP*
130:30 But naturally *TSaR*] Curiously *MS* But, naturally *PP*
130:31 evidences] ~, *PP*
130:35 mean little…in some] *Om. TSa*
130:40 evidence of…indeed! Even the word of a Theopompus is enough. *TScR*] evidence of…indeed!—even if that Word was a lie.—But the word of a Theopompus is enough. *MS* evidence of…indeed! Even the word of a Theopompus! *TSaR*
131:5 head-wreath—] head-/wreath, *PP*
131:8 convention] Convention, *TSa*
131:9 convention] Convention *TSa*
131:12 Typhon,] ~ *PP*
131:14 altogether: and…from classic…refers to…decadence. #———# It *TScR*] altogether. #———# P It *MS* altogether. # P It *TSa see also entries to* 131:17
131:14 altogether: *TSaR*] ~, *PP*
131:15 classic *TScR*] the classic *TSaR*
131:16 refers *TSbR*] refers only *TSaR*
131:17 decadence. #———# It *Ed.*] decadance. # P It *TSaR* decadence. # P It *TSbR*
131:21 surely *TSaR*] probably *MS*
131:23 and] ~, *PP*
131:24 big, *TScR*] *Om. MS* big *TSaR*
131:24 pale-pink *TSaR*] pale pink *MS, PP*
131:26 whitey-pink] whity-pink *PP*
131:29 there] *Om. TSa*
131:30 clean] clear *TSa*
131:38 grew rich as *TSaR*] were *MS*
132:6 "fattorie." *MS, PP*] "~". *TSa fattorie. E1*
132:14 villas,] ~ *TSa*

132:15 But] ~, *PP*
132:20 which *TSaR, TSbR*] which probably *MS, TSc*
132:21 Tarquinii,] ~ *PP*
132:23 drinking place] drinking-place *E1*
132:24 hill-top,] hill-top *PP* hilltop *E1*
132:25 inland,] ~ *PP*
132:26 far off] far-off *TSa*
132:26 town *TSa*] a town *MS*
132:26 hill-top] hilltop *E1*
132:27 hill] ~, *PP*
132:29 And we…[132:33] and loneliness. *TScR*] *Om. MS see also entries to* 132:32
132:29 the high…of Tarquinii *TScR*] what would be the arx of the vanished city *TSaR* the high…of a great city *TSbR*
132:31 moving *TSbR*] move *TSaR*
132:32 as much *TScR*] so much even *TSaR* as much even *TSbR*
132:32 of Tarquinii *TScR*] *Om. TSa*
132:32 two stones…and loneliness *TSbR*] even one stone. It is so lonely and open *TSaR*
132:35 of the present town across there…to calm *TScR*] *Om. MS* of the city today {to-day *PP*}…to calm *TSaR* of the dark town across there…to calm *TSbR*
132:39 Dazio *PP*] dazio *MS* Dazio *E1*
132:40 *morra TSaR*] morra *MS*
132:40 like] up like *TSa*
133:18 for no reason, *TSaR*] *Om. MS*
133:20 far-off] far off *PP*
133:22 defense] defence *TSa*
133:27 Pittsburgh *Ed.*] Pittsburg *MS*
133:27 chimney-stacks—*PP*] chimney-stacks——*MS* chimney stacks—*TSa*
133:29 are some *TSaR*] they are *MS*
133:30 age. *TSaR*] age, but where the people, perhaps, has not been vastly changed. *MS*

Vulci

The sequence of the states of the text is: *MS, TSa, TSb, TSc, TSaR, TSbR, TScR; PP* follows *TSaR* unless otherwise indicated, and *E1* follows *PP*. For *TSb* (and *TSc*) the retyped p. 12a (144:12–145:3) becomes base-text.

137:3 confederacy] Confederacy *TSaR*
137:5 city states] city-states *PP*
137:7 city states] city-states *PP*
137:9 Volci *Ed.*] Vulci *MS*
137:10 Volci *Ed.*] Vulci *MS*
137:10 Volci *Ed.*] Vulci *MS*
137:12 empire] Empire *PP*
137:17 Vulci *Ed.*] Volci *MS*
137:19 Vulci *Ed.*] Volci *MS*
137:23 village] ~, *PP*
137:27 Vulci *Ed.*] Volci *MS*
137:32 Bridge] bridge *PP*
137:32 Ponte] *Ponte E1*
137:33 Ponte della Badia *Ed.*] Ponte dell'Abbadia *MS Ponte dell'Abbadia E1*
137:34 Bridge] bridge *PP*
137:34 Monastery] monastery *PP*
138:1 kilometres…kilometres *PP*] kilometers…kilometers *MS*
138:3 twelve.] ~! *PP*
138:11 barroccino *Ed.*] barrocino *MS barrocino E1*
138:23 the road…two hours,] *Om. TSa*
138:28 Liras] liras *PP*
138:32 long?— *TSa*] ~?—/ — *MS*
138:32 *Subito!*—] Subito!— *TSa* "Subito!" *PP* "*Subito!*" *E1*~
138:32 *Subito!*] ~ *PP*
138:33 definite.—] ~— *TSa* ~. *PP*
138:36 food!] ~, *PP*
138:39 quicksilver] quick-/ silver *PP*
139:4 bread-cart *TSaR*] bread cart *MS* bread-/ cart *PP*
139:4 outside.—] ~— *TSa* ~. *PP*
139:7 patience, *TSaR*] ~ *MS*
139:11 shop—] ~ *PP*
139:14 finocchio] *finocchio E1*
139:18 attractive:] ~, *PP*
139:21 oh] Oh *PP*

139:21 where—] ~, *PP*
139:25 that] ~, *PP*
139:38 sparse] spare *E1*
139:40 part,] parts *E1*
140:1 mud holes] mud-holes *PP*
140:2 passable,] ~; *PP*
140:5 impatient] ~, *TSa*
140:11 horseback!] ~, *PP*
140:12 Always!] ~? *PP*
140:20 drainage-engineers,] ~; *PP*
140:26 day; *TSaR*] ~: *MS, TSb*
140:29 campagna] Campagna *TSa*
140:35 further] farther *PP*
140:36 umbrella pines] umbrella-pines, *PP*
140:37 arbutus *TSaR*] heaths *MS*
140:39 further] farther *PP*
140:40 silent and bosky *TSaR*] open and airy *MS*
141:1 So] ~, *PP*
141:6 mastic tree] mastic-tree *PP*
141:6 spiney] spiny *PP*
141:11 wild-boar] wild boar *PP*
141:11 herds,] ~; *PP*
141:12 roe-buck,] roebuck; *PP*
141:12 wild fowl,] wild-fowl *PP*
141:12 flamingoes] the flamingoes *TSa* the flamingos *PP*
141:13 pools,] ~ *PP*
141:19 government] Government *E1*
141:20 results,] ~— *PP*
141:20 farm-land] farm-/ land *TSa* farmland *PP*
141:22 still,] ~ *PP*
141:23 wheat; *TSaR*] ~: *MS, TSb*
141:24 carrion crows] carrion-crows *PP*
141:25 bareness; *TSaR*] ~: *MS, TSb*
141:25 ilex-oak; *TSaR*] ~: *MS, TSb*
141:26 wheat; *TSaR*] ~: *MS, TSb*
141:26 farm-house] farmhouse *PP*
141:29 youth *TSaR*] Youth *MS*

141:31 notice,] ~,/ *TSa* ~ *PP*
141:33 children,] ~ *PP*
141:33 past] by *TSa*
141:35 guardiano] *guardiano PP*
141:35 district—] ~, *PP*
141:37 lived *TSa*] *Om. MS see notes*
142:2 alert,] ~ *PP*
142:6 big *TSaR*] ~, *MS*
142:10 hand,] ~ *PP*
142:11 hot] ~, *PP*
142:13 much,] ~ *PP*
142:13 foot-hills] foot-/ hills *TSaR*
    foothills *PP*
142:17 winter time] winter-time *PP*
142:18 dogs] ~, *PP*
142:20 capriolo] *capriolo E1*
142:20 roe-deer,] roedeer *PP*
142:21 *résistance Ed.*] resistance *MS*
142:22 carcase] carcass *PP*
142:24 Soon,] ~ *PP*
142:26 maremma! *MS, TScR*]
    maremma. *TSa, PP*
    Maremma. *E1*
142:27 bridge of *TSaR*] Badia, *MS*
142:27 We *MS, PP*] we *TSa*
142:31 government] Government *E1*
142:33 cut *TSaR*] mow *MS*
142:35 big *TSaR*] big new *MS*
142:36 an] the *PP*
142:40 this!] ~" *PP*
143:2 maremma] *maremma E1*
143:2 cattle,] ~ *PP*
143:7 steam plough] steam-plough
    PP
143:13 went] *Om. TSa*
143:15 stony *MS, PP*] stoney *TSa*
143:15 path nipped…a gutter *TSaR*]
    road going *MS*
143:17 once was *MS*] was once *TSa*
143:17 castle of…gully…the bridge.
    TSaR] monastery. *MS* castle
    of…ravine…the bridge. *TScR*
143:28 an *MS, E1*] one *TSa*
143:31 castle *TSaR*] Badia *MS*
143:35 Volci *Ed.*] Vulci *MS*
143:35 tufo] *tufo E1*
144:1 castle *TSaR*] Badia *MS*
144:2 ruin] ruins *TSa*

144:3 reddish-black *TSaR*] black
    MS reddish black *PP*
144:5 castle *TSaR*] Badia *MS*
144:7 stream,] ~ *PP*
144:9 moorland, over…[145:3]
    much ravished. *TSbR*]
    moorland. *MS see also entries to*
    144:36
144:10 trees, *TSbR*] ~ *TSaR, TScR*
144:11 distance. *P* That *TSbR*] ~.
    That *TSaR*
144:12 Badia] *Badia E1*
144:13 It is…[144:18] maremma. *P*
    In *TSb*] But it has long been
    turned into a villa. The whole
    of this property belonged to
    Lucien Bonaparte, Prince of
    Canino, {Cassino, *PP*}
    brother of Napoleon. He lived
    here after the death of his
    brother, as an Italian prince.
    In *TSaR*
144:18 1828, *TSb*] ~ *TSaR*
144:19 through, and…containing
    TSb] through the surface of
    the earth, and sank into a
    tomb {tomb, *PP*} in which
    were *TSaR*
144:20 brought on *TSb*] led to *TSaR*
144:21 hey-day…urn." *Ed.*] time
    when the "Grecian urn" was
    most popular. *TSaR*
    hey-day…urn". *TSb*
144:22 vases, save…fetched. *TSb*]
    vases. *TSaR*
144:22 a boor of *TSb*] *Om. TSaR*
144:23 his excavations *TSb*] the
    excavating *TSaR*
144:25 cheapening *TSb*] the
    cheapening of *TSaR*
144:25 The *TSb*] So that the *TSaR*
144:25 rudely on. Vases *TSb*] savagely
    on, vases, *TSaR* savagely on,
    vases *PP*
144:26 things that…[144:34]
    smashed. *P* But *TSb*] the
    coarse, rough black etruscan
    {Etruscan *E1*} ware was

smashed to pieces {pieces, *PP*} as it was discovered, the overseer guarding the workmen with his gun over his knees. Dennis saw this still happening in 1846, when Lucien was dead. But the work was still going on, under the Princes's {Princess's *PP*} charge. And vainly Dennis asked the overseer to spare him some of the rough black ware. Not one! Smash they went to earth, while the overseer sat with his gun over his knees, {knees *PP*} ready to shoot. But *TSaR*

144:34 were *TSb*] were most *TSaR*
144:35 Princess' *TSb, TSaR*] Princess's *PP*
144:35 for a…cylix that *TSb*] some patera or amphora for a thousand crowns, which *TSaR*
144:36 Tombs that…[145:1] that some…[145:3] much ravished. *TSbR*] The tombs were opened, rifled, and then filled in with earth again. All the landed proprietors with property in the neighbourhood carried on excavations, and endless treasure was exhumed. Within two months of the time when he started excavating, Lucien Bonaparte had got more than two thousand etruscan {Etruscan *E1*} objects out of tombs occupying a few acres of ground. That the Etruscans should have left fortunes to the Bonapartes seems an irony: but so it was. Vulci had mines indeed: but mostly of painted vases, those "brides of quietness" which had been only two-much {too much *PP*} ravished. The tombs have

little to show now. *TSaR* Tombs that…the some…much ravished. *TSb*

145:6 across-stream] across stream *PP*
145:7 castle *TSaR*] monastery *MS, TSb*
145:8 corduroy-velveteens] corduroy velveteens *PP*
145:9 or two] *Om. TSa*
145:14 populous,] ~ *PP*
145:16 house *TSaR*] Badia *MS*
145:20 while,] ~ *PP*
145:20 back] ~, *PP*
145:24 no-one] no one *PP*
145:25 *dispensa TSaR*] dispensa *MS*
145:29 ruin *TSaR*] monastery *MS*
145:33 queer-looking,] queer-looking men, *TSa*
145:36 But] And *TSa*
145:37 queer] ~, *PP*
146:2 another] an *TSa*
146:4 castle *TSaR*] Badia *MS*
146:5 forlorn,] ~ *TSa*
146:6 stair-case] staircase *PP*
146:10 strong,] ~ *PP*
146:14 have *TSa*] has *MS*
146:18 *dispensa TSaR*] dispensa *MS*
146:20 dispensa] *dispensa PP*
146:31 Lira] lira *PP*
146:35 Lira] lira *PP*
146:36 away] *Om. TSa*
146:38 vaguely—] ~: *PP*
146:40 that] the *TSa*
147:3 anyhow!] ~, *PP*
147:5 maremmano] *maremmano E1*
147:6 Marco—] ~, *PP*
147:6 jacket,] ~ *E1*
147:7 determined seeming] determined-seeming *PP*
147:12 heathy, *MS, TSaR*] healthy, *TSa* heathy *PP*
147:12 stony] strong *TSa*
147:22 said, not] ~: "Not *PP*
147:23 said,] ~: *PP*
147:23 never!] ~. *PP*
147:28 admitted,] ~ *PP*
147:34 Marco,] ~ *PP*

147:35 said,] ~ *PP*
147:38 trees] ~, *PP*
147:39 castle *TSaR*] Badia *MS*
148:3 ominous] ~, *PP*
148:4 Volci *Ed.*] Vulci *MS*
148:5 across-stream] across stream *PP*
148:9 on] upon *TSa*
148:9 walls, to] walls, *TSa*
148:10 there.] there; some sign of where the walls had gone round. *E1*
148:10 said, nothing] ~: "Nothing *PP*
148:10 —some sign…round.] *Om. E1*
148:11 It had] It has *TSa*
148:13 thousands *TSaR*] hundreds, even thousands *MS*
148:14 taken from *TSbR*] found in *MS*
148:19 through,] ~ *PP*
148:20 river-side] riverside *PP*
148:27 rock houses] rock-houses *E1*
148:34 rubble:] ~, *PP*
148:35 black] ~, *PP*
148:37 behind,] ~, *PP*
149:5 roof tilts] roof-tilts *PP*
149:6 pale-brown,] pale brown *PP*
149:6 in bunches] ~ ~, *E1*
149:6 huge,] ~ *E1*
149:7 alive:] ~, *PP*
149:11 wing,] ~ *PP*
149:12 a] *Om. TSa*
149:15 fellow,] ~— *PP*
149:15 soft] ~, *PP*
149:17 old—] ~, *PP*
149:21 sores,] ~; *PP*
149:22 say!] ~. *PP*
149:25 about] ~, *PP*
149:27 damp—] ~, *PP*
149:28 top—] ~, *PP*
149:32 vases, mostly broken pieces, *TSaR*] vases *MS*
149:39 a stone *TSa*] stone *MS*
149:39 lies] lie *E1*
150:2 tomb,] ~ *PP*
150:3 Tomb *Ed.*] tomb *MS*

150:4 Museum. *Ed.*] museum, *MS* museum. *TSaR*
150:4 It was…A. François…very few…at Vulci. *TSbR*] and whence came the all-famous but rather boring François vase. *MS* It was…François… very very few {very, very few *PP*}…at Vulci. *TSaR*
150:13 stone-work] stonework *PP*
150:15 into] inside *TSa*
150:19 itself. Here…[150:23] passage? It *TSbR*] itself, following the candle-light in the narrow, winding passages. It *MS see also entries to* 150:23
150:21 nothing.— *TSbR*] ~. *TSaR* ~— *TScR*
150:22 gryphons *Ed.*] griffons *TSaR* griffins *PP*
150:22 find, *TSaR*] ~ *PP*
150:23 candle-light *TSaR*] candlelight *PP*
150:23 narrow *TSbR*] ~, *TSaR*
150:27 passages,] ~ *PP*
150:27 sign-post *TSa*] sign-/ post *MS* signpost *PP*
150:29 ceiling,] ~ *PP*
150:34 it, and] ~. And *PP*
150:36 passages—] ~. *PP*
150:36 But Dennis…[151:2] doubt collapsed. *TSbR*] *Om. MS see also entries to* 151:2
150:39 there no doubt *TSbR*] probably there *TSaR* probably these *PP*
150:39 phallic *TSbR*] *Om. TSaR*
150:40 monuments, *TSaR*] ~ *TScR*
150:40 or cippi, seen for miles around. *TSbR*] probably the phallic cippi. *TSaR*
151:1 chamber *TSaR*] chambers *TScR*
151:2 nothing. The *TSbR*] ~: the *TSaR* ~; the *PP*
151:2 has *TSbR*] is *TSaR*
151:3 burrowing *Ed.*] being burrowing *MS see notes*

151:6 shell:] ~— *PP*

151:7 people, *TSaR*] people, surely, *MS*

151:9 days,] ~ *PP*

151:10 pyramids. *TSaR*] pyramids, or something. *MS*

151:11 nowhere,] ~ *PP*

151:12 bramble-tangle] bramble tangle *PP*

151:15 We looked…[151:22] tomb-rifled earth. *TSbR*] And for the moment we turned our backs on the Etruscans. *MS* *see also entries to* 151:22

151:18 on *TSbR*] across *TSaR*

151:19 strange *TSbR*] strange, strange *TSaR*

151:21 cippi. *TSbR*] ~! *TSaR, TScR*

151:21 backs *TSbR*] back *TSaR*

151:22 it, *TSbR*] it all, *TSaR* it all *PP*

151:23 Vulci *E1*] Volci *MS*

151:28 *pure, no? Ed.*] pure no! *MS see notes*

151:29 bridge,] ~ *PP*

151:29 goodbye!] good-bye *PP*

151:30 side,] ~ *PP*

151:33 above:] ~, *PP*

151:35 Once this…Everything passes! *TSbR*] *Om. MS see also entries to* 151:38

151:35 aqueduct *PP*] acqueduct *TSaR*

151:36 like a beard *TSaR*] *Om. TScR*

151:37 mountain *TSbR*] mountains *TSaR, TScR*

151:37 aqueduct *PP*] acqueduct *TSaR*

151:37 is itself *TSbR*] itself is *TSaR* is *TScR*

151:38 passes! *TSaR*] ~. *TScR*

151:39 mare,] ~ *PP*

152:1 donkey:] ~— *PP*

152:9 malaria. All except for the] *Om. TSa*

152:12 rarely:] ~; *PP*

152:12 and] *Om. PP*

152:14 impassable,] ~— *PP*

152:14 off:] ~— *PP*

152:14 Luigi *TSaR*] he *MS*

152:15 tune,] ~: *PP*

152:15 more,] ~; *PP*

152:16 passable,] ~; *PP*

152:18 easily:] ~! *PP*

152:18 all, at all, *MS*] all, *TSaR* all *PP*

152:21 foot-hills] foothills *PP*

152:22 horses;] ~, *PP*

152:23 no-one] no one *PP*

152:28 solitary] ~, *PP*

152:29 peasants—] ~.— *TSa* ~. *PP*

152:31 there,] ~ *PP*

152:34 so-called *TSbR*] famous *MS*

152:35 whom Dennis thought was *TSaR*] *Om. MS*

152:36 straight *TSaR*] straight and just like Egypt *MS*

152:37 "Isis," *TSaR*] ~, *MS*

152:37 imported *TSaR*] Egyptian *MS*

152:40 Volci *Ed.*] Vulci *MS*

153:1 down in…Volci…called Polledrara, *Ed.*] *Om. MS* down in…Vulci…called Polledrara, *TSaR*

153:3 Anyhow she…Dennis Egyptian. *TSaR*] *Om. MS*

153:6 Volci *Ed.*] Vulci *MS*

153:6 was *TSa*] were *MS see notes*

153:7 owners, *TSaR*] owners, the Lucien Bonapartes, *MS*

153:9 again,] ~ *PP*

Volterra

The sequence of the states of the text is: *MS, TSa, TSc, TSaR, TScR, TScC, Per1, PP, E1; Per2* follows *TSaR* unless otherwise indicated.

157:3 west *TSaR*] maremma *MS*

157:6 Cecina] Cécina *Per2*

157:8 Pre-Apennines *PP*] Pre-appenines *MS*

157:10 Cecina] Cécina *MS, Per2*
157:16 *Saline di Volterra*] Saline di Volterra *PP*
157:17 salt-works] salt works *PP*
157:21 cog-and-ratchet *E1*] cog-and-racket *MS*
157:23 walking pace] walking-pace *PP*
157:26 south *MS, PP*] the south *TScC*
157:32 The hotel...[158:3] any alp. *MS, PP*] *Om. TScC see also entries to* 158:2
157:33 hap-hazard] haphazard *Per2, PP*
158:1 icy] ~, *PP*
158:2 1800] 1,800 *Per2*
158:6 tea] ~, *PP*
158:9 régime] regime *PP*
158:11 occasion,] ~ *PP*
158:12 cold] ~, *Per1*
158:20 and therefore *MS, PP*] ~, ~, *Per1*
158:23 whole-heartedly *MS, Per1, Per2*] whole-/ heartedly *TSa* wholeheartedly *PP*
158:23 anything:] ~; *Per2*
158:23 anything. And *MS, PP*] ~. *P* And *Per1*
158:26 party"? *TSa*] ~."? *MS*
158:30 are, *MS, PP*] ~ *Per1*
158:31 podestà] *podestà TScC, Per2*
158:33 Anyhow *MS, PP*] ~, *Per1*
158:36 Rome,] ~ *PP*
158:39 *Lenin: Death to Lenin:*] Lenin: Death to Lenin: *TSa* Lenin: Death to Lenin; *Per2* Lenin! (Death to Lenin!) *PP* Lenin! *E1*
159:2 *Mussolini is always right!*] *Mussolini is always right! Per1, Per2* (Mussolini is always right!) *PP Om. E1*
159:3 it] infallibility *E1*
159:3 infallibility] it *E1*
159:6 governed, *MS, PP*] ~ *Per1*
159:14 piazza:] ~; *Per2*
159:15 coats of arms] coats-of-arms *Per2*

159:16 it:] ~; *Per2*
159:16 nice *MS, PP*] ~, *Per1*
159:17 incense:] ~; *Per2*
159:19 bas reliefs] bas-reliefs *Per1*
159:21 long] ~, *PP*
159:22 all'Arco] dell'Arco *E1*
159:26 Up *MS, PP*] ~, *Per1*
159:26 round *MS, PP*] ~, *Per1*
159:29 inquiringly] ~, *Per1, Per2*
159:30 arch-bases] arch-/ bases *Per2* arch bases *PP*
159:30 out *MS*] and *TSa*
159:32 Strange, dark...[160:5] the watch. *MS, PP*] *Om. TScC see also entries to* 159:40
159:38 door-posts] doorposts *PP*
159:40 Unlike the...old position!—] (~ ~...~ ~!) *PP*
160:8 world:] ~; *Per2*
160:9 dump heaps] dump-heaps *PP*
160:15 irregularly-dropping *MS, PP*] irregularly dropping *Per1*
160:15 hill. And...[161:2] quick. *P* On *MS, PP*] hill. On *TScC see also entries to* 161:1
160:16 Santa Chiara *PP*] Santa-Chiara *MS*
160:18 olive gardens] olive-gardens *PP*
160:23 steeply] ~, *PP*
160:24 hill-top] hilltop *E1*
160:32 dale,] ~ *TSa*
160:34 merely occupies] occupies merely *PP*
160:35 city-site *TSaR*] city *MS* city site *Per2, PP*
161:1 olive orchards] olive-orchards *PP*
161:11 christian] Christian *Per1*
161:15 quarries. The...dark-grey... [161:22] down. *P* This] quarries. This *TScC* quarries. The...dark grey...down. *P* This *PP*
161:22 Le Balze *TSaR*] Le Balze *MS*
161:26 Badia] Badia *E1*
161:28 Le Balze] *Le Balze E1*
161:31 further] farther *PP*

161:33 gleam] gleams *TSa*
161:36 portentous:] ~; *Per2*
161:37 us:] ~; *Per2*
161:38 liquescence] liquescency *PP*
162:4 And] ~, *PP*
162:7 When we…[162:12] is
impervious. *MS, PP*] *Om.*
TScC
162:15 between-whiles *MS, Per1*]
between-/ whiles *TSa*
between whiles *PP*
162:17 chiffonnier cupboard]
chiffonier cupboard *Per2*
chiffonnier-cupboard *PP*
162:19 banquet room:] ~ ~; *Per2*
banquet-room: *PP*
162:22 enquiry] inquiry *TScC, Per2*
162:25 new podestà] podestà *TSa,*
Per2 podestà TScC, PP
officious *podestà Per1*
162:25 may *MS, PP*] may, by some
good chance, *Per1*
162:28 being] *Om. TSa*
162:28 bed. To] ~; to *Per2*
162:28 wakened] awakened *TSa*
162:30 unmistakeable] unmistakable
Per1, Per2
162:35 work-shops] workshops *PP*
162:36 half-awakenedness]
half-awakedness *PP*
162:38 so-called] so called *PP*
163:4 untinted, *MS, PP*] ~ *Per1*
163:4 around] *Om. TSa*
163:6 electric light] electric-light *PP*
163:7 Volterra] Volterran *TSa*
163:8 alabaster-worker] alabaster
worker *PP*
163:9 form, *MS, PP*] form, there is
no doubt that *Per1*
163:12 street,] ~ *PP*
163:15 dead cold] dead-cold *PP*
163:17 us] *Om. TSa*
163:18 —Why…museum!] ~…~!
Per1, Per2 "~…~!" *PP*
163:18 *Ah! Ah!*] *Ah! Ah! Per1, Per2*
"*Ah! Ah! PP*
163:18 *si—sì!*] *si, sì! TScC si, si! Per1*
si—sì! Per2 si—sì!" PP

163:18 on] upon *TSa*
163:19 Ah sì, si Signori!] Ah sì, sì
Signori! *TSa Ah sì, sì, Signori!*
TScC Ah si, si, Signori! Per1
"Ah si, si, Signori!" *PP* "*Ah*
si, si, Signori!" E1
163:20 tickets, *MS, PP*] ~ *Per1*
163:27 jar:] ~; *Per2*
163:28 Keats' *MS, TScC*] Keats *TSa*
Keats; *Per2*
163:28 "Ode on a Grecian Urn" *Ed.*]
"Ode to a Grecian Urn" *MS*
Ode to a Grecian Urn PP
163:33 alabaster *MS, PP*] soft
alabaster very near *Per1*
163:34 Anyhow *MS, PP*] ~, *Per1*
163:36 If] "~ *TScC, Per2*
163:39 after-life.—] ~." *TScC, Per2,*
E1 ~. *PP*
163:40 he too *MS, PP*] ~, ~, *Per1*
164:1 —"the *TSa*] —'the *MS* "The
TScC, PP "the *Per2*
164:5 museum *MS, PP*] Museum
TSa
164:7 'And *TScC, Per2, E1*] "~ *MS,*
PP
164:8 soul.'"— *Ed.*] ~."— *MS*
~.'" *TScC, Per2, E1* ~." *PP*
164:14 greekified] Greekified *PP*
164:14 Homer] *Homer PP*
164:19 For me…[164:31] of life. *MS,*
PP] *Om. TScC see also entries to*
164:29
164:24 consciousness *MS, E1*]
Consciousness *TSa*
164:25 day, ~ *PP*
164:26 period"] ~," *PP*
164:29 fascinating] ~, *PP*
164:34 fish tail] fish-tail *PP*
164:34 same:] ~; *Per2*
164:35 serpent legs] serpent-legs *PP*
164:37 If we…[165:16] of death. *MS,*
PP] *Om. TScC see also entries to*
165:16
164:37 world,] ~ *PP*
164:39 body:] ~, *Per2*
165:5 born:] ~; *Per2*
165:11 water deities] water-deities *PP*

165:16 down-pour] downpour *PP*
165:18 gryphons] griffins *E1*
165:18 asunder, and] ~ ~, *PP*
165:19 time, *MS*, *PP*] ~ *Per1*
165:22 consciousness *MS*, *E1*]
        Consciousness *TSa*
165:22 thieves *TSa*] theives *MS*
165:22 are] are the *Per2*
165:23 treasure:] ~; *Per2*
165:23 tearers-asunder] tearers
        asunder *PP*
165:25 It is...[165:36] the
        otherworld. *MS*, *PP*] *Om.*
        TScC see also entries to 165:36
165:25 man] men *TSa*
165:26 borders] border *PP*
165:27 sometimes:] ~; *Per2*
165:29 man:] ~; *Per2*
165:30 ocean:] ~; *Per2*
165:33 waters:] ~; *Per2*
165:36 otherworld] other world *Per2*
165:38 ash-chest,] ~ *Per1* ash-/ chest
        PP
166:2   earth?—] ~; *PP*
166:4   centaur:] ~; *Per2*
166:5   away.] ~? *TScC*, *Per2*
166:6   scenes,] ~ *Per1*
166:7   circus games] circus-games
        TSa circus-/ games *Per2*
166:9   sacrifices] sacrifice *TSa*
166:11 around;] ~: *PP*
166:12 fare-well] farewell *TScC*, *PP*
166:12 goodbye] good-by *TScC*
        good-bye *PP*
166:15 is *MS*, *PP*] ~, *TScC*
166:16 soul. I *MS*, *PP*] ~. P I *TScC*
166:17 no! he] ~! He *E1*
166:21 meant,] ~ *PP*
166:30 represented] represent *TSa*
166:35 The dogs...[167:5] symbolic
        opposition. *MS*, *PP*] *Om.*
        TScC see also entries to 167:4
166:35 double axe *MS*, *PP*]
        double-axe *TSa*
166:39 scene:] ~; *Per2*
167:1   gryphons] griffins *E1*
167:3   winter:] ~; *Per2*
167:4   vases,] ~ *PP*

167:6   departures,] ~; *Per2*
167:7   the driver on...horseback...by
        other *TScR*] wagoner and
        horses and dogs, met by *MS*
        wagons and horses and dogs,
        and by *TSa* driver
        on...horseback...by other
        TSaR the driver
        on...horse-back...by other
        Per2 driver on...horse-/
        back...by other *PP*
167:10 family:] ~; *Per2*
167:23 the dancing surety *TSaR*] that
        MS
167:24 Etruria; *TSaR*] ~, *MS*
167:25 In the...[168:19] east. *P* Very]
        The very *TScC see also entries*
        to 168:18
167:26 so-called] so called *PP*
167:27 Oedipus *E1*] Edipus *TSa*
        Œdipus *Per2*, *PP*
167:28 Sphinx *PP*] Sphynx *MS*
167:28 Polynices *PP*] Polynice *MS*
167:29 Iphigenia *PP*] Iphegenia *MS*
167:30 subjects,] ~ *PP*
167:38 recognisable,] ~ *TSa*
        recognizable *PP*
167:39 handling:] ~; *Per2*
168:1   as the *TSa*] the *MS*
168:1   in England] *Om. TSa*
168:2   alabaster-cutters] alabaster-/
        cutters *TSa* alabaster cutters
        PP
168:5   un-classic! *TSaR*] ~. *MS* un-/
        classic! *PP*
168:7   For] ~, *PP*
168:9   B.C.] B.C. *PP*
168:9   christian] Christian *TSa*
168:9   A.D.] A.D. *PP*
168:10 seem *TSa*] *Om. MS see note on*
        141:37
168:10 Volterra,] ~ *PP*
168:11 chests:] ~; *Per2*
168:11 christianity] Christianity *TSa*
168:13 christian *Ed.*] Christian *MS*
168:18 east:] East *PP*
168:22 end, *MS*, *PP*] ~ *Per1*
168:22 dead:] ~; *Per2*

168:24 oriental] Oriental *TScC, PP*
168:25 *show*] show *TSa*
168:28 east] East *TScC, PP*
168:29 untameable] untamable *Per1, Per2*
168:30 kept] ~, *PP*
168:30 keeps] ~, *PP*
168:36 oriental] Oriental *TScC, PP*
168:37 death effigy] death-effigy *PP*
168:39 portrait effigy] portrait-effigy *PP*
168:39 often, *MS, PP*] ~ *Per1*
169:2 portraiture:] ~; *Per2*
169:3 days,] ~ *Per1*
169:5 see:] ~; *Per2*
169:6 your ashes] *Om. Per2*
169:6 probably, *MS, PP*] ~ *Per1*
169:7 work-shops] workshops *Per1*
169:11 Or] So *TSa*
169:12 portrait bust] portrait-bust *PP*
169:14 assorted:] ~; *Per2*
169:14 found,] ~ *PP*
169:21 libation dish] libation-dish *PP*
169:23 up] *Om. TSa*
169:24 hand,] ~ *PP*
169:27 Etruscans] ~, *Per1*
169:28 It is…[169:36] ancient world. *P* In the…[170:6] ancient mysteries. *MS, PP*] It is…ancient world. *TScC Om. Per1 see also entries to* 170:5
169:28 ladies:] ~; *Per2*
169:29 ancient] *Om. TSa*
169:30 wine-cups or *TSaR*] *Om. MS*
170:2 upside-down] upside down *PP*
170:3 upside-down] upside-/ down

TSa upsidedown *Per2* upside down *PP*
170:4 upside-down] upside down *PP*
170:5 Vlathri] Velathri *PP*
170:8 courtyard *MS, Per1*] Courtyard *TSa*
170:9 and] to *PP*
170:16 tumuli:] ~, *Per2*
170:20 Archaeological Museum *Ed.*] archaeological museum *MS* archeological museum *TScC* archæological museum *Per2, PP*
170:21 Florence:] ~; *Per2*
170:24 Tomb *PP*] tomb *MS*
170:36 urns. *P* But…[171:25] useless. We *MS, PP*] urns. *P* We *TScC see also entries to* 171:19
170:37 Why] ~, *Per2, PP*
170:37 why] ~, *PP*
171:7 sickening?] ~! *PP*
171:17 Veio *Ed.*] Vei *MS* Veii *E1*
171:19 contact:] ~; *Per2*
171:27 state] State *E1*
171:27 prison. There…[171:31] ship, here…And behind *MS, PP*] prison. Behind *Per1* prison. There…ship; here…And behind *E1*
171:32 black] bleak *TSa*
171:34 piano: *MS, PP*] ~; *Per1, Per2*
172:1 life-like] lifelike *Per1*
172:2 There they…dogs!] "~ ~…~!" *PP*
172:6 rewarded, *MS, PP*] ~ *Per1*

The Florence Museum

MS is the only text of this essay. The entry to the left of the square bracket usually indicates the final *MS* reading, with the unidentified entry to the right giving the reading of the *MS* before DHL revised it; still earlier readings are indicated by pointed and half brackets. Word fragments of fewer than three letters have not been recorded.

⟨ ⟩, ⟪ ⟫ = First and second deletions
⌐ ⌐,⌐⌐ ⌐⌐ = First and second additions

175:2 Museum *Ed.*] ~.
175:30 Tyrrheni...the Etruscan.] Tyrrhenici
175:32 Etruria] And Etruria
175:32 case to England.] case.
176:4 culture] civilisation
176:9 emotions or culture-rhythms] emotions
176:15 death] hope
176:18 of worlds] of cosmos
176:20 religion, every] great religion, every great
176:22 goal] great goal
176:22 consciousness] cosmic consciousness
176:40 lived and who *were*,] were themselves
177:1 living and being.] being ourselves.
177:1 artistic or impulsive] artistic
177:2 culture-expression,] culture-revelation,
177:2 scientific or civilisation expression] religio-scientific revelation

177:3 people. The...on concepts.] people.
177:8 languages, vulgarly.] languages.
177:10 attempt on man's part] ⌐on man's part¬ attempt
177:27 ancient China...in Babylonia] Babylonia
177:28 Minor, in...the Teuton,] Minor,
177:34 etruscan] Etruscan
177:36 one absolute *Ed.*] a one ⟨typical⟩ ⌐absolute¬
178:25 Etruscans] Etruscans one
178:26 that] of that
179:2 from the...or Hittite] ⟨till the Etruscan is swamped by Greek or Roman⟩ ⌐from the... emerges ⟨⟨from⟩⟩ ⌐ ⌐out of¬¬ ...or Hittite¬
179:4 swamped] temporarily swamped

Italian Essays, 1919–27

The following symbols are used throughout (see Introduction for specific identification):

MS = Manuscript
TS = Typescript
TCC = Carbon typescript
G = Galley proofs
Per = Periodical publication
A1 = First American edition, Viking 1936
E1 = First English edition, Heinemann 1968

In the individual textual apparatus the base-text adopted for this edition appears within the square bracket with no symbol; only when the reading adopted for this edition differs from the base-text specified in the 'Note on the texts' is a symbol given. Variant readings follow the square bracket, in chronological sequence, with their respective source-symbols. When the reading of base-text corresponds to the reading of another text, their respective symbols are given within the square bracket.

When more than two documents survive and some of them match with each other, a symbol is given only for the first.

The following symbols are used editorially:

Ed. = Editor
Om. = Omitted
~ = Substitution for a word in recording an accidental variant
P = New paragraph
R = Changes by DHL
C = Corrections by another person
/ = Line break resulting in hyphenation error or ambiguity
{ } = Minor variant in a long passage in rejected readings
⟨ ⟩ = Original deleted *MS* reading (Appendix I)
⟨⟨ ⟩⟩ = Second deleted *MS* reading (Appendix I)
⌐ ¬ = Added *MS* reading
⌐⌐ ¬¬ = Second added *MS* reading

In order to reduce the difficulty of tracing DHL's revisions, some passages rejected in a state of the text are printed with variants internally recorded inside braces. When variants occur in revisions which replace these passages, they are indicated by the note '*see also entries to…*'.

David

The chronological sequence of the texts is: *TCCI, TCCIR, TCCII, A1*

185:3	café-au-lait] *café-au-lait TCCII*	186:1	river] ~, *TCCII*
185:3	olive trees *TCCI, A1*] olive-trees *TCCII*	186:2	night—] ~.— *TCCII* ~. *A1*
		186:4	cat-swirls] cat-/ swirls *A1*
185:4	the *TCCIR*] *Om. TCCI*	186:15	sun,] ~ *TCCII*
185:4	café-au-lait] *café-au-lait TCCII*	186:22	surcharge *TCCIR*] search surcharge *TCCI*
185:5	Café-au-lait] *Café-au-lait TCCII*	186:22	and] an *TCCII*
185:9	beneath a bright *TCCIR*] under a *TCCI*	186:25	Northerners] northerners *A1*
		186:27	lily's] Lily's *A1*
185:10	whip-thong *TCCII*] whip-/ thong *TCCI*	186:29	lily] Lily *A1*
		186:29	water-born] Water-born *A1*
185:11	arm in arm] arm-in-arm *TCCII*	186:31	Michelangelo's *A1*] Michael Angelo's *TCCI*
185:12	Midday] Mid-day *A1*	186:33	stark naked] stark-naked *TCCII*
185:12	Miniato] Ministo *TCCII*		
185:12	cannon-shots *TCCIR*] cannon shots *TCCI*	187:2	midwinter] mid-/ winter *A1*
185:13	cannon shots?—] canno shots? *TCCI* cannonshots?— *TCCIR* cannon-shots? *TCCII*	187:7	Hamadryads *A1*] hamadryads *TCCI*
		187:7	Silenus, *TCCII*] ~/ *TCCI*
		187:8	these] ~, *TCCII*
		187:8	Iacchos] Iacchus *A1*

187:9 reed-music *TCCII*] reed-/ music *TCCI*
187:10 grass",—] ~"— *TCCII*
187:11 Deliverer. *TCCII*] ~, *TCCI*
187:12 Michelangelo *A1*] Michael Angelo *TCCI*
187:13 self-realization] self-revelation *TCCII*
187:14 Michelangelo's… Michelangelo's *A1*] Michael Angelo's…Michael Angelo' *TCCI* Michel Angelo's… Michel Angelo's *TCCIR*
187:21 Cinquecento *Ed.*] Cinque-Cento *TCCI*
187:25 Married! *TCCIR*] ~. *TCCI*
187:26 Iacchos] Iacchus *A1*
187:28 fire] ~, *TCCII*
187:31 Lily. *TCCII*] ~, *TCCI*
187:34 Dithyrambus:] ~; *A1*
187:34 instant *TCCIR*] flux *TCCI*
187:35 combination *TCCIR*] conversation *TCCI*
187:38 Cinquecento *Ed.*] Cinque-Cento *TCCI*
188:2 Scallop-Shell *TCCIR*] scallop-shell *TCCI*
188:3 adolescence— *TCCII*] adolescene/— *TCCI* adolescence—/— *TCCIR*
188:3 subtle] ~, *TCCII*
188:4 women,] ~; *TCCII*
188:5 Michelangelo's *A1*] Michael Angelo's *TCCI*
188:19 Michelangelo *A1*] Michael Angelo's *TCCI*
188:22 listen *TCCIR*] listened *TCCI*
188:26 all *TCCIR*] all the *TCCI*
188:27 flame,] ~ *TCCII*
188:27 in *TCCIR*] by *TCCI*
188:28 Christ-like *TCCII*] Christi-like *TCCI* Christe-like *TCCIR*
189:1 David] ~, *TCCII*
189:2 may be] maybe *TCCII*
189:11 nipped,] ~; *TCCII*

Looking Down on the City

TCC is the only text of this essay. The entry to the left of the square bracket usually indicates the final *TCC* reading, with the unidentified entry to the right giving the reading of the *TCC* before DHL revised it; still earlier readings are indicated by pointed brackets. Word fragments of fewer than three letters have not been recorded.

193:1 Looking Down on the City *Ed.*] LOOKING DOWN ON THE CITY
193:3 the Pitti *Ed.*] The ~
193:4 door,] ~
193:5 *see*] see
193:15 me.] me. Yet
193:16 pearl-like,] ~
193:16 air-and-sea-clean] air and sea-clean
193:20 physically,] ~
193:22 probably is] seems
194:10 Michelangelo] Mich<a>el Angelo
194:11 each] every
194:15 one,] ~
194:20 roofs,] ~
194:23 Edinburgh *Ed.*] Edinborough
194:25 "The…Heaven—"] ~…~—
194:29 "The…Heaven—"] ~…~—
194:32 city!] ~.
194:34 Florence, even now.] Florence.
194:35 planes] plains
194:39 *Madonna of the Rocks*] Madonna of the Rocks
195:2 *Madonna of the Rocks*] Madonna of the Rocks
195:3 these] my
195:9 "Cursed…works,"] ~…~,

195:11 "cursed...works"?] ~...work.
195:14 consciousness,] ~
195:17 of] in
195:17 a] the
195:17 misery in] misery of
195:20 conscious,] ~

195:25 again;] ~,
196:4 "Viva Lenin,"] ~ ~,
196:11 palace] house
196:12 bluey-red] bluey red
196:14 perfect!] ~.

Europe Versus America

The chronological sequence of the texts is: *Per1, A1.*

199:1 Versus] *V. A1*
199:5 it.] ~? *A1*
199:12 bigger] better *A1*
199:15 Eve,] ~ *A1*
200:16 it,] ~ *A1*
200:20 Vogue la galère *Ed.*] Vogue la galere *Per* Vogue la galère *A1*

200:21 —It] ~ *A1*
200:24 man,] ~— *A1*
200:24 woman] ~, *A1*
200:24 still,] ~— *A1*
200:28 her fixed] fixed *A1*

Fireworks

The chronological sequence of the texts is: *Per1, Per2,* with a few corrections from *MS.*

203:2 June,] ~ *Per2*
203:2 St.] ~ *Per2*
203:2 day;] ~,— *Per2*
203:3 St.] ~ *Per2*
203:4 St.] ~ *Per2*
203:4 John moreover] ~, ~, *Per2*
203:5 Florence;] ~,— *Per2*
203:5 reasons *MS*] ~, *Per1*
203:9 roof,] ~ *Per2*
203:10 tower,] ~ *Per2*
203:11 orange-ruddy,] ~ *Per2*
203:12 midsummer's eve;] Midsummer's Eve, *Per2*
203:14 battlements,] ~ *Per2*
203:14 unrelenting] ~, *Per2*
203:16 mediaeval *MS*] mediæval *Per1* medieval *Per2*
203:18 long] ~, *Per2*
203:18 neck,] ~ *Per2*
203:19 silhouette-like] silhouette like *Per2*
203:20 Ages] ~, *Per2*

203:21 plumes. *P* It] ~. It *Per2*
203:22 hasn't *MS, Per2*] has not *Per1*
203:23 haughtiness. *P* But] ~. But *Per2*
203:25 stupid] ~, *Per2*
203:27 nail-heads] nail-/ heads *Per2*
203:29 pinion-tips *MS, Per2*] pinion-/ tips *Per1*
203:30 darknecked *MS*] dark-necked *Per1*
203:32 oil flare-lamps *MS*] oil-flare lamps *Per1*
204:1 living] ~, *Per2*
204:1 bodies,] ~ *Per2*
204:1 warm] ~, *Per2*
204:2 air,] ~ *Per2*
204:2 night;] ~ *Per2*
204:2 witches,] ~ *Per2*
204:2 Shiva] Siva *Per2*
204:3 her] his *Per2 see notes*
204:6 below. *P* How] ~. How *Per2*

204:8 same,] ~ *Per2*
204:10 dead-head] deadhead *Per2*
204:13 sunrays] sun rays *Per2*
204:14 Pyramids] pyramids *Per2*
204:16 Pyramid] pyramid *Per2*
204:18 queer little lively] ~, ~, ~, *Per2*
204:19 street-scenes *MS*] street-/ scenes *Per1* street scenes *Per2*
204:22 them. *P* Not] ~. Not *Per2*
204:25 storey] story *Per2*
204:26 York,] ~ *Per2*
204:31 naked] ~, *Per2*
204:32 Michelangelo's *Per2*] Michael Angelo's *Per1*
204:33 self-consciousness,] ~ *Per2*
204:34 do not;] don't, *Per2*
204:35 do not] don't *Per2*
204:39 neighbourhood] neighborhood *Per2*
205:4 do not] don't *Per2*
205:8 numbers, *MS*] ~ *Per1*
205:13 there. *P* In] ~. In *Per2*
205:17 part. *P* The] ~. The *Per2*
205:18 well behaved *MS*] well-behaved *Per1*
205:20 half-a-dozen *MS*, *Per2*] half a dozen *Per1*
205:21 alle *Ed.*] delle *Per1 see notes*
205:22 flare-lit] flare-/ lit *Per2*
205:22 stall,] ~ *Per2*
205:24 ice-cream,] ice-/ cream *Per2*
205:26 still-full *MS*] still full *Per1*
205:29 underworld. *P* Still] ~. Still *Per2*
205:31 summer] Summer *Per2*
205:34 women *MS*] ~, *Per1*
205:37 *Bang!* up *MS*] *Bang! Up Per1*
206:1 *Bang! Bang! Crackle! MS*] ~! ~! ~! *Per1*

206:4 further...further] farther...farther *Per2*
206:10 air-raid, *MS*] air raid *Per1* air-/ raid *Per2*
206:11 else. *P* So] ~. So *Per2*
206:18 earth,] ~ *Per2*
206:19 look,] ~ *Per2*
206:20 *Bish! Ed.*] bish! *MS* Bish! *Per1*
206:20 the sky-asters] The ~ *Per2*
206:24 ears,] ~ *Per2*
206:30 someone] some one *Per2*
206:32 by, and] ~ ~, *Per2*
206:34 bello! bello! bellezza!— *Ed.*] ~! ~! ~! *MS* Bello! bello! *bellezza!– Per1* "Bello! bello! *bellezza!"— Per2*
206:34 irony. As *MS*] ~. *P* As *Per1*
206:35 sky-line] skyline *Per2*
207:3 Piazzale, *MS*] ~ *Per1*
207:3 figure-pieces: *MS*] figure pieces, *Per1*
207:5 smoke, *MS*] ~ *Per1*
207:6 piece: *MS*] ~; *Per1*
207:11 fume. *P* More] ~. More *Per2*
207:13 spider-lilies *MS*] spider lilies *Per1*
207:13 long *MS*] ~, *Per1*
207:13 out-curving] out-/ curving *Per2*
207:14 petal, *MS*] ~ *Per1*
207:18 grey] gray *Per2*
207:19 out. *P* And] ~. And *Per2*
207:23 numb] ~, *Per2*
207:26 many-petalled] many-petaled *Per2*
207:27 at] At *Per2*
207:27 once! *P* And] ~. And *Per2*
207:28 marvellous] marvelous *Per2*
208:1 sparks,] ~ *Per2*
208:2 still,] ~ *Per2*
208:2 soft,] ~ *Per2*

The Nightingale

The chronological sequence of the texts is: *MS, Per1, G, Per2, A1*, but *A1* follows *Per1* unless otherwise indicated. *TS* and *A2* – see Introduction, p. lxiii – always follow *MS* unless otherwise indicated.

211:2 spring *MS, G, A1*] Spring *Per1*

211:2 summer *MS, G, A1*] Summer *Per1*

211:4 little *MS, G*] ~, *Per1*

211:4 towards *MS, G, A1*] toward *Per1, TSC*

211:6 again *Per1*] Om. *MS*

211:7 Hello! Hello! Hello!] "*Hello! Hello! Hello!*" *Per1* "Hello! Hello! Hello!" *A1*

211:7 sound *Per1*] sound, perhaps, of all sounds *MS*

211:7 world: a...up.] world, a...up. *Per1* world. *G*

211:8 Every] And every *G*

211:8 it,] ~ *G*

211:8 wonder *Per1*] a wonder *MS*

211:9 said *Per1*] confessed *MS*

211:9 it has *Per1*] and it has *MS* and has *G*

211:10 so much *Per1*] such *MS, G*

211:11 nightingale! *MS, G*] ~, *Per1*

211:11 yourself. It...half-dawn *Per1*] yourself: and it is *MS*

211:14 But the...you wonder *Per1*] And every single time you hear the nightingale afresh, your second thought is *MS*

211:15 "Now...bird?"] ~...~? *G*

211:18 *Ode to a Nightingale* with] "Ode to a Nightingale" ~: *Per1* "Ode to a Nightingale" ~ *A2*

211:19 senses—"] senses," *Per1* senses" *G* sense" *Per2* senses..." *TS* senses....." *A2*

211:19 is a...song. You *Per1*] —well, I for one don't know. You can *MS*

211:21 What *MS, G*] ~, *Per1, Per2*

211:22 pains?—] ~? *Per1* ~....? *G* ~...? *Per2*

211:22 tra-la-la!—] tra-la-la! *Per1* Tra-la-la! *G, A1* tra-la-la!- *A2*

211:22 tri-li-lilylilyly.] tri-li-lilylilylilyly! *Per1* Tri-li-lilylilylilyly! *G, A1*

tri-li-lilylilyly! *TS* tri-li-lily-lilyly! *A2*

211:23 he—] ~, *Per1*

211:23 she—] ~, *Per1*

211:24 Jug-jug-jug! *MS, G*] "~!" *Per1*

211:24 mediaeval *MS, G*] medieval *Per1*

211:26 wild] ~, *Per1*

211:27 tail.— *P* "And *Ed.*] ~.—"And *MS* ~: *P* And *Per1* ~! *P* "And *G* ~. *P* "And *TS, A2*

211:28 amorous] ~, *Per1*

211:29 Itylus—" *MS, G*] ~. *Per1* ~." *Per2*

211:30 say,] ~— *G*

211:30 jug! jug! jug!— *MS, G*] "Jug! ~! ~!", *Per1* "Jug! ~! ~!," *A1* jug! ~! ~! *TS, A2*

211:30 How they...don't know *Per1*] It really is mysterious, what people hear. You'd think they had their ears on upside down. Anyone who ever heard the nightingale "sobbing" must have quite a different hearing-faculty from the one I've got *MS see also entries to 212:1*

211:31 it, *Per1*] ~ *G, A1*

211:31 anyone *G, A1*] any one *Per1*

212:1 sobbing," *A1*] ~", *Per1* ~" *G*

212:2 Anyhow, *MS, G*] ~ *Per1*

212:3 A *Per1*] And *MS*

212:3 nor a *Per1*] nor *MS*

212:4 bell. *MS, G*] ~! *Per1*

212:4 in the world] Om. *Per2*

212:6 Perhaps that...[212:13] discrepancy. *P* Because *Ed.*] Om. *G see also entries to 212:10*

212:7 "Forlorn] ~ *Per1*

212:8 self!"] ~! *Per1*

212:9 it:] ~; *Per1*

212:10 when the...of small *Per1*] where any really normal listening mortal hears the silver ringing shouts of *MS*

212:13 Because in sober *Ed.*] Because

212:13 as a matter of *MS* Because, in sober *Per1* In sober *G* Because, as a matter of *TS, A2*

212:13 fact] ~, *Per1, TS, A2*

212:14 punching *MS, G*] pinching *Per1*

212:14 assertiveness] ~, *G*

212:14 that makes...still. A *Per1*] that makes a mere man sit down and consider. It is the *MS* a *G*

212:16 glittering] *Om. G*

212:16 such as *Per1*] which *MS*

212:17 created, and...knew it *Per1*] created in brightness, and found themselves able to shout aloud *MS*

212:19 to-do...heaven! *G*] nightingaleish to-do! *MS* to-do...heaven: *Per1*

212:19 Hello! Hello...mar-mar-marvellous occurrence! What?] "~! ~...mar-mar-marvelous ~! ~!" *Per1 Om. G* "~! ~...mar-mar-marvellous ~! ~!" *A1*

212:22 splendidness *Per1*] splendid splendidness *MS*

212:22 *Lo! It is I!*—] "Lo! It is I!" *Per1* "Lo! It is I!" *G Lo! It is I! TS, A2*

212:22 have to] must *G*

212:24 assertion,] ~ *G*

212:24 to look] a look *A1*

212:25 the *Per1*] *Om. MS, G*

212:25 final *Per1*] positive *MS*

212:25 splendour,] splendor, *Per1* splendour *G*

212:26 finally *Per1*] *Om. MS*

212:26 perfect: *MS, G*] ~; *Per1*

212:26 is *Per1*] in *MS, G*

212:27 other is *Per1*] other in *MS, G*

212:28 grey-brown *MS, G, A1*] gray-brown *Per1*

212:28 him:] ~, *Per1*

212:28 he's] he has *G*

212:29 him,] ~ *G*

212:30 Just as...[213:17] is sad. *Per1* *Om. Per2 see also entries to* 213:16

212:34 seethes] seeths *TS, A2*

212:35 perhaps,] ~ *Per1*

212:35 reason:] ~,— *Per1* reason— *G, A1*

212:35 pure] ~, *Per1*

212:36 or...self; *Ed.*] self-assertion; *MS* or...self,— *Per1* or...self— *G, A1*

212:36 makes] does make *G*

212:37 sad, and...peacock often...him angry...The birds *Per1*] sad, and...peacock so often...him feel angry. Because they *MS* sad—with a sadness that is half envy. The birds *G*

212:39 rich *MS, G*] ~, *Per1*

213:1 The nightingale ripples... perfection *Per1*] The nightingale simply ripples... perfection *MS Om. G*

213:3 This,—this...[213:17] is sad. *Per1*] *Om. G see also entries to* 213:16

213:3 This,— *Per1*] ~, *MS* ~— *A1*

213:3 a perfect...creation,—this green *Per1*] perfection, this emerald *MS* a perfect... creation—this green *A1*

213:4 beauty in a bird, *Ed.*] self, *MS* beauty in a bird,— *Per1* beauty in a bird— *A1*

213:5 ear. The] ~. P The *Per1*

213:6 I] "~ *Per1*

213:7 awfully:] ~, *Per1*

213:7 morning!] ~," *Per1*

213:7 she will *Per1*] they'll *MS*

213:11 it is *Per1*] it will be *MS*

213:11 immediately *Per1*] instantly *MS*

213:13 reason,] ~ *Per1*

213:13 get *Per1*] see *MS*

213:13 all *Per1*] *Om. MS*

213:13 showy] ~, *Per1*

213:14 self-assertion:] ~; *Per1*

213:14 Fine...birds!] "~...~!" *Per1*
213:16 sad: forlorn!] ~, ~. *Per1*
213:18 The] Yet the *G*
213:18 us] me *G*
213:18 most unsad] least sad *G*
213:19 world: even...gleam.] world;
    even...gleam. *Per1* world. *G*
213:19 He *Per1*] The nightingale
    MS
213:21 life-perfect] life perfect *A2*
213:21 out,] ~,— *Per1* ~: *G* ~—*A1*
213:21 trills, gives...mock-plaintive
    ...assertions *G*] calls, declares,
    asserts *MS* trills, gives...
    mock-plaintiff...assertions
    Per1
213:23 triumphs,] ~; *Per1*
213:23 he *Per1*] *Om. MS*
213:25 No! *MS, G*] ~, *Per1*
213:25 even] Even *G*
213:27 purer *Per1*] more pure *MS*
213:27 words, which...say, *Per1*]
    words. But *MS* words,
    which...say *G*
213:28 life-perfection. *G, A1*]
    life-perfection. *P* Keats feels
    this, all through his ode. *MS*
    life perfection. *Per1* life
    perfection. Keats feels this all,
    through his ode. *A2*
213:30 "'Tis *Per2*] —~ *MS* "~ *G* '~
    Per1, TSC '*Tis A2*
213:31 thine] thy *Per2, TSC* thy *A2*
213:31 happiness,—] ~— *G*
    happiness,— A2
213:32 light-winged] light-wingèd
    Per2, A1 light-wingéd *TSC*
    light-wingéd A2
213:35 ease.—"] ~. *Per1* ~." *G* ~..."
    TS ease...A2
213:36 Poor Keats, he...he wants
    Per1] It is beautiful poetry, of
    a truthful poet. And Keats
    keeps it up, in the next stanza,
    wanting *MS* Poor Keats!
    He...he wants *G*
213:38 Hippocrene] ~, *Per1*
213:39 dim.] ~:— *G*

214:1 "Fade *MS, G*] ~ *Per1* Fade
    A2
214:3 fret—" *MS, G*] ~. *Per1* ~."
    Per2 ~. ...*A1* fret..." *TS*
    fret...A2
214:4 It is...[214:13] of Poesy—"
    Per1] *Om. G see also entries to*
    214:13
214:4 sad, beautiful...Yet *Per1*]
    lovely poetry! But *MS*
214:5 strikes me as *Per1*] is *MS*
214:5 ridiculous. *Per1*] ridiculous, so
    I won't quote it. Yes, I will:
    MS
214:6 "Here] ~ *Per1 Here A2*
214:7 grey] gray *Per1, TSC* gray *A2*
214:7 hairs—" etc.] hairs. *Per1*
    hairs. ...*A1* hairs..." etc. *TS*
    hairs...etc. A2
214:8 at all *Per1*] *Om. MS*
214:8 the sad human male *Per1*]
    Keats *MS*
214:9 Wine will...go. *Per1*] *Om. MS*
214:11 "Away] ~ *Per1 Away A2*
214:11 thee] ~, *Per1, TSC* thee, *A2*
214:13 Poesy—"] ~. *Per1* ~. ...*A1*
    ~..." *TSC Poesy...A2*
214:16 outside.] ~:— *G*
214:17 "Darkling *MS, G*] ~ *Per1*
    Darkling A2
214:17 listen: *MS, G*] ~; *Per1, TSC*
    listen; A2
214:17 and,] ~ *Per1, TSC and A2*
214:18 Death,—"] Death. *Per1*
    death,—" *G* death." *Per2*
    Death. ...*A1* Death..." *TSC*
    Death ...A2
214:19 The *Per1*] I am sure the
    sound of the *MS*
214:20 death—] ~, *Per1*
214:21 self-aliveness, *Per1*]
    self-perfection, *MS*
    self-aliveness *G*
214:21 flickering of yearning *Per1*]
    flame of waning *MS*
214:22 forever] for ever *A1*
214:22 yearning for...Keats: *Per1*]
    reaching out to be something

not himself, in the poet! *MS*
yearning for...Keats:— *G*

214:24 "To *MS, G*] ~ *Per1* To *A2*

214:27 vain— *MS, G*] ~,— *Per1*
vain— *A2*

214:28 sod."—] ~. *Per1* ~." *G, TS*
sod. *A2*

214:30 realise] realize *Per1*

214:30 sort of answer] *Om. G*

214:30 song! *MS, G*] ~. *Per1*

214:33 in *Per1*] in the *MS*

214:34 neighbouring *MS, G, A1*]
neighboring *Per1*

214:34 bushes— *MS, G, A1*] ~,— *Per1*

214:34 do—then *MS, G*] ~. Then
Per1

215:2 tongues] tongs *A1*

215:3 at] *Om. TS, A2*

215:3 third act, *MS, G*] Third
Act,— *Per1* Third Act— *A1*

215:4 down: *MS, G*] ~, *Per1*

215:5 quarrel. *Per1*] quarrel, and
you have to laugh. *MS*

215:6 Caruso, *MS, G*] ~,— *Per1*
~—*A1*

215:7 bird-like bursting *MS, G*] ~,
~, *Per1*

215:7 song, and fullness of himself
Per1] song and self-utterance
MS song, the fulness of
himself *G*

215:8 self-luxuriance.] ~:— *G*

215:9 "Thou *MS, G*] ~ *Per1* Thou
A2

215:10 down;"] ~. *Per1* ~;—" *G* ~."
Per2, TS ~..." *TSC down...*
A2

215:12 Whereas *Per1*] And *MS*

215:12 low-voiced] low-/ voiced *G*

215:12 his *Per1*] *Om. MS*

215:13 half-secretive call *G*]
half-secretive, even *MS* half
secretive call *Per1*

215:13 it really *Per1*] really it *MS*

215:14 England.] ~:— *G*

215:15 "The *MS, G*] ~ *Per1* The *A2*

215:15 hear *Per1*] heard *MS* heard *A2*

215:18 home] ~, *Per1, TS home, A2*

215:19 corn;"—] ~. *Per1* ~:—" *G*
~." *Per2, TS corn. A2*

215:20 And why...tears.
Did...Aesop...[215:23]
nightingale singing *Per1*] I
wonder what sort of answer
they all made! Diocletian, for
instance! And Aesop! {Æsop!
A2} And Mademoiselle Ruth!
I strongly suspect the last
young lady of giving the
nightingale occasion to sing
MS But why...tears!
Did...Aesop...nightingale
singing *Per2* But why...tears.
Did...Æsop...nightingale
singing *A1*

215:24 Boccaccio's *Per1*] the
Boccaccio *MS*

215:24 lively bird *Per1*] nightingale
MS

215:25 hand: *TS*] ~. *MS, G* ~, *Per1*
see notes

215:25 "tua] "—tua *Per1* "tua *A2*

215:25 è] e *TS* é *A2*

215:25 sì *MS, GR*] si *G, TS* si *A2*.

215:25 ch'ella *A1*] che ella *MS, G*
Ch'ella *Per1* che ella *A2 see*
notes

215:26 mano.] ~! *Per1* mano. *A2*

215:27 what does *Per1*] I wonder
what *MS*

215:27 think *Per1*] thinks *MS*

215:29 it] ~, *Per1, TS, A2*

215:29 as jaunty as ever *Per1*] true to
type *MS*

215:30 prefers...humble moan: *Per1*]
likes it better than if, like the
poet, he humbly warbled: *MS*
prefers...humble moan:— *G*

215:31 "Now *MS, G*] ~ *Per1* Now *A2*

215:31 seems it *Per2, A1, TSC*] it
seems *MS seems it A2*

215:32 pain—" *MS, G*] ~. *Per1* ~."
Per2 ~. ... *A1* ~..." *TSC*
pain... A2

215:33 That wouldn't...And one
Per1] One *MS*

215:34 sympathises] sympathizes *Per1*
215:34 Keats's *Per1, GR*] Keats' *MS*
 Keat's *G*
215:35 good such...*her!* Perhaps *Ed.*]
 she'd have got out of such a
 midnight! Perhaps *MS* good
 such...*her! P* Perhaps *Per1*
215:36 gets more out of life *Per1*]
 prefers it *MS*
215:37 isn't wanting...cosy...[216:4]
 of her. *G*] of the species is full
 of his own bright life, and
 warbles her into the spell of
 himself. In the end, she gets
 more out of it that way. *MS*
 isn't wanting...cozy...of her.
 Per1
216:5 Of *Per1*] Because, of *MS*
216:5 course, *Per1*] course, though
 MS
216:6 hen *MS, G*] ~, *Per1*

216:6 sings. And...But *Per1*] sings,
 MS
216:6 she] she *A1*
216:7 she knows *Per1*] Om. *MS*
216:8 him. *Per1*] his. *MS*
216:8 in *Per1*] Om. *MS, G*
216:10 poking into...it up. *Per1*] to
 come nestling down on his
 song and smothering it, or
 muffling it. *MS*
216:11 hers.] ~: *Per1* ~! *G*
216:12 "Adieu! Adieu! *MS, G*] ~; ~;
 Per1 ~! adieu! *A1* "~! adieu!
 TSC Adieu! adieu! A2
216:12 fades—" *MS, G*] ~. *Per1* ~."
 Per2 ~. ... ... *A1* ~ ..." *TS*
 fades... A2
216:13 anthem,] ~,— *Per1* ~; *G* ~—
 A1
216:13 jauntiest *Per1*] best *MS*
216:14 try to *Per1*] Om. *MS*

Man is a Hunter

The chronological sequence of the texts is: *MS, TCCI, TCCIR, TCCII, A1*.

219:3 think *TCCI*] imagine *MS*
219:5 dawn *TCCI*] the dawn *MS*
219:6 a *TCCI*] the *MS*
219:7 irritating *TCCI*] Om. *MS*
219:7 scattering *TCCI*] Om. *MS*
219:7 olive gardens *MS, A1*]
 olive-gardens *TCCII*
219:9 huntsmen *TCCI*] "hunters"
 MS
219:9 abroad:] ~; *TCCII*
219:11 *cacciatore TCCI*] "cacciatore"
 MS
219:11 Oh Nimrod...arrows! *TCCI*]
 Nimrod and Bahram, where
 are your arrows? *MS* Oh
 Nimrod...arrows: *TCCII*
219:13 hunter; *TCCI*] ~: *MS,*
 TCCII
219:14 head] bed *TCCII*
219:15 an *TCCI*] it is an *MS*
219:15 asses *TCCI*] asses that *MS*
219:16 wood, *TCCI*] ~ *MS, A1*

219:16 berries, and *TCCI*] ~. And
 MS
219:17 never fail...have been. *TCCI*]
 invariably wake my sleeping
 ire. *MS*
219:18 *L'uomo è cacciatore! TCCI*]
 "L'uomo è cacciatore!" *MS*
 L'uomo è cacciatore: TCCII
219:18 The] the *TCCII*
219:18 are *TCCI*] used to be *MS*
219:20 in the...lion.— *TCCI*] upon
 the bloody trail of the lion he
 has wounded.— *MS* in
 the...lion. *TCCII*
219:20 it is...who has *TCCI*] a young
 man had *MS*
219:21 *l'uomo è cacciatore!* man is a
 hunter! *TCCI*] oh well, *man is*
 a hunter! MS "L'uomo è
 cacciatore"—"man is a hunter"
 — *TCCII* "L'uomo è cacciatore"
 —"man is a hunter"— *A1*

219:22 what can you expect? *TCCI*]
       Om. MS
219:23 out for...hunter! *TCCI*] out.
       L'uomo è cacciatore. *MS*
219:24 go,] ~ *TCCII*
219:25 go!"] ~", *TCCII* ~." *A1*
219:26 run!"— *TCCI*] ~—" *MS* ~."
       TCCII
219:27 erect, *TCCI*] *Om. MS*
219:28 alert. *TCCI*] ~! *MS*
219:28 bang] *bang TCCII*
219:28 they have...of noise! *TCCI*]
       —it is amazing what a loud
       noise they make. *MS* they
       have...of noise. *TCCII*
219:30 predatory *TCCI*] predative
       MS
219:30 strides, to the spot. *TCCI*]
       strides. *MS*
219:31 There is...La caccia! where
       TCCIR] And even then, they
       have missed. Where is the
       "game"? Where *MS* And
       there is...La caccia! where
       TCCI There is...*La
       caccia!*—where *TCCII* There
       is...*La caccia!*—where *A1*
220:2 could not *TCCI*] couldn't *MS*
220:2 blanker and more spooky
       TCCI] more blank and spooky
       MS
220:3 see *TCCI*] see at least *MS*
220:3 side] ~, *TCCII*
220:3 trunk; *TCCI*] ~: *MS*
220:4 wild *TCCI*] wicked wild *MS*
220:4 ploughing *TCCI*] plowing *MS*
220:4 death-agony *TCCI*] death
       agony *MS*
220:5 nothing, *TCCI*] *Om. MS*
220:5 all! *TCCI*] ~. *MS*, *TCCII*
220:5 Man, being...bad shot *TCCI*]
       They are amazing bad shots
       MS
220:7 Nimrod, in...[220:17] shoot
       straight. *P A TCCI*] The
       hunter, the great nimrod, in a
       corduroy velveteen shooting
       suit, gun, bandolier and all,

strides importantly up to the
spot where the wounded boar
should lie, and gazes for a
moment downwards, at some
imaginary point in space.
Then hitching his game-bag
more determinedly over his
shoulder, he sets off up the
hill again, virile as Hector—
perhaps that is really his
name, Italianised to
Ettore—determined on death.
P Now a *MS see also entries to*
220:13

220:7 game bag *TCCI*] game-/ bag
       TCCII game-bag *A1*
220:8 hand *TCCI*] his hand *TCCII*
220:8 apart, *TCCI*] ~ *TCCII*
220:8 virilissimo *TCCI*] *virilissimo*
       TCCII
220:13 game bag *TCCI*] game-bag
       TCCII
220:18 umbrella pines] umbrella-
       pines *TCCII*
220:18 with *TCCI*] with all *MS*
220:18 open, and...scattered *TCCI*]
       open. And they are by no
       means crowded *MS*
220:19 is allowed...so, then it *TCCI*]
       Om. MS is allowed...so; then
       it *TCCII*
220:22 for cooking Nimrod's
       macaroni *TCCI*] as soon as it
       gets big enough to be worth it
       MS
220:22 a *pineta TCCI*] the "pineta"
       MS
220:22 piney] piny *A1*
220:23 rest,] ~ *TCCII*
220:24 There is...bumble bee. *TCCI*]
       Om. MS There
       is...bumble-bee. *TCCII*
220:25 the game be, that...the
       lions...these Nimrods? *TCCI*]
       they be, the lions and tigers,
       the wolves and wild-boars that
       should make it worth while to
       all these "huntsmen." *MS* the

game be that…The
lions…these Nimrods? *TCCII*
220:28 Or not *TCCI*] Not *MS*
220:28 home, between…olive trees…
the open, *TCCI*] home—the
huntsmen are banging away in
the open *MS* home,
between…olive-trees…the
open, *TCCII*
220:30 wood: *TCCI*] ~, *MS*
220:31 bull-finch, with *TCCI*]
bull-finch. And it will have
MS bull-/ finch, with *TCCII*
bullfinch, with *A1*
220:32 side, *TCCI*] ~ *MS*
220:32 frail feet *TCCI*] paws *MS*
220:33 Nimrod, having…his quarry
TCCI] Nimrod has been
abroad *MS*
220:35 Or] So *TCCII*
220:36 game?"— *TCCIR*] game?" *MS*
game?" *TCCI, TCCII*
220:36 splendid idea! a *TCCI*]
splendid! a *MS* Splendid idea!
A *TCCII*
220:37 rabbit? *TCCI*] ~! *MS*
220:37 Why] ~, *TCCII*
220:38 in triumph *TCCI*] *Om. MS*
220:38 not very bulky *TCCI*] *Om. MS*
220:39 inside *TCCI*] in *MS*
220:39 Aha!— *TCCI*] ~! *MS*
221:1 coloured, feathery *TCCI*]
feathery, coloured *MS*
221:2 small *TCCI*] little *MS*
221:2 rolling *TCCI*] dropping *MS*
221:2 away!] ~, *TCCII*
221:3 tipping *TCCI*] picking *MS*
221:4 roughly *TCCI*] *Om. MS*

221:4 ones! *TCCIR*] ~. *MS, TCCII*
221:4 these either *TCCI*] those
either *MS* these, either,
TCCII
221:5 "No?" she…*more…you!* And
disgusted…the game *TCCI*]
And she goes off with the
"game", in rather angry
disgust *MS* "No?"
she…*"more…you!"* And,
disgusted…the game *TCCII*
"No?" she…*"More…you!"*
And, disgusted…the game *A1*
221:9 yard-lengths *TCCI*] rows *MS*
221:10 bull-finches] bullfinches
TCCII
221:10 gold-finches] goldfinches
TCCII
221:11 along with…the show *TCCI*]
Om. MS
221:12 the birds *TCCI*] them *MS*
221:13 ornament, *TCCI*] *Om. MS*
221:13 be more conceivable *TCCI*]
seem more bearable *MS*
221:14 different coloured]
different-coloured *TCCII*
221:14 tenpence] ten-/ pence *A1*
221:14 But *TCCI*] But to *MS*
221:15 bones *TCCI*] bones which *MS*
221:15 carcases] carcasses *A1*
221:16 must make! *TCCI*] makes, is
exasperating. *MS*
221:17 But after all *TCCI*] It is true
MS But, after all *TCCII*
221:18 And *TCCI*] ~, *MS*
221:18 game. *TCCI*] ~! *MS*
221:20 don't you *TCCIR*] do not *MS*
221:20 grunt,] ~; *TCCII*

Flowery Tuscany

The chronological sequence of the texts is: *MS, Per1, Per2, TCC, A1* for Parts
I–III (*A1* follows *Per1* unless otherwise indicated).

225:4 hawthorn *MS, A1*] hawthorne
Per1
225:5 America] ~, *TCC*

225:5 golden rod *MS, TCC*]
goldenrod *Per2, A1*
225:5 star-grass] stargrass

Per1, TCC star-/ grass
Per2
225:5   and maple] maple *Per1*
         Mayapple *A1*
225:6   michaelmas] Michaelmas *A1*
225:11   yucca *MS, A1*] zucca *Per1*
225:11   drooping] dropping *Per1*
225:14   myrtle] ~, *A1*
225:16   Paestum] Pæstum *A1*
225:19   north] North *A1*
225:22   understood,] ~ *Per1*
225:32   feet, *MS, TCC*] ~ *Per2*
226:10   neighbours *MS, TCC*]
         neighbors *Per2*
226:11   sculpt] sculp *A1*
226:11   gardens *MS, A1*] ~, *TCC*
226:13   modelling *MS, TCC*]
         modeling *Per2*
226:18   drystone *MS, TCC*] dry-/
         stone *Per2*
226:19   gentle, *MS, Per2*] ~ *Per1*,
         TCC
226:21   natural] ~, *Per1*
226:27   But] ~, *Per1*
226:31   grape-vine *MS, TCC*]
         grapevine *Per2* grape-/ vine
         A1
226:34   dry-stone *MS, Per2*] dry-/
         stone *Per1* drystone *TCC*
226:37   surface,] ~ *Per1*
227:4   tips] lips *Per1*
227:7   forever hanging] for ever
         hanging *Per1*
227:7   but forever] but for ever *A1*
227:10   terraces, *MS, TCC*] ~ *Per2*
227:15   "tazzette,"] '~', *Per1, TCC*
         tazzette, *Per2, A1*
227:19   of *MS, TCC*] on *Per2*
227:29   tramontana] *tramontana A1*
227:31   bubbles] ~, *Per1*
227:32   splendour *MS, TCC*] splendor
         Per2
227:34   honey-sweet *MS, Per2*]
         honey-/ sweet *Per1*
227:34   narcissus frosty]
         narcissus-frosty *A1*
227:35   bees. P Till *MS, TCC*] ~. Till
         Per2

227:38   But at...[228:5] shine forth.
         MS, TCC] *Om. Per2*
228:7   cosy nook] cosy-nook *Per1*,
         TCC cozy-nook *Per2*
228:8   on *MS, Per2*] in *Per1, TCC*
228:9   débris *MS, Per2*] debris *Per1*,
         TCC
228:9   stands *Ed.*] stand *MS*
228:9   hellebore] hellebores *A1*
228:10   places, *MS, Per2, A1*] ~ *Per1*,
         TCC
228:16   hand-mirror *MS, Per2*]
         hand-/ mirror *Per1*
228:17   short,] ~ *TCC*
228:17   lonely] lovely *Per1*
228:18   wintry-beautiful, *MS, TCC*] ~
         Per2
228:19   alone. But *MS, TCC*] ~. P
         But *Per2*
228:20   roses *MS, TCC*] ~, *Per2*
228:24   assertiveness. In...[228:28] of
         winter.] assertiveness. *Per2*
         assertiveness. P In...of winter.
         see also entries to 228:28
228:26   as you...primroses, *MS, A1*]
         Om. TCC
228:27   leaf,] ~ *TCC*
228:28   of] in *Per1*
228:29   balls] *Om. TCC*
228:32   sharp, *MS, Per2*] ~ *Per1, TCC*
228:36   pinewood] ~, *Per1, TCC*
         pine-/ wood, *Per2* pine-wood,
         A1
228:38   Apennines *Per2, A1*]
         Appenines *MS, TCC*
228:39   afternoon, *MS, TCC*] ~ *Per2*
229:1   tramontana] *tramontana A1*
229:3   again:] ~; *Per1*
229:6   funny *MS, Per2*] sunny *Per1*,
         TCC
229:8   sharp,] ~ *Per1*
229:9   single] *Om. TCC*
229:15   yield. South] ~, South *TCC*
         ~; south *A1*
229:18   day,] ~ *Per1*
229:21   even now...the Alps,] *Om.*
         TCC
229:22   forever] for ever *Per1*

229:23 especially, *MS, TCC*] ~ *Per2*
229:23 sides of *Per1, TCC*] sides *MS, Per2*
229:28 single] simple *Per1*
229:29 fields, *MS, TCC*] ~ *Per2*
229:35 tiny] being *Per1*
229:39 pine-slopes, *MS, TCC*] pine-/slopes, *Per2*
230:2 mightiest,] ~ *Per1*
230:3 bees, *MS, TCC*] ~ *Per2*
230:4 lavendar crocuses *MS, A1*] lavender-crocuses *Per1*
230:9 Apaches *MS, Per2*] apaches *Per1, TCC*
230:9 teepees *MS, TCC*] tepees *Per2, A1*
230:10 west *MS, TCC*] West *Per2, A1*
230:11 morning,] ~ *Per2*
230:14 then] there *Per1*
230:17 marvellous *MS, TCC*] marvelous *Per2*
230:28 some time *MS, Per2, A1*] sometime *Per1, TCC*
230:29 bee-bread *Per1, TCC*] bee-/bread *MS, Per2*
230:29 elbow joints] elbow-joints *Per1*
230:31 camp, *MS, TCC*] ~ *Per2*
230:38 bright,] ~ *Per1*
230:39 sun. With *MS, Per2*] ~, with *Per1, TCC*
231:1 March, *MS, TCC*] ~ *Per2*
231:2 sun] ~, *TCC*
231:3 briar] brier *A1*
231:9 and *MS, TCC*] ~, *Per2*
231:11 I know…[231:14] very unjust. *MS, TCC*] *Om. Per2*
231:15 towers] flowers *Per1*
231:20 grape hyacinth] grape-hyacinth *Per1*
231:22 that,] ~ *Per1*
231:22 their] the *Per1*
231:23 But] ~, *TCC*
231:23 first, *MS, TCC*] ~ *Per2*
231:28 nipples] ripples *Per1*
231:28 them. P As *MS, TCC*] ~. As *Per2*

231:31 breasts, *MS, Per2*] ~ *Per1, TCC*
231:35 deep-toned, *MS, TCC*] ~ *Per2*
231:36 individuals:] ~, *Per1*
231:38 "Oh…pink!" *MS, Per2, A1*] '~…~!' *Per1, TCC*
231:40 "vulgar" *MS, Per2, A1*] '~' *Per1, TCC*
232:1 peach-blossom] peach blossom *Per1, TCC* peach-/blossom *Per2*
232:3 landscape:] ~, *Per1*
232:4 asphodels. It *MS, Per2*] ~. P It *Per1, TCC*
232:5 spring. P Because *MS, Per2*] ~, because *Per1, TCC*
232:8 podere] *podere A1*
232:17 invisible. They *MS, TCC*] ~. P Anemones *Per2*
232:17 and *MS, TCC*] and perhaps *Per2*
232:18 them. P Altogether *MS, TCC*] ~. Altogether *Per2*
232:22 broad petalled *MS, TCC*] broad-petaled *Per2* broad-petalled *A1*
232:28 podere] *podere A1*
232:30 then] there *Per1*
232:32 invisible, *MS, TCC*] ~ *Per2*
232:33 Yet *MS, Per2*] ~, *Per1, TCC*
232:40 luminous, *MS, TCC*] ~ *Per2*
233:4 pure,] ~ *TCC*
233:7 apple-blossom] apple blossom *A1*
233:16 big-petalled *MS, TCC*] big-petaled *Per2*
233:16 are: *MS, Per2*] ~; *Per1, TCC*
233:19 these *MS, Per2*] the *Per1, TCC*
233:21 here *MS, TCC*] ~, *Per2*
233:23 on, *MS, TCC*] ~ *Per2*
233:28 spiky] ~, *TCC*
233:37 fig-trees] fig-/trees *TCC* fig trees *A1*
234:3 time, *MS, TCC*] ~ *Per2*
234:6 flower *MS, TCC*] flowers *Per2*

234:14 summer, *MS, Per2, A1*] ~ *Per1, TCC*
234:15 tender, *MS, Per2*] ~ *Per1, TCC*
234:18 cherry-blossom] cherry blossom *A1*
234:19 year:] ~; *A1*
234:21 fruit-trees *MS, TCC*] fruit trees *Per2, A1*
234:22 pear-tree] pear tree *A1*
234:23 fulness] fullness *A1*
234:24 greens] green *Per1*
234:27 stone pines] stone-pines *A1*
234:31 brilliant,] ~ *Per1*
234:35 pear-tree] pear tree *A1*
235:1 pre-eminent *MS, TCC*] preeminent *Per2*
235:5 Christmas, *MS, TCC*] ~ *Per2*
235:6 beautiful, when] ~. When *Per1*
235:8 lavender. Then *MS, Per2*] ~, then *Per1*
235:8 mid-winter *MS, TCC*] midwinter *Per2*
235:14 wintry,] ~ *Per1*
235:15 dull tall] ~, ~ *Per1*
235:18 it. But *MS, Per2*] it, *Per1, TCC*
235:18 not, *MS, A1*] ~ *TCC*
235:20 hoar-frost *MS, Per2*] hoarfrost *Per1, TCC*
235:20 whitish *MS, Per2*] a whitish *Per1, TCC*
235:21 ghostly *MS, Per2, A1*] ~, *Per1, TCC*
235:25 fulness] fullness *A1*
235:26 honied *MS, TCC*] honeyed *Per2, A1*
235:29 pin-head *MS, TCC*] pinhead *Per2*
235:30 sun,] ~ *Per1*
235:34 heath-fingers *MS, TCC*] heath-/ fingers *Per2*
235:35 pine-woods *MS, TCC*] pine-/ woods *Per2*
235:37 little,] ~ *TCC*
235:40 ragged,] ~ *Per1*
235:40 conceited] concerted *Per1*

236:3 odd *MS, A1*] off *TCC*
236:5 orchids,] ~ *TCC*
236:13 wild-thyme *MS, Per2*] wild-/ thyme *Per1* wild thyme *A1*
236:14 month, *MS, TCC*] ~ *Per2*
236:14 wild thyme *MS, A1*] wild-thyme *Per1*
236:18 buffeted *MS, Per2, A1*] buffetted *Per1, TCC*
236:22 cold,] ~ *A1*
236:23 burnt *MS, TCC*] burned *Per2*
236:24 rock-rose *MS, TCC*] rock-/ rose *Per2*
236:26 May, *MS, TCC*] ~ *Per2*
236:28 barely-audible *MS, TCC*] barely audible *Per2, A1*
236:34 root, orris powder…used. *MS, Per2*] ~ (~ ~…~). *Per1, TCC*
236:36 air, *MS, TCC*] ~ *Per2*
237:1 June, *MS, TCC*] ~ *Per2*
237:5 bean-fields *MS, TCC*] bean-/ fields *Per1*
237:10 pea-harvest] pea-/ harvest *A1*
237:13 countries, *MS, TCC*] ~ *Per2*
237:13 vivid, *MS, TCC*] ~ *Per2*
237:13 complete,] ~ *Per1*
237:16 England, *MS, TCC*] ~ *Per2*
237:20 countries, *MS, TCC*] ~ *Per2*
237:20 reality,] ~ *Per1*
237:21 north] North *A1*
237:23 day, *MS, TCC*] ~ *Per2, A1*
237:26 temporal,] ~ *TCC*
237:29 southerner, *MS, TCC*] ~ *Per2*
237:32 shadow, *MS, TCC*] ~ *Per2*
237:36 body, therefore] ~. Therefore *Per1*
237:38 argument. We *MS, TCC*] ~, we *Per2*
238:1 short-sighted] shortsighted *Per1, TCC* short-/ sighted *Per2*
238:9 shadow,] ~ *Per2*
238:12 underworld *MS, Per2*] under-/ world *Per1* under-world *TCC*
238:14 dark, *MS, Per2*] ~ *Per1, TCC*

238:23 "Where are...yesteryear?"
   MS, Per2, A1] '~ ~...~?'
   Per1, TCC

238:26 sunny,] ~ *Per1*

IV

The chronological sequence is: *TCCI, TCCII, A1.*

238:38 pre-disposed] predisposed
   A1
238:39 To-morrow] Tomorrow
   TCCII
239:2 on to] onto *A1*
239:3 dark-haired *A1*] dark-/ haired
   TCCI
239:3 blondes] blonds *A1*
239:6 back,] ~ *A1*
239:6 brown *TCCI, A1*] ~, *TCCII*
239:7 breast] ~, *TCCII*
239:8 sun-darkened] sun-/
   darkened *A1*
239:21 halt,] ~ *A1*
239:22 swans,] ~ *A1*
239:23 wedge-shaped] ~, *TCCII*

239:28 Frankfurt-am-Main *Ed.*]
   Frankfort-am-Main *TCCI*
239:29 far off] far-off *A1*
239:35 Lungarno *A1*] Lung'arno
   TCCI
240:1 Doppelgänger] *Doppelgänger*
   A1
240:18 Drachen] *Drachen A1*
240:18 Greifen] *Greifen A1*
241:11 Wandervögel *Ed.*]
   Wandervögeln *TCCI*
   Wandervögel A1
241:26 that] that it *TCCII* That *A1*
241:39 sorts *TCCI, A1*] sort *TCCII*
242:18 mass consciousness]
   mass-consciousness *A1*

Germans and English

The chronological sequence of the texts is: *TS, E1*

247:1 **Germans and English** *Ed.*]
   E S S A Y—(No Title). *TS*
   [Germans and English] *E1*
247:7 rucksack *Ed.*] Rucksack *TS*
247:16 rucksacks *Ed.*] Rucksacks *TS*
247:30 no one *E1*] no-one *TS*
248:12 the mysterious] mysterious *E1*
248:38 Wandervögel *Ed.*]
   Wandervogel *TS*
249:4 little *E1*] Little *TS*
249:7 slave-market *E1*] slave-/
   market *TS*
249:11 Wandervögel *Ed.*]
   Wandervogel *TS*

249:35 Schwindelfrei *Ed.*] Swindelfrei
   TS
249:37 und *E1*] and *TS*
249:40 Charakterlosigkeit *E1*]
   Charakter-Losigkeit *TS*
249:40 Schwäche *E1*] Schuäche *TS*
250:9 pure *E1*] Pure *TS*
250:16 lamentable *E1*] ~, *TS*
250:30 "Warum *E1*] ~ *TS*
251:10 no one *E1*] no-one *TS*
251:22 [*ab ovo*] *Ed.*] *above TS alone E1*
   see notes
252:20 destiny. *E1*] destiny./ D.H.
   LAWRENCE. *TS*

The Painted Tombs of Tarquinia, First version

MS is the text of the first version. The entry to the left of the square bracket usually
indicates the final *MS* reading, with the unidentified entry to the right giving the

384   *Textual apparatus*

reading of the *MS* before DHL revised it; still earlier readings are indicated by pointed and half brackets. Word fragments of fewer than three letters usually have not been recorded.

⟨ ⟩, ⟨⟨ ⟩⟩ = First and second deletions
⌜ ⌝, ⌜⌜ ⌝⌝ = First and second additions

255:3   The Painted] The
255:11 Viterbo, inland.] Volterra.
255:16 almost close up to] within half a mile of
255:19 people.] people⟨.⟩ ⌜⌜.⌝⌝ ⌜since no tomb was made within the girdle of the city walls.—⌝
255:22 wild] grass of the wild
255:25 hill-crest] hillside
255:26 away to…the sun,] under the sun, on the right,
255:34 The] In the
256:7   hole, after…world!] hole.
256:9   some] some grim
256:13 hunting] the Chase and hunting
256:21 in it three] three
256:32 is the…Italians] is ⟨exactly⟩ the colour ⟨the⟩ ⌜⌜of⌝⌝ ⌜many⌝ Italians ⟨go⟩ ⟨⟨⌜are⌝⟩⟩
256:36 and] ⟨and⟩/ and
256:36 sling is] sling,
256:37 birds which rise] birds ⟨.⟩, that are
256:40 bows with…others, and] bows ⟨⌜and⌝⟩ ⌜⌜with…others, and⌝⌝
257:1   prow] bows
257:9   the quick ripple of] delight in
257:9   it is.] is your ticket.
257:14 these] this
257:25 the symbol either of] ⟨ey [?]⟩ either
257:26 organ] symbol
257:27 or] or it could be the symbol
257:31 According…meanings,] And so,
257:33 deeps of death,] deeps,
257:35 from] by
257:40 will, and…slinger [who]…flying birds] ⟨⟨will⟨.⟩⌜,⌝⟩⟩ ⌜⌜will, and⌝⌝ ⟨So

that⟩ ⟨⟨the slinger who is about to bring down a⟩⟩ ⟨⟨⌜So that⟩⟩ the priests, the augurs who watched, ⟨⟨c⟩⟩⌜ ⌜w⌝ ⌝ould send the divine will⟨⟨. And in the picture,⌝⟩⟩ ⌜⌜from their flight. In the picture, the slinger is about to bring down one of these flying⌝⌝ bird⌜ ⌜s⌝ ⌝
258:6   how to read] something
258:12 reclines] lies
258:20 playing on the] with a dish or
258:21 apparently. A] apparently, a
258:21 wall;] wall, though I doubt if it is a cage,
258:22 with garlands, sit,] sit with garlands,
258:23 pair, the…it all.] pair.
258:25 but they…love, and] or the crown of life and death—the same thing. But the garland, or wreath
258:29 a man] man
258:30 In this] Such a
258:30 is] so
258:31 death,] death, ⟨⌜after a gay life,⌝⟩
258:32 So all the creatures] And everyone
258:33 seem *Ed.*] seems ⟨so⟩
258:34 There is…movement, they] They
258:38 tomb,] picture,
259:1   quick, bright] full-flowing
259:4   uneasy,] gloomy,
259:4   Roman] overbearing Roman
259:5   a herd…cattle, or] or
259:7   it, with…humanity.] it.
259:8   hunting and *Ed.*] the hunting and ⟨the⟩
259:9   out-of-doors] leaves

259:10 immoral, any…produce it] immoral⟨.⟩⌜, any more…immoral.⌝ ⟨⟨It⟩⟩⌜ ⌜To produce it⌝ ⌝
259:12 vaunting,] overbearing;
259:14 sure] quite sure
259:14 *ambiente*,] *ambiente*, excellently,
259:17 accept] ⟨control⟩ ⟨⟨⌜direct⌝⟩⟩ ⌜⌜accept⌝ ⌝
259:17 living thing] thing
259:24 people of] of
259:24 on the whole] also
259:25 near to] near
259:28 vibration.] vibration, from the Latin.
259:30 Italic or non-Italic, long-skulls] long-skulls
259:35 people.] them.
260:1 characters.] natures.
260:2 overcome.] come.
260:8 earlier and more] more
260:13 new *awareness*] *awareness*
260:17 people] race
260:18 modern Frenchman…American.] ⟨Norman in France.⟩ ⌜modern Frenchman …or the ⟨⟨modern Russian⟩⟩ American.⌝
260:20 race] races
260:21 when an] when
260:21 gets] gets a
260:23 begin] start
260:24 Samnites and] and
260:26 European tribes] tribes
260:27 diverse] different/ [?]
260:28 caught…and roused] roused
260:29 a continuous] a
260:35 slug] caterpillar
260:37 of a sensitive] sensitive
261:11 little] covered
261:12 small] little
261:20 As it…scattered] Scattered
261:20 we dive] one dives
261:21 rabbits] a rabbit
261:22 It] And it
261:26 confederacy…states loosely] loosely
261:30 the] a
261:35 family,] family, and
261:38 we] one
261:39 conception] idea
262:9 left] left open
262:9 like common holes, when] when
262:15 putting] half putting
262:19 in each,] each time,
262:20 Hetaerae *Ed.*] Hetairae
262:22 with] as they
262:24 at the end on] on the end at
262:27 forefinger of the right hand,] forefinger,
262:27 a] the
262:31 It…say, the] The
262:34 this] this old
262:35 The second…making a] On the side walls there are most beautiful
263:3 real…style.] non-photographic.
263:6 them.] them alert and alive.
263:7 isn't *Ed.*] isnt
263:9 seize.] seize. *P* It is very interesting to compare, in F. Weege's most excellent book, ⟨on⟩ *Etruskische Malerei*—published in Leipzig at about 20 Mark—to compare the old drawings of these paintings in this tomb, done before photography was ⟨recent⟩ ⌜fully⌝ developed, with Weeges own photographs, taken, I believe, just before the war. Both are reproduced. The old drawings are very good, and interesting because they contain details that have now disappeared, the tomb having suffered further damage. Especially there is a fascinating little cat just curling round a tree trunk
263:14 Greek] greek
263:16 etruscan] Etruscan

263:16 modern] real
265:21 as usual] the same
263:24 rock walls] walls of
263:24 thinly stuccoed and frescoed]
 thin stucco⌐ed⌐ frescoed
263:25 with] with so
263:34 men] man
263:38 compare, in F. Weege's...20
 M),] compare
263:40 more recently.] recently, in F.
 Weege's excellent book,
 Etruskische Malerei (Etruscan
 Painting—published in
 Leipzig at about 20 Mark).
264:1 photographs, and the]
 photographs. The
264:6 etruscan] Etruscan
264:20 about] over
264:31 etruscan] Etruscan
264:34 intense temporary] intense
265:1 But this] This

265:2 etruscan] Etruscan
265:3 bulls, facing...an animal.]
 bulls.
265:4 elemental] passionate
265:5 death; and ready...its
 elements.] death, the short
 altar on which the individual
 life has been sacrificed, or the
 tree of life.
265:9 blood-stream, which...
 [265:14] etruscan artists.]
 blood-stream. *P* The lionesses
 with their udders remind one
 a little of the famous bronze
 Capitoline Wolf, that nurses
 Remus and Romulus, and that
 surely was made by etruscan
 craftsmen.
265:20 Crete] crete
265:21 the urn...soul-treasure, and]
 and

Fireworks [Fireworks in Florence]

The chronological sequence of the texts is: *MS, TCC, A1.*

287:3 day] Day *TCC*
287:3 24th.] 24th *TCC*
287:3 June;] ~, *TCC*
287:4 Florence;] ~: *TCC*
287:5 flames;] ~: *TCC*
287:7 sort,] ~ *TCC*
287:8 midsummer day] Midsummer
 Day *TCC* Mid-/ summer Day
 A1
287:17 mediaeval] medieval *A1*
287:26 midsummer night]
 Midsummer Night *TCC*
287:27 bulb-lights] bulb lights *TCC*
288:2 darknecked] dark-necked
 TCC
288:4 torch-lamps] torch lamps
 TCC
288:20 pictures;] ~: *TCC*
288:24 Then] There *TCC*
288:31 nakedness;] ~, *TCC*
288:31 Michelangelo's *A1*] Michal
 Angelo's *MS*

288:31 David] *David A1*
288:36 big-headed] big-/ headed *A1*
288:37 nude] male *TCC*
288:38 Piazza] ~, *TCC*
289:1 Tell them...an instant.] *Om.*
 TCC
289:5 theatre-pit] theatre pit *TCC*
289:7 numbers,] ~ *TCC*
289:10 plateau] platform *TCC*
289:16 well behaved] well-behaved
 TCC
289:18 toy] *Om. TCC*
289:21 ice-cream,] ~ *TCC*
289:23 still-full] still full *TCC*
289:25 gravel,] ~ *TCC*
289:28 stroll] ~, *TCC*
289:32 up] Up *A1*
290:5 air-raid,] ~ *TCC*
290:6 psyche,] ~ *TCC*
290:8 he] He *TCC*
290:11 fireworks,] ~ *A1*
290:21 say:] ~ *TCC*

290:22 bello! bello! bellezza!] *bello!*
  bello! bellezza! TCC
290:25 motionless] ~, *TCC*
290:36 water-tower] water-/ tower
  A1
291:2 spider-lilies] spider lilies *TCC*
291:2 out-curving] out-/ curving
  TCC outcurving *A1*
291:6 fire-lily] fire lily *TCC*
291:9 explosions] explosion *TCC*
291:14 sky,] ~ *TCC*

291:27 Giotto's] Giotti's *TCC*
291:27 lily stem] lily-/ stem *TCC*
  lily-stem *A1*
291:31 dome,] ~ *TCC*
291:31 night sky] night-sky *TCC*
291:33 group,] ~; *TCC*
291:34 the lily] ~ Lily *TCC*
291:34 Florence.—] ~— *TCC*
291:34 The lily] ~ Lily *TCC*
291:35 Rovezzano *Ed.*] Rovenzano
  MS see notes

Line-end hyphenation

Of the compound words which are hyphenated at the end of a line in this edition, only the following hyphenated forms should be retained in quotation:

10:1	such-like	193:18	pearl-trade
12:26	non-moral	194:20	far-spreading
21:14	ante-chambers	195:10	flower-town
30:36	Corneto-Tarquinia	212:35	angel-keen
31:38	butter-muslin	213:28	life-perfection
34:25	machine-parts	220:40	hedge-sparrows
37:24	monument-carver	226:31	grape-vine
39:4	still-unravished	235:28	brown-purple
39:9	red-and-black	235:31	vetch-bush
59:20	pure-bred	235:39	bee-orchid
64:10	blood-streams	236:1	thick-flowering
115:32	gay-coloured	237:10	pea-harvest
127:3	grip-handle	239:6	shirt-breast
130:30	non-etruscan	239:28	Frankfurt-am-Main
131:6	Greek-Roman	240:30	shirt-sleeves
131:38	metal-workers	241:39	half-translations
142:6	meadow-larks	247:7	shirt-sleeves
145:8	corduroy-velveteens	247:9	sun-darkened
153:4	east-Mediterranean	249:2	insolent-indifferent
158:13	black-dressed	260:9	pre-Hellenic
171:6	co-ordinated	265:31	women-dancers
176:32	lake-dwellings	288:4	torch-lamps
177:19	simple-minded	288:32	self-consciously
185:5	Café-au-lait	291:14	fire-blossoms
187:13	self-realization		